THE

AMERICAN HOUSE-CARPENTER:

A TREATISE UPON

ARCHITECTURE,

CORNICES AND MOULDINGS

FRAMING,

DOORS, WINDOWS, AND STAIRS.

TOGETHER WITH

THE MOST IMPORTANT PRINCIPLES

OF

PRACTICAL GEOMETRY.

BY R. G. HATFIELD,

ARCHITECT.

FOURTH EDITION, WITH ADDITIONS.

Illustrated by more than three hundred Engravings.

NEW YORK:
JOHN WILEY, 161 BROADWAY,
AND 13 PATERNOSTER ROW, LONDON.

1850.

PREFACE.

THIS book is intended for carpenters—for masters, journeymen and apprentices. It has long been the complaint of this class that architectural books, intended for their instruction, are of a price so high as to be placed beyond their reach. This is owing, in a great measure, to the costliness of the plates with which they are illustrated: an unnecessary expense, as illustrations upon wood, printed on good paper, answer every useful purpose. Wood engravings, too, can be distributed among the letter-press; an advantage which plates but partially possess, and one of great importance to the reader.

Considerations of this kind induced the author to undertake the preparation of this volume. The subject matter has been gleaned from works of the first authority, and subjected to the most careful examination. The explanations have all been written out from the figures themselves, and not taken from any other work; and the figures have all been drawn expressly for this book. In doing this, the utmost care has been taken to make every thing as plain as the nature of the case would admit.

The attention of the reader is particularly directed to the following new inventions, viz: an easy method of describing the curves of mouldings through three given points; a rule to determine the projection of eave cornices; a new method of proportioning a cornice to a larger given one; a way to determine the lengths and bevils of rafters for hip-roofs; a way to proportion the rise to the tread in stairs; to determine the true position of butt-joints in hand-rails; to find the bevils for splayed-work; a general rule for scrolls, &c. Many problems in geometry, also, have been simplified, and new ones introduced. Much labour has been bestowed upon the section on stairs, in which the subject of hand-railing is presented, in many respects, in a new, and, it is hoped, more practical form than in previous treatises on that subject.

The author has endeavoured to present a fund of useful information to the *American house-carpenter* that would enable him to excel in his vocation; how far he has been successful in that object, the book itself must determine.

PREFACE TO THE SECOND EDITION.

In preparing a second edition, the author regrets his want of leisure to give the work that thorough revision, which is demanded by the importance and intricacy of the subjects treated of. He has corrected all the typographical errors in the references, &c., that he could discover, and added a Section on the subject of Shadows. He cannot refrain from giving expression to the satisfaction which he feels at the unexpected success of his undertaking. But it is evident that in a wide-spread, *new* country like ours, works of a practical character, adapted to the wants of the people, and calculated to instruct our operative citizens in the every-day employment of their heads and hands, cannot but meet with a favourable reception. In another edition, perhaps, opportunity will be given for additions and improvements of a still more important nature.

TABLE OF CONTENTS.

INTRODUCTION.

	Art.		Art.
Articles necessary for drawing,	2	To use the set-square, -	11
To prepare the paper, -	5	Directions for drawing, -	13

SECT. I.—PRACTICAL GEOMETRY.

DEFINITIONS.

Lines, - - - - 17
Angles, - - - 23
Angular point, - - - 27
Polygons, - - - 28
The circle, - - - 47
The cone, - - - 56
Conic sections, - - - 58
The ellipsis, - - - 61
The cylinder, - - - 68

PROBLEMS.

To bisect a line, - - 71
To erect a perpendicular, - 72
To let fall a perpendicular, 73
To erect ditto on end of line, 74
Six, eight and ten rule, - 74
To square end of board, - 74
To square foundations, &c., 74
To let fall a perpendicular near the end of a line, - 75
To make equal angles, - 76
To bisect an angle, - - 77
To trisect a right angle, 78
To draw parallel lines, - 79
To divide a line into equal parts, - - - - - 80
To find the centre of a circle, 81
To draw tangent to circle, 82
Do. without using centre, 83
To find the point of contact, 84
To draw a circle through three given points, - - 85
To find a fourth point in circle, 86
To describe a segment of a circle by a set-triangle, - 87
Do. by intersection of lines, 88
To curve an angle, - 89
To inscribe a circle within a given triangle, - - 90
To make triangle about circle, 91
To find the length of a circumference, - - 92
To describe a triangle, hexagon, &c., - - - - 93
To draw an octagon, - 94
To eight-square a rail, &c., 94
To describe any polygon in a circle, - - - - 95
To draw equilateral triangle, 96
To draw a square by compasses, - - - 97
To draw any polygon on a given line, - - - 98
To form a triangle of required size, - - - - 99
To copy any right-lined figure, 100
To make a parallelogram equal to a triangle, - 101
To find the area of a triangle, 101
To make one parallelogram equal another, - - 102
To make one square equal to two others, - - - 103
To find the length of a rafter, 103

	Art.
To find the length of a brace,	103
To ascertain the pitch of a roof,	103
To ascertain the rake of a step-ladder,	103
To describe one circle equal to two others,	104
To make one polygon equal to two or more,	104
To make a square equal to a rectangle,	105
To make a square equal to a triangle,	106
To find a third proportional,	107
To find a fourth proportional,	108
To proportion one ellipsis to another,	108
To divide a line as another,	109
To find a mean proportional,	110
Definitions of conic sections,	111
To find the axes of an elliptical section,	112
To find the axes and base of the parabola,	113
To find the height, base and axes of the hyperbola,	114
To find foci of ellipsis,	115
To describe an ellipsis with a string,	115
To describe an ellipsis with a trammel,	116
To construct a trammel,	116
To describe an ellipsis by ordinates,	117
To trace a curve through given points,	117
To describe an ellipsis by intersection of lines,	118
Do. from conjugate diameters,	118
Do. by intersecting arcs,	119
To describe an oval by compasses,	120
Do. in the proportion, 7 × 9, 5 × 7, &c.,	121
To draw a tangent to an ellipsis,	122
To find the point of contact,	123
To find a conjugate to the given diameter,	124
To find the axes from given diameters,	125
To find axes proportionate to given ones,	126
To describe a parabola by intersection of lines,	127
To describe hyperbola by do.,	128

DEMONSTRATIONS.

Definitions, axioms, &c.,	130. 139
Addition of angles,	140
Equal triangles,	141
Angles at base of isoceles triangle equal,	142
Parallelograms divided equally by diagonal,	143
Equal parallelograms,	144
Parallelogram equal triangles,	146
To make triangle equal polygon,	147
Opposite angles equal,	148
Angles of triangle equal two right angles,	149
Corollaries from do.,	150. 155
Angle in semi-circle a right angle,	156
Hecatomb problem,	157

SECT. II.—ARCHITECTURE.

HISTORY.

Antiquity of its origin,	159
Its cultivation among the ancients,	160
Among the Greeks,	161
Among the Romans,	162
Ruin caused by Goths and Vandals,	163
Of the Gothic,	164
Of the Lombard,	165

	Art.
Of the Byzantine and Oriental,	166
Moorish, Arabian and Modern Gothic, - - - -	167
Of the English, - -	168
Revival of the art in the sixth century, - - -	169
The art improved in the 14th and 15th centuries, -	170
Roman styles cultivated,	171
STYLES.	
Origin of different styles,	172
Stylobate and pedestal, -	173
Definitions of an *order*, -	174
Of the several parts of an order, - - 175.	185
To proportion an order, -	186
The Grecian orders, -	187
Origin of the Doric, - -	188
Intercolumniation, - -	189
Adaptation, - - -	190
Origin of the Ionic, -	191
Characteristics, - -	192
Intercolumniation, - -	193
Adaptation, - - -	194
To describe the volute, -	195
Origin of the Corinthian, -	196
Adaptation, - - -	197
Persians, - - - -	199
Caryatides, - - -	200
The Roman orders, - -	202
Extent of Roman structures,	202
Roman styles copied from Grecian, - - -	203
Origin of the Tuscan, -	204
Adaptation, - - -	205
Characteristics of the Egyptian, - - - - -	206
Extent of Egyptian structures,	206
Adaptation, - - -	207
Appropriateness of design, 208.	211
Durable structures, - -	212
Plans of dwellings, &c.,	213
Directions for designing, 213,	214
PRINCIPLES.	
Origin of the art, - -	215
Arrangement and design, -	216
Ventilation and cleanliness,	217
Stability, - - -	218
Ornaments, - - -	219
Scientific knowledge necessary, - - - -	220
The foundation, - -	221
The column, - - -	222
The wall, - - -	223
The lintel, - - -	224
The arch, - - -	225
The vault, - - -	226
The dome, - - -	227
The roof, - - -	228

SECT. III.—MOULDINGS, CORNICES, &c.

MOULDINGS, &c.	
Elementary forms, - -	229
Characteristics, - -	230
Grecian and Roman, - -	231
Profile, - - -	232
To describe the torus and scotia, - - - - -	233
To describe the echinus,	234
To describe the cavetto,	235
To describe the cyma-recta,	236
To describe the cyma-reversa,	237
Roman mouldings, -	238
Modern mouldings, - -	239
Antæ caps, - - -	240
CORNICES.	
Designs, - - - -	241
To proportion an eave cornice,	242
Do. from a smaller given one, - - - -	243
Do. from a larger given one, - - - - -	244
To find shape of angle-bracket,	245
To find form of raking cornice,	246

SECT. IV.—FRAMING.

	Art.
Laws of pressure, - -	248
Parallelogram of forces, -	248
To measure the pressure on rafters, - - -	249
Do. on tie-beams, -	250
The effect of position, -	251
The composition of forces,	252
Best position for a strut, -	253
Nature of ties and struts, -	254
To distinguish ties from struts,	255
Lattice-work framing, -	256
Direction of pressure in rafters, - - - -	257
Oblique thrust of lean-to roofs,	258
Pressure on floor-beams, -	259
Kinds of pressure, - -	260
Resistance to compression,	261
Area of post, - -	261
Resistance to tension, -	262
Area of suspending piece,	262
Resistance to cross-strains,	263
Area of bearing timbers,	263
Area of stiffest beam, -	264
Bearers narrow and deep,	265
Principles of framing, -	266
FLOORS.	
Single-joisted, - -	267
To find area of floor-timbers,	268
Dimensions of trimmers, &c.,	269
Strutting between beams,	270
Cross-furring and deafening,	271
Double floors, - - -	272
Dimensions of binding-joists,	273
Do. of bridging-joists,	274
Do. of ceiling-joists, -	275
Framed floors, - - -	276
Dimensions of girders, -	277
Girders sawn and bolted, -	278
Trussed girders, - -	279
Floors in general, - -	280
PARTITIONS.	
Nature of their construction,	281
Designs for partitions, -	282
Superfluous timber, - -	282
Improved method, - -	283
Weight of partitioning, -	284
ROOFS.	
Lateral strains, - -	285
Pressure on roofs, - -	286
Weight of covering, -	286
Definitions, - - -	287
Relative size of timbers,	288
To find the area of a king-post,	289
Of a queen-post, - -	290
Of a tie-beam, - - -	291
Of a rafter, - - -	292
Of a straining-beam, -	294
Of braces, - - -	295
Of purlins, - - -	296
Of common rafters, -	297
To avoid shrinkage, - -	298
Roof with a built-rib, -	299
Badly-constructed roofs, -	300
To find the length and bevils in hip-roofs, - -	301
To find the backing of a hip-rafter, - - - -	302
DOMES.	
With horizontal ties, -	303
Ribbed dome, - - -	304
Area of the ribs, - -	305
Curve of equilibrium, -	306
To describe a cubic parabola,	307
Small domes for stairways,	308
To find the curves of the ribs,	309
To find the shape of the covering for spherical domes,	310
Do. when laid horizontally,	311
To find an angle-rib, - -	312
BRIDGES.	
Wooden bridge with tie-beam,	313
Do. without a tie-beam,	314
Do. with a built-rib,	315
Table of least rise in bridges,	315
Rule for built-ribs, - -	315
Pressure on arches, -	316
To form bent-ribs, - -	317
Elasticity of timber, -	317
To construct a framed rib,	318
Width of roadway, &c., -	319
Stone abutments and piers,	320
Piers constructed of piles,	321

	Art.
Piles in ancient bridges,	321
Centring for stone bridges,	322
Pressure of arch-stones, -	322
Centre without a tie at the base, - - -	323
Construction of centres, -	324
General directions, -	325
Lowering centres, - -	326
Relative size of timbers, -	327
Short rule for do. - -	328
Joints between arch-stones,	329
Do. in elliptical arch, -	330
Do. in parabolic arch, -	331

JOINTS.

	Art.
Scarfing, or splicing,	332. 334
To proportion the parts, -	335
Joints in beams and posts, -	336
Joints in floor-timbers, -	337
Timber weakened by framing,	338
Joints for rafters and braces,	339
Evil of shrinking avoided, -	340
Proper joint for collar-beam,	341
Pins, nails, bolts and straps,	342
Dimensions of straps, -	342
To prevent the rusting of straps, - - - -	342

SECT. V.—DOORS, WINDOWS, &c.

DOORS

Dimensions of doors, - -	343
To proportion height to width,	344
Width of stiles, rails and panels, - - -	345
Example of trimming, -	346
Elevation of a door and trimmings, - - -	347
General directions for hanging doors, - - -	348

WINDOWS.

To determine the size, -	349
To find dimensions of frame,	350
To proportion box to flap shutter, - - -	351
To proportion and arrange windows, - - -	352
Circular-headed windows,	353
To find the form of the soffit,	354
Do. in a circular wall, -	355

SECT. VI.—STAIRS.

Their position, - - -	356
Principles of the pitch-board,	357
To proportion the rise to the tread, - - -	358
The angle of ascent, - -	359
Length of steps, - -	360
To construct a pitch-board,	361
To lay-out the string, -	362
Section of step, - -	363

PLATFORM STAIRS.

To construct the cylinder, -	364
To cut the lower edge of do.,	365
To place the balusters, -	366
To find the moulds for the rail, - - - - -	367
Elucidation of this method,	368
Two other examples,	369, 370
To apply the mould to the plank, - - -	371
To bore for the balusters, -	372
Face-mould for moulded rail,	373
To apply this mould to plank,	374
To ascertain thickness of stuff,	375

WINDING STAIRS.

Flyers and winders, -	376
To construct winding stairs,	377

	Art.
Timbers to support winding stairs,	378
To find falling-mould of rail,	379
To find face-mould of do.,	380
Position of butt-joint,	380
To ascertain thickness of stuff,	381
To apply the mould to plank,	383
Elucidation of the butt-joint,	384
Quarter-circle stairs,	385
Falling-mould for do.,	386
Face-mould for do.,	387
Elucidation of this method,	388
To bevil edge of plank,	389
To apply moulds without bevilling plank,	390
To find bevils for splayed-work,	391
Another method for face-moulds,	392
To apply face-mould to plank,	394
To apply falling-mould,	395
SCROLLS.	
General rule,	396
To describe scroll for rail,	398
For curtail-step,	399
Balusters under scroll,	400
Falling-mould for scroll,	401
Face-mould for do.,	402
Round rails over winders,	403
To find form of newel-cap,	404

SECT. VII.—SHADOWS.

Inclination of line of shadow,	407
Shadows on mouldings,	408
Shadow of a shelf,	409
Of a shelf of varying width,	410
Of do. with oblique end,	411
Of an inclined shelf,	412
Of do. inclined in section,	413
Of do. having a curved edge,	414
Of do. curved in elevation,	415
Shadow on cylindrical wall,	416
Do. on inclined wall,	417
Shadow of a beam,	418
Shadow in a recess,	419
Do. with wall inclined,	420
Shadow in a fireplace,	421
Shadow of window lintel,	422
Shadow of step-nosing,	423
Of a pedestal upon steps,	424
Of square abacus on column,	425
Of circular abacus on do.	426
On the capital of a column,	427
Of column and entablature,	428
Shadows on Tuscan cornice,	429
Reflected light,	430

APPENDIX.

	Page.
Glossary of Architectural Terms,	3
Table of Squares, Cubes and Roots,	14
Rules for extending the use of the foregoing table,	21
Rule for finding the roots of whole numbers with decimals,	23
Rules for the reduction of Decimals,	23
Table of Areas and Circumferences of Circles,	25
Rules for extending the use of the foregoing table,	28
Table showing the Capacity of Wells, Cisterns, &c.,	29
Rules for finding the Areas, &c., of Polygons,	30
Table of Weights of Materials,	31

INTRODUCTION.

Art. 1.—A knowledge of the properties and principles of *lines* can best be acquired by practice. Although the various problems throughout this work may be understood by inspection, yet they will be impressed upon the mind with much greater force, if they are actually performed with pencil and paper by the student. Science is acquired by study—art by practice: he, therefore, who would have any thing more than a theoretical, (which must of necessity be a superficial,) knowledge of Carpentry, will attend to the following directions, provide himself with the articles here specified, and perform all the operations described in the following pages. Many of the problems may appear, at the first reading, somewhat confused and intricate; but by making one line at a time, according to the explanations, the student will not only succeed in copying the figures correctly, but by ordinary attention will learn the principles upon which they are based, and thus be able to make them available in any unexpected case to which they may apply.

2.—The following articles are necessary for drawing, viz: a drawing-board, paper, drawing-pins or mouth-glue, a sponge, a T-square, a set-square, two straight-edges, or flat rulers, a lead pencil, a piece of india-rubber, a cake of india-ink, a set of drawing-instruments, and a scale of equal parts.

3.—The size of the *drawing-board* must be regulated according to the size of the drawings which are to be made upon it. Yet for ordinary practice, in learning to draw, a board about 15 by 20 inches, and one inch thick, will be found large enough, and more convenient than a larger one. This board should be well-seasoned, perfectly square at the corners, and without clamps on the ends. A board is better without clamps, because the little service they are supposed to render by preventing the board from warping, is overbalanced by the consideration that the shrinking of the panel leaves the ends of the clamps projecting beyond the edge of the board, and thus interfering with the proper working of the stock of the T-square. When the stuff is well-seasoned, the warping of the board will be but trifling; and by exposing the rounding side to the fire, or to the sun, it may be brought back to its proper shape.

4.—For mere line drawings, the *paper* need not commonly be what is called drawing-paper; as this is rather costly, and will, where much is used, make quite an item of expense. Cartridge-paper, as it is called, of about 20 by 26 inches, and of as good a quality nearly as drawing-paper, can be bought for about 50 cts. a quire, or 2 pence a sheet; and each sheet may be cut in halves, or even quarters, for practising. If the drawing is to be much used, as working drawings generally are, cartridge-paper is much better than the other kind.

5.—A *drawing-pin* is a small brass button, having a steel pin projecting from the under side. By having one of these at each corner, the paper can be fixed to the board; but this can be done in a much better manner with *mouth-glue.* The pins will prevent the paper from changing its position on the board; but, more than this, the glue keeps the paper perfectly tight and smooth, thus making it so much the more pleasant to work on.

To attach the paper with mouth-glue, lay it with the bottom side up, on the board; and with a straight-edge and penknife, cut off the rough and uneven edge. With a sponge moderately wet, rub all the surface of the paper, except a strip around the edge about half an inch wide. As soon as the glistening of the water disappears, turn the sheet over, and place it upon the board just where you wish it glued. Commence upon one of the longest sides, and proceed thus: lay a flat ruler upon the paper, parallel to the edge, and within a quarter of an inch of it. With a knife, or any thing similar, turn up the edge of the paper against the edge of the ruler, and put one end of the cake of mouth-glue between your lips to dampen it. Then holding it upright, rub it against and along the entire edge of the paper that is turned up against the ruler, bearing moderately against the edge of the ruler, which must be held firmly with the left hand. Moisten the glue as often as it becomes dry, until a sufficiency of it is rubbed on the edge of the paper. Take away the ruler, restore the turned-up edge to the level of the board, and lay upon it a strip of pretty stiff paper. By rubbing upon this, not very hard but pretty rapidly, with the thumb nail of the right hand, so as to cause a gentle friction, and heat to be imparted to the glue that is on the edge of the paper, you will make it adhere to the board. The other edges in succession must be treated in the same manner.

Some short distances along one or more of the edges, may afterwards be found loose: if so, the glue must again be applied, and the paper rubbed until it adheres. The board must then be laid away in a warm or dry place; and in a short time, the surface of the paper will be drawn out, perfectly tight and smooth, and ready for use. The paper dries best when the board is laid level. When the drawing is finished, lay a straight-edge upon the paper, and cut it from the board, leaving the glued strip still attached. This may afterwards be taken off by wetting it freely with the sponge; which will soak the glue, and loosen the paper. Do this as soon as the drawing is taken off, in order that the board may be dry when it is wanted for use again. Care must be taken that, in applying the glue, the edge of the paper does not become damper than the rest: if it should, the paper must be laid aside to dry, (to use at another time,) and another sheet be used in its place.

Sometimes, especially when the drawing board is new, the paper will not stick very readily; but by persevering, this difficulty may be overcome. In the place of the mouth-glue, a strong solution of gum-arabic may be used, and on some accounts is to be preferred; for the edges of the paper need not be kept dry, and it adheres more readily. Dissolve the gum in a sufficiency of warm water to make it of the consistency of linseed oil. It must be applied to the paper with a brush, when the edge is turned up against the ruler, as was described for the mouth-glue. If two drawing-boards are used, one may be in use while the other is laid away to dry; and as they may be cheaply made, it is advisable to have two. The drawing-board having a frame around it, commonly called a panel-board, may afford rather more facility in attaching the paper when this is of the size to suit; yet it has objections which overbalance that con sideration.

6.—A *T-square* of mahogany, at once simple in its construction, and affording all necessary service, may be thus made. Let the stock or handle be seven inches long, two and a quarter inches wide, and three-eighths of an inch thick: the blade, twenty inches long, (exclusive of the stock,) two inches wide, and one-eighth of an inch thick. In joining the blade to the stock, a very firm and simple joint may be made by dovetailing it—as shown at *Fig*. 1.

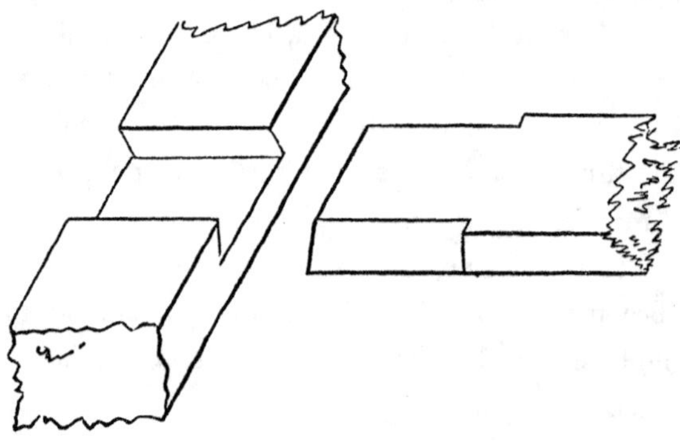

Fig. 1.

7.—The *set-square* is in the form of a right-angled triangle; and is commonly made of mahogany, one-eighth of an inch in thickness. The size that is most convenient for general use, is six inches and three inches respectively for the sides which contain the right angle; although a particular length for the sides is by no means necessary. Care should be taken to have the square corner exactly true. This, as also the T-square and rulers, should have a hole bored through them, by which to hang them upon a nail when not in use.

8.—One of the *rulers* may be about twenty inches long, and the other six inches. The *pencil* ought to be hard enough to retain a fine point, and yet not so hard as to leave ineffaceable marks. It should be used lightly, so that the extra marks that are not needed when the drawing is inked, may be easily rubbed off with the rubber. The best kind of *india-ink* is that which will easily rub off upon the plate; and, when the cake is rubbed against the teeth, will be free from grit.

9.—The *drawing-instruments* may be purchased of mathematical instrument makers at various prices: from one to one hundred dollars a set. In choosing a set, remember that the lowest price articles are not always the cheapest. A set, comprising a sufficient number of instruments for ordinary use, well made and fitted in a mahogany box, may be purchased at Pike and Son's, (Broadway, near Maiden-lane, N. Y.,) for three or four dollars. The compasses in this set have a *needle* point, which is much preferable to a common point.

10.—The best *scale of equal parts* for carpenters' use, is one that has one-eighth, three-sixteenths, one-fourth, three-eighths, one-half, five-eighths, three-fourths, and seven-eighths of an inch, and one inch, severally divided into *twelfths*, instead of being divided, as they usually are, into tenths. By this, if it be required to proportion a drawing so that every foot of the object represented will upon the paper measure one-fourth of an inch, use that part of the scale which is divided into one-fourths of an inch, taking for every foot one of those divisions, and for every inch one of the subdivisions into twelfths; and proceed in like manner in proportioning a drawing to any of the other divisions of the scale. An instrument in the form of a semi-circle, called a *protractor*, and used for laying down and measuring angles, is of much service to surveyors, but not much to carpenters.

11.—In drawing parallel lines, when they are to be parallel to either side of the board, use the T-square; but when it is required to draw lines parallel to a line which is drawn in a direction oblique to either side of the board, the set-square must be used. Let *a b*, (*Fig.* 2,) be a line, parallel to which it is

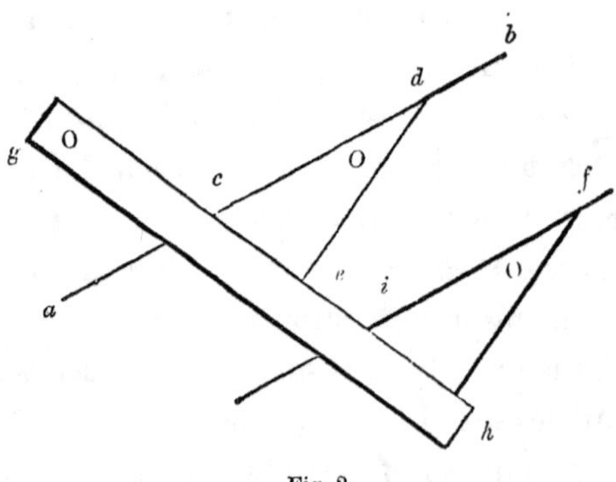

Fig. 2.

desired to draw one or more lines. Place any edge, as *c d*, of the set-square even with said line; then place the ruler, *g h*, against one of the other sides, as *c e*, and hold it firmly; slide the set-square along the edge of the ruler as far as it is desired, as at *f*; and a line drawn by the edge, *i f*, will be parallel to *a b*.

12.—To draw a line, as *k l*, (*Fig.* 3,) perpendicular to another, as *a b*, set the shortest edge of the set-square at the line, *a b*; place the ruler against the longest side, (the hypothenuse of the right-angled triangle;) hold the ruler firmly, and slide the set-square along until the side, *e d*, touches the point, *k*; then the line, *l k*, drawn by it, will be perpendicular to *a b*. In like manner, the drawing of other problems may be facilitated, as will be discovered in using the instruments.

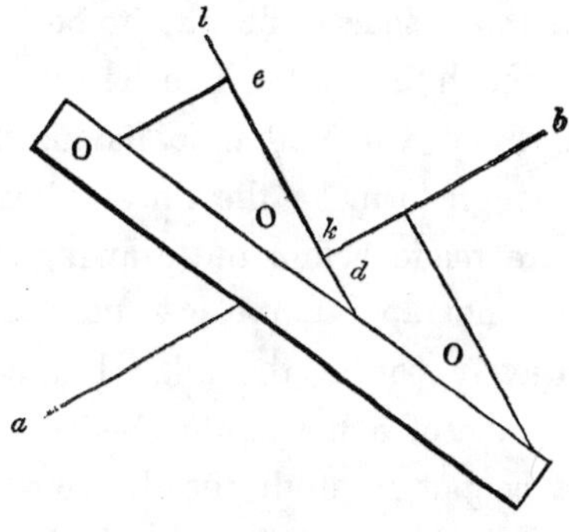

Fig. 3.

13.—In drawing a problem, proceed, with the pencil sharpened to a point, to lay down the several lines until the whole figure is completed; observing to let the lines cross each other at the several angles, instead of merely meeting. By this, the length of every line will be clearly defined. With a drop or two of water, rub one end of the cake of ink upon a plate or saucer, until a sufficiency adheres to it. Be careful to dry the cake of ink; because if it is left wet, it will crack and crumble in pieces. With an inferior camel's-hair pencil, add a little water to the ink that was rubbed on the plate, and mix it well. It should be diluted sufficiently to flow freely from the pen, and yet be thick enough to make a *black* line. With the hair pencil, place a little of the ink between the nibs of the drawing-pen, and screw the nibs together until the pen makes a fine line. Beginning with the curved lines, proceed to ink *all* the lines of the figure; being careful now to make every line of its requisite length. If they are a trifle too short or too long, the drawing will have a ragged appearance; and this is opposed to that neatness and accuracy which is indispensable to a good drawing. When the ink is dry, efface the pencil-marks with the india-rubber. If the pencil is used lightly, they will all rub off, leaving those lines only that were inked.

14.—In problems, all auxiliary lines are drawn light; while the lines given and those sought, in order to be distinguished at a glance, are made much heavier. The heavy lines are made so, by passing over them a second time, having the nibs of the pen separated far enough to make the lines as heavy as desired. If the heavy lines are made before the drawing is cleaned with the rubber, they will not appear so black and neat; because the india-rubber takes away part of the ink. If the drawing is a ground-plan or elevation of a house, the shade-lines, as they are termed, should not be put in until the drawing is shaded; as there is danger of the heavy lines spreading, when the brush, in shading or coloring, passes over them. If the lines are inked with common writing-ink, they will, however fine they may be made, be subject to the same evil; for which reason, india-ink is the only kind to be used.

THE

AMERICAN HOUSE-CARPENTER.

SECTION I.—PRACTICAL GEOMETRY.

DEFINITIONS.

15. —*Geometry* treats of the properties of magnitudes.

16.—A *point* has neither length, breadth, nor thickness.

17. —A *line* has length only.

18.—*Superficies* has length and breadth only.

19.—A *plane* is a surface, perfectly straight and even in every direction; as the face of a panel when not warped nor winding.

20.—A *solid* has length, breadth and thickness.

21.—A *right*, or *straight*, line is the shortest that can be drawn between two points.

22.—*Parallel lines* are equi-distant throughout their length.

23.—An *angle* is the inclination of two lines towards one another. (*Fig.* 4.)

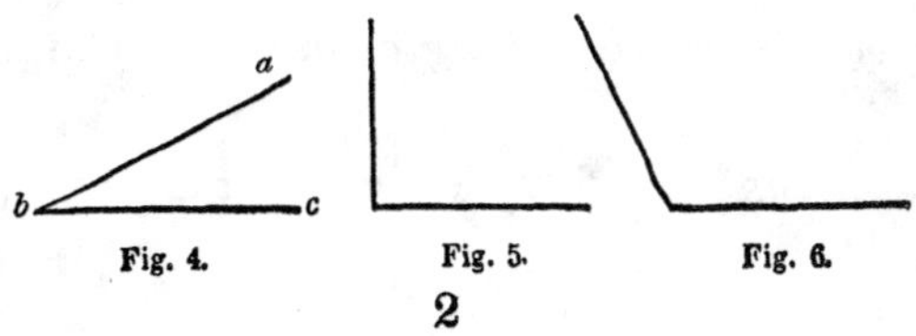

Fig. 4. Fig. 5. Fig. 6.

24.—A *right angle* has one line perpendicular to the other. (*Fig*. 5.)

25.—An *oblique angle* is either greater or less than a right angle. (*Fig*. 4 and 6.)

26.—An *acute angle* is less than a right angle. (*Fig*. 4.)

27.—An *obtuse angle* is greater than a right angle. (*Fig*. 6.)

When an angle is denoted by three letters, the middle one, in the order they stand, denotes the angular point, and the other two the sides containing the angle; thus, let *a b c*, (*Fig*. 4,) be the angle, then *b* will be the angular point, and *a b* and *b c* will be the two sides containing that angle.

28.—A *triangle* is a superficies having three sides and angles, (*Fig*. 7, 8, 9 and 10.)

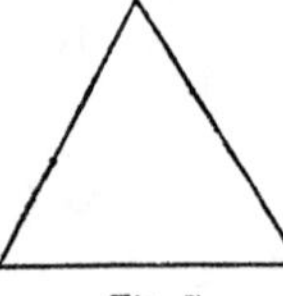
Fig. 7.

Fig. 8.

29.—An *equi-lateral triangle* has its three sides equal. (*Fig*. 7.)

30.—An *isoceles triangle* has only two sides equal. (*Fig*. 8.)

31.—A *scalene triangle* has all its sides unequal. (*Fig*. 9)

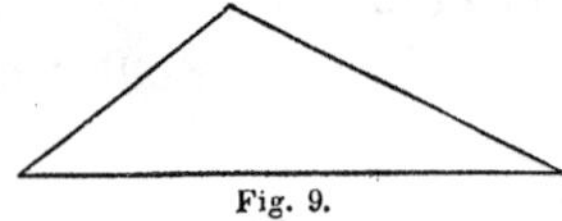
Fig. 9.

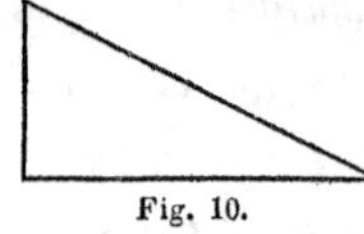
Fig. 10.

32.—A *right-angled triangle* has one right angle. (*Fig*. 10.)

33.—An *acute-angled triangle* has all its angles acute. (*Fig*. 7 and 8.)

34.—An *obtuse-angled triangle* has one obtuse angle. (*Fig*. 9.)

35.—A *quadrangle* has four sides and four angles. (*Fig*. 11 to 16.)

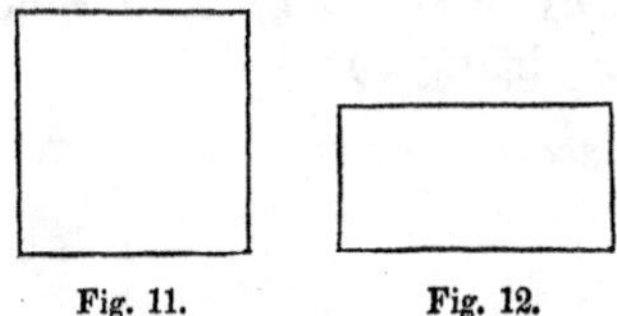

Fig. 11. Fig. 12.

36.—A *parallelogram* is a quadrangle having its opposite sides parallel. (*Fig.* 11 to 14.)

37.—A *rectangle* is a parallelogram, its angles being right angles. (*Fig.* 11 and 12.)

38.—A *square* is a rectangle having equal sides. (*Fig.* 11.)

39.—A *rhombus* is an equi-lateral parallelogram having oblique angles. (*Fig.* 13.)

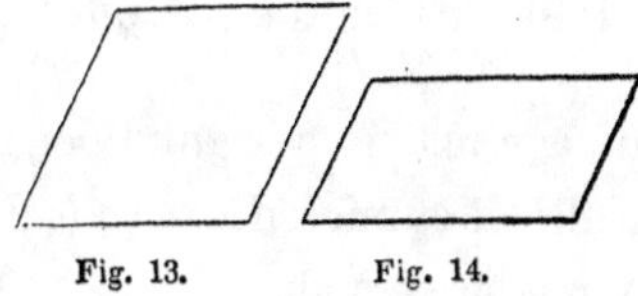

Fig. 13. Fig. 14.

40.—A *rhomboid* is a parallelogram having oblique angles. (*Fig.* 14.)

41.—A *trapezoid* is a quadrangle having only two of its sides parallel. (*Fig.* 15.)

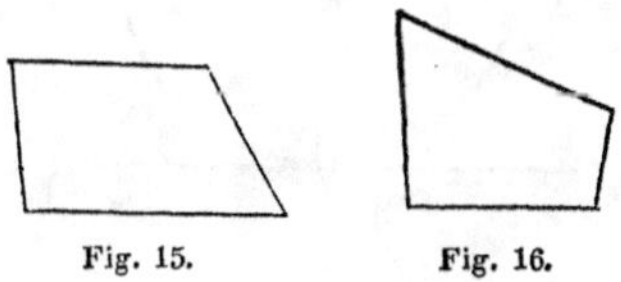

Fig. 15. Fig. 16.

42.—A *trapezium* is a quadrangle which has no two of its sides parallel. (*Fig.* 16.)

43.—A *polygon* is a figure bounded by right lines.

44.—A *regular polygon* has its sides and angles equal.

45.—An *irregular polygon* has its sides and angles unequal.

46.—A *trigon* is a polygon of three sides, (*Fig.* 7 to 10;) a *tetragon* has four sides, (*Fig.* 11 to 16;) a *pentagon* has five, (*Fig.* 17 ;) a *hexagon* six, (*Fig.* 18 ;) a *heptagon* seven, (*Fig.* 19 ;) an *octagon* eight, (*Fig.* 20 ;) a *nonagon* nine ; a *decagon* ten ; an *undecagon* eleven ; and a *dodecagon* twelve sides.

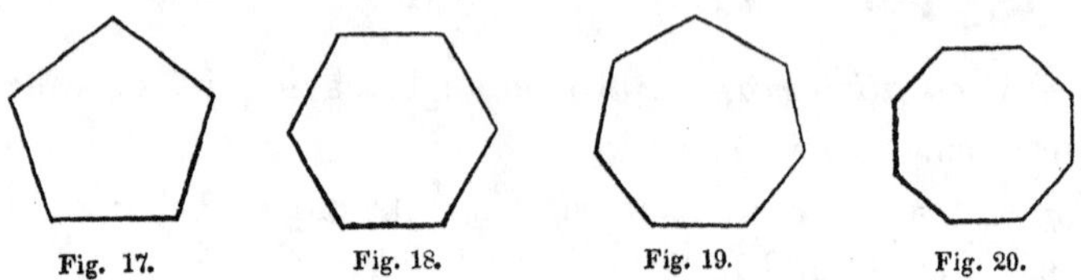

Fig. 17. Fig. 18. Fig. 19. Fig. 20.

47.—A *circle* is a figure bounded by a curved line, called the *circumference ;* which is every where equi-distant from a certain point within, called its *centre.*

The circumference is also called the *periphery*, and sometimes the *circle.*

48.—The *radius* of a circle is a right line drawn from the centre to any point in the circumference. (*a b*, *Fig.* 21.)

All the *radii* of a circle are equal.

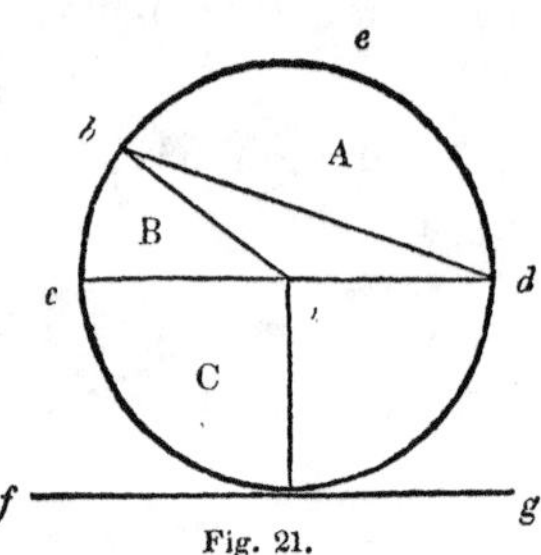

Fig. 21.

49.—The *diameter* is a right line passing through the centre, and terminating at two opposite points in the circumference. Hence it is twice the length of the radius. (*c d*, *Fig.* 21.)

50.—An *arc* of a circle is a part of the circumference. (*c b* or *b e d*, *Fig.* 21.)

51.—A *chord* is a right line joining the extremities of an arc. (*b d*, *Fig.* 21.)

52.—A *segment* is any part of a circle bounded by an arc and its chord. (*A*, *Fig.* 21.)

53.—A *sector* is any part of a circle bounded by an arc and two radii, drawn to its extremities. (*B*, *Fig.* 21.)

54.—A *quadrant*, or quarter of a circle, is a sector having a quarter of the circumference for its arc. (*C*, *Fig.* 21.)

55.—A *tangent* is a right line, which in passing a curve, touches, without cutting it. (*f g*, *Fig.* 21.)

56.—A *cone* is a solid figure standing upon a circular base diminishing in straight lines to a point at the top, called its vertex. (*Fig.* 22.)

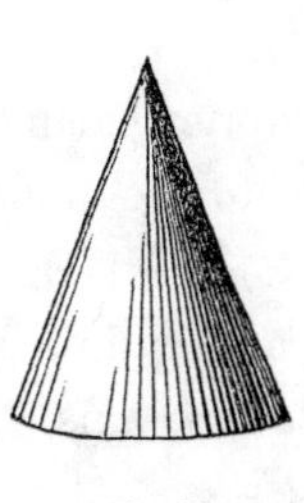

Fig. 22.

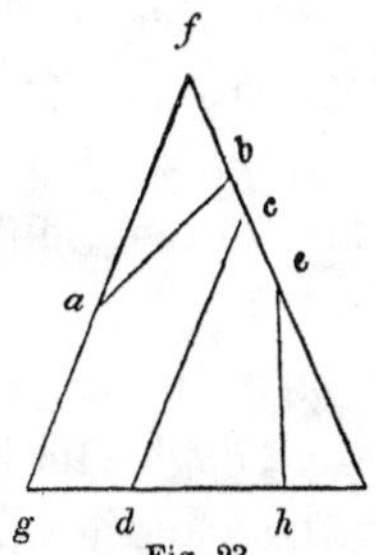

Fig. 23.

57.—The *axis* of a cone is a right line passing through it, from the vertex to the centre of the circle at the base.

58.—An *ellipsis* is described if a cone be cut by a plane, not parallel to its base, passing quite through the curved surface. (*a b*, *Fig.* 23.)

59.—A *parabola* is described if a cone be cut by a plane, parallel to a plane touching the curved surface. (*c d*, *Fig.* 23—*c d* being parallel to *f g*.)

60.—An *hyperbola* is described if a cone be cut by a plane, parallel to any plane within the cone that passes through its vertex. (*e h*, *Fig.* 23.)

61.—*Foci* are the points at which the pins are placed in describing an ellipse. (See *Art.* 115, and *f*, *f*, *Fig.* 24.)

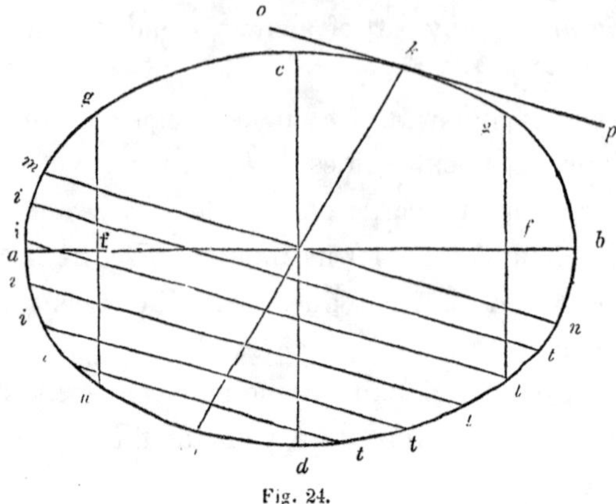

Fig. 24.

62.—The *transverse axis* is the longest diameter of the ellipsis. (*a b*, *Fig.* 24.)

63.—The *conjugate axis* is the shortest diameter of the ellipsis; and is, therefore, at right angles to the transverse axis. (*c d*, *Fig.* 24.)

64.—The *parameter* is a right line passing through the focus of an ellipsis, at right angles to the transverse axis, and terminated by the curve. (*g h* and *g t*, *Fig.* 24.)

65.—A *diameter of an ellipsis* is any right line passing through the centre, and terminated by the curve. (*k l*, or *m n*, *Fig.* 24.)

66.—A diameter is *conjugate* to another when it is parallel to a tangent drawn at the extremity of that other—thus, the diameter, *m n*, (*Fig.* 24,) being parallel to the tangent, *o p*, is therefore conjugate to the diameter, *k l*.

67.—A *double ordinate* is any right line, crossing a diameter of an ellipsis, and drawn parallel to a tangent at the extremity of that diameter. (*i t*, *Fig.* 24.)

68.—A *cylinder* is a solid generated by the revolution of a right-angled parallelogram, or rectangle, about one of its sides; and consequently the ends of the cylinder are equal circles. (*Fig.* 25.)

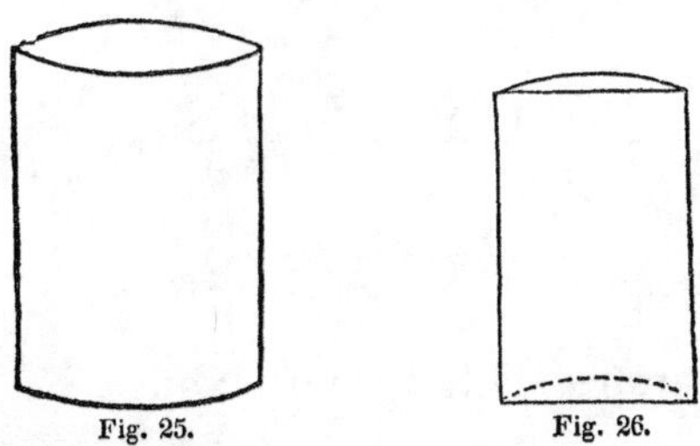

Fig. 25. Fig. 26.

69.—The *axis* of a cylinder is a right line passing through it, from the centres of the two circles which form the ends.

70.—A *segment* of a cylinder is comprehended under three planes, and the curved surface of the cylinder. Two of these are segments of circles: the other plane is a parallelogram, called by way of distinction, the *plane of the segment.* The circular segments are called, the ends of the cylinder. (*Fig.* 26.)

PROBLEMS.

RIGHT LINES AND ANGLES.

71.—*To bisect a line.* Upon the ends of the line, *a b*, (*Fig.* 27,) as centres, with any distance for radius greater than half

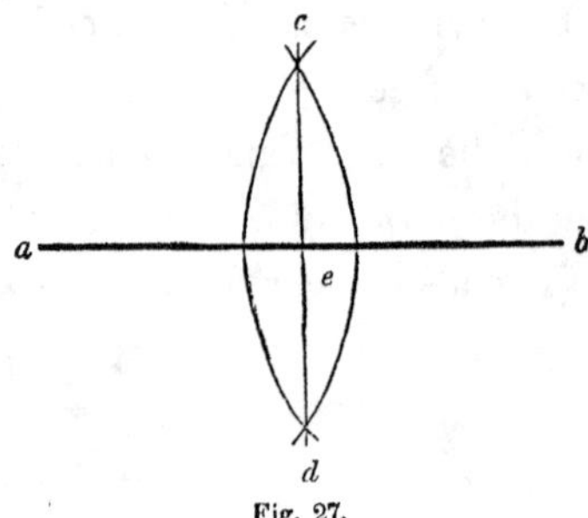

Fig. 27.

a b, describe arcs cutting each other in *c* and *d*; draw the line, *c d*, and the point, *e*, where it cuts *a b*, will be the middle of the line, *a b*.

In practice, a line is generally divided with the compasses, or dividers; but this problem is useful where it is desired to draw, at the middle of another line, one at right angles to it. (See *Art.* 85.)

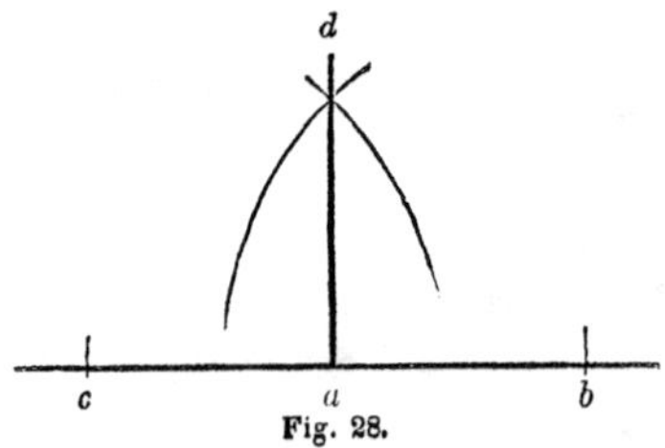

Fig. 28.

72.—*To erect a perpendicular.* From the point, *a*, (*Fig.* 28,) set off any distance, as *a b*, and the same distance from *a* to *c*; upon *c*, as a centre, with any distance for radius greater than *c a*, describe an arc at *d*; upon *b*, with the same radius, describe another at *d*; join *d* and *a*, and the line, *d a*, will be the perpendicular required.

This, and the three following problems, are more easily performed by the use of the set-square—(see *Art.* 12.) Yet they are useful when the operation is so large that a set-square cannot be used.

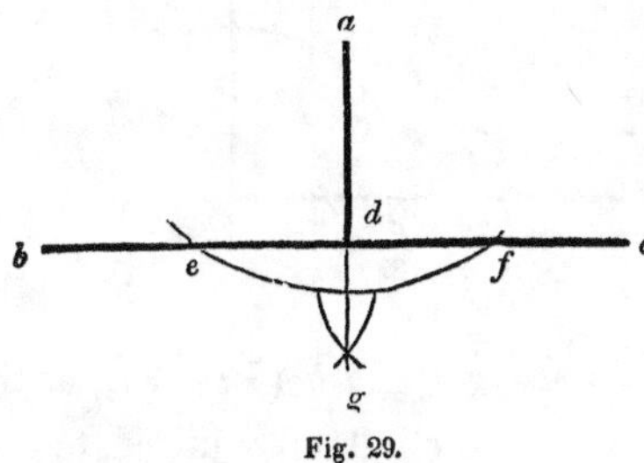

Fig. 29.

73.—*To let fall a perpendicular.* Let *a*, (*Fig.* 29,) be the point, above the line, *b c*, from which the perpendicular is required to fall. Upon *a*, with any radius greater than *a d*, describe an arc, cutting *b c* at *e* and *f*; upon the points, *e* and *f*, with any radius greater than *e d*, describe arcs, cutting each other at *g*; join *a* and *g*, and the line, *a d*, will be the perpendicular required.

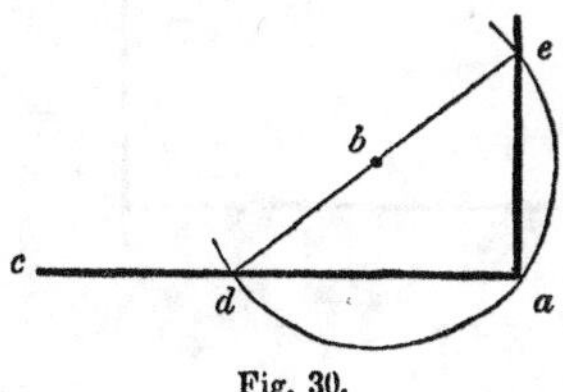

Fig. 30.

74.—*To erect a perpendicular at the end of a line.* Let *a*, (*Fig.* 30,) at the end of the line, *c a*, be the point at which the perpendicular is to be erected. Take any point, as *b*, above the line, *c a*, and with the radius, *b a*, describe the arc, *d a e*, through *d* and *b*, draw the line, *d e*; join *e* and *a*, then *e a* will be the perpendicular required.

The principle here made use of, is a very important one; and is applied in many other cases—(see *Art.* 81, *b*, and *Art.* 84. For proof of its correctness, see *Art.* 156.)

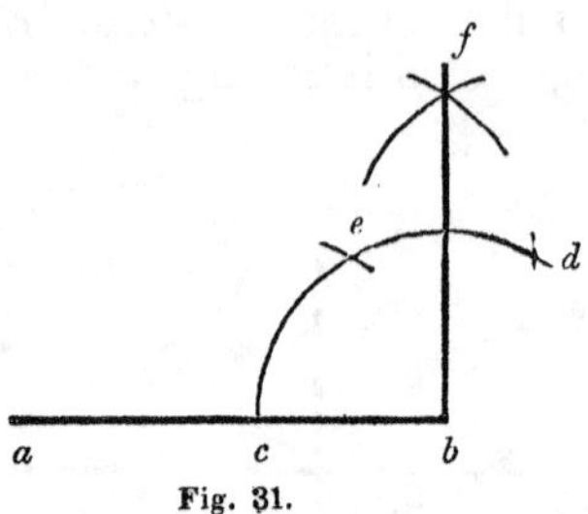

Fig. 31.

74, *a*.—*A second method.* Let *b*, (*Fig.* 31,) at the end of the line, *a b*, be the point at which it is required to erect a perpendicular. Upon *b*, with any radius less than *b a*, describe the arc, *c e d*; upon *c*, with the same radius, describe the small arc at *e*, and upon *e*, another at *d*; upon *e* and *d*, with the same or any other radius greater than half *e d*, describe arcs intersecting at *f*; join *f* and *b*, and the line, *f b*, will be the perpendicular required.

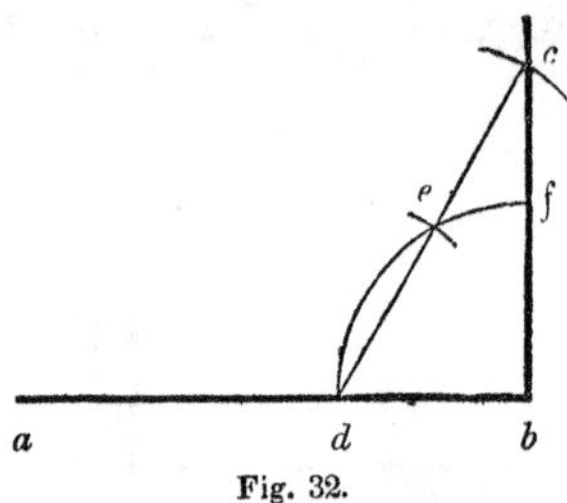

Fig. 32.

74, *b*.—*A third method.* Let *b*, (*Fig.* 32,) be the given point at which it is required to erect a perpendicular. Upon *b*, with any radius less than *b a*, describe the quadrant, *d e f*; upon *d*, with the same radius, describe an arc at *e*, and upon *e*, another at *c*;

through *d* and *e*, draw *d c*, cutting the arc in *c*; join *c* and *b*, then *c b* will be the perpendicular required.

This problem can be solved by the *six, eight and ten* rule, as it is called; which is founded upon the same principle as the problems at *Art.* 103, 104; and is applied as follows. Let *a d*, (*Fig.* 30,) equal eight, and *a e*, six; then, if *d e* equals ten, the angle, *e a d*, is a right angle. Because the square of six and that of eight, added together, equal the square of ten, thus: $6 \times 6 = 36$, and $8 \times 8 = 64$; $36 + 64 = 100$, and $10 \times 10 = 100$. Any sizes, taken in the same proportion, as six, eight and ten, will produce the same effect: as 3, 4 and 5, or 12, 16 and 20. (See note to *Art.* 103.)

By the process shown at *Fig.* 30, the end of a board may be squared without a carpenters'-square. All that is necessary is a pair of compasses and a ruler. Let *c a* be the edge of the board, and *a* the point at which it is required to be squared. Take the point, *b*, as near as possible at an angle of forty-five degrees, or on a *mitre*-line, from *a*, and at about the middle of the board. This is not necessary to the working of the problem, nor does it affect its accuracy, but the result is more easily obtained. Stretch the compasses from *b* to *a*, and then bring the leg at *a* around to *d*; draw a line from *d*, through *b*, out indefinitely; take the distance, *d b*, and place it from *b* to *e*; join *e* and *a*; then *e a* will be at right angles to *c a*. In squaring the foundation of a building, or laying-out a garden, a rod and chalk-line may be used instead of compasses and ruler.

75.—*To let fall a perpendicular near the end of a line.* Let *e*, (*Fig.* 30,) be the point above the line, *c a*, from which the perpendicular is required to fall. From *e*, draw any line, as *e d*, obliquely to the line, *c a*; bisect *e d* at *b*; upon *b*, with the radius, *b e*, describe the arc, *e a d*; join *e* and *a*; then *e a* will be the perpendicular required.

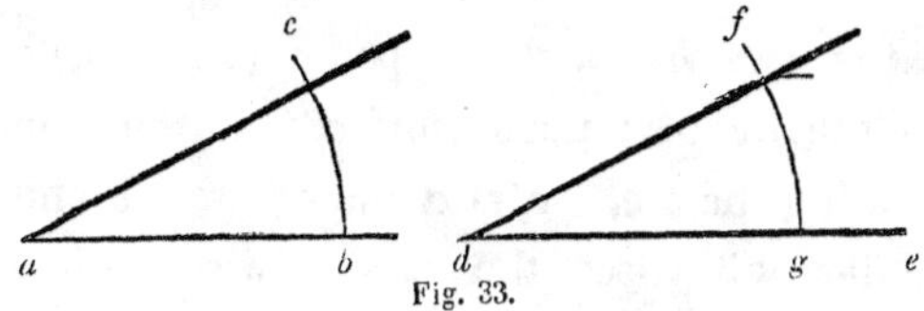

Fig. 33.

76.—*To make an angle,* (as *e d f*, *Fig.* 33,) *equal to a given angle,* (as *b a c*.) From the angular point, *a*, with any radius, describe the arc, *b c*; and with the same radius, on the line, *d e*, and from the point, *d*, describe the arc, *f g* ; take the distance, *b c*, and upon *g*, describe the small arc at *f* ; join *f* and *d* ; and the angle, *e d f*, will be equal to the angle, *b a c*.

If the given line upon which the angle is to be made, is situated parallel to the similar line of the given angle, this may be performed more readily with the set-square. (See *Art.* 11.)

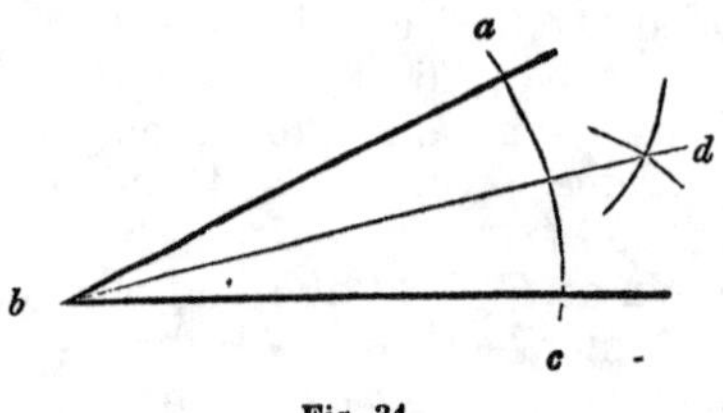

Fig. 34.

77.—*To bisect an angle.* Let *a b c*, (*Fig.* 34,) be the angle to be bisected. Upon *b*, with any radius, describe the arc, *a c* ; upon *a* and *c*, with a radius greater than half *a c*, describe arcs cutting each other at *d* ; join *b* and *d* ; and *b d* will bisect the angle, *a b c*, as was required.

This problem is frequently made use of in solving other problems ; it should therefore be well impressed upon the memory.

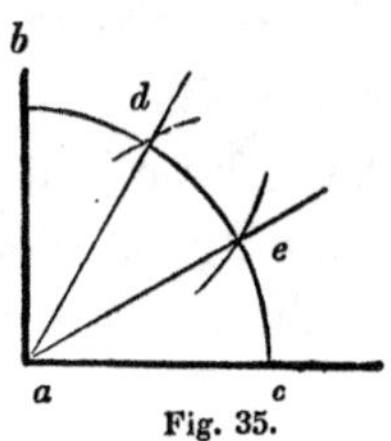

Fig. 35.

78.—*To trisect a right angle.* Upon *a*, (*Fig.* 35,) with any radius, describe the arc, *b c* ; upon *b* and *c*, with the same radius, describe arcs cutting the arc, *b c*, at *d* and *e* ; from *d* and *e*, draw lines to *a*, and they will trisect the angle as was required.

The truth of this is made evident by the following operation. Divide a circle into quadrants : also, take the radius in the dividers, and space off the circumference. This will divide the circumference into just six parts. A semi-circumference, therefore, is equal to three, and a quadrant to one and a half of those parts. The radius, therefore, is equal to $\frac{2}{3}$ of a quadrant; and this is equal to a right angle.

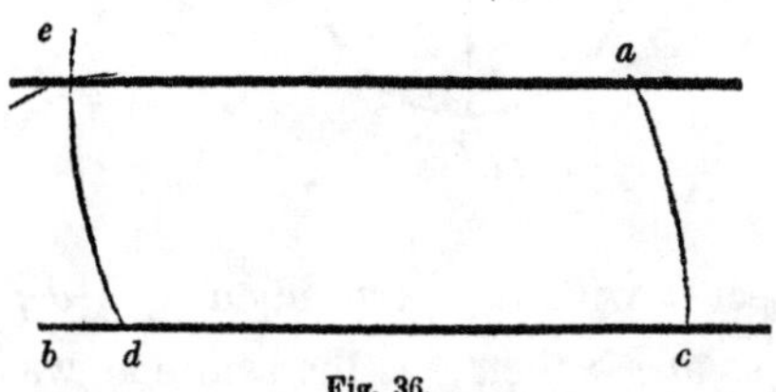

Fig. 36.

79.—*Through a given point, to draw a line parallel to a given line.* Let *a*, (*Fig.* 36,) be the given point, and *b c* the given line. Upon any point, as *d*, in the line, *b c*, with the radius, *d a*, describe the arc, *a c;* upon *a*, with the same radius, describe the arc, *d e;* make *d e* equal to *a c;* through *e* and *a*, draw the line, *e a;* which will be the line required.

This is upon the same principle as *Art.* 76.

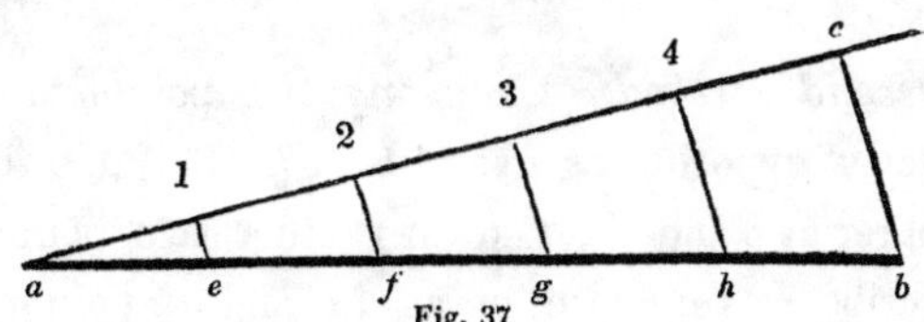

Fig. 37

80.—*To divide a given line into any number of equal parts.* Let *a b*, (*Fig.* 37,) be the given line, and 5 the number of parts. Draw *a c*, at any angle to *a b;* on *a c*, from *a*, set off 5 equal parts of any length, as at 1, 2, 3, 4 and *c;* join *c* and *b;* through the points, 1, 2, 3 and 4, draw 1 *e*, 2 *f*, 3 *g* and 4 *h*, parallel to *c b;* which will divide the line, *a b*, as was required.

The lines, *a b* and *a c*, are divided in the same proportion. (See *Art.* 109.)

THE CIRCLE.

81.—*To find the centre of a circle.* Draw any chord, as *a b*,

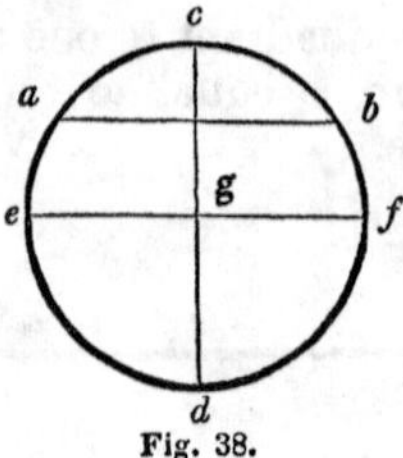

Fig. 38.

(*Fig.* 38,) and bisect it with the perpendicular, *c d;* bisect *c d* with the line, *e f*, as at *g;* then *g* is the centre as was required.

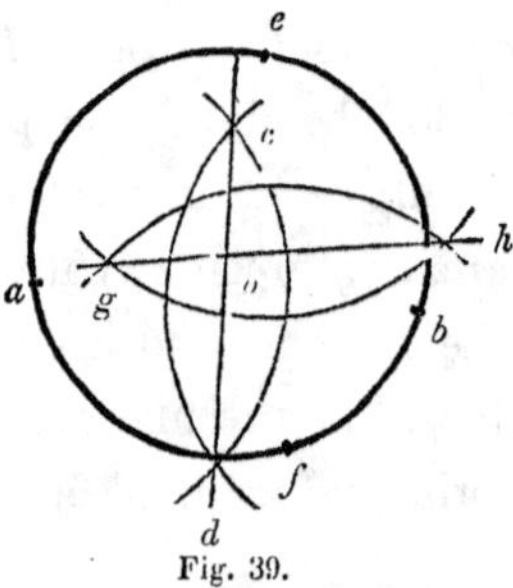

Fig. 39.

81, *a.*—*A second method.* Upon any two points in the circumference nearly opposite, as *a* and *b*, (*Fig.* 39,) describe arcs cutting each other at *c* and *d;* take any other two points, as *e* and *f*, and describe arcs intersecting as at *g* and *h;* join *g* and *h*, and *c* and *d;* the intersection, *o*, is the centre.

This is upon the same principle as *Art.* 85.

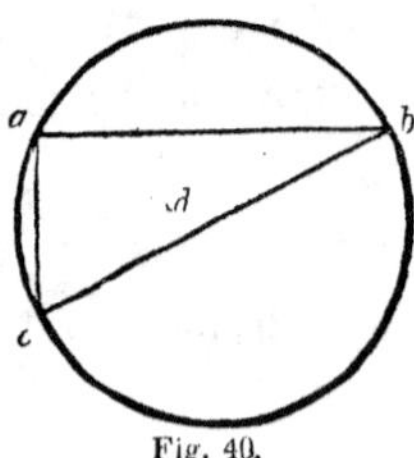

Fig. 40.

81, *b.*—*A third method.* Draw any chord, as *a b*, (*Fig.* 40,) and from the point, *a*, draw *a c*, at right angles to *a b*; join *c* and *b*; bisect *c b* at *d*—which will be the centre of the circle.

If a circle be not too large for the purpose, its centre may very readily be ascertained by the help of a carpenters'-square, thus: app'y the corner of the square to any point in the circumference, as at *a*; by the edges of the square, (which the lines, *a b* and *a c*, represent,) draw lines cutting the circle, as at *b* and *c*; join *b* and *c*; then if *b c* is bisected, as at *d*, the point, *d*, will be the centre. (See *Art.* 156.)

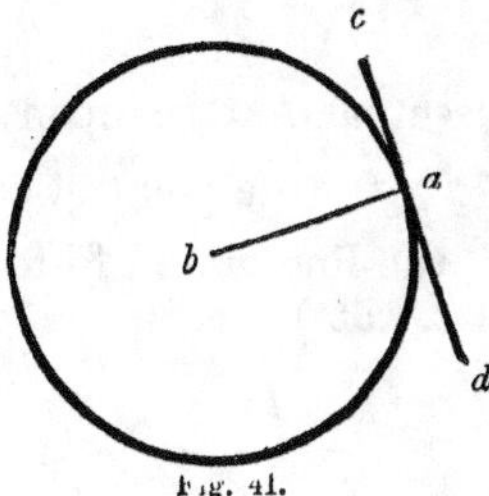

Fig. 41.

82.—*At a given point in a circle, to draw a tangent thereto.* Let *a*, (*Fig.* 41,) be the given point, and *b* the centre of the circle. Join *a* and *b*; through the point, *a*, and at right angles to *a b*, draw *c d*; *c d* is the tangent required.

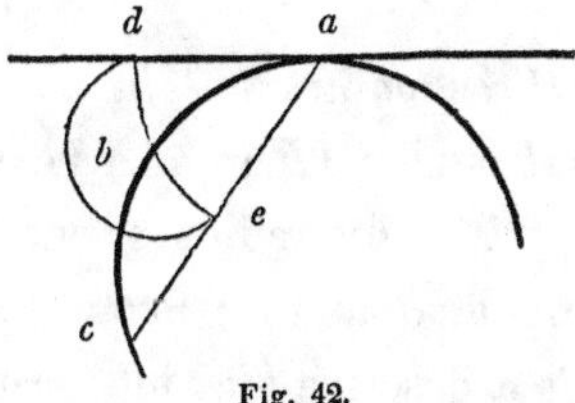

Fig. 42.

83.—*The same, without making use of the centre of the circle.* Let *a*, (*Fig.* 42,) be the given point. From *a*, set off any distance to *b*, and the same from *b* to *c*; join *a* and *c*; upon *a*, with *a b* for radius, describe the arc, *d b e*; make *d b* equal to *b e*; through *a* and *d*, draw a line; this will be the tangent required.

84.—*A circle and a tangent given, to find the point of contact.* From any point, as *a*, (*Fig.* 43,) in the tangent, *b c*, draw

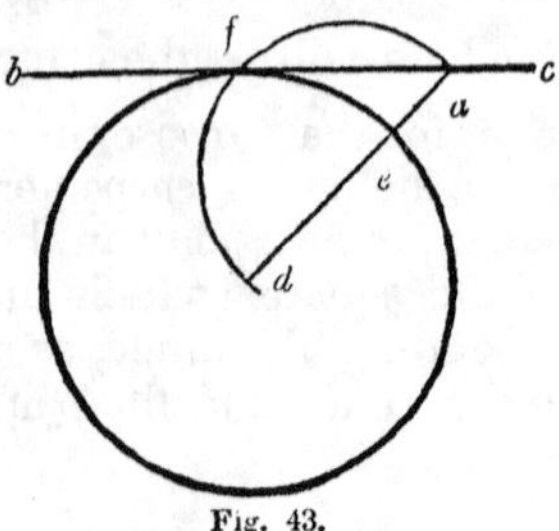

Fig. 43.

a line to the centre *d;* bisect *a d* at *e;* upon *e,* with the radius, *e a,* describe the arc, *a f d; f* is the point of contact required.

If *f* and *d* were joined, the line would form right angles with the tangent, *b c.* (See *Art.* 156.)

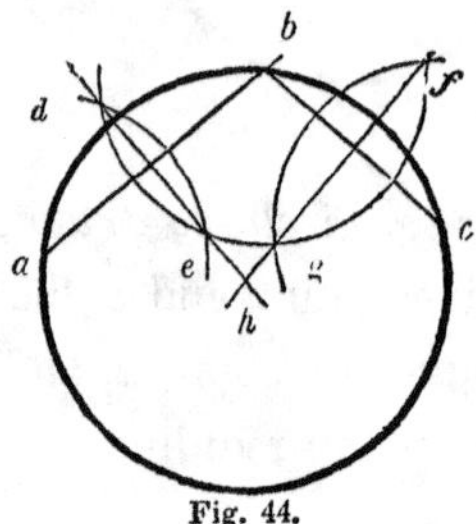

Fig. 44.

85.—*Through any three points not in a straight line, to draw a circle.* Let *a, b* and *c,* (*Fig.* 44,) be the three given points. Upon *a* and *b,* with any radius greater than half *a b,* describe arcs intersecting at *d* and *e;* upon *b* and *c,* with any radius greater than half *b c,* describe arcs intersecting at *f* and *g;* through *d* and *e,* draw a right line, also another through *f* and *g;* upon the intersection, *h,* with the radius, *h a,* describe the circle, *a b c,* and it will be the one required.

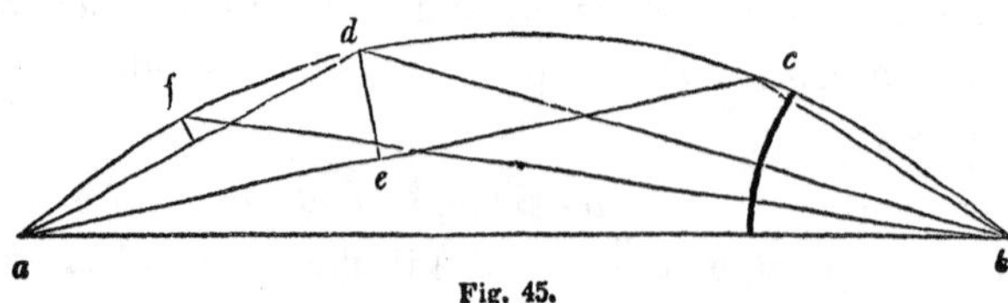

Fig. 45.

86.—*Three points not in a straight line being given, to find a fourth that shall, with the three, lie in the circumference of a circle.* Let *a b c*, (*Fig.* 45,) be the given points. Connect them with right lines, forming the triangle, *a c b*; bisect the angle, *c b a*, (*Art.* 77,) with the line, *b d*; also bisect *c a* in *e*, and erect *e d*, perpendicular to *a c*, cutting *b d* in *d*; then *d* is the *fourth* point required.

A fifth point may be found, as at *f*, by assuming *a*, *d* and *b*, as the three given points, and proceeding as before. So, also, any number of points may be found; simply by using any three already found. This problem will be serviceable in obtaining short pieces of very flat sweeps. (See *Art.* 311.)

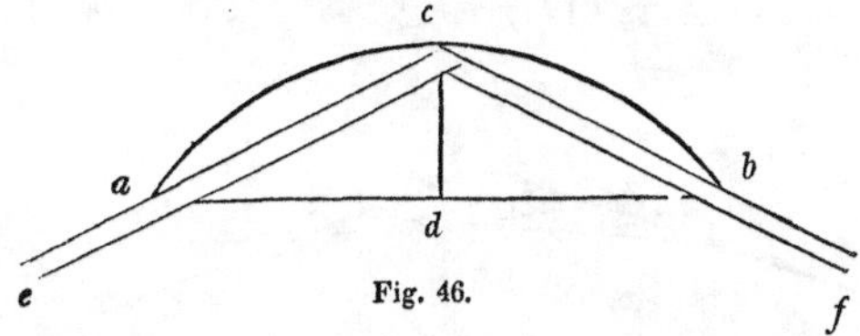

Fig. 46.

87.—*To describe a segment of a circle by a set-triangle.* Let *a b*, (*Fig.* 46,) be the chord, and *c d* the height of the segment. Secure two straight-edges, or rulers, in the position, *c e* and *c f*, by nailing them together at *c*, and affixing a brace from *e* to *f*; put in pins at *a* and *b*; move the angular point, *c*, in the direction, *a c b*; keeping the edges of the triangle hard against the pins, *a* and *b*; a pencil held at *c* will describe the arc, *a c b*.

If the angle formed by the rulers at *c* be a right angle, the segment described will be a semi-circle. This problem is useful in describing centres for brick arches, when they are required to be rather flat. Also, for the head hanging-stile of a window-frame, where a brick arch, instead of a stone lintel, is to be placed over it.

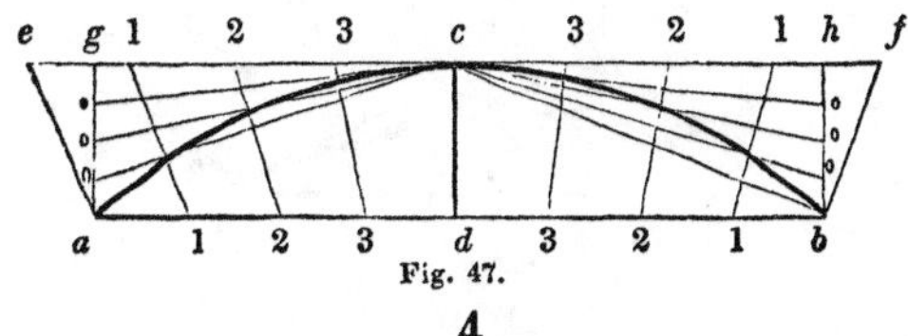

Fig. 47.

88.—*To describe the segment of a circle by intersection of lines.* Let *a b*, (*Fig.* 47,) be the chord, and *c d* the height of the segment. Through *c*, draw *e f*, parallel to *a b*; draw *b f* at right angles to *c b*; make *c e* equal to *c f*; draw *a g* and *b h*, at right angles to *a b*; divide *c e*, *c f*, *d a*, *d b*, *a g* and *b h*, each into a like number of equal parts, as four; draw the lines, 1 1, 2 2, &c., and from the points, *o*, *o* and *o*, draw lines to *c*; at the intersection of these lines, trace the curve, *a c b*, which will be the segment required.

In very large work, or in laying out ornamented gardens, &c., this will be found useful; and where the centre of the proposed arc of a circle is inaccessible, it will be invaluable. (To trace the curve, see note at *Art.* 117.)

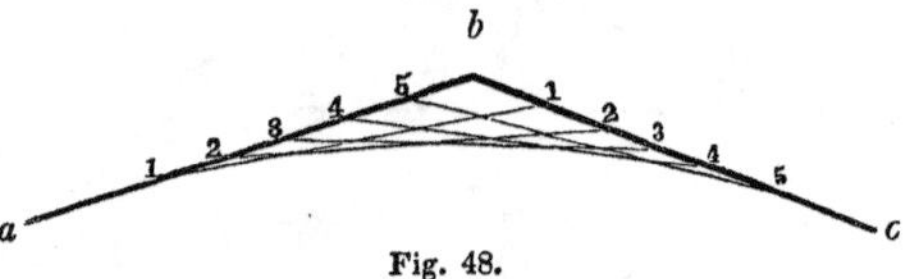

Fig. 48.

89.—*In a given angle, to describe a tanged curve.* Let *a b c*, (*Fig.* 48,) be the given angle, and 1 in the line, *a b*, and 5 in the line, *b c*, the termination of the curve. Divide 1 *b* and *b* 5 into a like number of equal parts, as at 1, 2, 3, 4 and 5; join 1 and 1, 2 and 2, 3 and 3, &c.; and a regular curve will be formed that will be tangical to the line, *a b*, at the point, 1, and to *b c* at 5.

This is of much use in stair-building, in easing the angles formed between the wall-string and base of the hall, also between the front string and level facia, and in many other instances. The curve is not circular, but of the form of the parabola, (*Fig.* 93;) yet in large angles the difference is not perceptible. This problem can be applied to describing segments of circles for door-

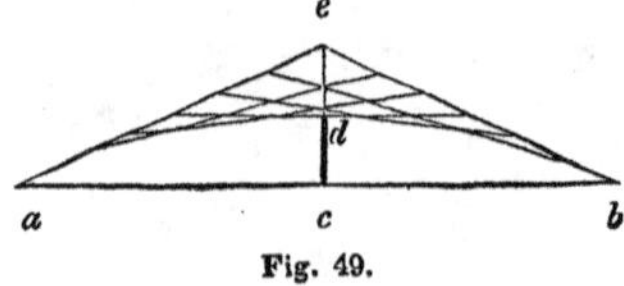

Fig. 49.

heads, window-heads, &c., to rather better advantage than *Art.* 87. For instance, let *a b*, (*Fig.* 49,) be the width of the opening, and *c d* the height of the arc. Extend *c d*, and make *d e* equal to *c d ;* join *a* and *e*, also *e* and *b ;* and proceed as directed at *Art* 89.

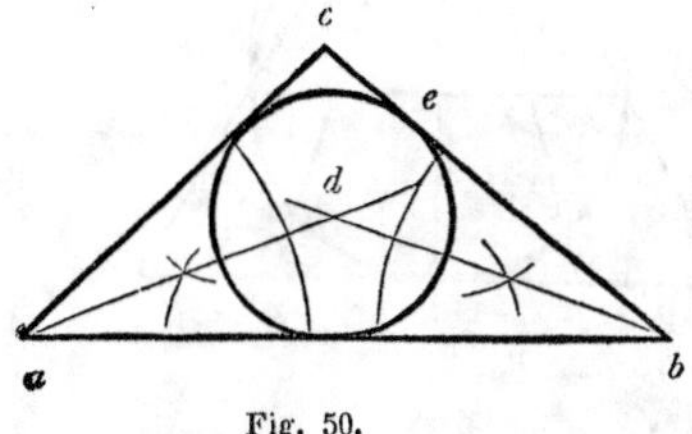

Fig. 50.

90.—*To describe a circle within any given triangle, so that the sides of the triangle shall be tangical.* Let *a b c*, (*Fig.* 50,) be the given triangle. Bisect the angles, *a* and *b*, according to *Art.* 77 ; upon *d*, the point of intersection of the bisecting lines, with the radius, *d e*, describe the required circle.

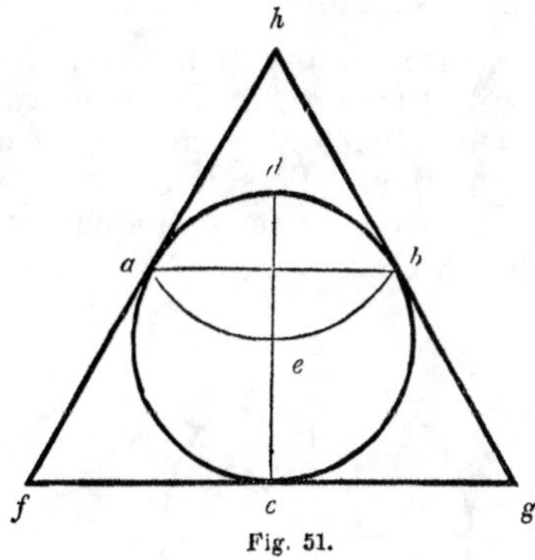

Fig. 51.

91.—*About a given circle, to describe an equi-lateral triangle.* Let *a d b c*, (*Fig.* 51,) be the given circle. Draw the diameter, *c d ;* upon *d*, with the radius of the given circle, describe the arc, *a e b ;* join *a* and *b ;* draw *f g*, at right angles to *d c ;* make *f c* and *c g*, each equal to *a b ;* from *f*, through *a*, draw *f h*, also from *g*, through *b*, draw *g h ;* then *f g h* will be the triangle required.

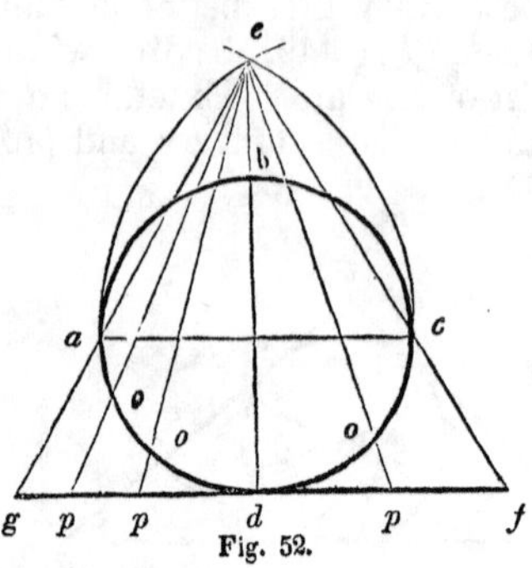

Fig. 52.

92.—*To find a right line nearly equal to the circumference of a circle.* Let *a b c d*, (*Fig.* 52,) be the given circle. Draw the diameter, *a c ;* on this erect an equi-lateral triangle, *a e c*, according to *Art.* 96 ; draw *g f*, parallel to *a c ;* extend *e c* to *f*, also *e a* to *g ;* then *g f* will be nearly the length of the semi-circle, *a d c ;* and twice *g f* will nearly equal the circumference of the circle, *a b c d*, as was required.

Lines drawn from *e*, through any points in the circle, as *o*, *o* and *o*, to *p*, *p* and *p*, will divide *g f* in the same way as the semi-circle, *a d c*, is divided. So, any portion of a circle may be transferred to a straight line. This is a very useful problem, and should be well studied; as it is frequently used to solve problems on stairs, domes, &c.

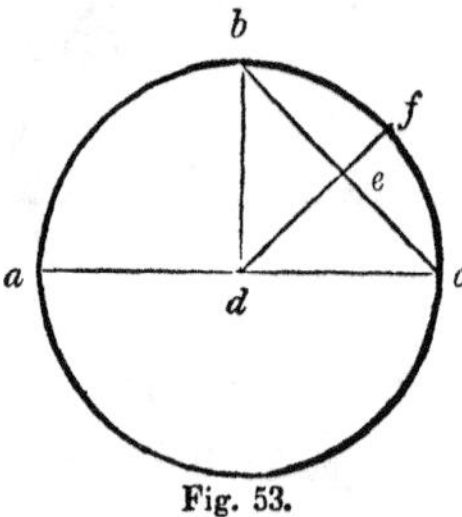

Fig. 53.

92, *a.*—*Another method.* Let *a b f c*, (*Fig.* 53,) be the given circle. Draw the diameter, *a c ;* from *d*, the centre, and at right angles to *a c*, draw *d b ;* join *b* and *c ;* bisect *b c* at *e ;* from *d*, through *e*, draw *d f ;* then *e f* added to three times the diameter, will equal the circumference of the circle within the $\frac{1}{4000}$ part of its length.

POLYGONS, &c.

93.—*Within a given circle, to inscribe an equi-lateral triangle, hexagon or dodecagon.* Let *a b c d*, (*Fig.* 54,) be the

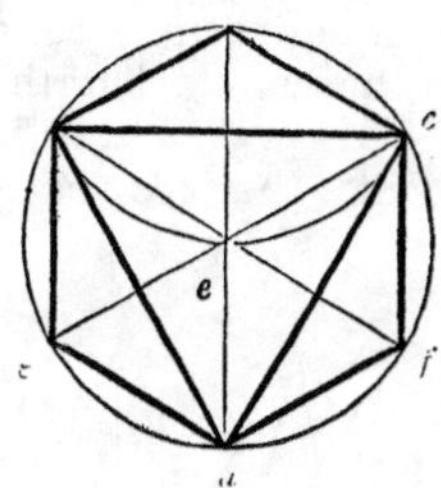

Fig. 54.

given circle. Draw the diameter, *b d ;* upon *b*, with the radius of the given circle, describe the arc, *a e c ;* join *a* and *c*, also *a* and *d*, and *c* and *d*—and the triangle is completed. For the hexagon: from *a*, also from *c*, through *e*, draw the lines, *a f* and *c g ;* join *a* and *b*, *b* and *c*, *c* and *f*, &c., and the hexagon is completed. The dodecagon may be formed by bisecting the sides of the hexagon.

Each side of a regular hexagon is exactly equal to the radius of the circle that circumscribes the figure. For the radius is equal to a chord of an arc of 60 degrees ; and, as every circle is supposed to be divided into 360 degrees, there is just 6 times 60, or 6 arcs of 60 degrees, in the whole circumference. A line drawn from each angle of the hexagon to the centre, (as in the figure,) divides it into six equal, equi-lateral triangles.

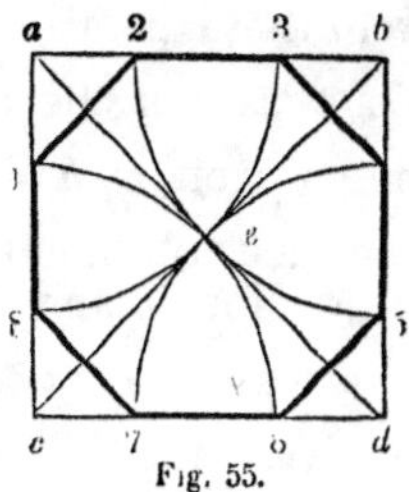

Fig. 55.

94.—*Within a square to inscribe an octagon.* Let *a b c d*, (*Fig.* 55,) be the given square. Draw the diagonals, *a d* and *b c*; upon *a*, *b*, *c* and *d*, with *a e* for radius, describe arcs cutting the sides of the square at 1, 2, 3, 4, 5, 6, 7 and 8; join 1 and 2, 3 and 4, 5 and 6, &c., and the figure is completed.

In order to eight-square a hand-rail, or any piece that is to be afterwards rounded, draw the diagonals, *a d* and *b c*, upon the end of it, after it has been squared-up. Set a gauge to the distance, *a e*, and run it upon the whole length of the stuff, from each corner both ways. This will show how much is to be chamfered off, in order to make the piece octagonal.

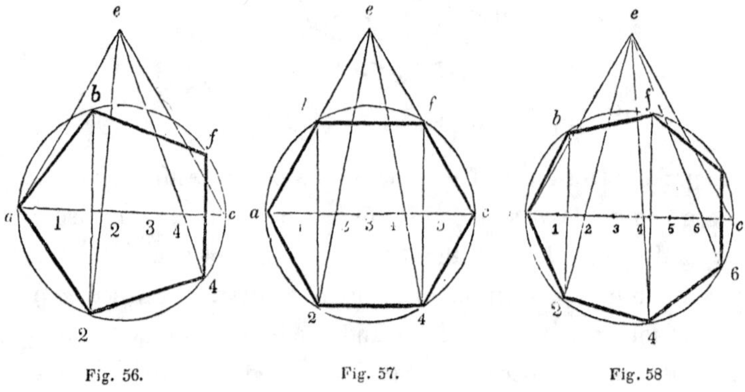

Fig. 56. Fig. 57. Fig. 58

95.—*Within a given circle to inscribe any regular polygon.* Let *a b c* 2, (*Fig.* 56, 57 and 58,) be given circles. Draw the diameter, *a c*; upon this, erect an equi-lateral triangle, *a e c*, according to *Art.* 96; divide *a c* into as many equal parts as the polygon is to have sides, as at 1, 2, 3, 4, &c.; from *e*, through each even number, as 2, 4, 6, &c., draw lines cutting the circle in the points, 2, 4, &c.; from these points and at right angles to *a c*, draw lines to the opposite part of the circle; this will give the remaining points for the polygon, as *b*, *f*, &c.

In forming a hexagon, the sides of the triangle erected upon *a c*, (as at *Fig.* 57,) mark the points, *b* and *f*.

96.—*Upon a given line to construct an equi-lateral triangle.* Let *a b*, (*Fig.* 59,) be the given line. Upon *a* and *b*, with *a b*

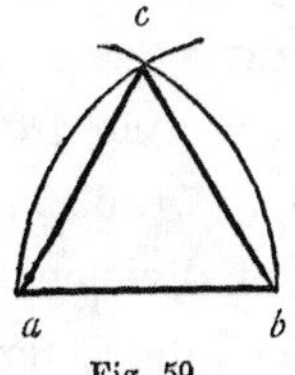

Fig. 59.

for radius, describe arcs intersecting at *c;* join *a* and *c*, also *c* and *b ;* then *a c b* will be the triangle required.

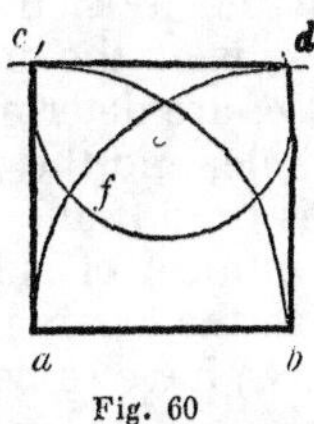

Fig. 60

97.—*To describe an equi-lateral rectangle, or square.* Let *a b*, (*Fig*. 60,) be the length of a side of the proposed square. Upon *a* and *b*, with *a b* for radius, describe the arcs, *a d* and *b c ;* bisect the arc, *a e*, in *f ;* upon *e*, with *e f* for radius, describe the arc, *c f d ;* join *a* and *c*, *c* and *d*, *d* and *b ;* then *a c d b* will be the square required.

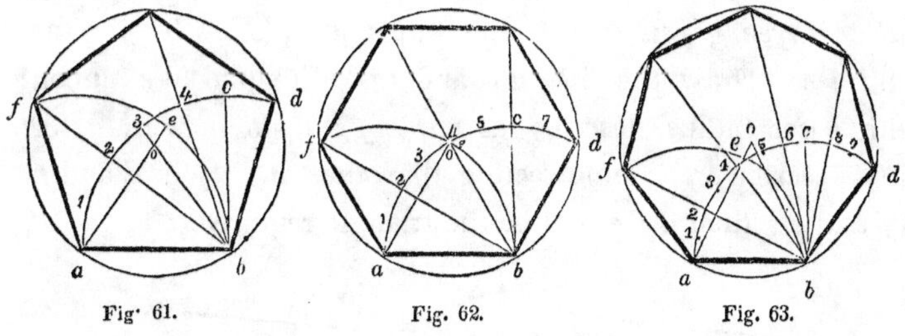
Fig. 61. Fig. 62. Fig. 63.

98.—*Upon a given line to describe any regular polygon.* Let *a b*, (*Fig*. 61, 62 and 63,) be given lines, equal to a side of the required figure. From *b*, draw *b c*, at right angles to *a b ;* upon *a* and *b*, with *a b* for radius, describe the arcs, *a c d* and *f e b*; divide *a c* into as many equal parts as the polygon is to have sides, and extend those divisions from *c* towards *d*; from the second point of division counting from *c* towards *a*, as 3, (*Fig.* 61,) 4, (*Fig.* 62,) and 5, (*Fig.* 63,) draw a line to *b*; take the distance from said point of division to *a*, and set it from *b* to *e*; join *e* and *a*; upon the intersection, *o*, with the radius, *o a*, describe the circle, *a f d b*; then radiating lines, drawn from *b* through the even numbers on the arc, *a d*, will cut the circle at the several angles of the required figure.

In the hexagon, (*Fig.* 62,) the divisions on the arc, *a d*, are not necessary; for the point, *o*, is at the intersection of the arcs, *a d* and *f b*, the points, *f* and *d*, are determined by the intersection of those arcs with the circle, and the points above, *g* and *h*, can be found by drawing lines from *a* and *b*, through the centre, *o*. In polygons of a greater number of sides than the hexagon, the intersection, *o*, comes above the arcs; in such case, therefore, the lines, *a e* and *b* 5, (*Fig.* 63,) have to be extended before they will intersect.

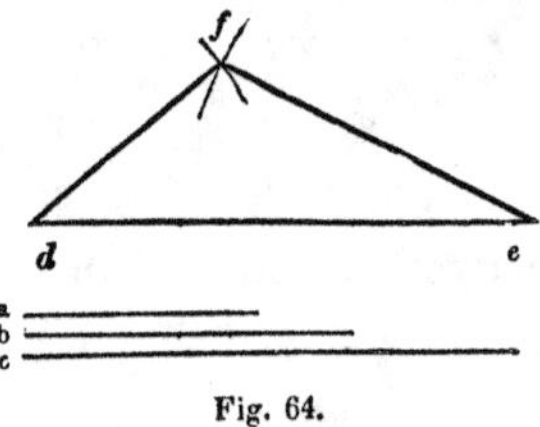

Fig. 64.

99.—*To construct a triangle whose sides shall be severally equal to three given lines.* Let *a*, *b* and *c*, (*Fig.* 64,) be the given lines. Draw the line, *d e*, and make it equal to *c*; upon *e*, with *b* for radius, describe an arc at *f*; upon *d*, with *a* for radius, describe an arc intersecting the other at *f*; join *d* and *f*, also *f* and *e*; then *d f e* will be the triangle required.

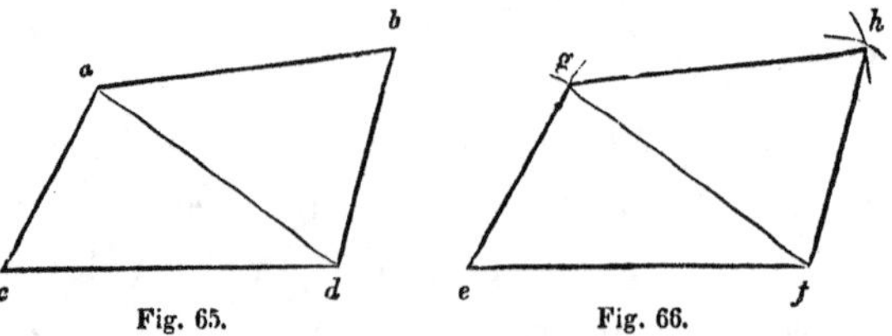

Fig. 65. Fig. 66.

100.—*To construct a figure equal to a given, right-lined figure.* Let *a b c d*, (*Fig.* 65,) be the given figure. Make *e f*, (*Fig.* 66,) equal to *c d ;* upon *f*, with *d a* for radius, describe an arc at *g ;* upon *e*, with *c a* for radius, describe an arc intersecting the other at *g ;* join *g* and *e ;* upon *f* and g, with *d b* and *a b* for radius, describe arcs intersecting at *h ;* join *g* and *h*, also *h* and *f ;* then *Fig.* 66 will every way equal *Fig.* 65.

So, right-lined figures of any number of sides may be copied, by first dividing them into triangles, and then proceeding as above. The shape of the floor of any room, or of any piece of land, &c., may be accurately laid out by this problem, at a scale upon paper; and the contents in square feet be ascertained by the next.

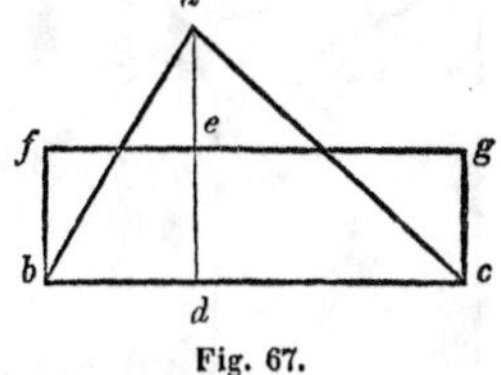

Fig. 67.

101.—*To make a parallelogram equal to a given triangle.* Let *a b* c, (*Fig.* 67,) be the given triangle. From *a*, draw *a d*, at right angles to *b c ;* bisect *a d* in *e ;* through *e*, draw *f g*, parallel to *b c ;* from *b* and *c*, draw *b f* and *c g*, parallel to *d e ;* then *b f g c* will be a parallelogram containing a surface exactly equal to that of the triangle, *a b c*.

Unless the parallelogram is required to be a rectangle, the lines, *b f* and *c g*, need not be drawn parallel to *d e*. If a rhomboid is desired, they may be drawn at an oblique angle, provided they be parallel to one another. To ascertain the area of a triangle, multiply the base, *b c*, by half the perpendicular height, *d a*. In doing this, it matters not which side is taken for base.

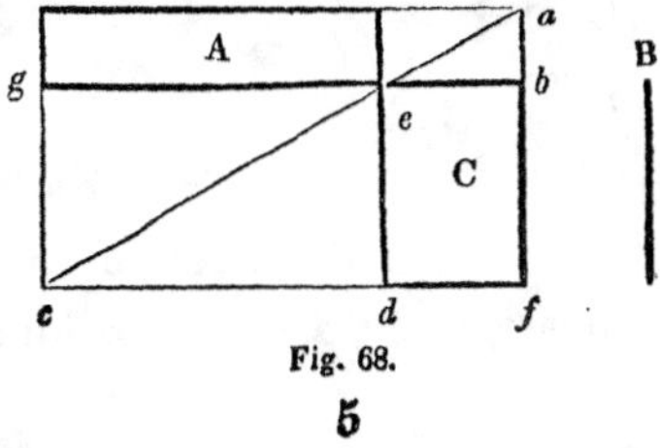

Fig. 68.

102.—*A parallelogram being given, to construct another equal to it, and having a side equal to a given line.* Let *A*, (*Fig.* 68,) be the given parallelogram, and *B* the given line Produce the sides of the parallelogram, as at *a*, *b*, *c* and *d*; make *e d* equal to *B*; through *d*, draw *c f*, parallel to *g b*; through *e*, draw the diagonal, *c a*; from *a*, draw *a f*, parallel to *e d* then *C* will be equal to *A*. (See *Art.* 144.)

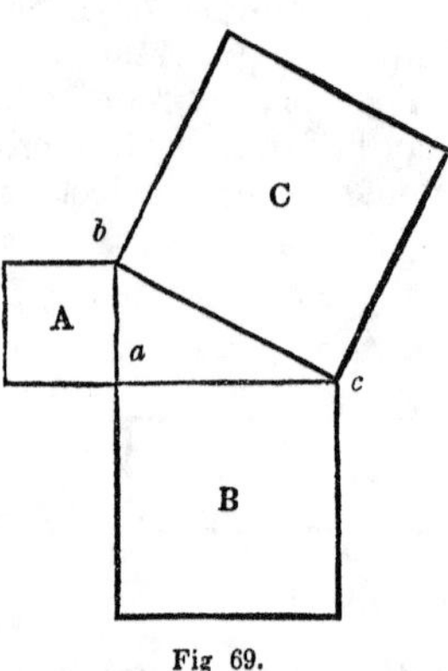

Fig 69.

103.—*To make a square equal to two or more given squares.* Let *A* and *B*, (*Fig.* 69,) be two given squares. Place them so as to form a right angle, as at *a*; join *b* and *c*; then the square, *C*, formed upon the line, *b c*, will be equal in extent to the squares, *A* and *B*, added together. Again: if *a b*, (*Fig.* 70,) be equal to

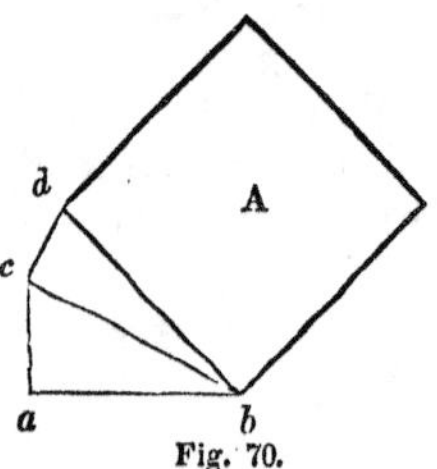

Fig. 70.

the side of a given square, *c a*, placed at right angles to *a b*, be the side of another given square, and *c d*, placed at right angles to *c b*, be the side of a third given square; then the square, *A*, formed upon the line, *d b*, will be equal to the three given squares. (See *Art.* 157.)

The usefulness and importance of this problem are proverbial. To ascertain the length of braces and of rafters in framing, the length of stair-strings, &c., are some of the purposes to which it may be applied in carpentry. (See note to *Art.* 74, *b.*) If the length of any two sides of a right-angled triangle is known, that of the third can be ascertained. Because the square of the hypothenuse is equal to the united squares of the two sides that contain the right angle.

(1.)—The two sides containing the right angle being known, to find the hypothenuse. *Rule.*—Square each given side, add the squares together, and from the product extract the square-root: this will be the answer. For instance, suppose it were required to find the length of a rafter for a house, 34 feet wide,—the ridge of the roof to be 9 feet high, above the level of the wall-plates. Then 17 feet, half of the span, is one, and 9 feet, the height, is the other of the sides that contain the right angle. Proceed as directed by the rule:

17	9
17	9
119	81 = square of 9.
17	289 = square of 17.
289 = square of 17.	370 Product.

1) 370 (19·235 + = square-root of 370; equal 19 feet, $2\frac{7}{8}$ in. nearly: which would be the required length of the rafter.
1 1
29) 270
9 261
382) · · 900
2 764
3843) 13600
3 11529
38465) · 207100
192325

(By reference to the table of square-roots in the appendix, the root of almost any number may be found ready calculated.)

Again: suppose it be required, in a frame building, to find the length of a brace, having a run of three feet each way from the point of the right angle. The length of the sides containing the right angle will be each 3 feet: then, as before—

```
              3
              3
             --
              9 = square of one side.
3 times 3  =  9 = square of the other side.
             --
             18 Product: the square-root of which is 4·2426 + ft.,
```

or 4 feet, 2 inches and $\frac{7}{8}$ths. full.

(2.)—The hypothenuse and one side being known, to find the other side. *Rule.*—Subtract the square of the given side from the square of the hypothenuse, and the square-root of the product will be the answer. Suppose it were required to ascertain the greatest perpendicular height a roof of a given span may have, when pieces of timber of a given length are to be used as rafters. Let the span be 20 feet, and the rafters of 3×4 hemlock joist. These come about 13 feet long. The known hypothenuse, then, is 13 feet, and the known side, 10 feet—that being half the span of the building.

```
                 13
                 13
                ---
                 39
                13
                ---
                169 = square of hypothenuse.
10 times 10  =  100 = square of the given side.
                ---
                 69 Product: the square-root of which is 8
```

·3066 + feet, or 8 feet, 3 inches and $\frac{5}{8}$ths. full. This will be the greatest perpendicular height, as required. Again: suppose that in a story of 8 feet, from floor to floor, a step-ladder is required, the strings of which are to be of plank, 12 feet long; and it is desirable to know the greatest run such a length of string will afford. In this case, the two given sides are—hypothenuse 12, perpendicular 8 feet.

```
12 times 12  =  144 = square of hypothenuse.
 8 times  8  =   64 = square of perpendicular.
                ---
                 80 Product: the square-root of which is 8·9442 +
```

feet, or 8 feet, 11 inches and $\frac{5}{16}$ths.—the answer, as required.

Many other cases might be adduced to show the utility of this problem. A practical and ready method of ascertaining the length of braces, rafters, &c., when not of a great length, is to apply a rule across the carpenters'-square. Suppose, for the length of a rafter, the base be 12 feet and the height 7. Apply the rule diagonally on the square, so that it touches 12 inches from the corner on one side, and 7 inches from the corner on the other. The number of inches on the rule, which are intercepted by the sides of the square, $13\frac{7}{8}$ nearly, will be the length of the rafter in feet; viz, 13 feet and $\frac{7}{8}$ths of a foot. If the dimensions are large, as 30 feet and 20, take the half of each on the sides of the square, viz, 15 and 10 inches; then the length in inches across, will be one-half the number of feet the rafter is long. This method is just as accurate as the preceding; but when the length of a very long rafter is sought, it requires great care and precision to ascertain the fractions. For the least variation on the square, or in the length taken on the rule, would make perhaps several inches difference in the length of the rafter. For shorter dimensions, however, the result will be true enough.

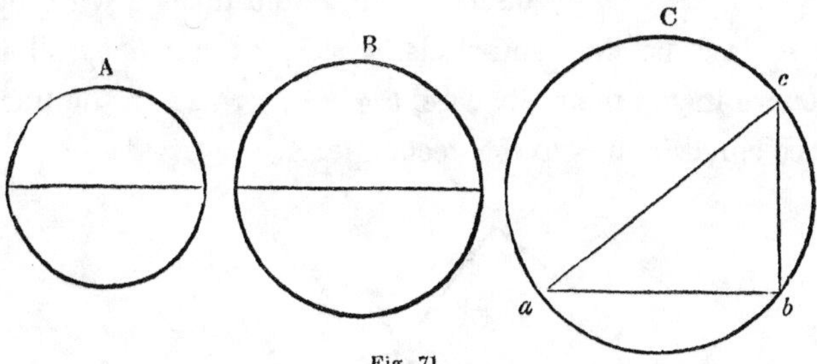

Fig. 71.

104.—*To make a circle equal to two given circles.* Let *A* and *B*, (*Fig.* 71,) be the given circles. In the right-angled triangle, *a b c*, make *a b* equal to the diameter of the circle, *B*, and *c b* equal to the diameter of the circle, *A*; then the hypothenuse,

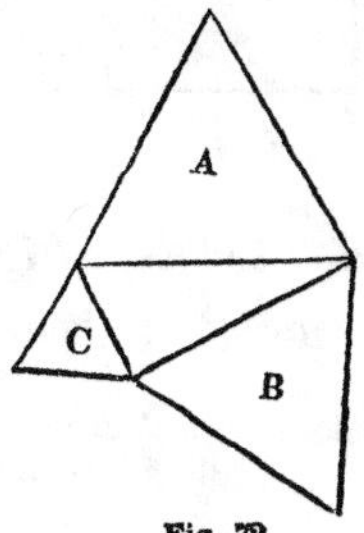

Fig. 72.

a c, will be the diameter of a circle, *C*, which will be equal in area to the two circles, *A* and *B*, added together.

Any polygonal figure, as *A*, (*Fig.* 72,) formed on the hypothenuse of a right-angled triangle, will be equal to two similar figures,* as *B* and *C*, formed on the two legs of the triangle.

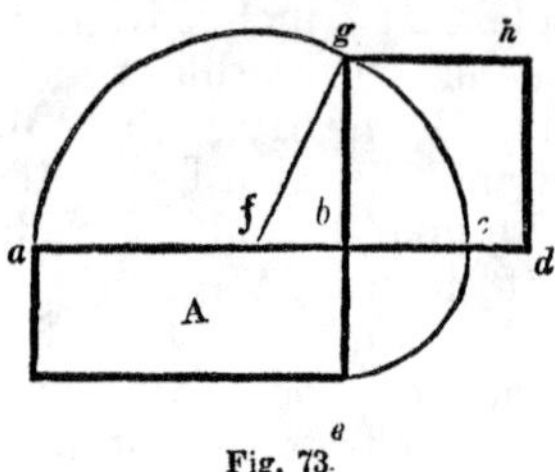

Fig. 73.

105.—*To construct a square equal to a given rectangle.* Let *A*, (*Fig.* 73,) be the given rectangle. Extend the side, *a b*, and make *b c* equal to *b e*; bisect *a c* in *f*, and upon *f*, with the radius, *f a*, describe the semi-circle, *a g c*; extend *e b*, till it cuts the curve in *g*; then a square, *b g h d*, formed on the line, *b g*, will be equal in area to the rectangle, *A*.

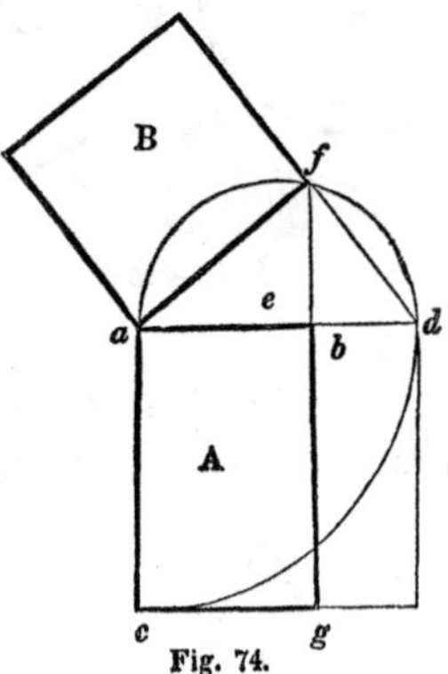

Fig. 74.

105, *a.*—*Another method.* Let *A*, (*Fig.* 74,) be the given rectangle. Extend the side, *a b*, and make *a d* equal to *a c*;

* Similar figures are such as have their several angles respectively equal, and their sides respectively proportionate.

bisect *a d* in *e;* upon *e*, with the radius, *e a*, describe the semicircle, *a f d;* extend *g b* till it cuts the curve in *f;* join *a* and *f;* then the square, *B*, formed on the line, *a f*, will be equal in area to the rectangle, *A*. (See *Art.* 156 and 157.)

106.—*To form a square equal to a given triangle.* Let *a b*, (*Fig.* 73,) equal the base of the given triangle, and *b e* equal half its perpendicular height, (see *Fig.* 67;) then proceed as directed at *Art.* 105.

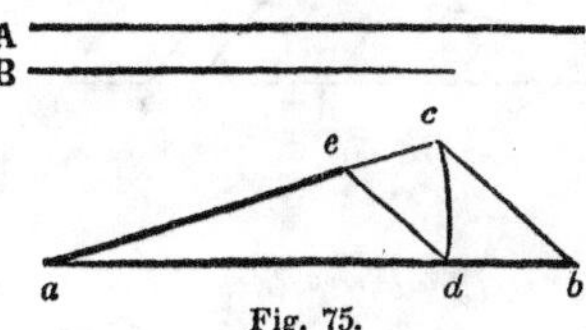

Fig. 75.

107.—*Two right lines being given, to find a third proportional thereto.* Let *A* and *B*, (*Fig.* 75,) be the given lines. Make *a b* equal to *A;* from *a*, draw *a c*, at any angle with *a b;* make *a c* and *a d* each equal to *B;* join *c* and *b;* from *d*, draw *d e*, parallel to *c b;* then *a e* will be the third proportional required. That is, *a e* bears the same proportion to *B*, as *B* does to *A*.

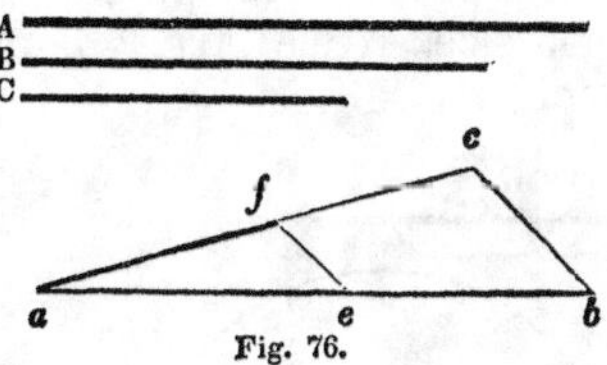

Fig. 76.

108.—*Three right lines being given, to find a fourth proportional thereto.* Let *A*, *B* and *C*, (*Fig.* 76,) be the given lines. Make *a b* equal to *A;* from *a*, draw *a c*, at any angle with *a b;* make *a c* equal to *B*, and *a e* equal to *C;* join c and *b;* from *e*, draw *e f*, parallel to *c b;* then *a f* will be the fourth proportional required. That is, *a f* bears the same proportion to *C*, as *B* does to *A*.

To apply this problem, suppose the two axes of a given ellipsis, and the longer axis of a proposed ellipsis are given. Then, by this problem, the length of the shorter axis to the proposed ellipsis, can be found; so that it will bear the same proportion to the longer axis, as the shorter of the given ellipsis does to its longer. (See also, *Art.* 126.)

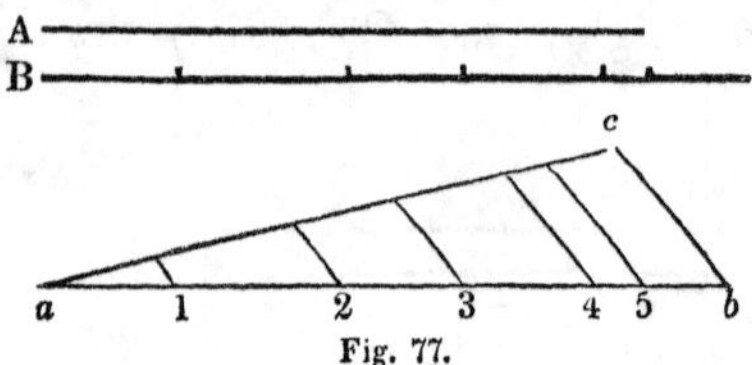

Fig. 77.

109.—*A line with certain divisions being given, to divide another, longer or shorter, given line in the same proportion.* Let *A*, (*Fig.* 77,) be the line to be divided, and *B* the line with its divisions. Make *a b* equal to *B*, with all its divisions, as at 1, 2, 3, &c.; from *a*, draw *a c*, at any angle with *a b;* make *a c* equal to *A;* join *c* and *b;* from the points, 1, 2, 3, &c., draw lines, parallel to *c b;* then these will divide the line, *a c*, in the same proportion as *B* is divided—as was required.

This problem will be found useful in proportioning the members of a proposed cornice, in the same proportion as those of a given cornice of another size. (See *Art.* 243 and 244.) So of a pilaster, architrave, &c.

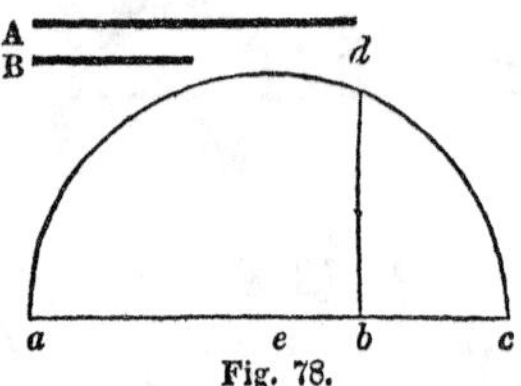

Fig. 78.

110.—*Between two given right lines, to find a mean proportional.* Let *A* and *B*, (*Fig.* 78,) be the given lines. On the line, *a c*, make *a b* equal to *A*, and *b c* equal to *B;* bisect *a c* in *e;* upon *e*, with *e a* for radius, describe the semi-circle, *a d c;* at *b*, erect *b d*, at right angles to *a c;* then *b d* will be the mean proportional between *A* and *B*.

For an application of this problem, see *Art.* 105.

CONIC SECTIONS.

111.—If a cone, standing upon a base that is at right angles with its axis, be cut by a plane, perpendicular to its base and passing through its axis, the section will be an isoceles triangle; (as *a b c*, *Fig.* 79;) and the base will be a semi-circle. If a cone be cut by a plane in the direction, *e f*, the section will be an *ellipsis;* if in the direction, *m l*, the section will be a *parabola;* and if in the direction, *r o*, an *hyperbola.* (See *Art.* 56 to 60.) If the cutting planes be at right angles with the plane, *a b c*, then—

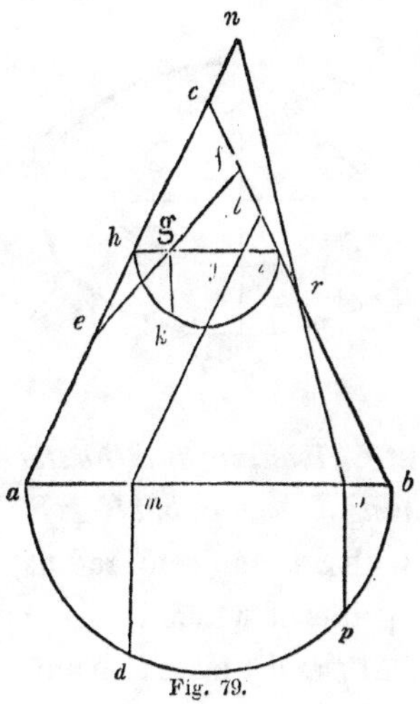

Fig. 79.

112.—*To find the axes of the ellipsis*, bisect *e f*, (*Fig.* 79,) in *g;* through *g*, draw *h i*, parallel to *a b;* bisect *h i* in *j;* upon *j*, with *j h* for radius, describe the semi-circle, *h k i;* from *g*, draw *g k*, at right angles to *h i;* then twice *g k* will be the conjugate axis, and *e f* the transverse.

113.—*To find the axis and base of the parabola.* Let *m l*, (*Fig.* 79,) parallel to *a c*, be the direction of the cutting plane. From *m*, draw *m d*, at right angles to *a b* ; then *l m* will be the axis and height, and *m d* an ordinate and half the base; as at *Fig.* 92, 93.

114.—*To find the height, base and transverse axis of an hyperbola.* Let *o r*, (*Fig.* 79,) be the direction of the cutting plane. Extend *o r* and *a c* till they meet at *n* ; from *o*, draw *o p*, at right angles to *a b*; then *r o* will be the height, *n r* the transverse axis, and *o p* half the base; as at *Fig.* 94.

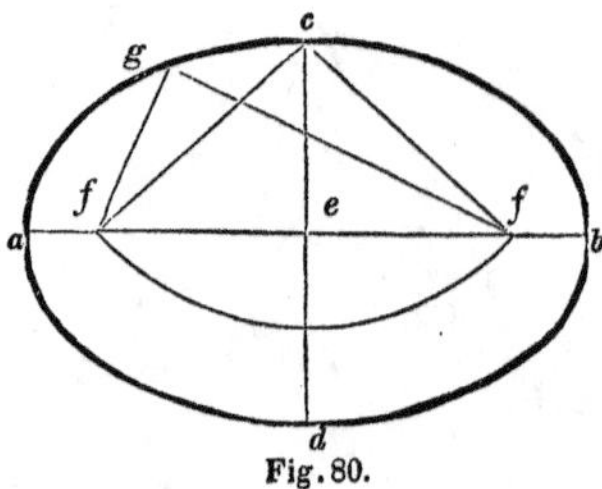

Fig. 80.

115.—*The axes being given, to find the foci, and to describe an ellipsis with a string.* Let *a b*, (*Fig.* 80,) and *c d*, be the given axes. Upon *c*, with *a e* or *b e* for radius, describe the arc, *f f* ; then *f* and *f*, the points at which the arc cuts the transverse axis, will be the *foci*. At *f* and *f* place two pins, and another at *c* ; tie a string about the three pins, so as to form the triangle, *f f c* ; remove the pin from *c*, and place a pencil in its stead; keeping the string taut, move the pencil in the direction, *c g a* ; it will then describe the required ellipsis. The lines, *f g* and *g f*, show the position of the string when the pencil arrives at *g*.

This method, when performed correctly, is perfectly accurate; but the string is liable to stretch, and is, therefore, not so good to use as the trammel. In making an ellipse by a string or twine, that kind should be used which has the least tendency to elasticity. For this reason, a cotton cord, such as chalk-lines are commonly made of, is not proper for the purpose: a linen, or flaxen cord is much better.

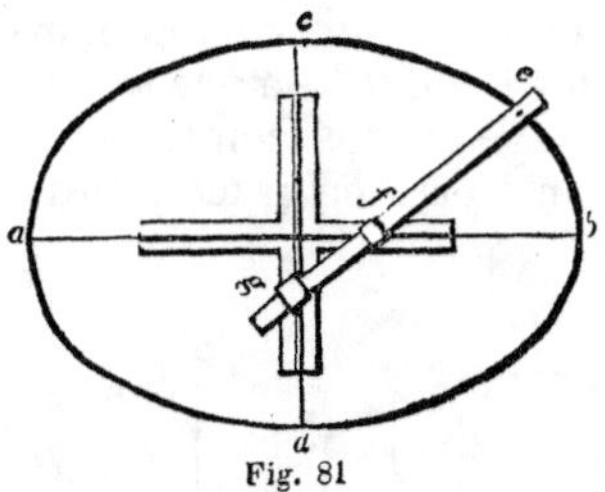

Fig. 81

116.—*The axes being given, to describe an ellipsis with a trammel.* Let *a b* and *c d*, (*Fig.* 81,) be the given axes. Place the trammel so that a line passing through the centre of the grooves, would coincide with the axes; make the distance from the pencil, *e*, to the nut, *f*, equal to half *c d*; also, from the pencil, *e*, to the nut, *g*, equal to half *a b;* letting the pins under the nuts slide in the grooves, move the trammel, *e g*, in the direction, *c b d;* then the pencil at *e* will describe the required ellipse.

A trammel may be constructed thus: take two straight strips of board, and make a groove on their face, in the centre of their width; join them together, in the middle of their length, at right angles to one another; as is seen at *Fig.* 81. A rod is then to be prepared, having two moveable nuts made of wood, with a mortice through them of the size of the rod, and pins under them large enough to fill the grooves. Make a hole at one end of the rod, in which to place a pencil. In the absence of a regular trammel, a temporary one may be made, which, for any short job, will answer every purpose. Fasten two straight-edges at right angles to one another. Lay them so as to coincide with the axes of the proposed ellipse, having the angular point at the centre. Then, in a rod having a hole for the pencil at one end, place two brad-awls at the distances described at *Art.* 116. While the pencil is moved in the direction of the curve, keep the brad-awls hard against the straight-edges, as directed for using the trammel-rod, and one-quarter of the ellipse will be drawn. Then, by shifting the straight-edges, the other three quarters in succession may be drawn. If the required ellipse be not too large, a carpenters'-square may be made use of, in place of the straight-edges.

An improved method of constructing the trammel, is as follows: make the sides of the grooves bevilling from the face of the stuff, or dove-tailing instead of square. Prepare two slips of wood, each about two inches long, which shall be of a shape to just fill the groove when slipped in at the end. These, instead of pins, are to be attached one to each of the moveable nuts with a screw, loose enough for the nut to move freely about the screw as an axis. The advantage of this contrivance is, in preventing the nuts from slipping out of their places, during the operation of describing the curve.

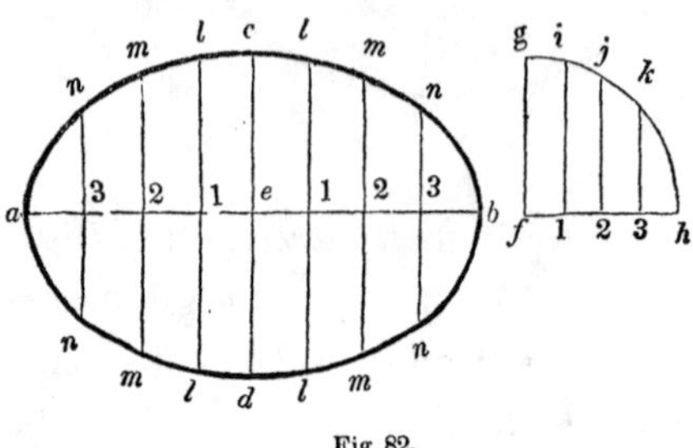

Fig. 82.

117.—*To describe an ellipsis by ordinates.* Let *a b* and *c d*, (*Fig.* 82,) be given axes. With *c e* or *e d* for radius, describe the quadrant, *f g h;* divide *f h*, *a e* and *e b*, each into a like number of equal parts, as at 1, 2 and 3; through these points, draw ordinates, parallel to *c d* and *f g;* take the distance, 1 *i*, and place it at 1 *l*, transfer 2 *j* to 2 *m*, and 3 *k* to 3 *n;* through the points, *a*, *n*, *m*, *l* and *c*, trace a curve, and the ellipsis will be completed.

The greater the number of divisions on *a e*, &c., in this and the following problem, the more points in the curve can be found, and the more accurate the curve can be traced. If pins are placed in the points, *n*, *m*, *l*, &c., and a thin slip of wood bent around by them, the curve can be made quite correct. This method is mostly used in tracing face-moulds for stair hand-railing.

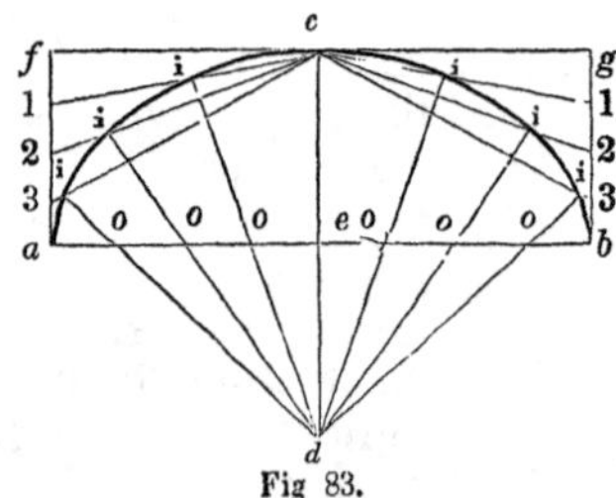

Fig 83.

118.—*To describe an ellipsis by intersection of lines.* Let

a b and ***c d***, (*Fig.* 83,) be given axes. Through *c*, draw *f g*, parallel to *a b;* from *a* and *b*, draw *a f* and *b g*, at right angles to *a b;* divide *f a*, *g b*, *a e* and *e b*, each into a like number of equal parts, as at 1, 2, 3 and *o*, *o*, *o;* from 1, 2 and 3, draw lines to *c;* through *o*, *o* and *o*, draw lines from *d*, intersecting those drawn to *c;* then a curve, traced through the points, *i*, *i*, *i*, will be that of an ellipsis.

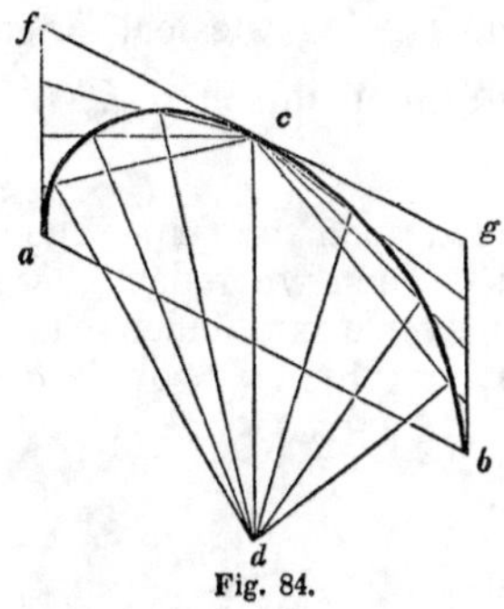

Fig. 84.

Where neither trammel nor string is at hand, this, perhaps, is the most ready method of drawing an ellipsis. The divisions should be small, where accuracy is desirable. By this method, an ellipsis may be traced without the axes, provided that a diameter and its conjugate be given. Thus, *a b* and *c d*, (*Fig.* 84,) are conjugate diameters: *f g* is drawn parallel to *a b*, instead of being at right angles to *c d;* also, *f a* and *g b* are drawn parallel to *c d*, instead of being at right angles to *a b*.

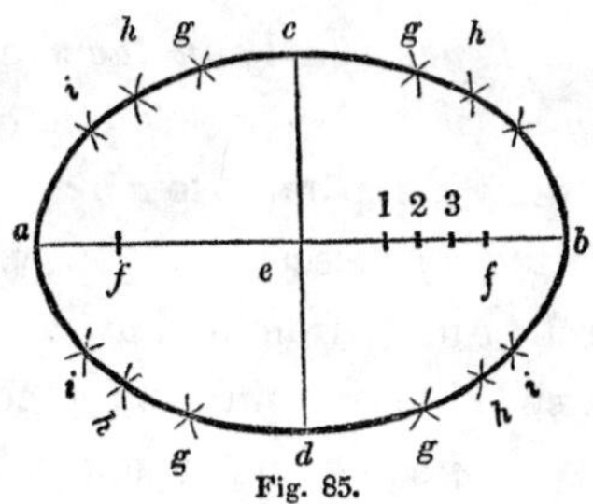

Fig. 85.

119.—***To describe an ellipsis by intersecting arcs.*** Let ***a b***

and *c d*, (*Fig.* 85,) be given axes. Between one of the foci, *f* and *f*, and the centre, *e*, mark any number of points, at random, as 1, 2 and 3; upon *f* and *f*, with *b* 1 for radius, describe arcs at *g*, *g*, *g* and *g*; upon *f* and *f*, with *a* 1 for radius, describe arcs intersecting the others at *g*, *g*, *g* and *g*; then these points of intersection will be in the curve of the ellipsis. The other points, *h* and *i*, are found in like manner, viz: *h* is found by taking *b* 2 for one radius, and *a* 2 for the other; *i* is found by taking *b* 3 for one radius, and *a* 3 for the other, always using the foci for centres. Then by tracing a curve through the points, *c*, *g*, *h*, *i*, *b*, &c., the ellipse will be completed.

This problem is founded upon the same principle as that of the string. This is obvious, when we reflect that the length of the string is equal to the transverse axis, added to the distance between the foci. See *Fig.* 80; in which *c f* equals *a e*, the half of the transverse axis.

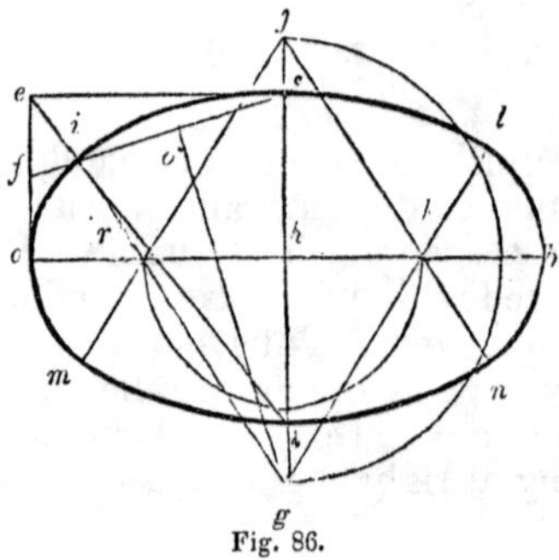

Fig. 86.

120.—*To describe a figure nearly in the shape of an ellipsis, by a pair of compasses.* Let *a b* and *c d*, (*Fig.* 86,) be given axes. From *c*, draw *c e*, parallel to *a b*; from *a*, draw *a e*, parallel to *c d*; join *e* and *d*; bisect *e a* in *f*; join *f* and *c*, intersecting *e d* in *i*; bisect *i c* in *o*; from *o*, draw *o g*, at right angles to *i c*, meeting *c d* extended to *g*; join *i* and *g*, cutting the transverse axis in *r*; make *h j* equal to *h g*, and *h k* equal to *h r*; from *j*, through *r* and *k*, draw *j m* and *j n*; also, from *g*, through *k*, draw *g l*; upon *g* and *j*, with *g c* for radius, describe the arcs, *i l* and *m n;* upon *r* and *k*, with *r a* for radius, describe the arcs, *m i* and *l n;* this will complete the figure.

When the axes are proportioned to one another as 2 to 3, the extremities, *c* and *d*, of the shortest axis, will be the centres for describing the arcs, *i l* and *m n;* and the intersection of *e d* with the transverse axis, will be the centre for describing the arc, *m i*, &c. As the elliptic curve is continually changing its course from that of a circle, a true ellipsis cannot be described with a pair of compasses. The above, therefore, is only an approximation.

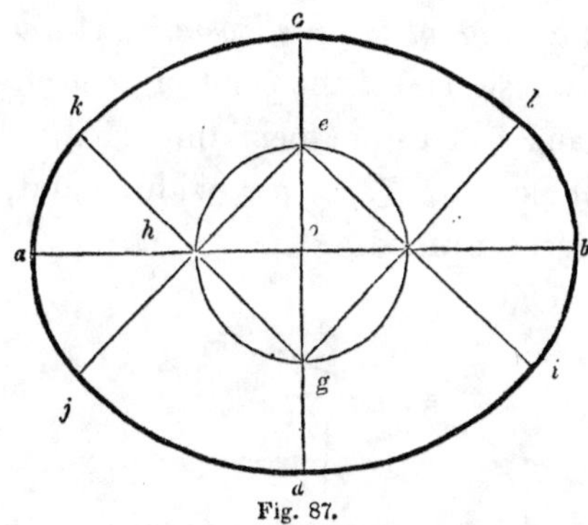

Fig. 87.

121.—*To draw an oval in the proportion, seven by nine.* Let *c d*, (*Fig.* 87,) be the given conjugate axis. Bisect *c d* in *o*, and through *o*, draw *a b*, at right angles to *c d;* bisect *c o* in *e;* upon *o*, with *o e* for radius, describe the circle, *e f g h;* from *e*, through *h* and *f*, draw *e j* and *e i;* also, from *g*, through *h* and *f*, draw *g k* and *g l;* upon *g*, with *g c* for radius, describe the arc, *k l;* upon *e*, with *e d* for radius, describe the arc, *j i;* upon *h* and *f*, with *h k* for radius, describe the arcs, *j k* and *l i;* this will complete the figure.

This is a very near approximation to an ellipsis; and perhaps no method can be found, by which a well-shaped oval can be drawn with greater facility. By a little variation in the process, ovals of different proportions may be obtained. If quarter of the transverse axis is taken for the radius of the circle, *e f g h*, one will be drawn in the proportion, five by seven.

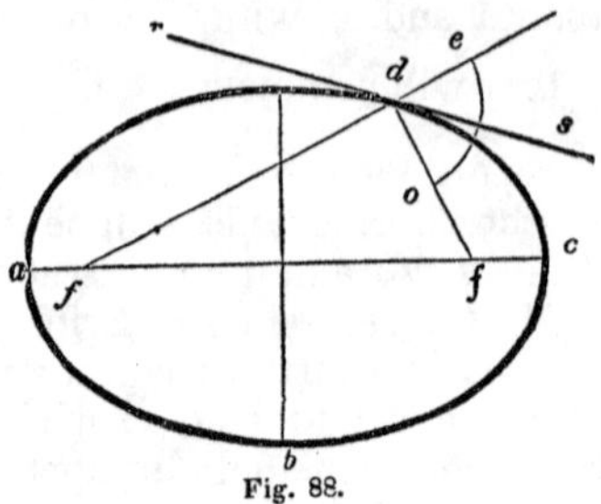

Fig. 88.

122.—*To draw a tangent to an ellipsis.* Let *a b c d*, (*Fig.* 88,) be the given ellipsis, and *d* the point of contact. Find the foci, (*Art.* 115,) *f* and *f*, and from them, through *d*, draw *f e* and *f d;* bisect the angle, (*Art.* 77,) *e d o*, with the line, *s r;* then *s r* will be the tangent required.

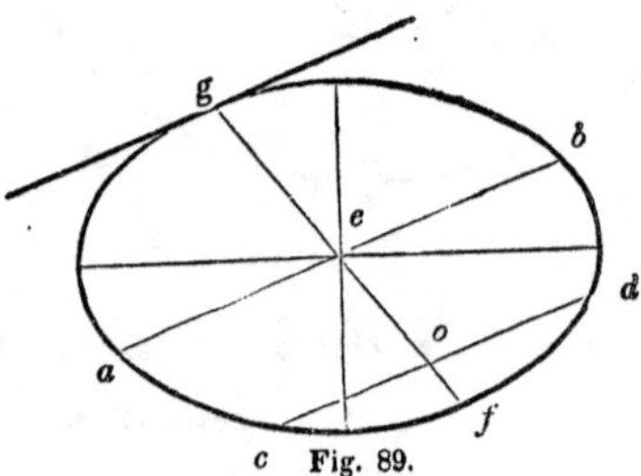

Fig. 89.

123.—*An ellipsis with a tangent given, to detect the point of contact.* Let *a g b f*, (*Fig.* 89,) be the given ellipsis and tangent. Through the centre, *e*, draw *a b*, parallel to the tangent; any where between *e* and *f*, draw *c d*, parallel to *a b;* bisect *c d* in *o;* through *o* and *e*, draw *f g;* then *g* will be the point of contact required.

124.—*A diameter of an ellipsis given, to find its conjugate.* Let *a b*, (*Fig.* 89,) be the given diameter. Find the line, *f g*, by the last problem; then *f g* will be the diameter required.

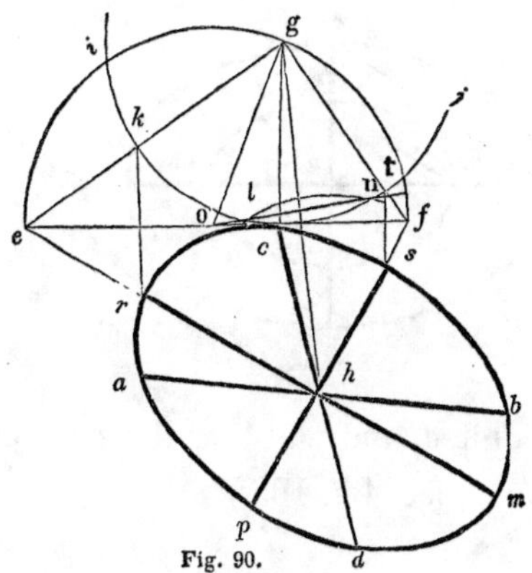

Fig. 90.

125.—*Any diameter and its conjugate being given, to ascertain the two axes, and thence to describe the ellipsis.* Let *a b* and *c d*, (*Fig.* 90,) be the given diameters, conjugate to one another. Through *c*, draw *e f*, parallel to *a b*; from *c*, draw *c g*, at right angles to *e f*; make *c g* equal to *a h* or *h b*; join *g* and *h*; upon *g*, with *g c* for radius, describe the arc, *i k c j*; upon *h*, with the same radius, describe the arc, *l n*; through the intersections, *l* and *n*, draw *n o*, cutting the tangent, *e f*, in *o*; upon *o*, with *o g* for radius, describe the semi-circle, *e i g f*; join *e* and *g*, also *g* and *f*, cutting the arc, *i c j*, in *k* and *t*; from *e*, through *h*, draw *e m*, also from *f*, through *h*, draw *f p*; from *k* and *t*, draw *k r* and *t s*, parallel to *g h*, cutting *e m* in *r*, and *f p* in *s*; make *h m* equal to *h r*, and *h p* equal to *h s*; then *r m* and *s p* will be the axes required, by which the ellipsis may be drawn in the usual way.

126.—*To describe an ellipsis, whose axes shall be proportionate to the axes of a larger or smaller given one.* Let *a c b d*, (*Fig.* 91,) be the given ellipsis and axes, and *i j* the transverse axis of a proposed smaller one. Join *a* and *c*; from *i*, lraw *i e*, parallel to *a c*; make *o f* equal to *o e*; then *e f* will be

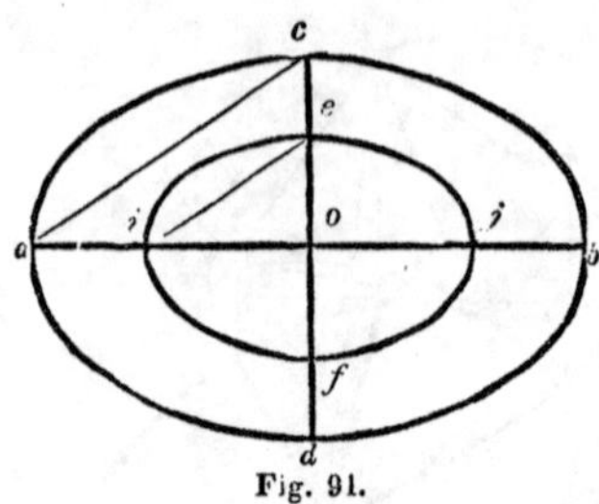

Fig. 91.

the conjugate axis required, and will bear the same proportion to *i j*, as *c d* does to *a b*. (See *Art.* 108.)

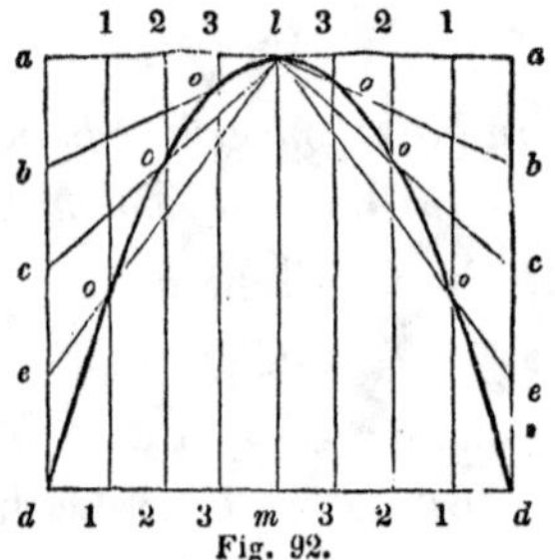

Fig. 92.

127.—*To describe a parabola by intersection of lines.* Let *m l*, (*Fig.* 92,) be the axis and height, (see *Fig.* 79,) and *d d*, a double ordinate and base of the proposed parabola. Through *l*, draw *a a*, parallel to *d d*; through *d* and *d*, draw *d a* and *d a*, parallel to *m l*; divide *a d* and *d m*, each into a like number of equal parts; from each point of division in *d m*, draw the lines, 1 1, 2 2, &c., parallel to *m l*; from each point of division in *d a*, draw lines to *l*; then a curve traced through the points of intersection, *o*, *o* and *o*, will be that of a parabola.

127, *a.*—*Another method.* Let *m l*, (*Fig.* 93,) be the axis and height, and *d d* the base. Extend *m l*, and make *l a* equal to *m l*; join *a* and *d*, and *a* and *d*; divide *a d* and *a d*, each into a like number of equal parts, as at 1, 2, 3, &c.; join 1 and 1, 2 and 2, &c., and the parabola will be completed.

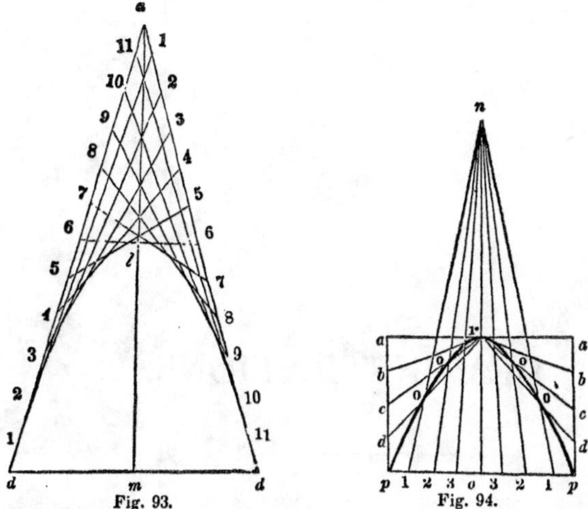

Fig. 93.

Fig. 94.

128.—*To describe an hyperbola by intersection of lines.* Let *r o*, (*Fig.* 94,) be the height, *p p* the base, and *n r* the transverse axis. (See *Fig.* 79.) Through *r*, draw *a a*, parallel to *p p;* from *p*, draw *a p*, parallel to *r o;* divide *a p* and *p o*, each into a like number of equal parts; from each of the points of divisions in the base, draw lines to *n;* from each of the points of division in *a p*, draw lines to *r;* then a curve traced through the points of intersection, *o*, *o*, &c., will be that of an hyperbola.

The parabola and hyperbola afford handsome curves for various mouldings.

DEMONSTRATIONS.

129.—To impress more deeply upon the mind of the learner some of the more important of the preceding problems, and to indulge a very common and praiseworthy curiosity to discover the cause of things, are some of the reasons why the following exercises are introduced. In all reasoning, definitions are necessary; in order to insure, in the minds of the proponent and respondent, identity of ideas. A *corollary* is an inference deduced from a previous course of reasoning. An *axiom* is a proposition evident at first sight. In the following demonstrations, there are many axioms taken for granted; (such as, things equal to the same thing are equal to one another, &c.;) these it was thought not necessary to introduce in form.

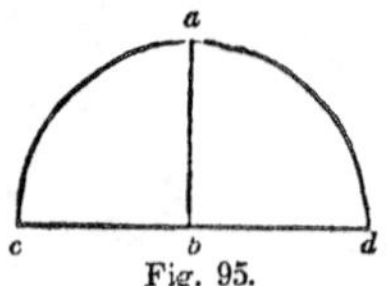

Fig. 95.

130.—*Definition.* If a straight line, as $a\ b$, (*Fig.* 95,) stand upon another straight line, as $c\ d$, so that the two angles made at the point, *b*, are equal—*a b c* to *a b d*, (see note to *Art.* 27,) then each of the two angles is called *a right angle.*

131.—*Definition.* The circumference of every circle is supposed to be divided into 360 equal parts, called *degrees ;* hence a semi-circle contains 180 degrees, a quadrant 90, &c.

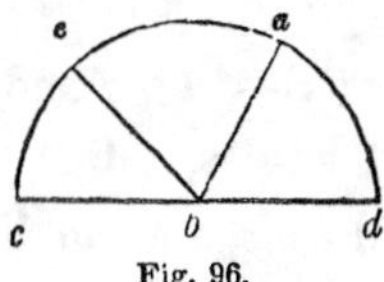

Fig. 96.

132.—*Definition.* The *measure of an angle* is the number of degrees contained between its two sides, using the angular point as a centre upon which to describe the arc. Thus the arc, *c e*, (*Fig.* 96,) is the measure of the angle, *c b e ; e a*, of the angle, *e b a ;* and *a d*, of the angle, *a b d.*

133.—*Corollary.* As the two angles at *b*, (*Fig.* 95,) are right angles, and as the semi-circle, *c a d*, contains 180 degrees, (*Art.* 131,) the measure of two right angles, therefore, is 180 degrees ; of one right angle, 90 degrees ; of half a right angle, 45 ; of one-third of a right angle, 30, &c.

134.—*Definition.* In measuring an angle, (*Art.* 132,) no regard is to be had to the length of its sides, but only to the degree of their inclination. Hence *equal angles* are such as have the same degree of inclination, without regard to the length of their sides.

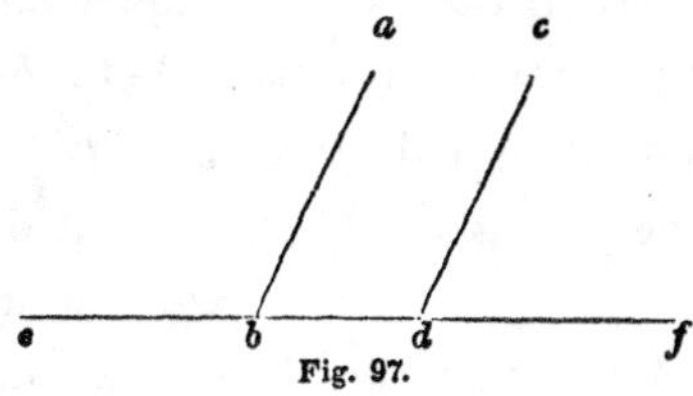

Fig. 97.

135.—*Axiom.* If two straight lines, parallel to one another, as *a b* and *c d*, (*Fig.* 97,) stand upon another straight line, as *e f*, the angles, *a b f* and *c d f*, are equal; and the angle, *a b e*, is equal to the angle, *c d e*.

136.—*Definition.* If a straight line, as *a b*, (*Fig.* 96,) stand obliquely upon another straight line, as *c d*, then one of the angles, as *a b c*, is called *an obtuse angle*, and the other, as *a b d*, *an acute angle.*

137.—*Axiom.* The two angles, *a b d* and *a b c*, (*Fig.* 96,) are together equal to two right angles, (*Art.* 130, 133;) also, the three angles, *a b d*, *e b a* and *c b e*, are together equal to two right angles.

138.—*Corollary.* Hence all the angles that can be made upon one side of a line, meeting in a point in that line, are together equal to two right angles.

139.—*Corollary.* Hence all the angles that can be made on both sides of a line, at a point in that line, or all the angles that can be made about a point, are together equal to four right angles.

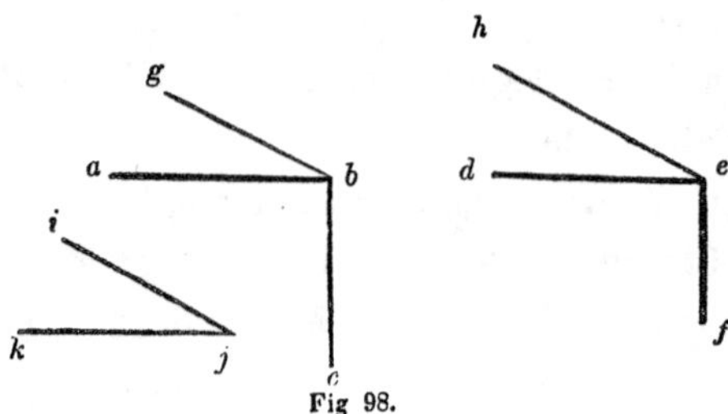

Fig 98.

140.—*Proposition.* If to each of two equal angles a third angle be added, their sums will be equal. Let *a b c* and *d e f*, (*Fig.* 98,) be equal angles, and the angle, *i j k*, the one to be added. Make the angles, *g b a* and *h e d*, each equal to the given angle, *i j k;* then the angle, *g b c*, will be equal to the angle, *h e f;* for, if *a b c* and *d e f* be angles of 90 degrees, and *i j k*, 30, then the angles, *g b c* and *h e f*, will be each equal to 90 and 30 added, viz: 120 degrees.

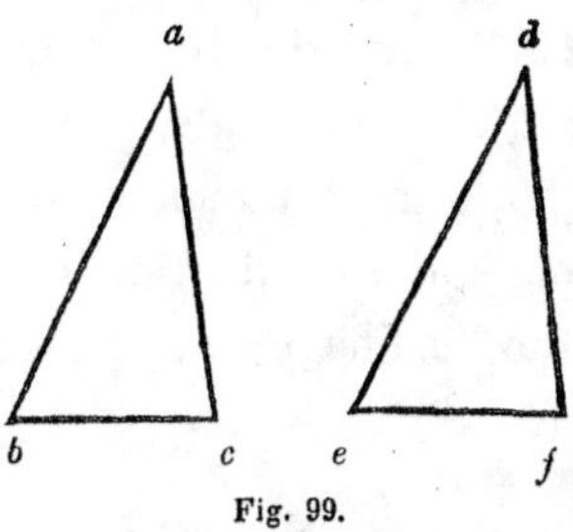

Fig. 99.

141.—*Proposition.* Triangles that have two of their sides and the angle contained between them respectively equal, have also their third sides and the two remaining angles equal; and consequently one triangle will every way equal the other. Let *a b c*, (*Fig.* 99,) and *d e f* be two given triangles, having the angle at *a* equal to the angle at *d*, the side, *a b*, equal to the side, *d e*, and the side, *a c*, equal to the side, *d f*; then the third side of one, *b c*, is equal to the third side of the other, *e f*; the angle at *b* is equal to the angle at *e*, and the angle at *c* is equal to the angle at *f*. For, if one triangle be applied to the other, the three points, *b*, *a*, *c*, coinciding with the three points, *e*, *d*, *f*, the line, *b c*, must coincide with the line, *e f*; the angle at *b* with the angle at *e*; the angle at *c* with the angle at *f*; and the triangle, *b a c*, be every way equal to the triangle, *e d f*.

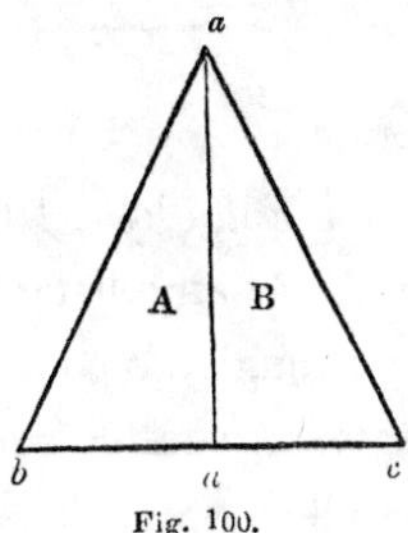

Fig. 100.

142.—*Proposition.* The two angles at the base of an isoceles triangle are equal. Let *a b c*, (*Fig.* 100,) be an isoceles triangle, of which the sides, *a b* and *a c*, are equal. Bisect the angle, (*Art.*

77,) *b a c*, by the line, *a d*. Then the line, *b a*, being equal to the line, *a c*; the line, *a d*, of the triangle, *A*, being equal to the line, *a d*, of the triangle, *B*, being common to each; the angle, *b a d*, being equal to the angle, *d a c*; the line, *b d*, must, according to *Art.* 141, be equal to the line, *d c*; and the angle at *b* must be equal to the angle at *c*.

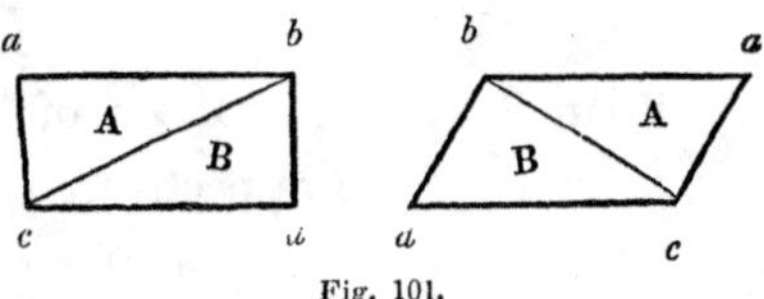

Fig. 101.

143.—*Proposition.* A diagonal crossing a parallelogram divides it into two equal triangles. Let *a b c d*, (*Fig.* 101,) be a given parallelogram, and *b c*, a line crossing it diagonally. Then, as *a c* is equal to *b d*, and *a b* to *c d*, the angle at *a* to the angle at *d*, the triangle, *A*, must, according to *Art.* 141, be equal to the triangle, *B*.

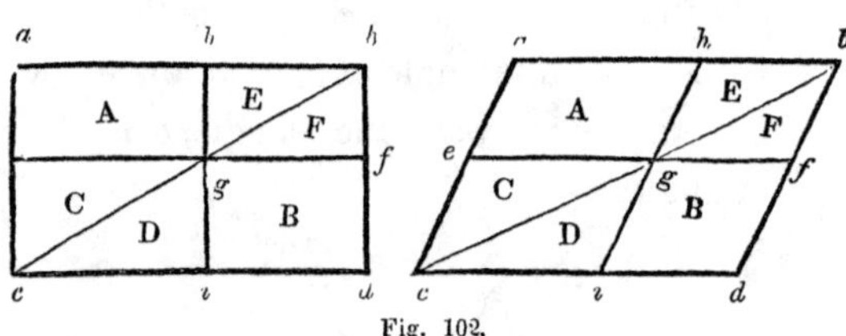

Fig. 102.

144.—*Proposition.* Let *a b c d*, (*Fig.* 102,) be a given parallelogram, and *b c* a diagonal. At any distance between *a b* and *c d*, draw *e f*, parallel to *a b*; through the point, *g*, the intersection of the lines, *b c* and *e f*, draw *h i*, parallel to *b d*. In every parallelogram thus divided, the parallelogram, *A*, is equal to the parallelogram, *B*. According to *Art.* 143, the triangle, *a b c*, is equal to the triangle, *b c d*; the triangle, *C*, to the triangle, *D*; and *E* to *F*; this being the case, take *D* and *F* from the triangle, *b c d*, and *C* and *E* from the triangle, *a b c*, and what remains in one must be equal to what remains in the other; therefore, the parallelogram, *A*, is equal to the parallelogram, *B*.

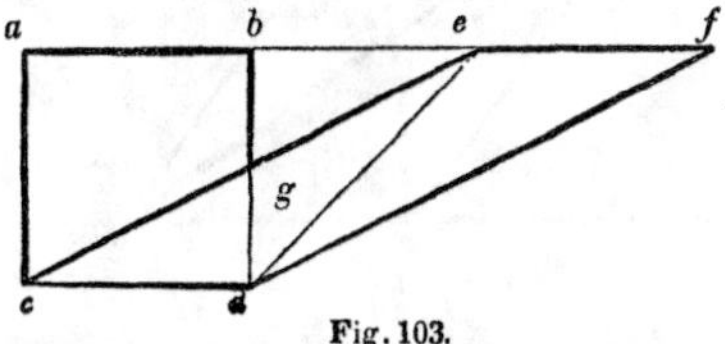

Fig. 103.

145.—*Proposition.* Parallelograms standing upon the same base and between the same parallels, are equal. Let *a b c d* and *e f c d*, (*Fig.* 103,) be given parallelograms, standing upon the same base, *c d*, and between the same parallels, *a f* and *c d*. Then, *a b* and *e f* being equal to *c d*, are equal to one another; *b e* being added to both *a b* and *e f*, *a e* equals *b f;* the line, *a c*, being equal to *b d*, and *a e* to *b f*, and the angle, *c a e*, being equal, (*Art.* 135,) to the angle, *d b f*, the triangle, *a e c*, must be equal, (*Art.* 141,) to the triangle, *b f d;* these two triangles being equal, take the same amount, the triangle, *b e g*, from each, and what remains in one, *a b g c*, must be equal to what remains in the other, *e f d g;* these two quadrangles being equal, add the same amount, the triangle, *c g d*, to each, and they must still be equal; therefore, the parallelogram, *a b c d*, is equal to the parallelogram, *e f c d*.

146.—*Corollary.* Hence, if a parallelogram and triangle stand upon the same base and between the same parallels, the parallelogram will be equal to double the triangle. Thus, the parallelogram, *a d*, (*Fig.* 103,) is double, (*Art.* 143,) the triangle, *c e d*.

147.—*Proposition.* Let *a b c d*, (*Fig.* 104,) be a given quadrangle with the diagonal, *a d*. From *b*, draw *b e*, parallel to *a d;* extend *c d* to *e;* join *a* and *e;* then the triangle, *a e c*, will be equal in area to the quadrangle, *a b c d*. Since the triangles, *a d b* and *a d e*, stand upon the same base, *a d*, and between the same paral-

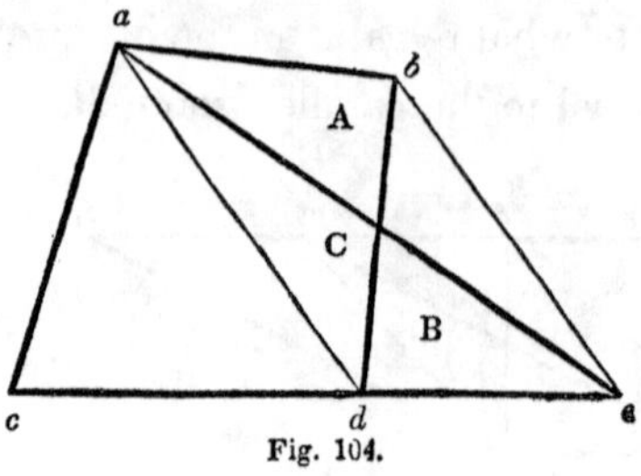

Fig. 104.

lels, *a d* and *b e*, they are therefore equal, (*Art.* 145, 146 ;) and since the triangle, *C*, is common to both, the remaining triangles, *A* and *B*, are therefore equal; then *B* being equal to *A*, the triangle, *a e c*, is equal to the quadrangle, *a b c d*.

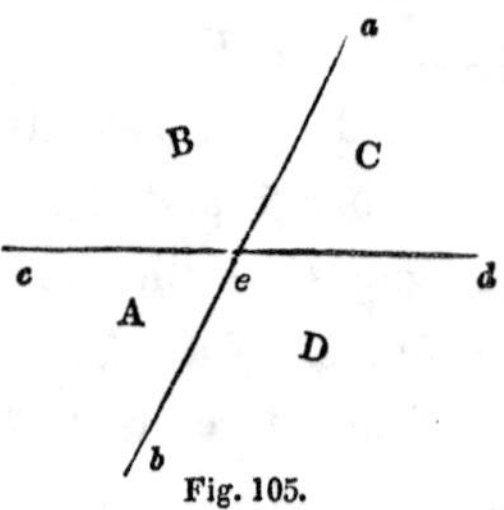

Fig. 105.

148.—*Proposition.* If two straight lines cut each other, as *a b* and *c d*, (*Fig.* 105,) the vertical, or opposite angles, *A* and *C*, are equal. Thus, *a e*, standing upon *c d*, forms the angles, *B* and *C*, which together amount, (*Art.* 137,) to two right angles; in the same manner, the angles, *A* and *B*, form two right angles; since the angles, *A* and *B*, are equal to *B* and *C*, take the same amount, the angle, *B*, from each pair, and what remains of one pair is equal to what remains of the other; therefore, the angle, *A*, is equal to the angle, *C*. The same can be proved of the opposite angles, *B* and *D*.

149.—*Proposition.* The three angles of any triangle are equal to two right angles. Let *a b c*, (*Fig.* 106,) be a given triangle, with its sides extended to *f*, *e*, and *d*, and the line, *c g*,

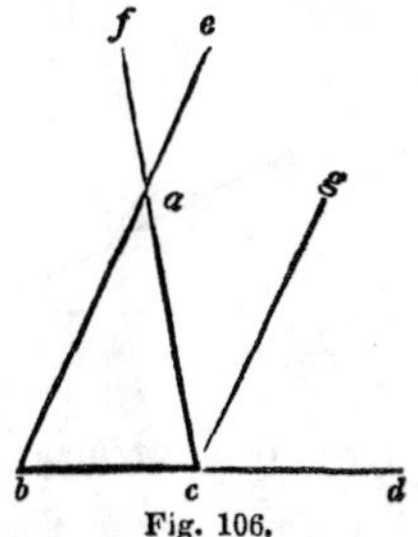

Fig. 106.

drawn parallel to *b e*. As *g c* is parallel to *e b*, the angle, *g c d*, is, equal, (*Art.* 135,) to the angle, *e b d;* as the lines, *f c* and *b e*, cut one another at *a*, the opposite angles, *f a e* and *b a c*, are equal, (*Art.* 148 ;) as the angle, *f a e*, is equal, (*Art.* 135,) to the angle, *a c g*, the angle, *a c g*, is equal to the angle, *b a c;* therefore, the three angles meeting at *c*, are equal to the three angles of the triangle, *a b c;* and since the three angles at *c* are equal, (*Art.* 137,) to two right angles, the three angles of the triangle, *a b c*, must likewise be equal to two right angles. Any triangle can be subjected to the same proof.

150.—*Corollary.* Hence, if one angle of a triangle be a right angle, the other two angles amount to just one right angle.

151.—*Corollary.* If one angle of a triangle be a right angle, and the two remaining angles are equal to one another, these are each equal to half a right angle.

152.—*Corollary.* If any two angles of a triangle amount to a right angle, the remaining angle is a right angle.

153.—*Corollary.* If any two angles of a triangle are together equal to the remaining angle, that remaining angle is a right angle.

154.—*Corollary.* If any two angles of a triangle are each equal to two-thirds of a right angle, the remaining angle is also equal to two-thirds of a right angle.

155.—*Corollary.* Hence, the angles of an equi-lateral triangle, are each equal to two-thirds of a right angle.

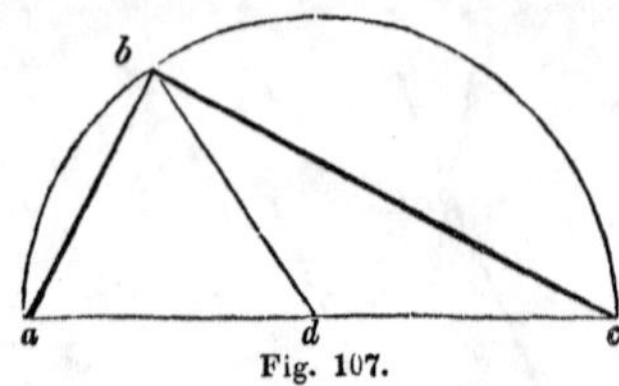

Fig. 107.

156.—*Proposition.* If from the extremities of the diameter of a semi-circle, two straight lines be drawn to any point in the circumference, the angle formed by them at that point will be a right angle. Let *a b c*, (*Fig.* 107,) be a given semi-circle; and *a b* and *b c*, lines drawn from the extremities of the diameter, *a c*, to the given point, *b*; the angle formed at that point by these lines, is a right angle. Join the point, *b*, and the centre, *d*; the lines, *d a*, *d b* and *d c*, being radii of the same circle, are equal; the angle at *a* is therefore equal, (*Art.* 142,) to the angle, *a b d*, also, the angle at *c* is, for the same reason, equal to the angle, *d b c*; the angle, *a b c*, being equal to the angles at *a* and *c* taken together, must therefore, (*Art.* 153,) be a right angle.

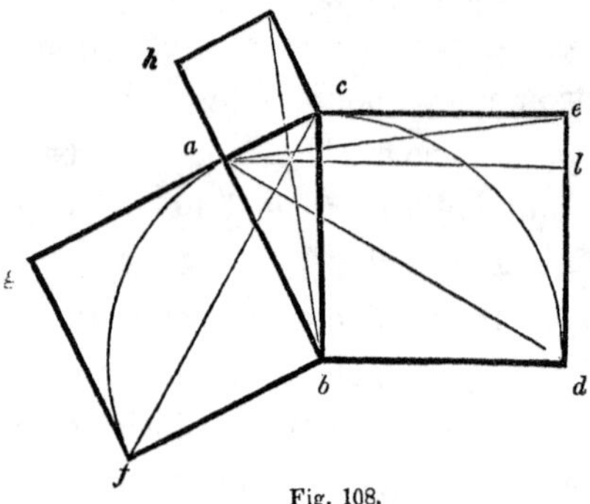

Fig. 108.

157.—*Proposition.* The square of the hypothenuse of a right-angled triangle, is equal to the squares of the two remaining sides: Let *a b c*, (*Fig.* 108,) be a given right-angled triangle, having a square formed on each of its sides: then, the square, *b e*, is equal to the squares, *h c* and *g b*, taken together. This can be proved by showing that the parallelogram, *b l*, is equal to the square, *g b ;* and that the parallelogram, *c l*, is equal to the square, *h c*. The angle, *c b d*, is a right angle, and the angle, *a b f*, is a right angle ; add to each of these the angle, *a b c ;* then the angle, *f b c*, will evidently be equal, (*Art.* 140,) to the angle, *a b d ;* the triangle, *f b c*, and the square, *g b*, being both upon the same base, *f b*, and between the same parallels, *f b* and *g c*, the square, *g b*, is equal, (*Art.* 146,) to twice the triangle, *f b c ;* the triangle, *a b d*, and the parallelogram, *b l*, being both upon the same base, *b d*, and between the same parallels, *b d* and *a l*, the parallelogram, *b l*, is equal to twice the triangle, *a b d ;* the triangles, *f b c* and *a b d*, being equal to one another, (*Art.* 141,) the square, *g b*, is equal to the parallelogram, *b l*, either being equal to twice the triangle, *f b c* or *a b d*. The method of proving *h c* equal to *c l* is exactly similar—thus proving the square, *b e*, equal to the squares, *h c* and *g b*, taken together.

This problem, which is the 47th of the First Book of Euclid, is said to have been demonstrated first by Pythagoras. It is stated, (but the story is of doubtful authority,) that as a thank-offering for its discovery he sacrificed a hundred oxen to the gods. From this circumstance, it is sometimes called the *hecatomb* problem. It is of great value in the exact sciences, more especially in Mensuration and Astronomy, in which many otherwise intricate calculations are by it made easy of solution.

These demonstrations, which relate mostly to the problems previously given, are introduced to satisfy the learner in regard to their mathematical accuracy. By studying and thoroughly understanding them, he will soonest arrive at a knowledge of their importance, and be likely the longer to retain them in memory. Should he have a relish for such exercises, and wish to continue them farther, he may consult Euclid's Elements, in which the whole subject of theoretical geometry is treated of in a manner sufficiently intelligible to be understood by the young mechanic.

The house-carpenter, especially, needs information of this kind, and were he thoroughly acquainted with the principles of geometry, he would be much less liable to commit mistakes, and be better qualified to excel in the execution of his often difficult undertakings.

SECTION II.—ARCHITECTURE.

HISTORY OF ARCHITECTURE.

158.—Architecture has been defined to be—"the art of building;" but, in its common acceptation, it is—"the art of designing and constructing buildings, in accordance with such principles as constitute stability, utility and beauty." The literal signification of the Greek word *archi-tecton*, from which the word *architect* is derived, is chief-carpenter; but the architect has always been known as the chief *designer* rather than the chief *builder*. Of the three classes into which architecture has been divided—viz., Civil, Military, and Naval, the first is that which refers to the construction of edifices known as dwellings, churches and other public buildings, bridges, &c., for the accommodation of civilized man—and is the subject of the remarks which follow.

159.—This is one of the most ancient of the arts: the scriptures inform us of its existence at a very early period. Cain, the son of Adam,—"builded a city, and called the name of the city after the name of his son, Enoch"—but of the peculiar style or manner of building we are not informed. It is presumed that it was not remarkable for beauty, but that utility and perhaps stability were its characteristics. Soon after the deluge—that memorable event, which removed from existence all traces of the works of man—the Tower of Babel was commenced. This was a work of such magnitude that the gathering of the materials, according to some writers, occupied three years; the period from its commencement until the work was abandoned, was twenty-two years; and the bricks were like blocks of stone, being twenty feet long, fifteen broad and seven thick. Learned men have given it as their opinion, that the tower in the temple of Belus at Babylon was the same as that which in the scriptures is called the Tower of Babel. The tower of the temple of Belus was square at its base, each side measuring one furlong, and consequently half a mile in circumference. Its form was that of a pyramid, and its height was 660 feet. It had a winding passage on the outside from the base to the summit, which was wide enough for two carriages.

160.—Historical accounts of ancient cities, of which there are now but few remains—such as Babylon, Palmyra and Ninevah of the Assyrians; Sidon, Tyre, Aradus and Serepta of the Phœnicians; and Jerusalem, with its splendid temple, of the Israelites—show that architecture among them had made great advances. Ancient monuments of the art are found also among other nations; the subterraneous temples of the Hindoos upon the islands, Elephanta and Salsetta; the ruins of Persepolis in Persia; pyramids, obelisks, temples, palaces and sepulchres in Egypt—all prove that the architects of those early times were possessed of skill and judgment highly cultivated. The principal characteristics of their works, are gigantic dimensions, immoveable solidity, and, in some instances, harmonious splendour. The extraordinary size of some is illustrated in the pyramids of Egypt. The largest of these stands not far from the city of Cairo: its base, which is square, covers about 11¼ acres, and its height is nearly 500 feet. The stones of which it is built are immense—the smallest being full thirty feet long.

161.—Among the Greeks, architecture was cultivated as a fine art, and rapidly advanced towards perfection. Dignity and grace were added to stability and magnificence. In the Doric order, their first style of building, this is fully exemplified. Phidias, Ictinus and Callicrates, are spoken of as masters in the art at this period: the encouragement and support of Pericles stimulated them to a noble emulation. The beautiful temple of Minerva, erected upon the acropolis of Athens, the Propyleum, the Odeum and others, were lasting monuments of their success. The Ionic and Corinthian orders were added to the Doric, and many magnificent edifices arose. These exemplified, in their chaste proportions, the elegant refinement of Grecian taste. Improvement in Grecian architecture continued to advance, until perfection seems to have been attained. The specimens which have been partially preserved, exhibit a combination of elegant proportion, dignified simplicity and majestic grandeur. Architecture among the Greeks was at the height of its glory at the period immediately preceding the Peloponnesian war; after which the art declined. An excess of enrichment succeeded its former simple grandeur; yet a strict regularity was maintained amid the profusion of ornament. After the death of Alexander, 323 B. C., a love of gaudy splendour increased: the consequent decline of the art was visible, and the Greeks afterwards paid but little attention to the science.

162.—While the Greeks were masters in architecture, which they applied mostly to their temples and other public buildings, the Romans gave their attention to the science in the construction of the many aqueducts and sewers with which Rome abounded; building no such splendid edifices as adorned Athens, Corinth and Ephesus, until about 200 years B. C., when their intercourse with the Greeks became more extended. Grecian architecture was introduced into Rome by Sylla; by whom, as also by Marius and Cæsar, many large edifices were erected in various cities of Italy. But under Cæsar Augustus, at about the beginning of the christian era, the art arose to the greatest perfection it ever attained in Italy. Under his patronage, Grecian artists were encouraged, and many emigrated to Rome. It was at about this time that Solomon's temple at Jerusalem was rebuilt by Herod—a Roman. This was 46 years in the erection, and was most probably of the Grecian style of building—perhaps of the Corinthian order. Some of the stones of which it was built were 46 feet long, 21 feet high and 14 thick; and others were of the astonishing length of 82 feet. The porch rose to a great height; the whole being built of white marble exquisitely polished. This is the building concerning which it was remarked—"Master, see what manner of stones, and what buildings are here." For the construction of private habitations also, finished artists were employed by the Romans: their dwellings being often built with the finest marble, and their villas splendidly adorned. After Augustus, his successors continued to beautify the city, until the reign of Constantine; who, having removed the imperial residence to Constantinople, neglected to add to the splendour of Rome; and the art, in consequence, soon fell from its high excellence.

Thus we find that Rome was indebted to Greece for what she possessed of architecture—not only for the knowledge of its principles, but also for many of the best buildings themselves; these having been originally erected in Greece, and stolen by the unprincipled conquerors—taken down and removed to Rome. Greece was thus robbed of her best monuments of architecture. Touched by the Romans, Grecian architecture lost much of its elegance and dignity. The Romans, though justly celebrated for their scientific knowledge as displayed in the construction of their various edifices, were not capable of appreciating the simple grandeur, the refined elegance of the Grecian style; but sought to improve upon it by the addition of luxurious enrichment, and thus deprived it of true elegance. In the days of Nero, whose palace of gold is so celebrated, buildings were lavishly adorned. Adrian did much to encourage the art; but not satisfied with the simplicity of the Grecian style, the artists of his time aimed at inventing new ones, and added to the already redundant embellishments of the previous age. Hence the origin of the pedestal, the great variety of intricate ornaments, the convex frieze, the round and the open pediments, &c. The rage for luxury continued until Alexander Severus, who made some improvement; but very soon after his reign, the art began rapidly to decline, as particularly evidenced in the mean and trifling character of the ornaments.

163.—The Goths and Vandals, when they overran the countries of Italy, Greece, Asia and Africa, destroyed most of the works of ancient architecture. Cultivating no art but that of war, these savage hordes could not be expected to take any interest in the beautiful forms and proportions of their habitations. From this time, architecture assumed an entirely different aspect. The celebrated styles of Greece were unappreciated and forgotten; and modern architecture took its first step on the platform of existence. The Goths, in their conquering invasions, gradually extended it over Italy, France, Spain, Portugal and Germany, into England. From the reign of Gallienus may be reckoned the total extinction of the arts among the Romans. From his time until the 6th or 7th century, architecture was almost entirely neglected. The buildings which were erected during this suspension of the arts, were very rude. Being constructed of the fragments of the edifices which had been demolished by the Visigoths in their unrestrained fury, and the builders being destitute of a proper knowledge of architecture, many sad blunders and extensive patchwork might have been seen in their construction—entablatures inverted, columns standing on their wrong ends, and other ridiculous arrangements characterized their clumsy work. The vast number of columns which the ruins around them afforded, they used as piers in the construction of arcades—which by some is thought, after having passed through various changes, to have been the origin of the plan of the Gothic cathedral. Buildings generally, which are not of the classical styles, and which were erected after the fall of the Roman empire, have by some been indiscriminately included under the term *Gothic.* But the changes which architecture underwent during the dark ages, show that there were several distinct modes of building.

164.—Theodoric, king of the Ostrogoths, a friend of the arts, who reigned in Italy from A. D. 493 to 525, endeavoured to restore and preserve some of the ancient buildings; and erected others, the ruins of which are still seen at Verona and Ravenna. Simplicity and strength are the characteristics of the structures erected by him; they are, however, devoid of grandeur and elegance, or fine proportions. These are properly of the GOTHIC style; by some called the *old* Gothic to distinguish it from the pointed style, which is generally called *modern* Gothic.

165.—The Lombards, who ruled in Italy from A. D. 568, had no taste for architecture nor respect for antiquities. Accordingly, they pulled down the splendid monuments of classic architecture which they found standing, and erected in their stead huge buildings of stone which were greatly destitute of proportion, elegance or utility—their characteristics being scarcely any thing more than stability and immensity combined with ornaments of a puerile character. Their churches were disfigured with rows of small columns along the cornice of the pediment, small doors and windows with circular heads, roofs supported by arches having arched buttresses to resist their thrust, and a lavish display of incongruous ornaments. This kind of architecture is called, the LOMBARD style, and was employed in the 7th century in Pavia, the chief city of the Lombards; at which city, as also at many other places, a great many edifices were erected in accordance with its inelegant forms.

166.—The Byzantine architects, from Byzantium, Constantinople, erected many spacious edifices; among which are included the cathedrals of Bamberg, Worms and Mentz, and the most ancient part of the minster at Strasburg; in all of these they combined the Roman-Ionic order with the Gothic of the Lombards.

This style is called the LOMBARD-BYZANTINE. To the last style there were afterwards added cupolas similar to those used in the east, together with numerous slender pillars with tasteless capitals, and the many minarets which are the characteristics of the proper *Byzantine*, or *Oriental* style.

167.—In the eighth century, when the Arabs and Moors destroyed the kingdom of the Goths, the arts and sciences were mostly in possession of the Musselmen-conquerors; at which time there were three kinds of architecture practised; viz: the Arabian, the Moorish and the modern-Gothic. The ARABIAN style was formed from Greek models, having circular arches added, and towers which terminated with globes and minarets. The MOORISH is very similar to the Arabian, being distinguished from it by arches in the form of a horse-shoe. It originated in Spain in the erection of buildings with the ruins of Roman architecture, and is seen in all its splendour in the ancient palace of the Mohammedan monarchs at Grenada, called the *Alhambra*, or *red-house.* The MODERN-GOTHIC was originated by the Visigoths in Spain by a combination of the Arabian and Moorish styles; and introduced by Charlemagne into Germany. On account of the changes and improvements it there underwent, it was, at about the 13th or 14th century, termed the *German*, or *romantic* style. It is exhibited in great perfection in the towers of the minster of Strasburgh, the cathedral of Cologne and other edifices. The most remarkable features of this lofty and aspiring style, are the lancet or pointed arch, clustered pillars, lofty towers and flying buttresses. It was principally employed in ecclesiastical architecture, and in this capacity introduced into France, Italy, Spain, and England.

168.—The Gothic architecture of England is divided into the *Norman*, the *Early-English*, the *Decorated*, and the *Perpendicular* styles. The Norman is principally distinguished by the character of its ornaments—the chevron, or *zigzag*, being the most common. Buildings in this style were erected in the 12th century. The Early-English is celebrated for the beauty of its edifices, the chaste simplicity and purity of design which they display, and the peculiarly graceful character of its foliage. This style is of the 13th century. The Decorated style, as its name implies, is characterized by a great profusion of enrichment, which consists principally of the crocket, or feathered-ornament, and ball-flower. It was mostly in use in the 14th century. The Perpendicular style, which dates from the 15th century, is distinguished by its high towers, and parapets surmounted with spires similar in number and grouping to oriental minarets.

169.—Thus these several styles, which have been erroneously termed *Gothic*, were distinguished by peculiar characteristics as well as by different names. The first symptoms of a desire to return to a pure style in architecture, after the ruin caused by the Goths, was manifested in the character of the art as displayed in the church of St. Sophia at Constantinople, which was erected by Justinian in the 6th century. The church of St. Mark at Venice, which arose in the 10th or 11th century, was the work of Grecian architects, and resembles in magnificence the forms of ancient architecture. The cathedral at Pisa, a wonderful structure for the age, was erected by a Grecian architect in 1016. The marble with which the walls of this building were faced, and of which the four rows of columns that support the roof are composed, is said to be of an excellent character. The Campanile, or leaning-tower as it is usually called, was erected near the cathedral in the 12th century. Its inclination is generally supposed to have arisen from a poor foundation; although by some it is said to have been thus constructed originally, in order to inspire in the minds of the beholder sensations of sublimity and awe. In the 13th century, the science in Italy was slowly progressing; many fine churches were erected, the style of which displayed a decided advance in the progress towards pure classical architecture. In other parts of Europe, the Gothic, or pointed style, was prevalent. The cathedral at Strasburg, designed by Irwin Steinbeck, was erected in the 13th and 14th centuries. In France and England during the 14th century, many very superior edifices were erected in this style.

170.—In the 14th and 15th centuries, and particularly in the latter, architecture in Italy was greatly revived. The masters began to study the remains of ancient Roman edifices; and many splendid buildings were erected, which displayed a purer taste in the science. Among others, St. Peter's of Rome, which was built about this time, is a lasting monument of the architectural skill of the age. Giocondo, Michael Angelo, Palladio, Vignola, and other celebrated architects, each in their turn, did much to restore the art to its former excellence. In the edifices which were erected under their direction, however, it is plainly to be seen that they studied not from the pure models of Greece, but from the remains of the deteriorated architecture of Rome. The high pedestal, the coupled columns, the rounded pediment, the many curved-and-twisted enrichments, and the convex frieze, were unknown to pure Grecian architecture. Yet their efforts were serviceable in correcting, to a good degree, the very impure taste that had prevailed since the overthrow of the Roman empire.

171.—At about this time, the Italian masters and numerous artists who had visited Italy for the purpose, spread the Roman style over various countries of Europe; which was gradually received into favor in place of the modern-Gothic. This fell into disuse; although it has of late years been again cultivated. It requires a building of great magnitude and complexity for a perfect display of its beauties. In America at the present time, the pure Grecian style is more or less studied; and perhaps the simplicity of its principles is better adapted to a republican country, than the intricacy and extent of those of the Gothic.

STYLES OF ARCHITECTURE.

172.—It is generally acknowledged that the various styles in architecture, were originated in accordance with the different pursuits of the early inhabitants of the earth; and were brought by their descendants to their present state of perfection, through the propensity for imitation and desire of emulation which are found more or less among all nations. Those that followed agricultural pursuits, from being employed constantly upon the same piece of land, needed a permanent residence, and the wooden *hut* was the offspring of their wants; while the shepherd, who followed his flocks and was compelled to traverse large tracts of country for pasture, found the *tent* to be the most portable habitation; again, the man devoted to hunting and fishing—an idle and vagabond way of living—is naturally supposed to have been content with the *cavern* as a place of shelter. The latter is said to have been the origin of the Egyptian style; while the curved roof of Chinese structures gives a strong indication of their having had the tent for their model; and the simplicity of the original style of the Greeks, (the Doric,) shows quite conclusively, as is generally conceded, that its original was of wood. The modern-Gothic, or pointed style, which was most generally confined to ecclesiastical structures, is said by some to have originated in an attempt to imitate the bower, or grove of trees, in which the ancients performed their idol-worship.

173.—There are numerous styles, or orders, in architecture; and a knowledge of the peculiarities of each, is important to the student in the art. The STYLOBATE is the substructure, or basement, upon which the columns of an order are arranged. In Roman architecture—especially in the interior of an edifice—it frequently occurs that each column has a separate substructure; this is called a *pedestal.* If possible, the pedestal should be avoided in all cases; because it gives to the column the appearance of having been originally designed for a small building, and afterwards pieced-out to make it long enough for a larger one.

174.—An ORDER, in architecture, is composed of tw) principal parts, viz: the column and the entablature.

175.—The Column is composed of the base, shaft and capital.

176.—The Entablature, above and supported by the columns, is horizontal; and is composed of the architrave, frieze and cornice. These principal parts are again divided into various members and mouldings. (See *Sect.* III.)

177.—The Base of a column is so called from *basis*, a foundation, or footing.

178.—The Shaft, the upright part of a column standing upon the base and crowned with the capital, is from *shafto*, to dig—in the manner of a well, whose inside is not unlike the form of a column.

179.—The Capital, from *kephale* or *caput*, the head, is the uppermost and crowning part of the column.

180.—The Architrave, from *archi*, chief or principal, and *trahs*, a beam, is that part of the entablature which lies in immediate connection with the column.

181.—The Frieze, from *fibron*, a fringe or border, is that part of the entablature which is immediately above the architrave and beneath the cornice. It was called by some of the ancients, *zophorus*, because it was usually enriched with sculptured animals.

182.—The Cornice, from *corona*, to crown, is the upper and projecting part of the entablature—being also the uppermost and crowning part of the whole order.

183.—The Pediment, above the entablature, is the triangular portion which is formed by the inclined edges of the roof at the end of the building. In Gothic architecture, the pediment is called, a *gable*.

184.—The Tympanum is the perpendicular triangular surface which is enclosed by the cornice of the pediment.

185.—The Attic is a small order, consisting of pilasters and entablature, raised above a larger order, instead of a pediment. An attic story is the upper story, its windows being usually square.

186.—An order, in architecture, has its several parts and members proportioned to one another by a scale of 60 equal parts, which are called minutes. If the height of buildings were always the same, the scale of equal parts would be a fixed quantity—an exact number of feet and inches. But as buildings are erected of different heights, the column and its accompaniments are required to be of different dimensions. To ascertain the scale of equal parts, it is necessary to know the height to which the whole order is to be erected. This must be divided by the number of diameters which is directed for the order under consideration. Then the quotient obtained by such division, is the length of the scale of equal parts—and is, also, the diameter of the column next above the base. For instance, in the Grecian Doric order the whole height, including column and entablature, is 8 diameters. Suppose now it were desirable to construct an example of this order, forty feet high. Then 40 feet divided by 8, gives 5 feet for the length of the scale; and this being divided by 60, the scale is completed. The upright columns of figures, marked *H* and *P*, by the side of the drawings illustrating the orders, designate the height and the projection of the members. The projection of each member is reckoned from a line passing through the axis of the column, and extending above it to the top of the entablature. The figures represent minutes, or 60ths, of the major diameter of the shaft of the column.

187.—Grecian Styles. The original method of building among the Greeks, was in what is called the *Doric* order: to this were afterwards added the *Ionic* and the *Corinthian.* These three were the only styles known among them. Each is distinguished from the other two, by not only a peculiarity of some one or more of its principal parts, but also by a particular destination. The character of the Doric is robust, manly and Herculean-like; that of the Ionic is more delicate, feminine, matronly; while that of the Corinthian is extremely delicate, youthful and virgin-like. However they may differ in their general character, they are alike famous for grace and dignity, elegance and grandeur, to a high degree of perfection.

188.—The Doric Order is so ancient that its origin is unknown—although some have pretended to have discovered it. But the most general opinion is, that it is an improvement upon the original log huts of the Grecians. These no doubt were very rude, and perhaps not unlike the following figure.

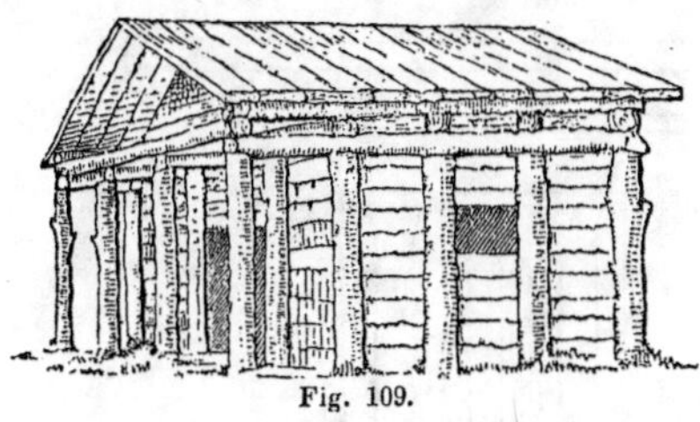
Fig. 109.

The trunks of trees, set perpendicularly to support the roof, may be taken for columns; the tree laid upon the tops of the perpendicular ones, the architrave; the ends of the cross-beams which rest upon the architrave, the triglyphs; the tree laid on the cross-beams as a support for the ends of the rafters, the bed-moulding of the cornice; the ends of the rafters which project beyond the bed-moulding, the mutules; and perhaps the projection of the roof in front, to screen the entrance from the weather, gave origin to the portico.

The peculiarities of the Doric order are the triglyphs—those parts of the frieze which have perpendicular channels cut in their surface; the absence of a base to the column—as also of fillets between the flutings of the column, and the plainness of the capital. The triglyphs are to be so disposed that the width of the metopes—the spaces between the triglyphs—shall be equal to their height.

189.—The *intercolumniation*, or space between the columns, is regulated by placing the centres of the columns under the centres of the triglyphs—except at the angle of the building; where, as may be seen in *Fig.* 110, one edge of the triglyph must be over the centre of the column.* Where the columns are so disposed that one of them stands beneath every other triglyph, the arrangement is called, *mono-triglyph*, and is most common.

* See note, page 108.

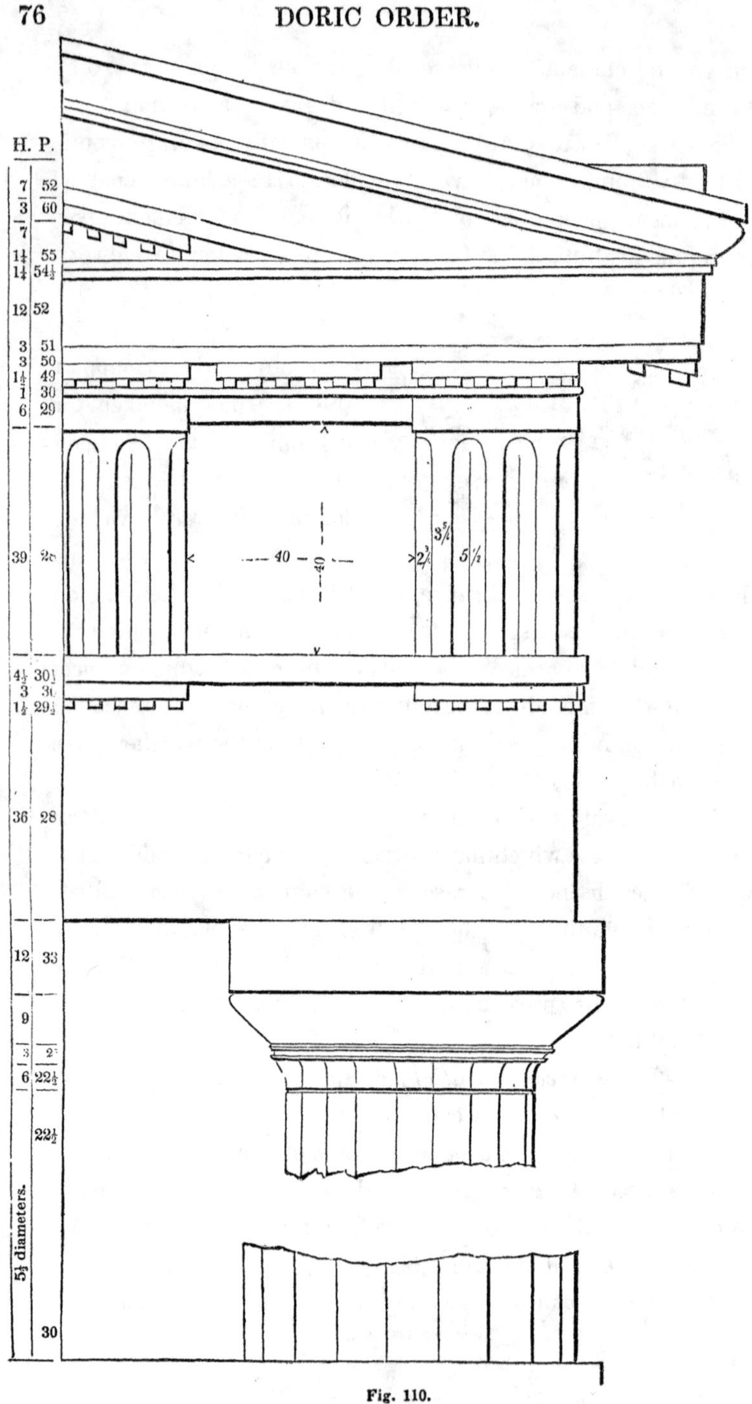

Fig. 110.

When a column is placed beneath every third triglyph, the arrangement is called *diastyle;* and when beneath every fourth, *aræostyle.* This last style is the worst, and is seldom practised.

190.—The Doric order is suitable for buildings that are destined for national purposes, for banking-houses, &c. Its appearance, though massive and grand, is nevertheless rich and graceful. The Custom-House and the Union Bank, in New-York city, are good specimens of this order.

191.—The Ionic Order. The Doric was for some time the only order in use among the Greeks. They gave their attention to the cultivation of it, until perfection seems to have been attained. Their temples were the principal objects upon which their skill in the art was displayed; and as the Doric order seems to have been well fitted, by its massive proportions, to represent the character of their male deities rather than the female, there seems to have been a necessity for another style which should be emblematical of feminine graces, and with which they might decorate such temples as were dedicated to the goddesses. Hence the origin of the Ionic order. This was invented, according to historians, by Hermogenes of Alabanda; and he being a native of Caria, then in the possession of the Ionians, the order was called, the Ionic.

192.—The distinguishing features of this order are the *volutes,* or spirals of the capital; and the *dentils* among the bed-mouldings of the cornice: although in some instances, dentils are wanting. The volutes are said to have been designed as a representation of curls of hair on the head of a matron, of whom the whole column is taken as a semblance.

193.—The intercolumniation of this and the other orders—both Roman and Grecian, with the exception of the Doric—are distinguished as follows. When the interval is one and a half diameters, it is called, *pycnostyle,* or columns thick-set; when two diameters, *systyle;* when two and a quarter diameters, *eustyle;* when three diameters, *diastyle;* and when more than

H. P.
2½ 66
9
2 60
2½ 59
12 57
39 3
9 29
4½ 7 4½ 7 7
3 30
45 27
1 31
2 30½
4
1 28¼
21 27½
21 27
4 31
2 3-10 31½
10 7-10
4
30
7 30
2 27
1 26
25
39
7 dia. 33m
30
1 33
5 35½
1½ 36
7 33½
25
1½ 40
10 45

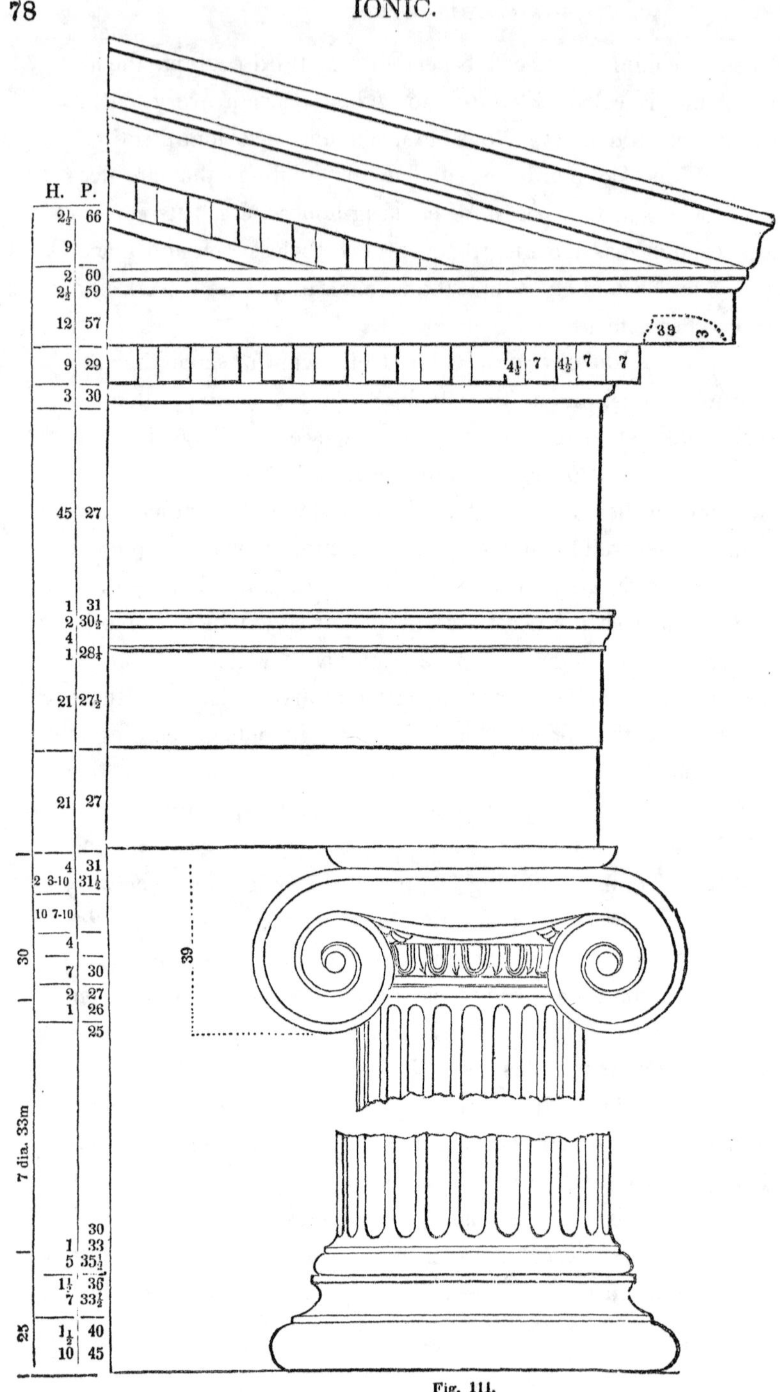

Fig. 111.

three diameters, *arœostyle*, or columns thin-set. In all the orders, when there are four columns in one row, the arrangement is called, *tetrastyle;* when there are six in a row, *hexastyle;* and when eight, *octastyle.*

194.—The Ionic order is appropriate for churches, colleges, seminaries, libraries, all edifices dedicated to literature and the arts, and all places of peace and tranquillity. The front of the Merchants' Exchange, New-York city, is a good specimen of this order.

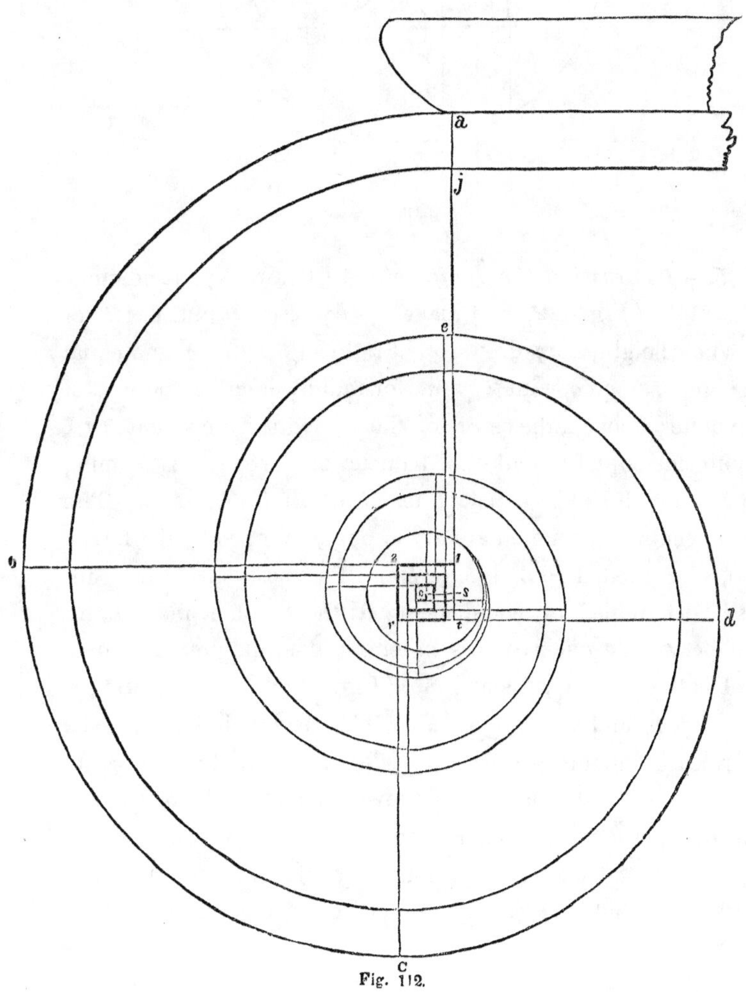

Fig. 112.

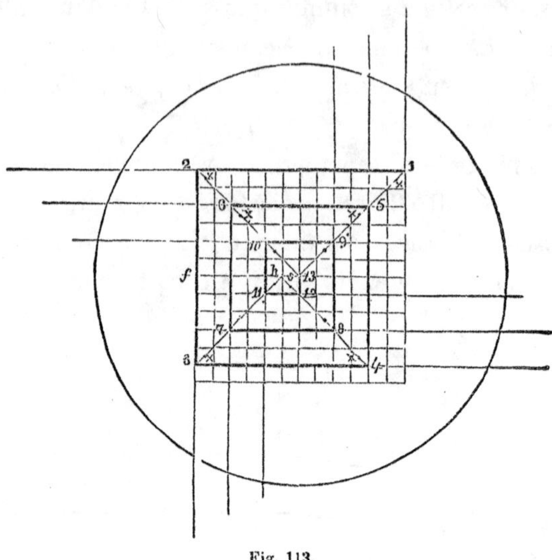

Fig. 113.

195.—*To describe the Ionic volute.* Draw a perpendicular from *a* to *s*, (*Fig.* 112,) and make *a s* equal to 20 min. or to $\frac{4}{7}$ of the whole height, *a c;* draw *s o*, at right angles to *s a*, and equal to $1\frac{1}{4}$ min.; upon *o*, with $2\frac{1}{2}$ min. for radius, describe the eye of the volute; about *o*, the centre of the eye, draw the square, *r t* 1 2, with sides equal to half the diameter of the eye, viz., $2\frac{1}{2}$ min., and divide it into 144 equal parts, as shown at *Fig.* 113. The several centres in rotation are at the angles formed by the heavy lines, as figured, 1, 2, 3, 4, 5, 6, &c. The position of these angles is determined by commencing at the point, 1, and making each heavy line one part less in length than the preceding one. No. 1 is the centre for the arc, *a b*, (*Fig.* 112;) 2 is the centre for the arc, *b c;* and so on to the last. The inside spiral line is to be described from the centres, *x*, *x*, *x*, &c., (*Fig.* 113,) being the centre of the first small square towards the middle of the eye from the centre for the outside arc. The breadth of the fillet at *a j*, is to be made equal to $2\frac{3}{10}$ min. This is for a spiral of *three* revolutions; but one of any number of revolutions, as 4 or 6, may be drawn, by dividing *o f*, (*Fig.* 113,) into a corresponding number of equal parts. Then divide the part nearest the centre, *o*, into two parts, as at *h*; join *o* and 1, also *o* and 2; draw *h* 3, parallel to *o* 1, and *h* 4, parallel to *o* 2; then the lines, *o* 1, *o* 2, *h* 3, *h* 4, will determine the length of the heavy lines, and the place of the centres. (See *Art.* 396.)

196.—The CORINTHIAN ORDER is in general like the Ionic, though the proportions are lighter. The Corinthian displays a more airy elegance, a richer appearance; but its distinguishing feature is its beautiful capital. This is generally supposed to have had its origin in the capitals of the columns of Egyptian temples; which, though not approaching it in elegance, have yet a similarity of form with the Corinthian. The oft-repeated story of its origin which is told by Vitruvius—an architect who flourished in Rome, in the days of Augustus Cæsar—though pretty generally considered to be fabulous, is nevertheless worthy of being again recited. It is this: a young lady of Corinth was sick, and finally died. Her nurse gathered into a deep basket, such trinkets and keepsakes as the lady had been fond of when alive, and placed them upon her grave; covering the basket with a flat stone or tile, that its contents might not be disturbed. The basket was placed accidentally upon the stem of an acanthus plant, which, shooting forth, enclosed the basket with its foliage; some of which, reaching the tile, turned gracefully over in the form of a volute.

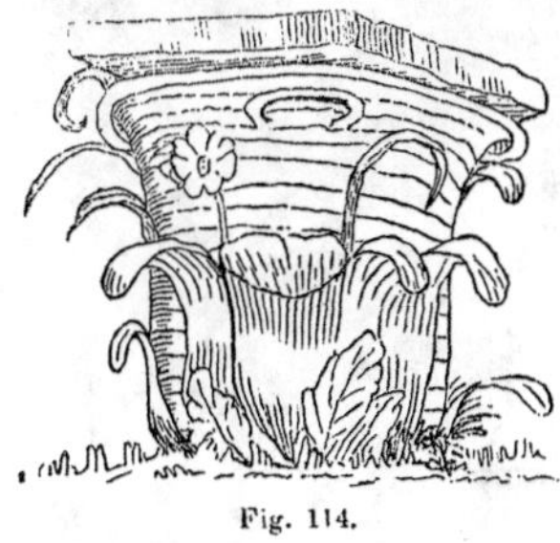
Fig. 114.

A celebrated sculptor, Calimachus, saw the basket thus decorated, and from the hint which it suggested, conceived and constructed a capital for a column. This was called Corinthian from the fact that it was invented and first made use of at Corinth.

197.—The Corinthian being the gayest, the richest and most lovely of all the orders, it is appropriate for edifices which are

H. P.
2 78
9 1/2
1 1/2 71
2 70
13 68
3 39
12 30
4 1/2 32
2 1/2 28
39 26
2 30
4
1 26 1/2
13 25 1/2
13 25
13 24 1/2
4 45
1 41
5 39
4
6
5
5
5 45
15
5 37
15 27
3 1/2 28 1/4
1 1/2 27
25
30
2 33
4 35
1 1/2 35
7 1/2 33
2 38
10 43
1 Dia. 10.
8 Dia. 25.
25
44 5
5 8 8

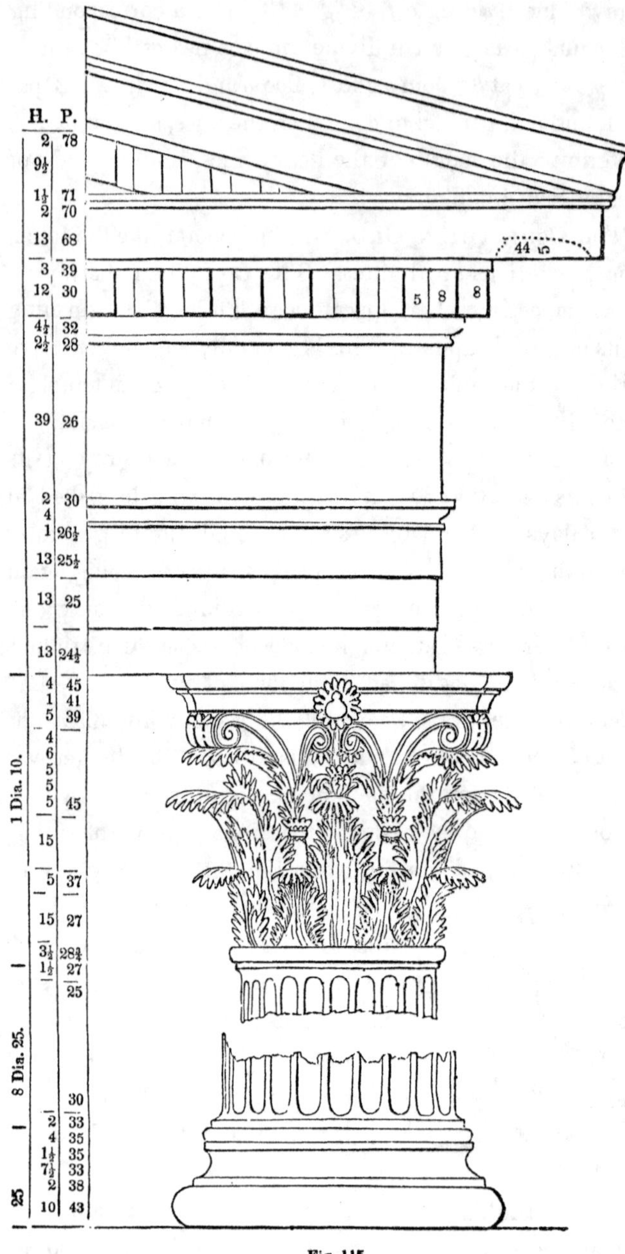

Fig. 115

dedicated to amusement, banqueting and festivity—for all places where delicacy, gayety and splendour are desirable.

198.—In addition to the three regular orders of architecture, it was sometimes customary among the Greeks—and afterwards among other nations—to employ representations of the human form, instead of columns, to support entablatures; these were called *Persians* and *Caryatides*.

199.—PERSIANS are statues of men, and are so called in commemoration of a victory gained over the Persians by Pausanias. The Persian prisoners were brought to Athens and condemned to abject slavery; and in order to represent them in the lowest state of servitude and degradation, the statues were loaded with the heaviest entablature, the Doric.

200.—CARYATIDES are statues of women dressed in long robes after the Asiatic manner. Their origin is as follows. In a war between the Greeks and the Caryans, the latter were totally vanquished, their male population extinguished, and their females carried to Athens. To perpetuate the memory of this event, statues of females, having the form and dress of the Caryans, were erected, and crowned with the Ionic or Corinthian entablature. The caryatides were generally formed of about the human size, but the persians much larger; in order to produce the greater awe and astonishment in the beholder. The entablatures were proportioned to a statue in like manner as to a column of the same height.

201.—These semblances of slavery have been in frequent use among moderns as well as ancients; and as a relief from the stateliness and formality of the regular orders, are capable of forming a thousand varieties; yet in a land of liberty such marks of human degradation ought not to be perpetuated.

202.—ROMAN STYLES. Strictly speaking, Rome had no architecture of her own—all she possessed was borrowed from other nations. Before the Romans exchanged intercourse with the Greeks, they possessed some edifices of considerable extent and merit, which were erected by architects from Etruria; but Rome was principally indebted to Greece for what she acquired of the art. Although there is no such thing as an architecture of Roman invention, yet no nation, perhaps, ever was so devoted to the cultivation of the art as the Roman. Whether we consider the number and extent of their structures, or the lavish richness and splendour with which they were adorned, we are compelled to yield to them our admiration and praise. At one time, under the consuls and emperors, Rome employed 400 architects. The public works—such as theatres, circuses, baths, aqueducts, &c.—were, in extent and grandeur, beyond any thing attempted in modern times. Aqueducts were built to convey water from a distance of 60 miles or more. In the prosecution of this work, rocks and mountains were tunnelled, and valleys bridged. Some of the latter descended 200 feet below the level of the water; and in passing them the canals were supported by an arcade, or succession of arches. Public baths are spoken of as large as cities; being fitted up with numerous conveniences for exercise and amusement. Their decorations were most splendid; indeed, the exuberance of the ornaments alone was offensive to good taste. So overloaded with enrichments were the baths of Diocletian, that on an occasion of public festivity, great quantities of sculpture fell from the ceilings and entablatures, killing many of the people.

203.—The three orders of Greece were introduced into Rome in all the richness and elegance of their perfection. But the luxurious Romans, not satisfied with the simple elegance of their refined proportions, sought to improve upon them by lavish displays of ornament. They transformed in many instances, the true elegance of the Grecian art into a gaudy splendour, better suited to their less refined taste. The Romans remodelled each of the orders: the Doric was modified by increasing the height of the column to 8 diameters; by changing the echinus of the capital for an ovolo, or quarter-round, and adding an astragal and neck below it; by placing the centre of the first triglyph, instead of one edge, over the centre of the column; and introducing horizontal instead of inclined mutules in the cornice. The Ionic was modified by diminishing the size of the volutes, and, in some specimens, introducing a new capital in which the volutes were diagonally arranged. This new capital has been termed *modern* Ionic. The favorite order at Rome and her colonies was the Corinthian. The Roman artists, in their search for novelty, subjected it to many alterations—especially in the foliage of its capital. Into the upper part of this, they introduced the modified Ionic capital; thus combining the two in one. This change was dignified with the importance of an *order*, and received the appellation COMPOSITE, or *Roman:* the best specimen of which is found in the Arch of Titus. This style was not much used among the Romans themselves, and is but slightly appreciated now. Its decorations are too profuse—a standing monument of the luxury of the age in which it was invented.

204.—The TUSCAN ORDER is said to have been introduced to the Romans by the Etruscan architects, and to have been the only style used in Italy before the introduction of the Grecian orders. However this may be, its similarity to the Doric order gives strong indications of its having been a rude imitation of that style: this is very probable, since history informs us that the Etruscans held intercourse with the Greeks at a remote period. The rudeness of this order prevented its extensive use in Italy. All that is known concerning it is from Vitruvius—no remains of buildings in this style being found among ancient ruins.

205. For mills, factories, markets, barns, stables, &c., where utility and strength are of more importance than beauty, the improved modification of this order, called the *modern* Tuscan, (*Fig.* 116,) will be useful; and its simplicity recommends it where economy is desirable.

206.—EGYPTIAN STYLE. The architecture of the ancient

H. P.
3 70
9
1½ 63
13 61
11½ 31
7 26½
30 25
6 30
24 25
10 39
8
2 28
10 25
3 27
25
30
3 35
12
15 41
45
1 Dia.
30
6 Dia.
30
10
17½
9
20

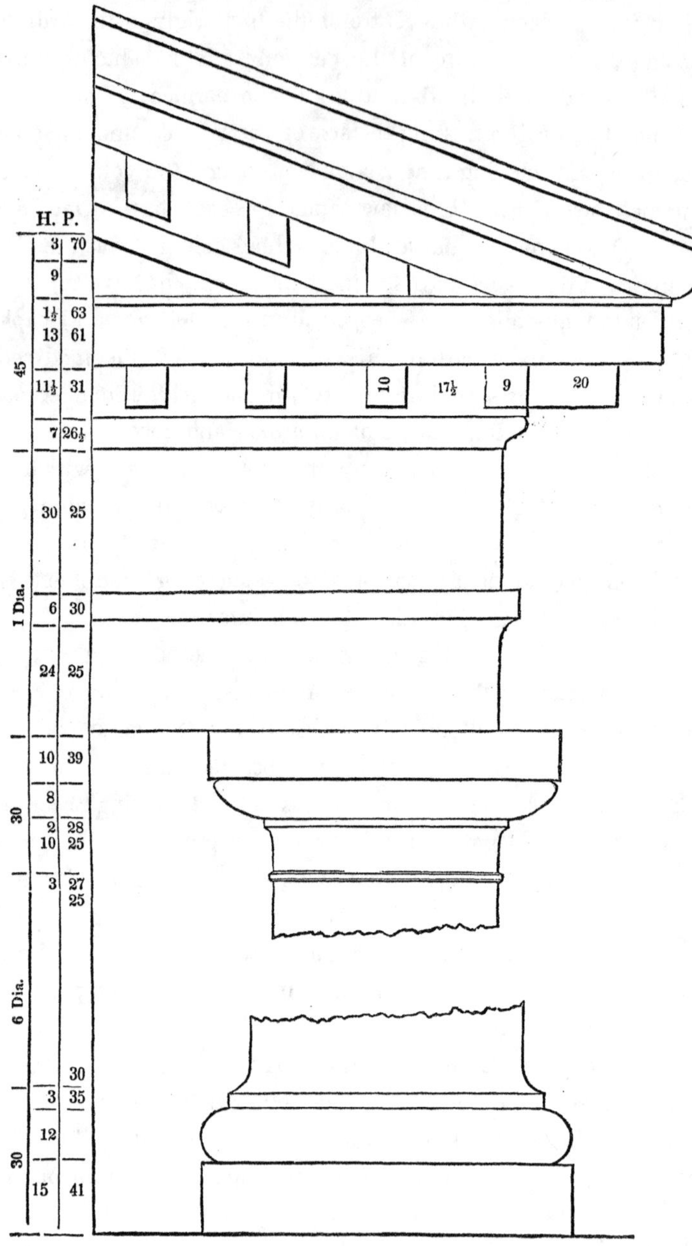

Fig. 116.

Egyptians—to which that of the ancient Hindoos bears some resemblance—is characterized by boldness of outline, solidity and grandeur. The amazing labyrinths and extensive artificial lakes, the splendid palaces and gloomy cemeteries, the gigantic pyramids and towering obelisks, of the Egyptians, were works of immensity and durability; and their extensive remains are enduring proofs of the enlightened skill of this once-powerful, but long since extinct nation. The principal features of the Egyptian Style of architecture are—uniformity of plan, never deviating from right lines and angles; thick walls, having the outer surface slightly deviating inwardly from the perpendicular; the whole building low; roof flat, composed of stones reaching in one piece from pier to pier, these being supported by enormous columns, very short in proportion to their height; the shaft sometimes polygonal, having no base but with a great variety of handsome capitals, the foliage of these being of the palm, lotus and other leaves; entablatures having simply an architrave, crowned with a huge cavetto ornamented with sculpture; and the intercolumniation very narrow, usually 1½ diameters and seldom exceeding 2½. In the remains of a temple, the walls were found to be 24 feet thick; and at the gates of Thebes, the walls at the foundation were 50 feet thick and perfectly solid. The immense stones of which these, as well as Egyptian walls generally, were built, had both their inside and outside surfaces faced, and the joints throughout the body of the wall as perfectly close as upon the outer surface. For this reason, as well as that the buildings generally partake of the pyramidal form, arise their great solidity and durability. The dimensions and extent of the buildings may be judged from the temple of Jupiter at Thebes, which was 1400 feet long and 300 feet wide—exclusive of the porticos, of which there was a great number.

It is estimated by Mr. Gliddon, U. S. consul in Egypt, that not less than 25,000,000 tons of hewn stone were employed in the erection of the Pyramids of Memphis alone,—or enough to construct 3,000 Bunker-Hill monuments. Some of the blocks are 40

H. P.
12 55
50
100
8 26
30
26
12 20
9 38
49 25
20
20
20
30
400
70
50
30
25 32½
15 30
30

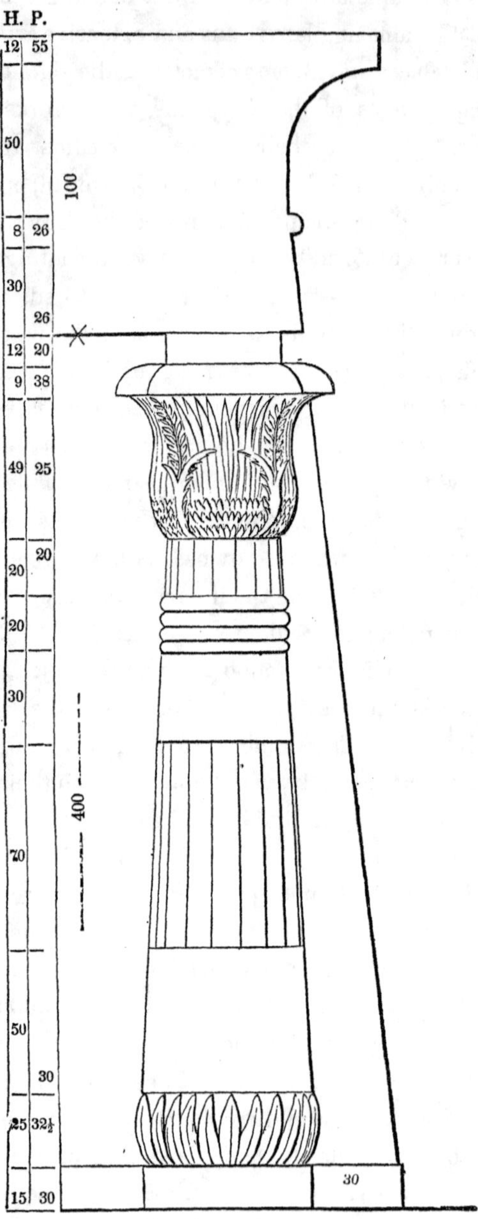

Fig. 117.

feet long, and polished with emery to a surprising degree. It is conjectured that the stone for these pyramids was brought, by rafts and canals, from a distance of 6 or 7 hundred miles.

207.—The general appearance of the Egyptian style of architecture is that of solemn grandeur—amounting sometimes to sepulchral gloom. For this reason it is appropriate for cemeteries, prisons, &c.; and being adopted for these purposes, it is gradually gaining favour.

A great dissimilarity exists in the proportion, form and general features of Egyptian columns. In some instances, there is no uniformity even in those of the same building, each differing from the others either in its shaft or capital. For practical use in this country, *Fig.* 117 may be taken as a standard of this style. The Halls of Justice in Centre-street, New-York city, is a building in general accordance with the principles of Egyptian architecture.

Buildings in General.

208.—That style of architecture is to be preferred in which utility, stability and regularity, are gracefully blended with grandeur and elegance. But as an arrangement designed for a warm country would be inappropriate for a colder climate, it would seem that the style of building ought to be modified to suit the wants of the people for whom it is designed. High roofs to resist the pressure of heavy snows, and arrangements for artificial heat, are indispensable in northern climes; while they would be regarded as entirely out of place in buildings at the equator.

209.—Among the Greeks, architecture was employed chiefly upon their temples and other large buildings; and the proportions of the orders, as determined by them, when executed to such large dimensions, have the happiest effect. But when used for small buildings, porticos, porches, &c., especially in country-places, they are rather heavy and clumsy; in such cases, more slender proportions will be found to produce a better effect. The

English cottage-style is rather more appropriate, and is becoming extensively practised for small buildings in the country.

210.—Every building should bear an expression suited to its destination. If it be intended for national purposes, it should be magnificent—grand; for a private residence, neat and modest; for a banqueting-house, gay and splendid; for a monument or cemetery, gloomy—melancholy; or, if for a church, majestic and graceful. By some it has been said—"somewhat dark and gloomy, as being favourable to a devotional state of feeling;" but such impressions can only result from a misapprehension of the nature of true devotion. "Her ways are ways of *pleasantness*, and all her paths are peace." The church should rather be a type of that brighter world to which it leads.

211.—However happily the several parts of an edifice may be disposed, and however pleasing it may appear as a whole, yet much depends upon its *site*, as also upon the character and style of the structures in its immediate vicinity, and the degree of cultivation of the adjacent country. A splendid country-seat should have the out-houses and fences in the same style with itself, the trees and shrubbery neatly trimmed, and the grounds well cultivated.

212.—Europeans express surprise that so many houses in this country are built of wood. And yet, in a new country, where wood is plenty, that this should be so is no cause for wonder. Still, the practice should not be encouraged. Buildings erected with brick or stone are far preferable to those of wood; they are more durable; not so liable to injury by fire, nor to need repairs; and will be found in the end quite as economical. A wooden house is suitable for a temporary residence only; and those who would bequeath a dwelling to their children, will endeavour to build with a more durable material. Wooden cornices and gutters, attached to brick houses, are objectionable—not only on account of their frail nature, but also because they render the building liable to destruction by fire.

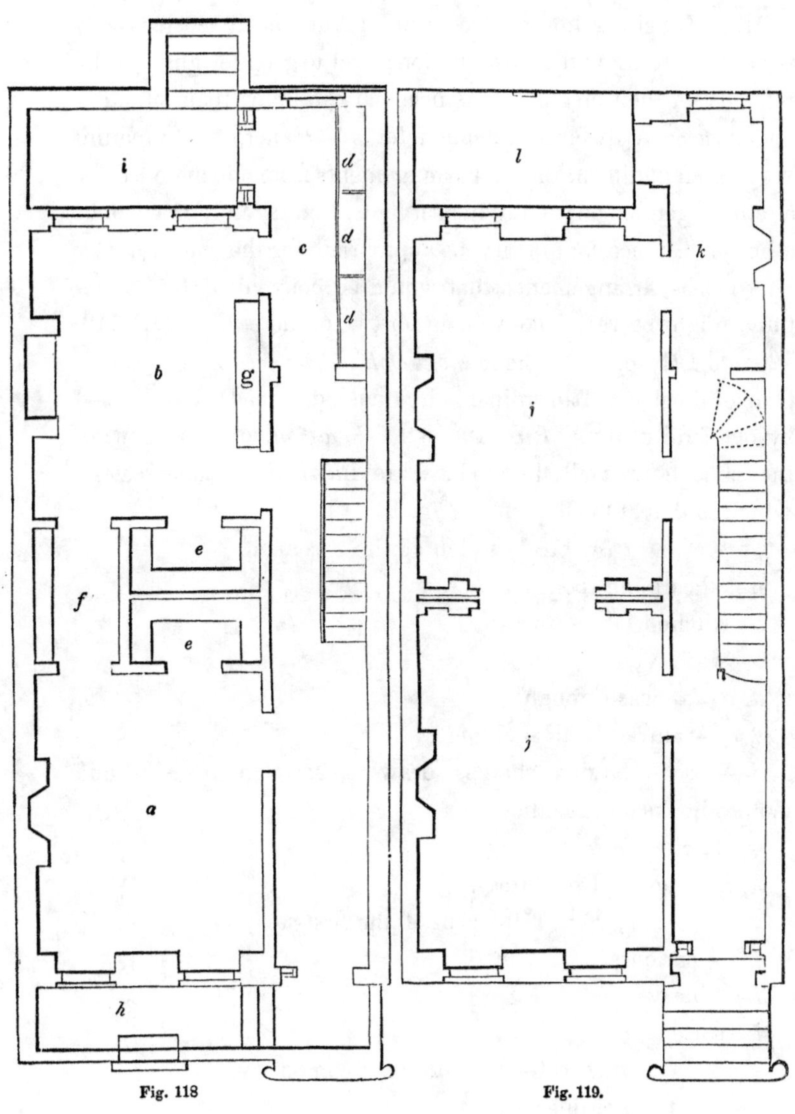

Fig. 118

Fig. 119.

213.—Dwelling houses are built of various dimensions and styles, according to their destination; and to give designs and directions for their erection, it is necessary to know their situation and object. A dwelling intended for a gardener, would require very different dimensions and arrangements from one intended for a retired gentleman—with his servants, horses, &c.; nor would a house designed for the city, be appropriate for the country. For city houses, arrangements that would be convenient for one family, might be very inconvenient for two or more. *Fig.* 118, 119, 120 and 121, represent the *ichnographical projection*, or ground-plan, of the floors of an ordinary city house, designed to be occupied by one family only. *Fig.* 122 is an *elevation*, or front-view, of the same house: all these plans are drawn at the same scale—which is that at the bottom of *Fig.* 122.

Fig. 118 is a plan of the basement.

a is the dining-room.

b—kitchen.

c—wash-room.

d, d, d,—wash-troughs.

e, e,—pantries with shelving.

f—passage having shelves, drawers, &c., on one side, and clothes-hooks on the other.

g—kitchen-dresser.

h, i,—front and rear areas.

Fig. 119—plan of the first-story.

j, j,—parlours.

k—library.

l—portico.

Fig. 120—plan of the second-story.

a—toilet and sitting room.

b—principal bed-chamber.

c—bath-room.

d, d,—bed-chambers.

e—passage with wardrobe and clothes-hooks.

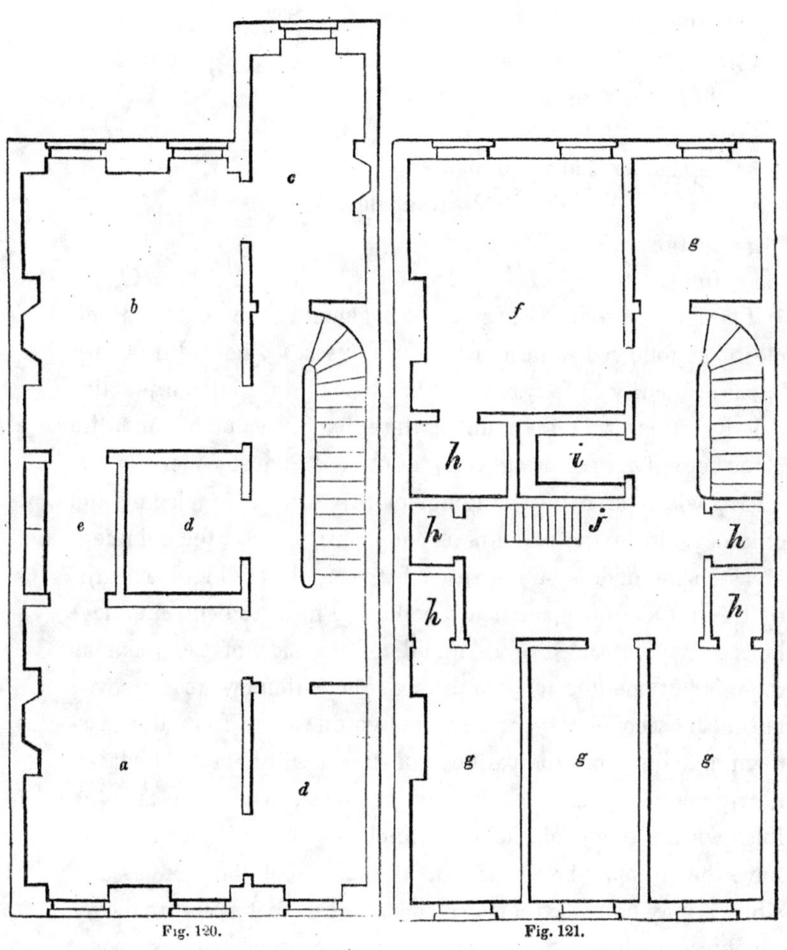

Fig. 120.

Fig. 121.

Fig. 121—plan of the attic-story.

f—nursery,

g, *g*, *g*, *g*,—bed-chambers,

h, *h*, *h*, *h*, *h*,—wardrobes,

i—pantry with shelves,

j—step-ladder leading to roof.

Fig. 122—front elevation.

a—section,

b—front,

These are introduced to give some general ideas of the principles to be followed in designing city houses. The width of city lots is ordinarily 25 feet, but as it has become a common practice to reduce this size, on account of the enhanced value of land, the plans here given are designed for a lot only 20 feet wide—the ordinary width of many buildings of this class. In placing the chimneys, make the parlours of equal size, and set the chimney-breast in the middle of the space between the sliding-door partition and the front (and rear) walls. The basement chimney-breasts may be placed in the middle of the side of the room, as there is but one flue to pass through the chimney-breast above; but in the second-story, as there are two flues, one from the basement and one from the parlour, the breast will have to be placed nearly perpendicular over the parlour breast, so as to receive the flues within the jambs of the fire-place. As it is desirable to have the chimney-breast as near the middle of the room as possible, it may be placed a few inches towards that point from over the breast below. So in arranging those of the stories above, always make provision for the flues from below.

214.—In placing the stairs, there should be at least as much room in the passage at the side of the stairs, as upon them; and in regard to the length of the passage in the second story, there must be room for the doors which open from each of the principal rooms into the hall, and more if the stairs require it. Having assigned a position for the stairs of the second story, let the winders of

Fig. 122.

the other stories be placed perpendicularly over and under them; and be careful to provide for head-room. To ascertain this, when it is doubtful, it is well to draw a vertical section of the whole stairs; but in ordinary cases, this is not necessary. To dispose the windows properly, the middle window of each story should be exactly in the middle of the front; but the pier between the two windows which light the parlour, should be in the centre of that room; because when chandeliers or any similar ornaments, hang from the centre-pieces of the parlour ceilings, it is important, in order to give the better effect, that the pier-glasses at the front and rear, be in a range with them. If both these objects cannot be attained, an approximation to each must be attempted. The piers should in no case be less in width than the window openings, else the blinds or shutters when thrown open will interfere with one another; in general practice, it is well to make the outside piers $\frac{2}{3}$ of the width of one of the middle piers. When this is desirable, deduct the amount of the three openings from the width of the front, and the remainder will be the amount of the width of all the piers; divide this by 10, and the product will be $\frac{1}{3}$ of a middle pier; and then, if the parlour arrangements do not interfere, give twice this amount to each corner pier, and three times the same amount to each of the middle piers.

PRINCIPLES OF ARCHITECTURE.

215.—In the construction of the first habitations of men, frail and rude as they must have been, the first and principal object was, doubtless, utility—a mere shelter from sun and rain. But as successive storms shattered the poor tenement, man was taught by experience the necessity of building with an idea to durability. And when in his walks abroad, the symmetry, proportion and beauty of nature met his admiring gaze, contrasting so strangely with the misshapen and disproportioned work of his own hands, he was led to make gradual changes; till his abode was rendered not only commodious and durable, but pleasant in its appearance; and building became a fine-art, having utility for its basis.

216.—In all designs for buildings of importance, utility, durability and beauty, the first great principles of architecture, should be pre-eminent. In order that the edifice be useful, commodious and comfortable, the arrangement of the apartments should be such as to fit them for their several destinations; for public assemblies, oratory, state, visitors, retiring, eating, reading, sleeping, bathing, dressing, &c.—these should each have its own peculiar form and situation. To accomplish this, and at the same time to make their relative situation agreeable and pleasant, producing regularity and harmony, require in some instances much skill and sound judgment. Convenience and regularity are very important, and each should have due attention; yet when both cannot be obtained, the latter should in most cases give place to the former. A building that is neither convenient nor regular, whatever other good qualities it may possess, will be sure of disapprobation.

217.—The utmost importance should be attached to such arrangements as are calculated to promote health: among these, *ventilation* is by no means the least. For this purpose, the ceilings of the apartments should have a respectable height; and the skylight, or any part of the roof that can be made moveable, should be arranged with cord and pullies, so as to be easily raised and lowered. Small openings near the ceiling, that may be closed at pleasure, should be made in the partitions that separate the rooms from the passages—especially for those rooms which are used for sleeping apartments. All the apartments should be so arranged as to secure their being easily kept *dry* and *clean*. In dwellings, suitable apartments should be fitted up for *bathing*, with all the necessary apparatus for conveying the water.

218.—To insure stability in an edifice, it should be designed upon well-known geometrical principles: such as science has demonstrated to be necessary and sufficient for firmness and durability. It is well, also, that it have the *appearance* of stability as well as the *reality ;* for should it seem tottering and unsafe, the sensation of fear, rather than those of admiration and pleasure, will be excited in the beholder. To secure certainty and accuracy in the application of those principles, a knowledge of the strength and other properties of the materials used, is indispensable; and in order that the whole design be so made as to be capable of execution, a practical knowledge of the requisite mechanical operations is quite important.

219.—The elegance of an architectural design, although chiefly depending upon a just proportion and harmony of the parts, will be promoted by the introduction of ornaments—provided this be judiciously performed. For enrichments should not only be of a proper character to suit the style of the building, but should also have their true position, and be bestowed in proper quantity. The most common fault, and one which is prominent in Roman architecture, is an excess of enrichment: an error which is carefully to be guarded against. But those who take the Grecian models for their standard, will not be liable to go to that extreme. In ornamenting a cornice, or any other assemblage of mouldings, at least every alternate member should be left plain; and those that are near the eye should be more finished than those which are distant. Although the characteristics of good architecture are utility and elegance, in connection with durability, yet some buildings are designed expressly for use, and others again for ornament: in the former, utility, and in the latter, beauty, should be the governing principle.

220.—The builder should be intimately acquainted with the principles upon which the essential, elementary parts of a building are founded. A scientific knowledge of these will insure certainty and security, and enable the mechanic to erect the most extensive and lofty edifices with confidence. The more important parts are the foundation, the column, the wall, the lintel, the arch, the vault, the dome and the roof. A separate description of the peculiarities of each, would seem to be necessary; and cannot perhaps be better expressed than in the following language of a modern writer on this subject.

221.—"In laying the FOUNDATION of any building, it is necessary to dig to a certain depth in the earth, to secure a solid basis, below the reach of frost and common accidents. The most solid basis is rock, or gravel which has not been moved. Next to these are clay and sand, provided no other excavations have been made in the immediate neighbourhood. From this basis a stone wall is carried up to the surface of the ground, and constitutes the foundation. Where it is intended that the superstructure shall press unequally, as at its piers, chimneys, or columns, it is sometimes of use to occupy the space between the points of pressure by an inverted arch. This distributes the pressure equally, and prevents the foundation from springing between the different points. In loose or muddy situations, it is always unsafe to build, unless we can reach the solid bottom below. In salt marshes and flats, this is done by depositing timbers, or driving wooden piles into the earth, and raising walls upon them. The preservative quality of the salt will keep these timbers unimpaired for a great length of time, and makes the foundation equally secure with one of brick or stone.

222.—The simplest member in any building, though by no means an essential one to all, is the COLUMN, or *pillar*. This is a perpendicular part, commonly of equal breadth and thickness, not intended for the purpose of enclosure, but simply for the support of some part of the superstructure. The principal force which a column has to resist, is that of perpendicular pressure. In its shape, the shaft of a column should not be exactly cylindrical, but, since the lower part must support the weight of the superior part, in addition to the weight which presses equally on the whole column, the thickness should gradually decrease from bottom to top. The outline of columns should be a little curved, so as to represent a portion of a very long spheroid, or paraboloid, rather than of a cone. This figure is the joint result of two calculations, independent of beauty of appearance. One of these is, that the form best adapted for stability of base is that of a cone; the other is, that the figure, which would be of equal strength throughout for supporting a superincumbent weight, would be generated by the revolution of two parabolas round the axis of the column, the vertices of the curves being at its extremities. The swell of the shafts of columns was called the *entasis* by the ancients. It has been lately found, that the columns of the Parthenon, at Athens, which have been commonly supposed straight, deviate about an inch from a straight line, and that their greatest swell is at about one third of their height. Columns in the antique orders are usually made to diminish one sixth or one seventh of their diameter, and sometimes even one fourth. The Gothic pillar is commonly of equal thickness throughout.

223.—The WALL, another elementary part of a building, may be considered as the lateral continuation of the column, answering the purpose both of enclosure and support. A wall must diminish as it rises, for the same reasons, and in the same proportion, as the column. It must diminish still more rapidly if it extends through several stories, supporting weights at different heights. A wall, to possess the greatest strength, must also consist of pieces, the upper and lower surfaces of which are horizontal and regular, not rounded nor oblique. The walls of most of the ancient structures which have stood to the present time, are constructed in this manner, and frequently have their stones bound together with bolts and cramps of iron. The same method is adopted in such modern structures as are intended to possess great strength and durability, and, in some cases, the stones are even dove-tailed together, as in the light-houses at Eddystone and Bell Rock. But many of our modern stone walls, for the sake of cheapness, have only one face of the stones squared, the inner half of the wall being completed with brick; so that they can, in reality, be considered only as brick walls faced with stone. Such walls are said to be liable to become convex outwardly, from the difference in the shrinking of the cement. *Rubble* walls are made of rough, irregular stones, laid in mortar. The stones should be broken, if possible, so as to produce horizontal surfaces. The *coffer* walls of the ancient Romans were made by enclosing successive portions of the intended wall in a box, and filling it with stones, sand, and mortar, promiscuously. This kind of structure must have been extremely insecure. The Pantheon, and various other Roman buildings, are surrounded with a double brick wall, having its vacancy filled up with loose bricks and cement. The whole has gradually consolidated into a mass of great firmness.

The *reticulated* walls of the Romans, having bricks with oblique surfaces, would, at the present day, be thought highly unphilosophical. Indeed, they could not long have stood, had it not been for the great strength of their cement. Modern brick walls are laid with great precision, and depend for firmness more upon their position than upon the strength of their cement. The bricks being laid in horizontal courses, and continually overlaying each other, or *breaking joints*, the whole mass is strongly interwoven, and bound together. Wooden walls, composed of timbers covered with boards, are a common, but more perishable kind. They require to be constantly covered with a coating of a foreign substance, as paint or plaster, to preserve them from spontaneous decomposition. In some parts of France, and elsewhere, a kind of wall is made of earth, rendered compact by ramming it in moulds or cases. This method is called building in *pisé*, and is much more durable than the nature of the material would lead us to suppose. Walls of all kinds are greatly strengthened by angles and curves, also by projections, such as pilasters, chimneys and buttresses. These projections serve to increase the breadth of the foundation, and are always to be made use of in large buildings, and in walls of considerable length.

224.—The LINTEL, or *beam*, extends in a right line over a vacant space, from one column or wall to another. The strength of the lintel will be greater in proportion as its transverse vertical diameter exceeds the horizontal, the strength being always as the square of the depth. The *floor* is the lateral continuation or connection of beams by means of a covering of boards.

225.—The ARCH is a transverse member of a building, answering the same purpose as the lintel, but vastly exceeding it in strength. The arch, unlike the lintel, may consist of any number of constituent pieces, without impairing its strength. It is, however, necessary that all the pieces should possess a uniform shape,—the shape of a portion of a wedge,—and that the joints, formed by the contact of their surfaces, should point towards a common centre. In this case, no one portion of the arch can be displaced or forced inward; and the arch cannot be broken by any force which is not sufficient to crush the materials of which it is made. In arches made of common bricks, the sides of which are parallel, any *one* of the bricks might be forced inward, were it not for the adhesion of the cement. Any *two* of the bricks, however, by the disposition of their mortar, cannot collectively be forced inward. An arch of the proper form, when complete, is rendered stronger, instead of weaker, by the pressure of a considerable weight, provided this pressure be uniform. While building, however, it requires to be supported by a centring of the shape of its internal surface, until it is complete. The upper stone of an arch is called the *key-stone*, but is not more essential than any other. In regard to the shape of the arch, its most simple form is that of the semi-circle. It is, however, very frequently a smaller arc of a circle, and, still more frequently, a portion of an ellipse. The simplest theory of an arch supporting itself only, is that of Dr. Hooke. The arch, when it has only its own weight to bear, may be considered as the inversion of a chain, suspended at each end. The chain hangs in such a form, that the weight of each link or portion is held in equilibrium by the result of two forces acting at its extremities; and these forces, or tensions, are produced, the one by the weight of the portion of the chain below the link, the other by the same weight increased by that of the link itself, both of them acting originally in a vertical direction. Now, supposing the chain inverted, so as to constitute an arch of the same form and weight, the relative situations of the forces will be the same, only they will act in contrary directions, so that they are compounded in a similar manner, and balance each other on the same conditions.

The arch thus formed is denominated a *catenary* arch. In common cases, it differs but little from a circular arch of the extent of about one third of a whole circle, and rising from the abutments with an obliquity of about 30 degrees from a perpendicular. But though the catenary arch is the best form for supporting its own weight, and also all additional weight which presses in a vertical direction, it is not the best form to resist lateral pressure, or pressure like that of fluids, acting equally in all directions. Thus the arches of bridges and similar structures, when covered with loose stones and earth, are pressed sideways, as well as vertically, in the same manner as if they supported a weight of fluid. In this case, it is necessary that the arch should arise more perpendicularly from the abutment, and that its general figure should be that of the longitudinal segment of an ellipse. In small arches, in common buildings, where the disturbing force is not great, it is of little consequence what is the shape of the curve. The outlines may even be perfectly straight, as in the tier of bricks which we frequently see over a window. This is, strictly speaking, a real arch, provided the surfaces of the bricks tend towards a common centre. It is the weakest kind of arch, and a part of it is necessarily superfluous, since no greater portion can act in supporting a weight above it, than can be included between two curved or arched lines.

Besides the arches already mentioned, various others are in use. The *acute* or *lancet* arch, much used in Gothic architecture, is described usually from two centres outside the arch. It is a strong arch for supporting vertical pressure. The *rampant* arch is one in which the two ends spring from unequal heights. The *horse-shoe* or *Moorish* arch is described from one or more centres placed above the base line. In this arch, the lower parts are in danger of being forced inward. The *ogee* arch is concavo-convex, and therefore fit only for ornament. In describing arches, the upper surface is called the *extrados*, and the inner, the *intrados*. The springing lines are those where the intrados meets the abutments, or supporting walls. The *span* is the distance from one springing line to the other. The wedge-shaped stones, which form an arch, are sometimes called *voussoirs*, the uppermost being the key-stone. The part of a pier from which an arch springs is called the *impost*, and the curve formed by the upper side of the voussoirs, the *archivolt*. It is necessary that the walls, abutments and piers, on which arches are supported, should be so firm as to resist the lateral *thrust*, as well as vertical pressure, of the arch. It will at once be seen, that the lateral or sideway pressure of an arch is very considerable, when we recollect that every stone, or portion of the arch, is a wedge, a part of whose force acts to separate the abutments. For want of attention to this circumstance, important mistakes have been committed, the strength of buildings materially impaired, and their ruin accelerated. In some cases, the want of lateral firmness in the walls is compensated by a bar of iron stretched across the span of the arch, and connecting the abutments, like the tie-beam of a roof. This is the case in the cathedral of Milan and some other Gothic buildings.

In an arcade, or continuation of arches, it is only necessary that the outer supports of the terminal arches should be strong enough to resist horizontal pressure. In the intermediate arches, the lateral force of each arch is counteracted by the opposing lateral force of the one contiguous to it. In bridges, however, where individual arches are liable to be destroyed by accident, it is desirable that each of the piers should possess sufficient horizontal strength to resist the lateral pressure of the adjoining arches.

226.—The VAULT is the lateral continuation of an arch, serving to cover an area or passage, and bearing the same relation to the arch that the wall does to the column. A simple vault is constructed on the principles of the arch, and distributes its pressure equally along the walls or abutments. A complex or *groined* vault is made by two vaults intersecting each other, in which case the pressure is thrown upon springing points, and is greatly increased at those points. The groined vault is common in Gothic architecture.

227.—The DOME, sometimes called *cupola,* is a concave covering to a building, or part of it, and may be either a segment of a sphere, of a spheroid, or of any similar figure. When built of stone, it is a very strong kind of structure, even more so than the arch, since the tendency of each part to fall is counteracted, not only by those above and below it, but also by those on each side. It is only necessary that the constituent pieces should have a common form, and that this form should be somewhat like the frustum of a pyramid, so that, when placed in its situation, its four angles may point toward the centre, or axis, of the dome. During the erection of a dome, it is not necessary that it should be supported by a centring, until complete, as is done in the arch. Each circle of stones, when laid, is capable of supporting itself without aid from those above it. It follows that the dome may be left open at top, without a key-stone, and yet be perfectly secure in this respect, being the reverse of the arch. The dome of the Pantheon, at Rome, has been always open at top, and yet has stood unimpaired for nearly 2000 years. The upper circle of stones, though apparently the weakest, is nevertheless often made to support the additional weight of a lantern or tower above it. In several of the largest cathedrals, there are two domes, one within the other, which contribute their joint support to the lantern, which rests upon the top. In these buildings, the dome

14

rests upon a circular wall, which is supported, in its turn, by arches upon massive pillars or piers. This construction is called building upon *pendentives*, and gives open space and room for passage beneath the dome. The remarks which have been made in regard to the abutments of the arch, apply equally to the walls immediately supporting a dome. They must be of sufficient thickness and solidity to resist the lateral pressure of the dome, which is very great. The walls of the Roman Pantheon are of great depth and solidity. In order that a dome in itself should be perfectly secure, its lower parts must not be too nearly vertical, since, in this case, they partake of the nature of perpendicular walls, and are acted upon by the spreading force of the parts above them. The dome of St. Paul's church, in London, and some others of similar construction, are bound with chains or hoops of iron, to prevent them from spreading at bottom. Domes which are made of wood depend, in part, for their strength, on their internal carpentry. The Halle du Bled, in Paris, had originally a wooden dome more than 200 feet in diameter, and only one foot in thickness. This has since been replaced by a dome of iron. (See *Art.* 303.)

228.—The Roof is the most common and cheap method of covering buildings, to protect them from rain and other effects of the weather. It is sometimes flat, but more frequently oblique, in its shape. The flat or platform-roof is the least advantageous for shedding rain, and is seldom used in northern countries. The *pent* roof, consisting of two oblique sides meeting at top, is the most common form. These roofs are made steepest in cold climates, where they are liable to be loaded with snow. Where the four sides of the roof are all oblique, it is denominated a *hipped* roof, and where there are two portions to the roof, of different obliquity, it is a *curb*, or *mansard* roof. In modern times, roofs are made almost exclusively of wood, though frequently covered with incombustible materials. The internal structure or carpentry of roofs is a subject of considerable mechanical contrivance.

The roof is supported by *rafters*, which abut on the walls on each side, like the extremities of an arch. If no other timbers existed, except the rafters, they would exert a strong lateral pressure on the walls, tending to separate and overthrow them. To counteract this lateral force, a *tie-beam*, as it is called, extends across, receiving the ends of the rafters, and protecting the wall from their horizontal thrust. To prevent the tie-beam from *sagging*, or bending downward with its own weight, a *king-post* is erected from this beam, to the upper angle of the rafters, serving to connect the whole, and to suspend the weight of the beam. This is called *trussing*. *Queen-posts* are sometimes added, parallel to the king-post, in large roofs; also various other connecting timbers. In Gothic buildings, where the vaults do not admit of the use of a tie-beam, the rafters are prevented from spreading, as in an arch, by the strength of the buttresses.

In comparing the lateral pressure of a high roof with that of a low one, the length of the tie-beam being the same, it will be seen that a high roof, from its containing most materials, may produce the greatest pressure, as far as weight is concerned. On the other hand, if the weight of both be equal, then the low roof will exert the greater pressure; and this will increase in proportion to the distance of the point at which perpendiculars, drawn from the end of each rafter, would meet. In roofs, as well as in wooden domes and bridges, the materials are subjected to an internal strain, to resist which, the cohesive strength of the material is relied on. On this account, beams should, when possible, be of one piece. Where this cannot be effected, two or more beams are connected together by *splicing*. Spliced beams are never so strong as whole ones, yet they may be made to approach the same strength, by affixing lateral pieces, or by making the ends overlay each other, and connecting them with bolts and straps of iron. The tendency to separate is also resisted, by letting the two pieces into each other by the process called *scarfing*. *Mortices*, intended to *truss* or suspend one piece by another, should be formed upon similar principles.

Roofs in the United States, after being boarded, receive a secondary covering of shingles. When intended to be incombustible, they are covered with slates or earthern tiles, or with sheets of lead, copper or tinned iron. Slates are preferable to tiles, being lighter, and absorbing less moisture. Metallic sheets are chiefly used for flat roofs, wooden domes, and curved and angular surfaces, which require a flexible material to cover them, or have not a sufficient pitch to shed the rain from slates or shingles. Various artificial compositions are occasionally used to cover roofs, the most common of which are mixtures of tar with lime, and sometimes with sand and gravel."—*Ency. Am.* (See *Art.* 285.)

NOTE TO ARTICLE 189.

GRECIAN DORIC ORDER. *When the width to be occupied by the whole front is limited; to determine the diameter of the column.*

The relation between the parts may be expressed thus:

$$x = \frac{60\,a}{d\,(b + c) + (60 - c)}$$

Where a equals the width in feet occupied by the columns, and their intercolumniations taken collectively, measured at the base; b equals the width of the metope, in minutes; c equals the width of the triglyphs in minutes; d equals the number of metopes, and x equals the diameter in feet.

Example.—A front of six columns—hexastyle—61 feet wide; the frieze having one triglyph over each intercolumniation, or mono-triglyph. In this case, there being five intercolumniations and two metopes over each, therefore there are $5 \times 2 = 10$ metopes. Let the metope equal 42 minutes and the triglyph equal 28. Then $a = 61$; $b = 42$; $c = 28$; and $d = 10$; and the formula above becomes,

$$x = \frac{60 \times 61}{10(42 + 28) + (60 - 28)} = \frac{60 \times 61}{10 \times 70 + 32} = \frac{3660}{732} = 5 \text{ feet} = \text{the diameter required.}$$

Example.—An octastyle front, 8 columns, 184 feet wide, three metopes over each intercolumniation, 21 in all, and the metope and triglyph 42 and 28, as before. Then,

$$x = \frac{60 \times 184}{21\,(42 + 28) + (60 - 28)} = \frac{11040}{1502} = 7{\cdot}35\tfrac{30}{1502} \text{ feet} = \text{the diameter required.}$$

SECTION III.—MOULDINGS, CORNICES, &c.

MOULDINGS.

229.—A moulding is so called, because of its being of the same determinate shape along its whole length, as though the whole of it had been cast in the same mould or form. The regular mouldings, as found in remains of ancient architecture, are eight in number; and are known by the following names:

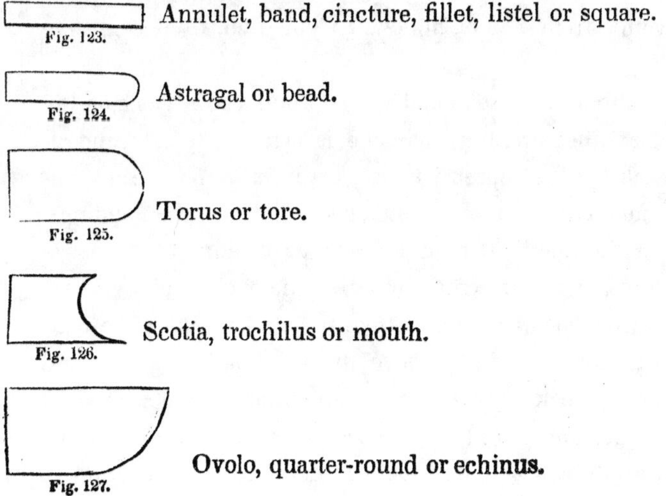

Fig. 123. Annulet, band, cincture, fillet, listel or square.

Fig. 124. Astragal or bead.

Fig. 125. Torus or tore.

Fig. 126. Scotia, trochilus or mouth.

Fig. 127. Ovolo, quarter-round or echinus.

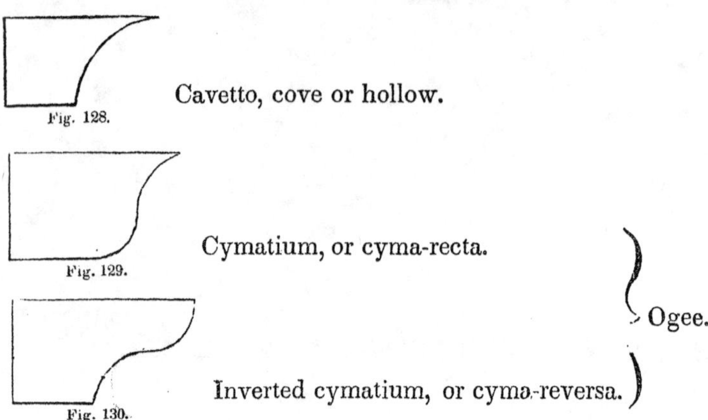

Fig. 128. Fig. 129. Fig. 130.

Some of the terms are derived thus: fillet, from the French word *fil*, thread. Astragal, from *astragalos*, a bone of the heel —or the curvature of the heel. Bead, because this moulding, when properly carved, resembles a string of beads. Torus, or tore, the Greek for *rope*, which it resembles, when on the base of a column. Scotia, from *shotia*, darkness, because of the strong shadow which its depth produces, and which is increased by the projection of the torus above it. Ovolo, from *ovum*, an egg, which this member resembles, when carved, as in the Ionic capital. Cavetto, from *cavus*, hollow. Cymatium, from *kumaton*, a wave.

230.—Neither of these mouldings is peculiar to any one of the orders of architecture, but each one is common to all; and although each has its appropriate use, yet it is by no means confined to any certain position in an assemblage of mouldings. The use of the fillet is to bind the parts, as also that of the astragal and torus, which resemble ropes. The ovolo and cyma-reversa are strong at their upper extremities, and are therefore used to support projecting parts above them. The cyma-recta and cavetto, being weak at their upper extremities, are not used as supporters, but are placed uppermost to cover and shelter the other parts. The scotia is introduced in the base of a column, to separate the upper and lower torus, and to produce a pleasing variety and relief. The form of the bead, and that of the torus, is the same; the reasons for giving distinct names to them are, that the torus, in every order, is always considerably larger than the bead, and is placed among the base mouldings, whereas the bead is never placed there, but on the capital or entablature; the torus, also, is never carved, whereas the bead is; and while the torus among the Greeks is frequently elliptical in its form, the bead retains its circular shape. While the scotia is the reverse of the torus, the cavetto is the reverse of the ovolo, and the cyma-recta and cyma-reversa are combinations of the ovolo and cavetto.

231.—The curves of mouldings, in Roman architecture, were most generally composed of parts of circles; while those of the Greeks were almost always elliptical, or of some one of the conic sections, but rarely circular, except in the case of the bead, which was always, among both Greeks and Romans, of the form of a semi-circle. Sections of the cone afford a greater variety of forms than those of the sphere; and perhaps this is one reason why the Grecian architecture so much excels the Roman. The quick turnings of the ovolo and cyma-reversa, in particular, when exposed to a bright sun, cause those narrow, well-defined streaks of light, which give life and splendour to the whole.

232.—A *profile* is an assemblage of essential parts and mouldings. That profile produces the happiest effect which is composed of but few members, varied in form and size, and arranged so that the plane and the curved surfaces succeed each other alternately.

233.—*To describe the Grecian torus and scotia.* Join the extremities, *a* and *b*, (*Fig.* 131;) and from *f*, the given projection of the moulding, draw *f o*, at right angles to the fillets; from *b*, draw *b h*, at right angles to *a b*; bisect *a b* in *c*; join *f* and *c*, and upon *c*, with the radius, *c f*, describe the arc, *f h*, cutting *b h* in *h*; through *c*, draw *d e*, parallel with the fillets; make *d c* and *c e*, each equal to *b h*; then *d e* and *a b* will be conjugate diame-

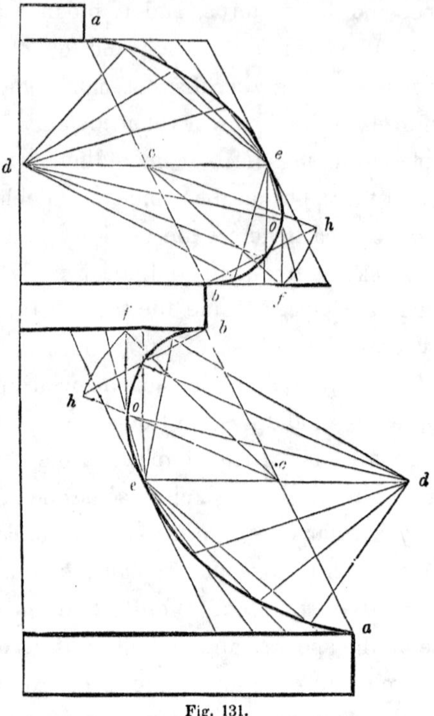

Fig. 131.

ters of the required ellipse. To describe the curve by intersection of lines, proceed as directed at *Art.* 118 and *note*; by a trammel, see *Art.* 125; and to find the foci, in order to describe it with a string, see *Art.* 115.

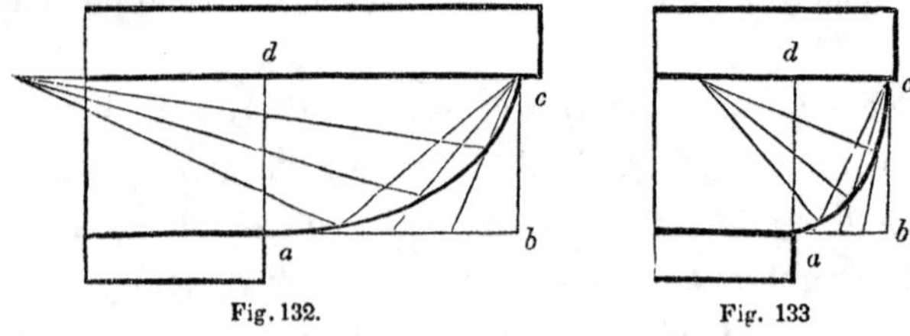

Fig. 132. Fig. 133

234.—*Fig.* 132 to 139 exhibit various modifications of the Grecian ovolo, sometimes called echinus. *Fig.* 132 to 136 are

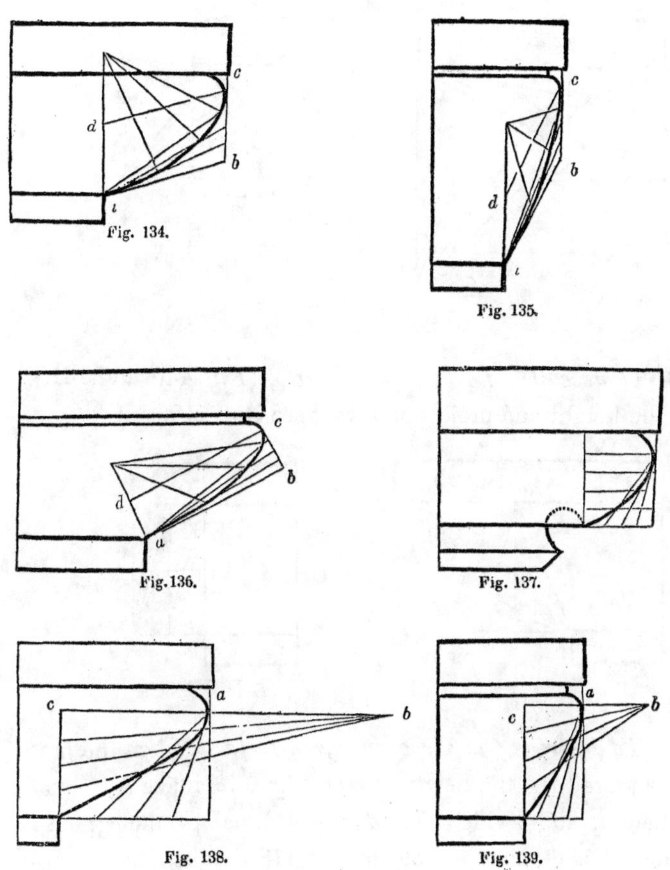

Fig. 134. Fig. 135. Fig. 136. Fig. 137. Fig. 138. Fig. 139.

elliptical, *a b* and *b c* being given tangents to the curve; parallel to which, the semi-conjugate diameters, *a d* and *d c*, are drawn. In *Fig.* 132 and 133, the lines, *a d* and *d c*, are semi-axes, the tangents, *a b* and *b c*, being at right angles to each other. To draw the curve, see *Art.* 118. In *Fig.* 137, the curve is parabolical, and is drawn according to *Art.* 127. In *Fig.* 138 and 139, the curve is hyperbolical, being described according to *Art.* 128. The length of the transverse axis, *a b*, being taken at pleasure, in order to flatten the curve, *a b* should be made short in proportion to *a c*.

15

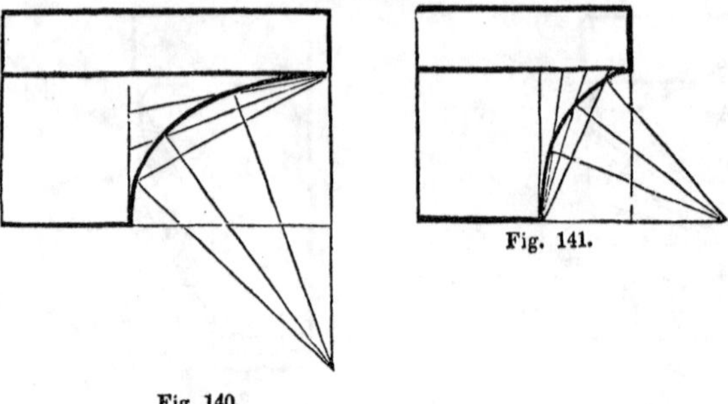
Fig. 140. Fig. 141.

235.—*To describe the Grecian cavetto,* (*Fig.* 140 and 141,) having the height and projection given, see *Art.* 118.

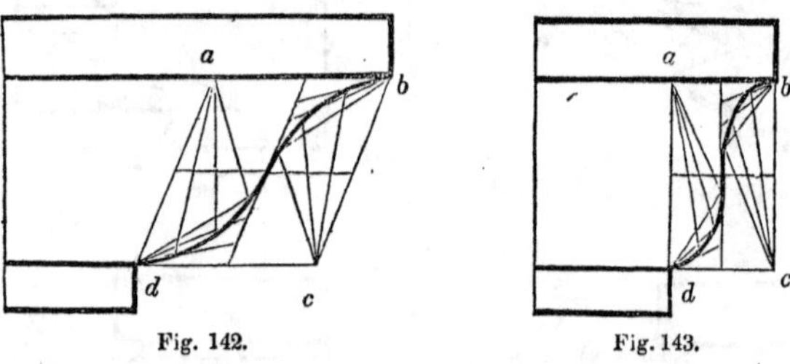

Fig. 142. Fig. 143.

236.—*To describe the Grecian cyma-recta.* When the projection is more than the height, as at *Fig.* 142, make *a b* equal to the height, and divide *a b c d* into 4 equal parallelograms; then proceed as directed in note to *Art.* 118. When the projection is less than the height, draw *d a*, (*Fig.* 143,) at right angles to *a b;* complete the rectangle, *a b c d;* divide this into 4 equal rectangles, and proceed according to *Art.* 118.

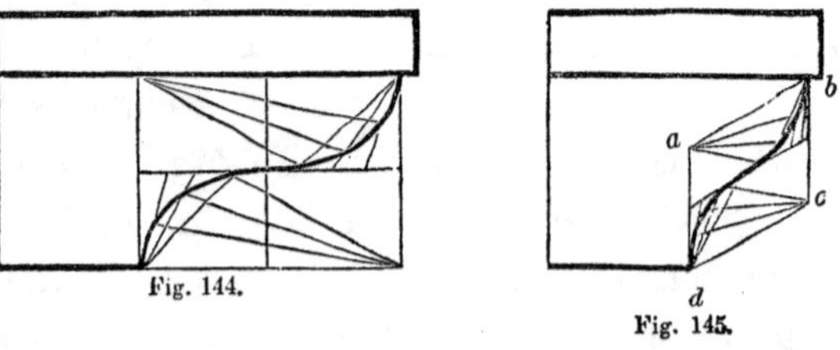

Fig. 144. Fig. 145.

237.—*To describe the Grecian cyma-reversa.* When the

projection is more than the height, as at *Fig.* 144, proceed as directed for the last figure; the curve being the same as that, the position only being changed. When the projection is less than the height, draw *a d*, (*Fig.* 145,) at right angles to the fillet; make *a d* equal to the projection of the moulding: then proceed as directed for *Fig.* 142.

238.—Roman mouldings are composed of parts of circles, and have, therefore, less beauty of form than the Grecian. The bead and torus are of the form of the semi-circle, and the scotia, also, in some instances; but the latter is often composed of two quadrants, having different radii, as at *Fig.* 146 and 147, which resemble the elliptical curve. The ovolo and cavetto are generally a quadrant, but often less. When they are less, as at *Fig.* 150, the centre is found thus: join the extremities, *a* and *b*, and bisect *a b* in *c;* from *c*, and at right angles to *a b*, draw *c d*, cutting a level line drawn from *a* in *d;* then *d* will be the centre. This moulding projects less than its height. When the projection is more than the height, as at *Fig.* 152, extend the line from *c* until

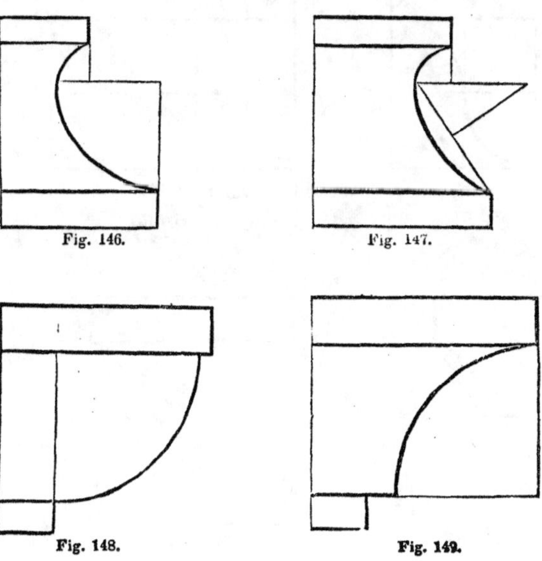

Fig. 146. Fig. 147.

Fig. 148. Fig. 149.

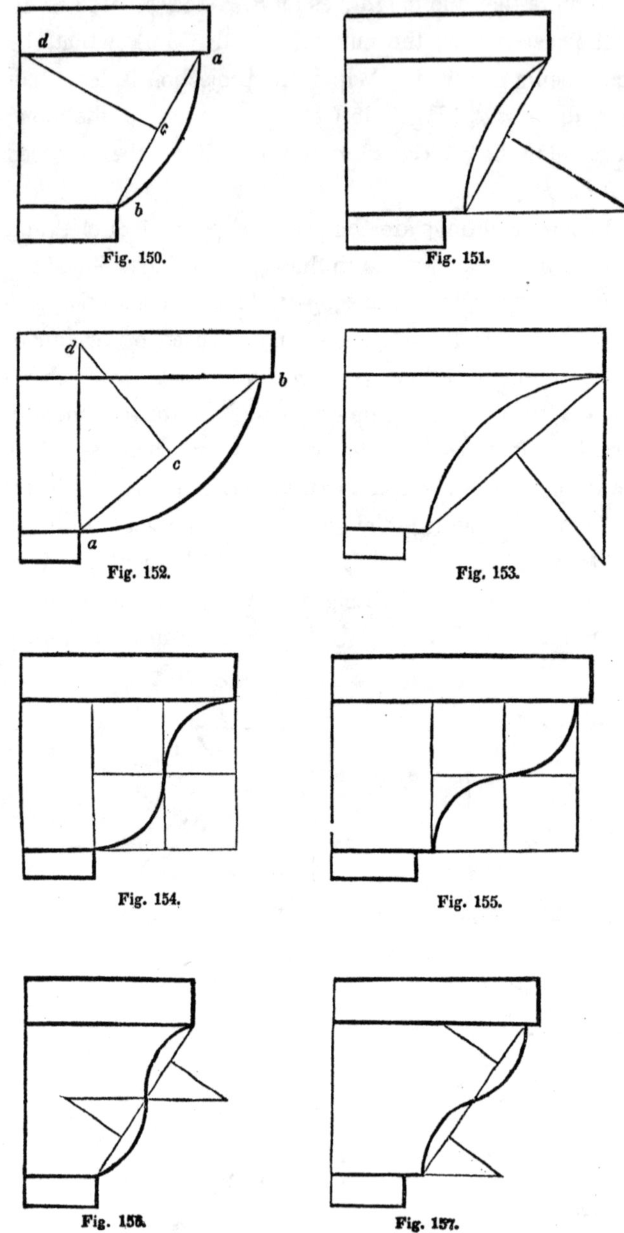

Fig. 150. Fig. 151.

Fig. 152. Fig. 153.

Fig. 154. Fig. 155.

Fig. 156. Fig. 157.

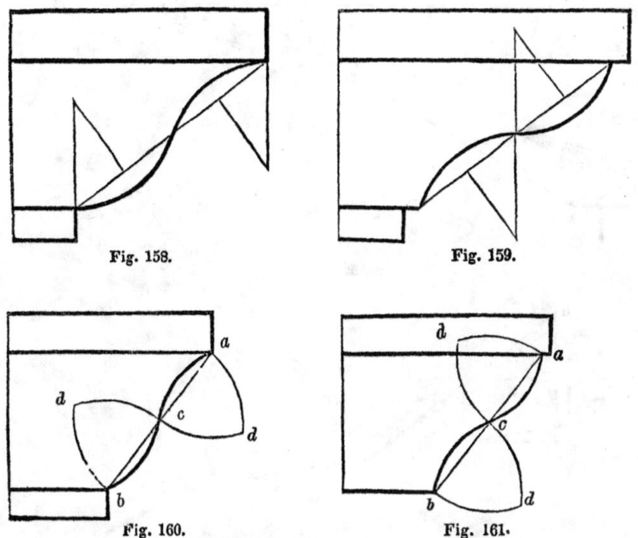

Fig. 158. Fig. 159.

Fig. 160. Fig. 161.

it cuts a perpendicular drawn from *a*, as at *d;* and that will be the centre of the curve. In a similar manner, the centres are found for the mouldings at *Fig.* 147, 151, 153, 156, 157, 158 and 159. The centres for the curves at *Fig.* 160 and 161, are found thus: bisect the line, *a b*, at *c;* upon *a*, *c* and *b*, successively, with *a c* or *c b* for radius, describe arcs intersecting at *d* and *d;* then those intersections will be the centres.

239.—*Fig.* 162 to 169 represent mouldings of modern invention. They have been quite extensively and successfully used in inside finishing. *Fig.* 162 is appropriate for a bed-moulding under a low, projecting shelf, and is frequently used under mantle-shelves. The tangent, *i h*, is found thus: bisect the line, *a b*, at *c*, and *b c* at *d;* from *d*, draw *d e*, at right angles to *e b;* from *b*, draw *b f*, parallel to *e d;* upon *b*, with *b d* for radius, describe the arc, *d f;* divide this arc into 7 equal parts, and set one of the parts from *s*, the limit of the projection, to *o;* make *o h* equal to *o e;* from *h*, through *c*, draw the tangent, *h i;* divide *b h*, *h c*, *c i* and *i a*, each into a like number of equal parts, and draw the in-

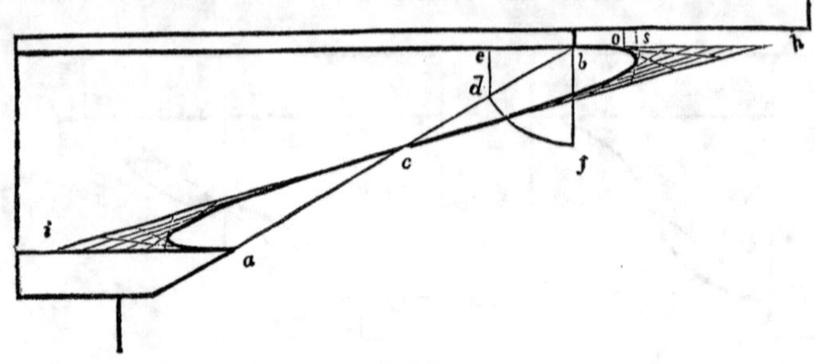

Fig. 162.

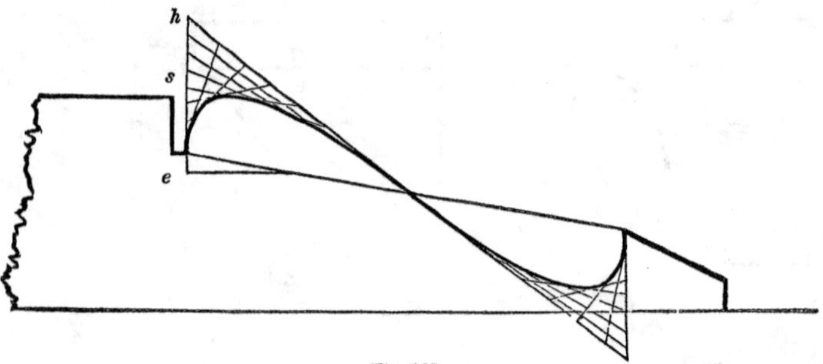

Fig. 163.

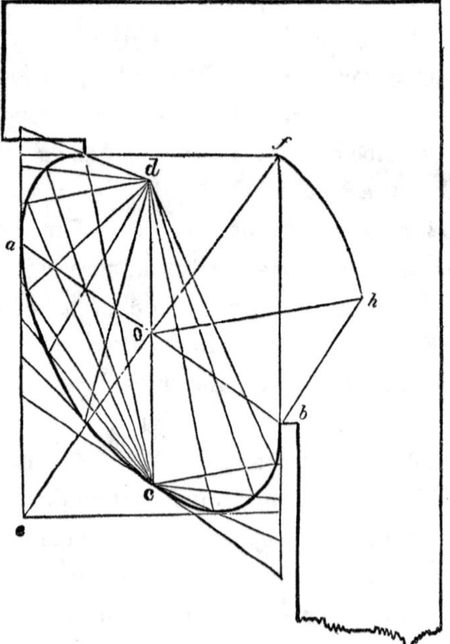

Fig. 164.

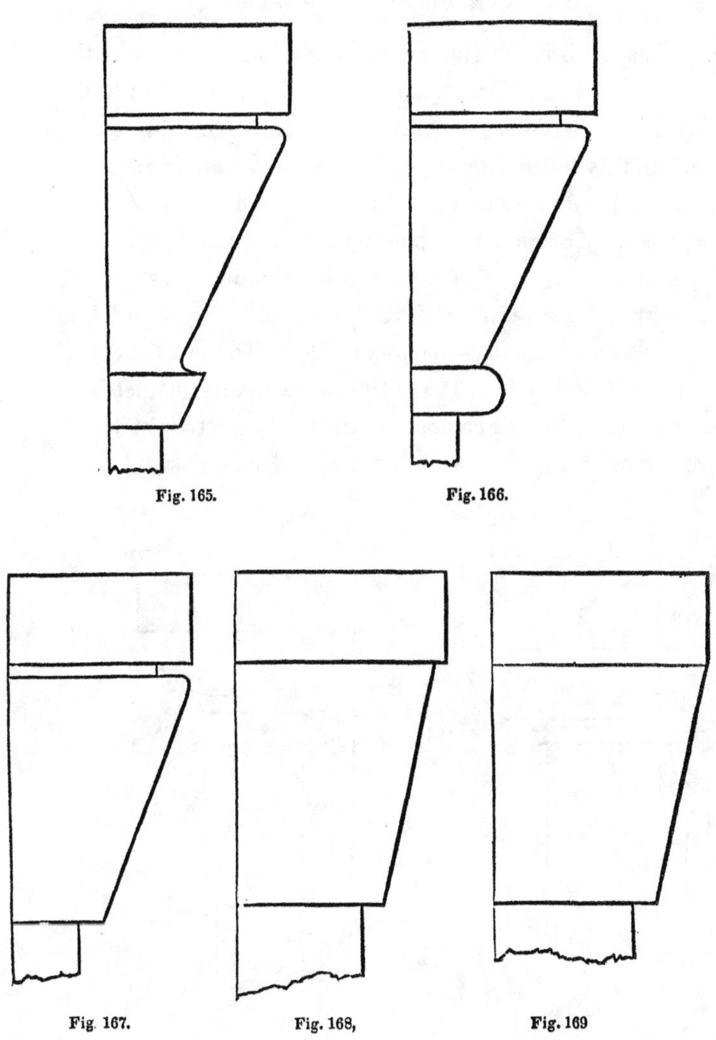

Fig. 165. Fig. 166.

Fig. 167. Fig. 168, Fig. 169

tersecting lines as directed at *Art.* 89. If a bolder form is desired, draw the tangent, *i h*, nearer horizontal, and describe an elliptic curve as shown in *Fig.* 131, 164, 175 and 176. *Fig.* 163 is much used on base, or skirting of rooms, and in deep panelling. The curve is found in the same manner as that of *Fig.* 162. In this case, however, where the moulding has so little projection in comparison with its height, the point, *e*, being found as in the last figure, *h s* may be made equal to *s e*, instead of *o e* as in the last figure. *Fig.* 164 is appropriate for a crown moulding of a cornice. In this figure the height and projection are given; the direction of the diameter, *a b*, drawn through the middle of the diagonal, *e f*, is taken at pleasure; and *d c* is parallel to *a e*. To find the length of *d c*, draw *b. h*, at right angles to *a b;* upon *o*, with *o f* for radius, describe the arc, *f h*, cutting *b h* in *h;* then make *o c* and *o d*, each equal to *b h*.* To draw the curve, see note to *Art.* 118. *Fig.* 165 to 169 are peculiarly distinct from ancient mouldings, being composed principally of straight lines; the few curves they possess are quite short and quick.

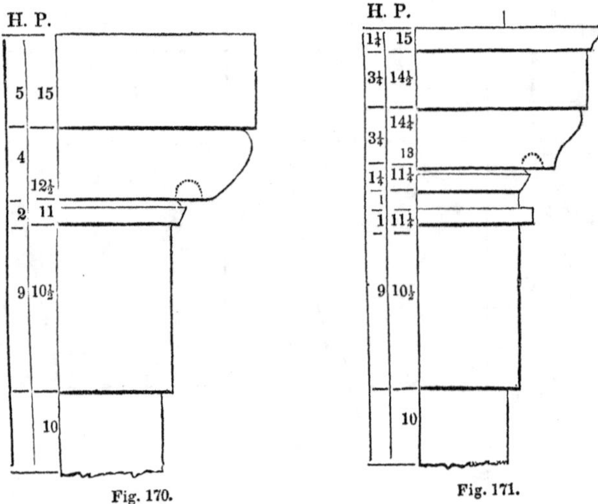

Fig. 170. Fig. 171.

240.—*Fig.* 170 and 171 are designs for antæ caps. The

* The manner of ascertaining the length of the conjugate diameter, *d c*, in this figure, and also in *Fig.* 131, 175 and 176, is new, and is important in this application. It is founded upon well-known mathematical principles, viz: All the parallelograms that may be circumscribed about an ellipsis are equal to one another, and consequently any one is equal to the rectangle of the two axes. And again: the sum of the squares of every pair of conjugate diameters is equal to the sum of the squares of the two axes.

diameter of the antæ is divided into 20 equal parts, and the height and projection of the members, are regulated in accordance with those parts, as denoted under *H* and *P*, height and projection. The projection is measured from the middle of the antæ. These will be found appropriate for porticos, door-ways, mantle-pieces, door and window trimmings, &c. The height of the antæ for mantle-pieces, should be from 5 to 6 diameters, having an entablature of from 2 to 2¼ diameters. This is a good proportion, it being similar to the Doric order. But for a portico these proportions are much too heavy; an antæ, 15 diameters high, and an entablature of 3 diameters, will have a better appearance.

CORNICES.

241.—*Fig*. 172, 173 and 174, are designs for eave cornices, and *Fig*. 175 and 176, for stucco cornices for the inside finish of rooms. The projection of the uppermost member from the facia, is divided into 20 equal parts, and the various members are proportioned according to those parts, as figured under *H* and *P*.

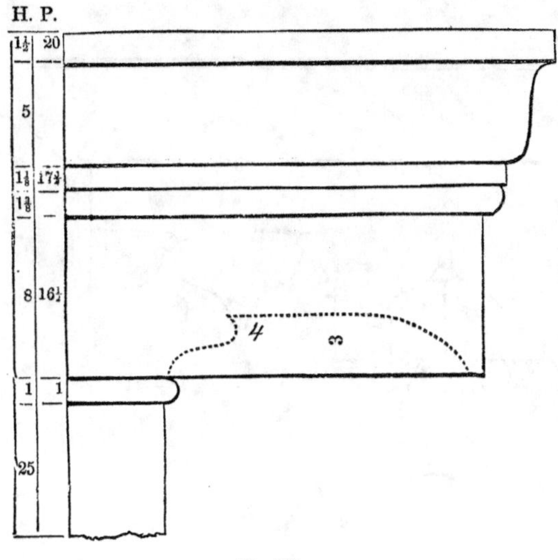

Fig. 172.

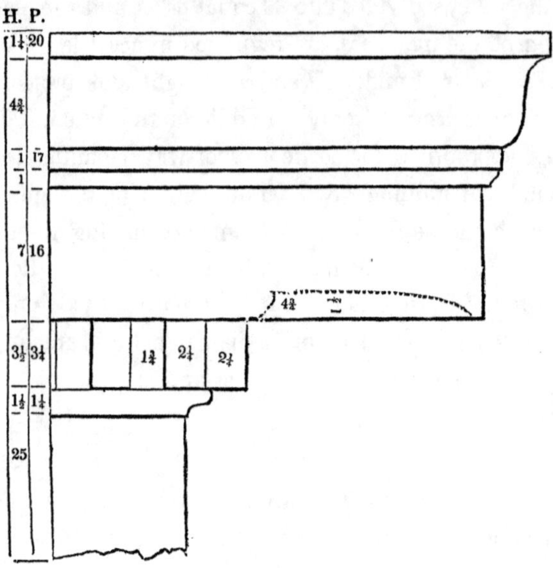

Fig. 173.

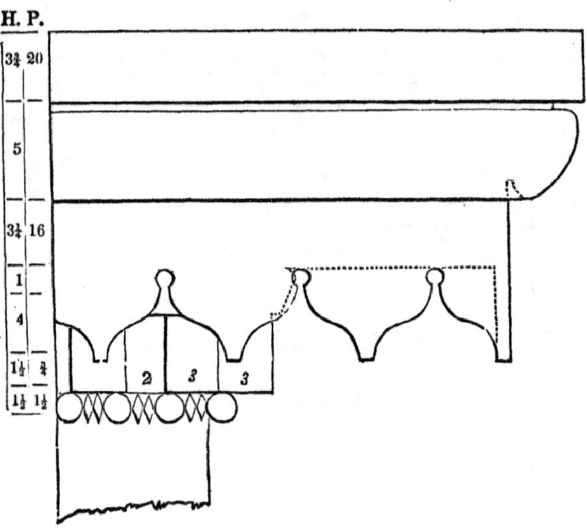

Fig. 174.

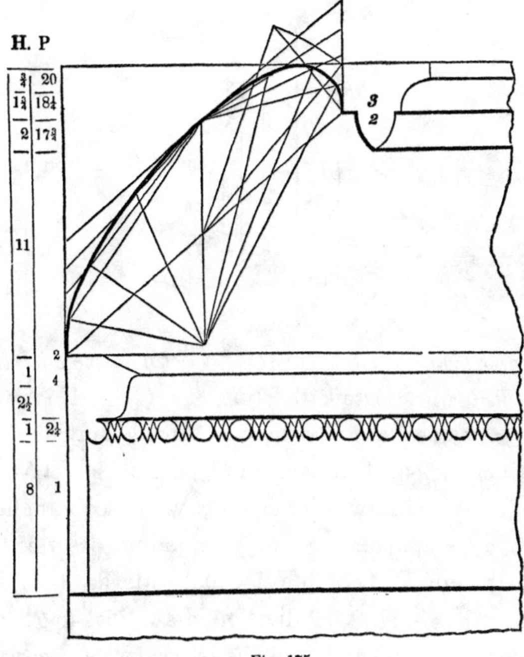

Fig. 175.

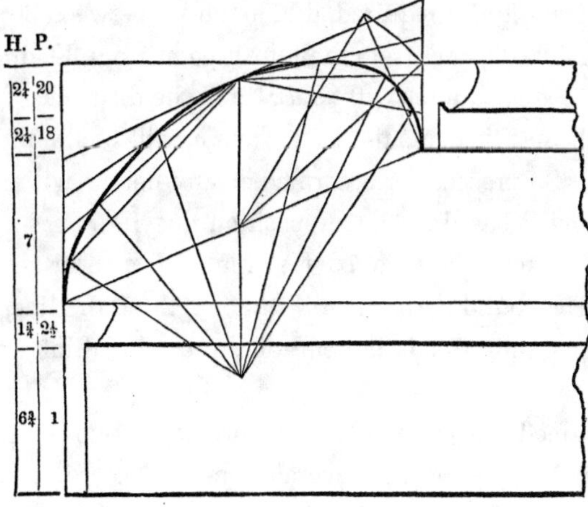

Fig. 176.

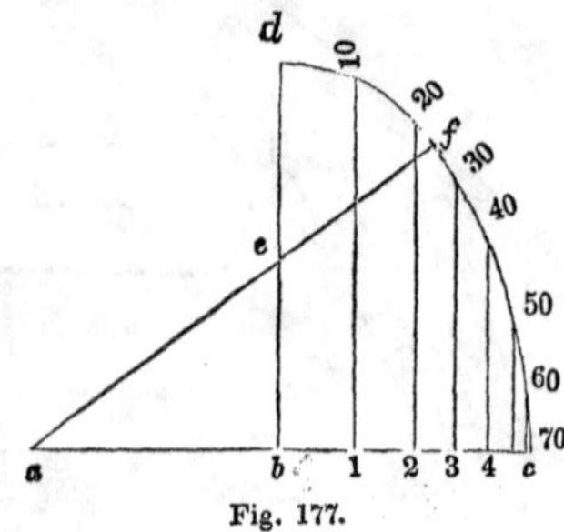

Fig. 177.

242.—*To proportion an eave cornice in accordance with the height of the building.* Draw the line, *a c*, (*Fig.* 177,) and make *b c* and *b a*, each equal to 18 inches; from *b*, draw *b d*, at right angles to *a c*, and equal in length to $\frac{3}{4}$ of *a c*; bisect *b d* in *e*, and from *a*, through *e*, draw *a f*; upon *a*, with *a c* for radius, describe the arc, *c f*, and upon *e*, with *e f* for radius, describe the arc, *f d*; divide the curve, *d f c*, into 7 equal parts, as at 10, 20, 30, &c., and from these points of division, draw lines to *b c*, parallel to *d b*; then the distance, *b* 1, is the projection of a cornice for a building 10 feet high; *b* 2, the projection at 20 feet high; *b* 3, the projection at 30 feet, &c. If the projection of a cornice for a building 34 feet high, is required, divide the arc between 30 and 40 into 10 equal parts, and from the fourth point from 30, draw a line to the base, *b c*, parallel with *b d*; then the distance of the point, at which that line cuts the base, from *b*, will be the projection required. So proceed for a cornice of any height within 70 feet. The above is based on the supposition that 18 inches is the proper projection for a cornice 70 feet high. This, for general purposes, will be found correct; still, the length of the line, *b c*, may be varied to suit the judgment of those who think differently.

Having obtained the projection of a cornice, divide it into 20 equal parts, and apportion the several members according to its destination—as is shown at *Fig.* 172, 173 and 174.

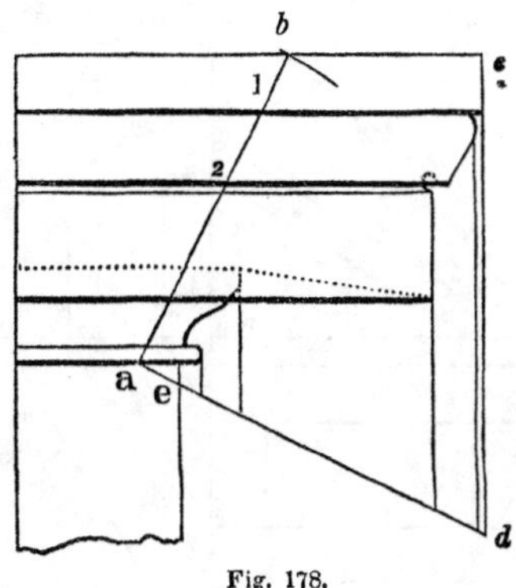

Fig. 178.

243.—*To proportion a cornice according to a smaller given one.* Let the cornice at *Fig.* 178 be the given one. Upon any point in the lowest line of the lowest member, as at *a*, with the height of the required cornice for radius, describe an intersecting arc across the uppermost line, as at *b*; join *a* and *b*; then *b* 1 will be the perpendicular height of the upper fillet for the proposed cornice, 1 2 the height of the crown moulding—and so of all the members requiring to be enlarged to the sizes indicated on this line. For the projection of the proposed cornice, draw *a d*, at right angles to *a b*, and *c d*, at right angles to *b c*; parallel with *c d*, draw lines from each projection of the given cornice to the line, *a d*; then *e d* will be the required projection for the proposed cornice, and the perpendicular lines falling upon *e d* will indicate the proper projection for the members.

244.—*To proportion a cornice according to a larger given one.* Let *A*, (*Fig.* 179,) be the given cornice. Extend *a o* to *b*, and draw *c d*, at right angles to *a b*; extend the horizontal lines of the cornice, *A*, until they touch *o d*; place the height of the proposed cornice from *o* to *e*, and join *f* and *e*; upon *o*, with the projection of the given cornice, *o a*, for radius, describe the quadrant, *a d*; from *d*, draw *d b*, parallel to *f e*; upon *o*, with *o b* for radius, describe the quadrant, *b c*; then *o c* will be the proper projection for the proposed cornice. Join *a* and *c*; draw lines from the

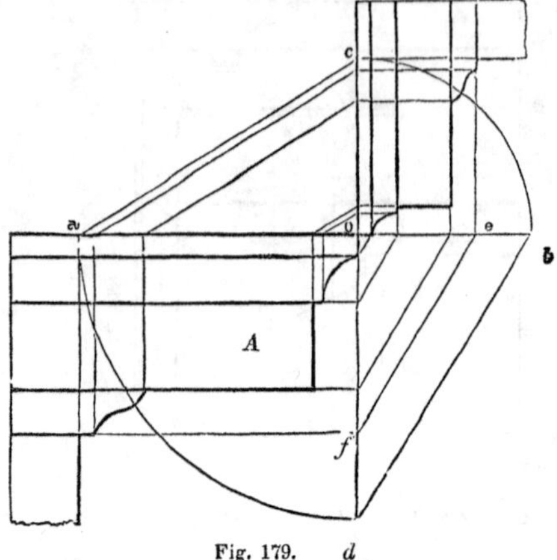

Fig. 179. d

projection of the different members of the given cornice to *a o*, parallel to *o d;* from these divisions on the line, *a o*, draw lines to the line, *o c*, parallel to *a c;* from the divisions on the line, *o f*, draw lines to the line, *o e*, parallel to the line, *f e;* then the divisions on the lines, *o e* and *o c*, will indicate the proper height and projection for the different members of the proposed cornice. In this process, we have assumed the height, *o e*, of the proposed cornice to be given; but if the projection, *o c*, alone be given, we can obtain the same result by a different process. Thus: upon *o*, with *o c* for radius, describe the quadrant, *c b;* upon *o*, with *o a* for radius, describe the quadrant, *a d;* join *d* and *b;* from *f*, draw *f e*, parallel to *d b;* then *o e* will be the proper height for the proposed cornice, and the height and projection of the different members can be obtained by the above directions. By this problem, a cornice can be proportioned according to a *smaller* given one as well as to a *larger;* but the method described in the previous article is much more simple for that purpose.

245.—*To find the angle-bracket for a cornice.* Let *A*, (*Fig.* 180,) be the wall of the building, and *B* the given bracket, which, for the present purpose, is turned down horizontally. The angle-bracket, *C*, is obtained thus: through the extremity, *a*, and paral-

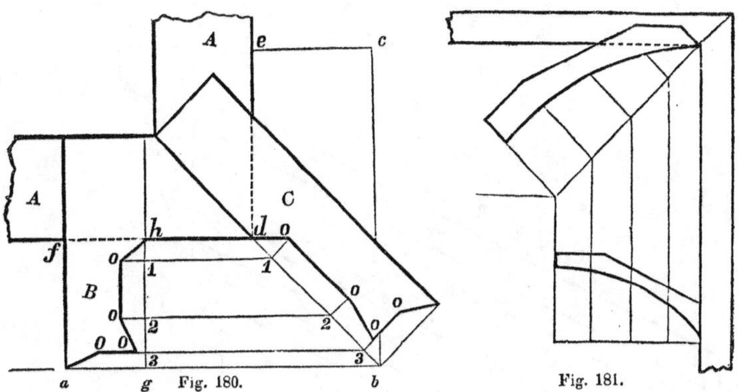

Fig. 180. Fig. 181.

lel with the wall, *f d*, draw the line, *a b;* make *e c* equal *a f*, and through *c*, draw *c b*, parallel with *e d;* join *d* and *b*, and from the several angular points in *B*, draw ordinates to cut *d b* in 1, 2 and 3; at those points erect lines perpendicular to *d b;* from *h*, draw *h g*, parallel to *f a;* take the ordinates, 1 *o*, 2 *o*, &c., at *B*, and transfer them to *C*, and the angle-bracket, *C*, will be defined. In the same manner, the angle-bracket for an internal cornice, or the angle-rib of a coved ceiling, or of groins, as at *Fig.* 181, can be found.

246.—*A level crown moulding being given, to find the raking moulding and a level return at the top.* Let *A*, (*Fig.* 182,) be the given moulding, and *A b* the rake of the roof. Divide the curve of the given moulding into any number of parts, equal or unequal, as at 1, 2, and 3; from these points, draw horizontal lines to a perpendicular erected from *c;* at any convenient place on the rake, as at *B*, draw *a c*, at right angles to *A b;* also, from *b*, draw the horizontal line, *b a;* place the thickness, *d a*, of the moulding at *A*, from *b* to *a*, and from *a*, draw the perpendicular line, *a e;* from the points, 1, 2, 3, at *A*, draw lines to *C*, parallel to *A b;* make *a* 1, *a* 2 and *a* 3, at *B* and at *C*, equal to *a* 1, &c., at *A;* through the points, 1, 2 and 3, at *B*, trace the curve—this will be the proper form for the raking moulding. From 1, 2 and

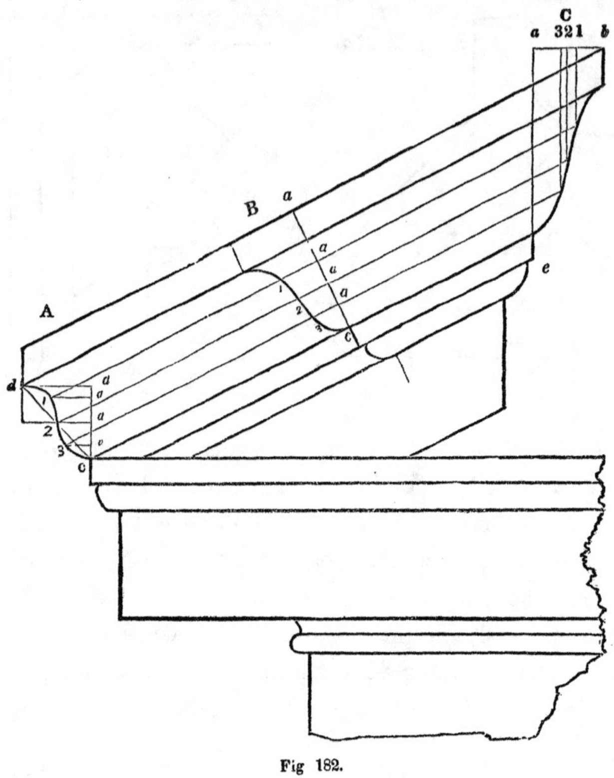

Fig 182.

3, at *C*, drop perpendiculars to the corresponding ordinates from 1, 2 and 3, at *A*; through the points of intersection, trace the curve—this will be the proper form for the *return* at the top.

SECTION IV.—FRAMING.

247.—This subject is, to the carpenter, of the highest importance; and deserves more attention and a larger place in a volume of this kind, than is generally allotted to it. Something, indeed, has been said upon the geometrical principles, by which the several lines for the joints and the lengths of timber, may be ascertained; yet, besides this, there is much to be learned. For however precise or workmanlike the joints may be made, what will it avail, should the system of framing, from an erroneous position of its timbers, &c., change its form, or become incapable of sustaining even its own weight? Hence the necessity for a knowledge of the laws of pressure and the strength of timber. These being once understood, we can with confidence determine the best position and dimensions for the several timbers which compose a floor or a roof, a partition or a bridge. As systems of framing are more or less exposed to heavy weights and strains, and, in case of failure, cause not only a loss of labour and material, but frequently that of life itself, it is very important that the materials employed be of the proper quantity and quality to serve their destination. And, on the other hand, any superfluous material is not only useless, but a positive injury, it being an unnecessary load upon the points of support. It is necessary, therefore, to know the *least* quantity of timber that will suffice for strength. The greatest fault in framing is that of using an excess of material. Economy, at least, would seem to require that this evil be abated.

Before proceeding to consider the principles upon which a system of framing should be constructed, let us attend to a few of the elementary laws in *Mechanics*, which will be found to be of great value in determining those principles.

248.—Laws of Pressure. (1.) A heavy body always exerts a pressure equal to its own weight in a vertical direction. Example: Suppose an iron ball, weighing 100 lbs., be supported upon the top of a perpendicular post, (*Fig.* 196;) then the pressure exerted upon that post will be equal to the weight of the ball; viz., 100 lbs. (2.) But if two inclined posts, (*Fig.* 183,) be substituted for the perpendicular support, the united pressures upon these posts will be more than equal to the weight, and will be in proportion to their position. The farther apart their feet are spread the greater will be the pressure, and *vice versa.* Hence tremendous strains may be exerted by a comparatively small weight. And it follows, therefore, that a piece of timber intended for a strut or post, should be so placed that its axis may coincide, as near as possible, with the direction of the pressure. The direction of the pressure of the weight, *W*, (*Fig.* 183,) is in the vertical line, *b d*; and the weight, *W*, would fall in that line, if the two posts were removed, hence the best position for a support

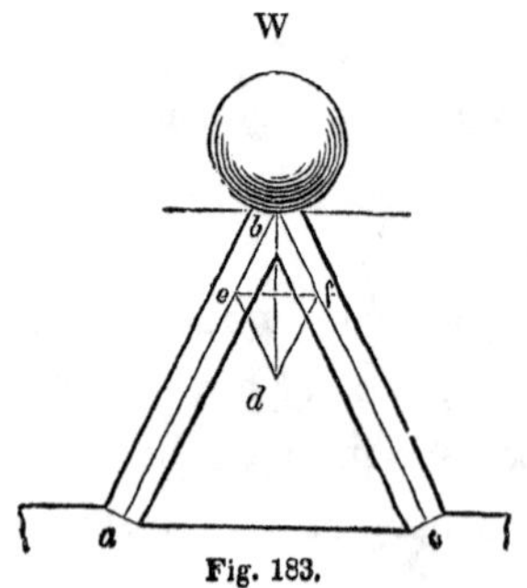

Fig. 183.

for the weight would be in that line. But, as it rarely occurs in systems of framing that weights can be supported by any single resistance, they requiring generally two or more supports, (as in the case of a roof supported by its rafters,) it becomes important, therefore, to know the exact amount of pressure any certain weight is capable of exerting upon oblique supports. This can be ascertained by the following process.

Let *a b* and *b c*, (*Fig.* 183,) represent the axes of two sticks of timber supporting the weight, *W;* and let the weight, *W*, be equal to 6 tons. Make the vertical line, *b d*, equal to 6 inches; from *d*, draw *d f*, parallel to *a b*, and *d e*, parallel to *c b;* then the line, *b e*, will be found to be 3½ inches long, which is equal to the number of tons that the weight, *W*, exerts upon the post, *a b*. The pressure upon the other post is represented by *b f*, which in this case is of the same length as *b e*. The posts being inclined at equal angles to the vertical line, *b d*, the pressure upon them is equal. Thus it will be found that the weight, which weighs only 6 tons, exerts a pressure of 7 tons; the amount being increased because of the oblique position of the supports. The lines, *e b*, *b f*, *f d* and *d e*, compose what is called the *parallelogram of forces*. The oblique strains exerted by any one force, therefore, may always be ascertained, by making *b d* equal, (upon any scale of equal parts,) to the number of lbs., cwts., or tons contained in the weight, *W*, and *b e* will then represent the number of lbs., cwts., or tons with which the timber, *a b*, is pressed, and *b f* that exerted upon *b c*.

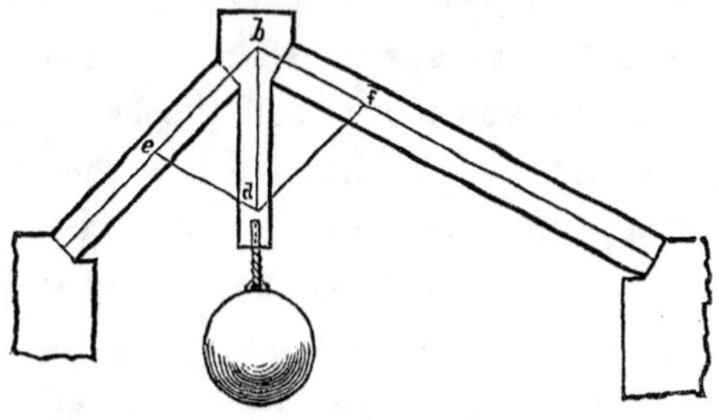

Fig. 184

Correct ideas of the comparative pressure exerted upon timbers according to their position, will be readily formed by drawing various designs of framing, and estimating the several strains in accordance with these principles. In *Fig.* 184, the struts are framed into a third piece, and the weight suspended from that. The struts are placed at a different angle to show the diverse pressures. The *length* of the timber used as struts, does not alter the amount of the pressure. But it may be observed that long timbers are not so capable of resistance as short ones.

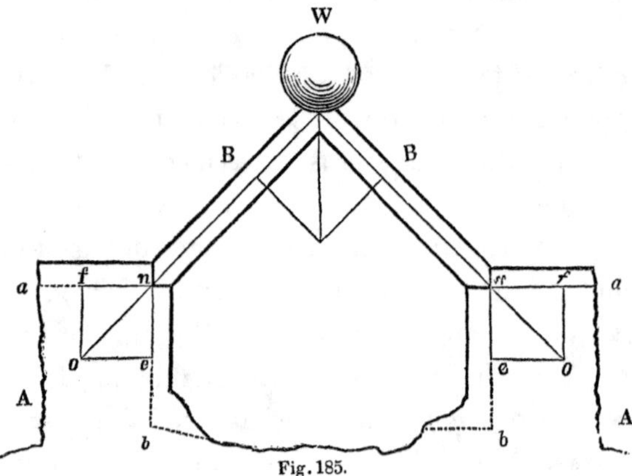

Fig. 185.

249.—In *Fig.* 185, the weight, *W*, exerts a pressure on the struts in the direction of their length; their feet, *n*, *n*, have, therefore, a tendency to move in the direction, *n o*, and would so move, were they not opposed by a sufficient resistance from the blocks, *A* and *A*. If a piece of each block be cut off at the horizontal line, *a n*, the feet of the struts would slide away from each other along that line, in the direction, *n a*; but if, instead of these, two pieces were cut off at the vertical line, *n b*, then the struts would descend vertically. To estimate the horizontal and the vertical pressures exerted by the struts, let *n o* be made equal (upon any scale of equal parts) to the number of tons (or pounds) with which the strut is pressed; construct the parallelogram of forces by drawing *o e* parallel to *a n*, and *o f* parallel to *b n*; then *n f*, (by the same scale,) shows the number of tons (or pounds) pressure that is exerted by the strut in the direction, *n a*, and *n e* shows the amount exerted in the direction, *n b*. By constructing designs similar to this, giving various and dissimilar positions to the struts, and then estimating the pressures, it will be found in every case that the horizontal pressure of one strut is exactly equal to that of the other, however much one strut may be inclined more than the other; and also, that the united vertical pressure of the two struts is exactly equal to the weight, *W*. (In this calculation, the weight of the timbers is not taken into consideration.)

250.—Suppose that the two struts, *B* and *B*, (*Fig*. 185,) were rafters of a roof, and that instead of the blocks, *A* and *A*, the walls of a building were the supports: then, to prevent the walls from being thrown over by the thrust of *B* and *B*, it would be desirable to remove the horizontal pressure. This may be done by uniting the feet of the rafters with a rope, iron rod, or piece of timber, as in *Fig*. 186. This figure is similar to the truss of a roof.

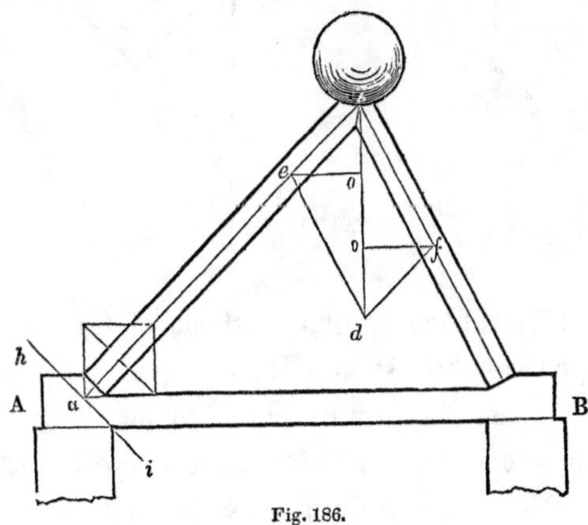

Fig. 186.

The horizontal strains on the tie-beam, tending to pull it asunder in the direction of its length, may be measured at the foot of the rafter, as was shown at *Fig.* 185; but it can be more readily and as accurately measured, by drawing from *f* and *e* horizontal lines to the vertical line, *b d*, meeting it in *o* and *o*; then *f o* will be the horizontal thrust at *B*, and *e o* at *A*; these will be found to equal one another. When the rafters of a roof are thus connected, all tendency to thrust the walls horizontally is removed, the only pressure on them is in a vertical direction, being equal to the weight of the roof and whatever it has to support. This pressure is beneficial rather than otherwise, as a roof thus formed tends to steady the walls.

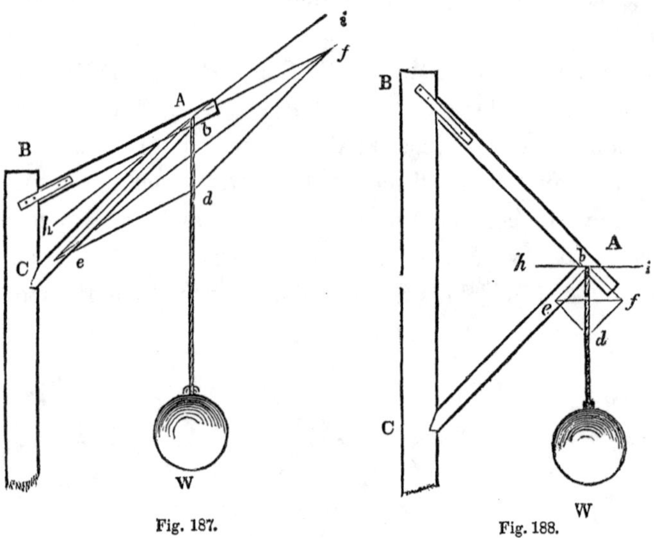

Fig. 187. Fig. 188.

251.—*Fig.* 187 and 188 exhibit methods of framing for supporting the equal weights, *W* and *W*. Suppose it be required to measure and compare the strains produced on the pieces, *A B* and *A C*. Construct the parallelogram of forces, *e b f d*, according to *Art.* 248. Then *b f* will show the strain on *A B*, and *b e* the strain on *A C*. By comparing the figures, *b d* being equal in each, it will be seen that the strains in *Fig.* 187 are about three times as great as those in *Fig.* 188: the position of the pieces, *A B* and *A C*, in *Fig.* 188, is therefore far preferable.

This and the preceding examples exemplify, in a measure, the *resolution of forces*; viz., the finding of *two or more* forces, which, acting in different directions, shall exactly balance the pressure of any given *single* force. Thus, in *Fig.* 185, supposing the weight, *W*, to be the greatest force that the two timbers, in their present position, are capable of sustaining, then the weight, *W*, is the *given* force, and the timbers are the *two* forces just equal to the given force.

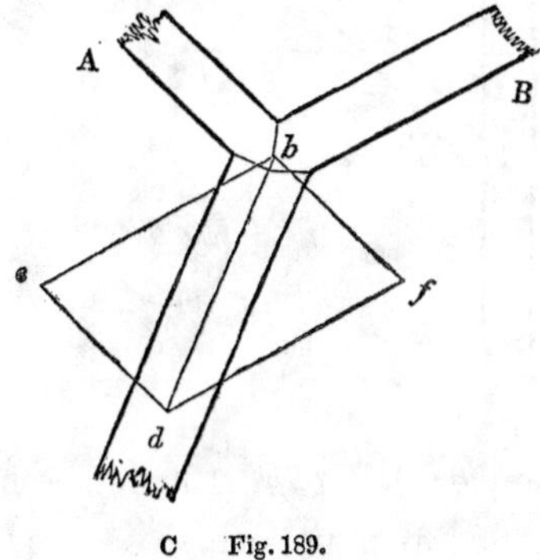

C Fig. 189.

252.—The *composition of forces* consists in ascertaining the direction and amount of *one* force, which shall be just capable of balancing *two or more* given forces, acting in different directions. This is only the reverse of the resolution of forces, and the two are founded on one and the same principle, and may be solved in the same manner. For example; let *A* and *B*, (*Fig.* 189,) be two pieces of timber, pressed in the direction of their length towards *b*—*A* by a force equal to 6 tons weight, and *B* equal to 9. To find the *direction* and *amount* of pressure they would unitedly exert, draw the lines, *b e* and *b f*, in a line with the axes of the timbers, and make *b e* equal to the pressure exerted by *B*, viz., 9; also make *b f* equal to the pressure on *A*, viz., 6, and complete the parallelogram of forces, *e b f d*; then *b d*, the diagonal of the parallelogram, will be the *direction*, and its length will be the *amount*, of the united pressures of *A* and of *B*. The line, *b d*, is termed the *resultant* of the two forces, *b f* and *b e*. If *A* and *B* are to be supported by one post, *C*, the best position for that post will be in the direction of the diagonal, *b d;* and it will require to be sufficiently strong to support the united pressures of *A* and of *B*.

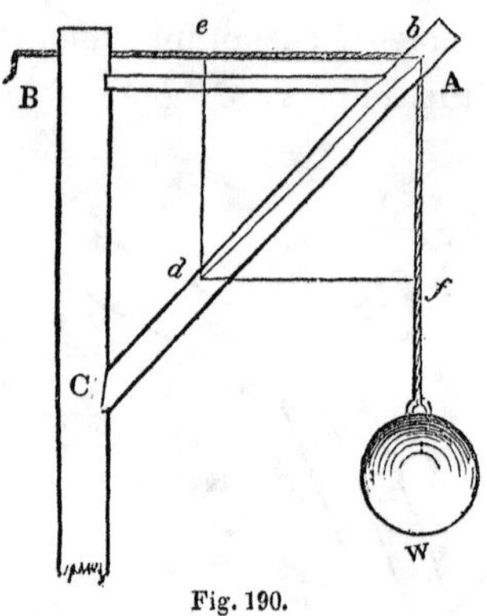

Fig. 190.

253.—Another example: let *Fig*. 190 represent a piece of framing commonly called a crane, which is used for hoisting heavy weights by means of the rope, *B b f*, which passes over a pulley at *b*. This is similar to *Fig*. 187 and 188, yet it is materially different. In those figures, the strain is in one direction only, viz., from *b* to *d ;* but in this there are two strains, from *A* to *B* and from *A* to *W*. The strain in the direction, *A B*, is evidently equal to that in the direction, *A W*. To ascertain the best position for the strut, *A C*, make *b e* equal to *b f*, and complete the parallelogram of forces, *e b f d ;* then draw the diagonal, *b d*, and it will be the position required. Should the foot, *C*, of the strut be placed either higher or lower, the strain on *A C* would be increased. In constructing cranes, it is advisable, in order that the piece, *B A*, may be under a gentle pressure, to place the foot of the strut a trifle lower than where the diagonal, *b d*, would indicate, but never higher

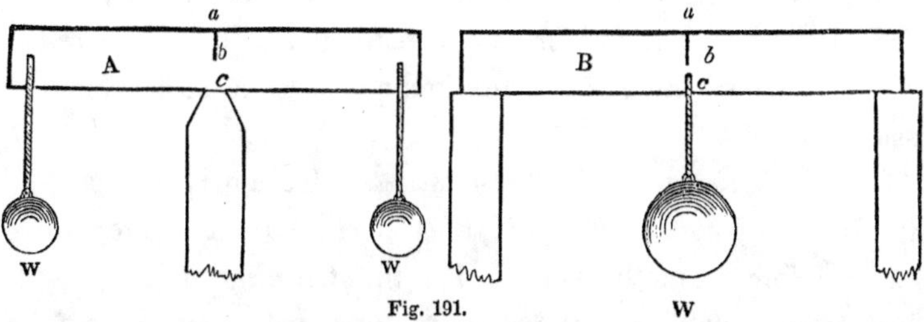

Fig. 191.

254.—*Ties and Struts.* Timbers in a state of tension are called *ties*, while such as are in a state of compression are termed *struts.* This subject can be illustrated in the following manner.

Let *A* and *B*, (*Fig.* 191,) represent beams of timber supporting the weights, *W*, *W* and *W; A* having but one support, which is in the middle of its length, and *B* two, one at each end. To show the nature of the strains, let each beam be sawed in the middle from *a* to *b*. The effects are obvious: the cut in the beam, *A*, will open, whereas that in *B* will close. If the weights are heavy enough, the beam, *A*, will break at *b;* while the cut in *B* will be closed perfectly tight at *a*, and the beam be very little injured by it. But if, on the other hand, the cuts be made in the bottom edge of the timbers, from *c* to *b*, *B* will be seriously injured, while *A* will scarcely be affected. By this it appears evident that, in a piece of timber subject to a pressure across the direction of its length, the fibres are exposed to contrary strains. If the timber is supported at both ends, as at *B*, those from the top edge down to the middle are compressed in the direction of their length, while those from the middle to the bottom edge are in a state of tension; but if the beam is supported as at *A*, the contrary effect is produced; while the fibres at the middle of either beam are not at all strained. The strains in a framed truss are of the same nature as those in a single beam. The truss for a roof, being supported at each end, has its tie-beam in a state of tension, while its rafters are compressed in the direction of their length. By this, it appears highly important that pieces in a state of tension should be distinguished

18

from such as are compressed, in order that the former may be preserved continuous. A strut may be constructed of two or more pieces; yet, where there are many joints, it will not resist compression so firmly.

255.—*To distinguish ties from struts.* This may be done by the following rule. In *Fig.* 183, the timbers, *a b* and *b c*, are the *sustaining* forces, and the weight, *W*, is the *straining* force; and, if the support be removed, the straining force would move from the point of support, *b*, towards *d*. Let it be required to ascertain whether the sustaining forces are *stretched* or *pressed* by the straining force. *Rule:* upon the direction of the straining force, *b d*, as a diagonal, construct a parallelogram, *e b f d*, whose sides shall be parallel with the direction of the sustaining forces, *a b* and *c b;* through the point, *b*, draw a line, parallel to the diagonal, *e f;* this may then be called the dividing line between ties and struts. Because all those supports which are on that side of the dividing line, which the straining force would occupy if unresisted, are compressed, while those on the other side of the dividing line are stretched.

In *Fig.* 183, the supports are both compressed, being on that side of the dividing line which the straining force would occupy if unresisted. In *Fig.* 187 and 188, in which *A B* and *A C* are the sustaining forces, *A C* is compressed, whereas *A B* is in a state of tension; *A C* being on that side of the line, *h i*, which the straining force would occupy if unresisted, and *A B* on the opposite side. The place of the latter might be supplied by a chain or rope. In *Fig.* 186, the foot of the rafter at *A* is sustained by two forces, the wall and the tie-beam, one perpendicular and the other horizontal: the direction of the straining force is indicated by the line, *b a*. The dividing line, *h i*, ascertained by the rule, shows that the wall is pressed and the tie-beam stretched.

256.—Another example: let *E A B F*, (*Fig.* 192,) represent a gate, supported by hinges at *A* and *E*. In this case, the *strain-*

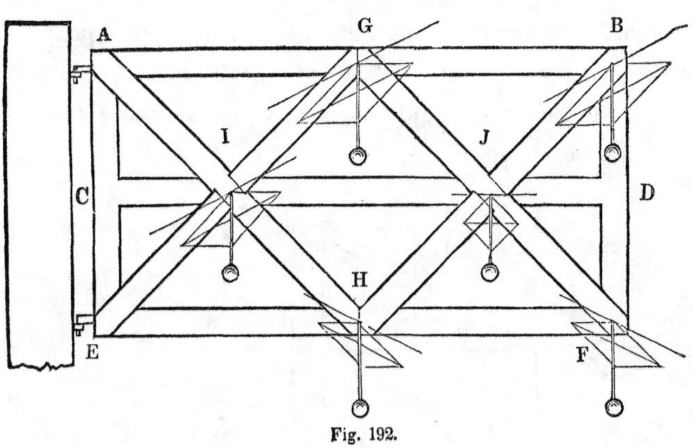

Fig. 192.

ing force is the weight of the materials, and the direction of course vertical. Ascertain the dividing line at the several points, *G*, *B*, *I*, *J*, *H* and *F*. It will then appear that the force at *G* is sustained by *A G* and *G E*, and the dividing line shows that the former is stretched and the latter compressed. The force at *H* is supported by *A H* and *H E*—the former stretched and the latter compressed. The force at *B* is opposed by *H B* and *A B*, one pressed—the other stretched. The force at *F* is sustained by *G F* and *F E*, *G F* being stretched and *F E* pressed. By this it appears that *A B* is in a state of tension, and *E F*, of compression; also, that *A H* and *G F* are stretched, while *B H* and *G E* are compressed: which shows the necessity of having *A H* and *G F*, each in one whole length, while *B H* and *G E* may be, as they are shown, each in two pieces. The force at *J* is sustained by *G J* and *J H*, the former stretched and the latter compressed. The piece, *C D*, is neither stretched nor pressed, and could be dispensed with if the joinings at *J* and *I* could be made as effectually without it. In case *A B* should fail, then *C D* would be in a state of tension.

257.—*The pressure of inclined beams.* The centre of gravity of a uniform prism or cylinder, is in its axis, at the middle of its length. In irregular bodies with plain sides, the centre of gravity may be found by balancing them upon the edge of a prism in two positions, making a line each time upon the body in a line with the edge of the prism, and the intersection of those lines will indicate the point required.

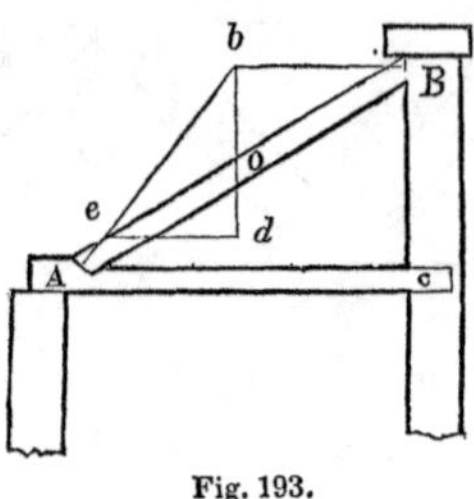

Fig. 193.

An inclined post or strut, supporting some heavy pressure applied at its upper end, as at *Fig.* 186, exerts a pressure at its foot in the direction of its length, or nearly so. But when such a beam is loaded uniformly over its whole length, as the rafter of a roof, the pressure at its foot varies considerably from the direction of its length. For example, let *A B*, (*Fig.* 193,) be a beam leaning against the wall, *B c*, and supported at its foot by the abutment, *A*, in the beam, *A c*, and let *o* be the centre of gravity of the beam. Through *o*, draw the vertical line, *b d*, and from *B*, draw the horizontal line, *B b*, cutting *b d* in *b;* join *b* and *A*, and *b A* will be the *direction* of the thrust. To prevent the beam from loosing its footing, the joint at *A* should be made at right angles to *b A*. The *amount* of pressure will be found thus: let *b d*, (by any scale of equal parts,) equal the number of tons, cwts., or pounds weight upon the beam, *A B;* draw *d e*, parallel to *B b;* then *b e*, (by the same scale,) equals the pressure in the direction, *b A;* and *e d*, the pressure against the wall at *B*—and also the horizontal thrust at *A*, as these are always equal in a construction of this kind. *Fig.* 194 represents two equal beams, supported at their feet by the abutments in the tie-beam. This case is similar to the last; for it is obvious that each beam is in precisely the position of the beam in *Fig.* 193. The horizontal

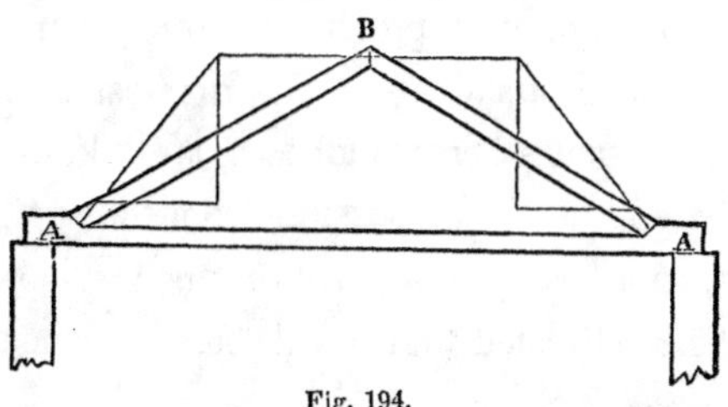

Fig. 194.

pressures at *B*, being equal and opposite, balance one another; and their horizontal thrusts at the tie-beam are also equal. (See *Art.* 250—*Fig.* 186.) When the inclination of a roof, (*Fig.* 194,) is one-fourth of the span, or of a shed, (*Fig.* 193,) is one-half the span, the horizontal thrust of a rafter, whose centre of gravity is at the middle of its length, is exactly equal to the weight distributed uniformly over its surface. The inclination, in a rafter uniformly loaded, which will produce the least oblique pressure, (*b e*, *Fig.* 193,) is 35 degrees and 16 minutes.

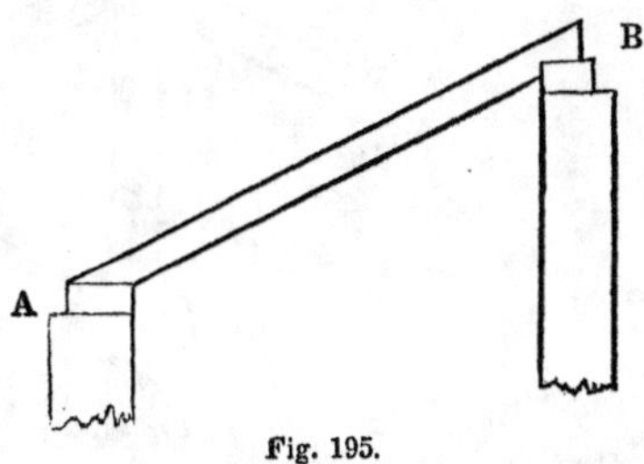

Fig. 195.

258.—In shed, or *lean-to* roofs, as *Fig.* 193, the horizontal pressure will be entirely removed, if the bearings of the rafters, as *A*, *B*, (*Fig.* 195,) are made horizontal—provided, however, that the rafters and other framing do not bend between the points of support. If a beam or rafter have a natural curve, the convex or rounding edge should be laid uppermost.

259.—A beam laid horizontally supported at each end and uniformly loaded, is subject to the greatest strain at the middle of its length. The amount of pressure at that point is equal to half of the whole load sustained. The greatest strain coming upon the middle of such a beam, mortices, large knots and other defects, should be kept as far as possible from that point; and, in resting a load upon a beam, as a partition upon a floor beam, the weight should be so adjusted that it will bear at or near the ends. (See *Art.* 282.)

260.—*The resistance of timber.* When the stress that a given load exerts in any particular direction, has been ascertained, before the proper size of the timber can be determined for the resistance of that pressure, the strength of the kind of timber to be used must be known. The following rules for calculating the resistance of timber, are based upon the supposition that the timber used be of what is called "merchantable" quality—that is, strait-grained, seasoned, and free from large knots, splits, decay, &c.

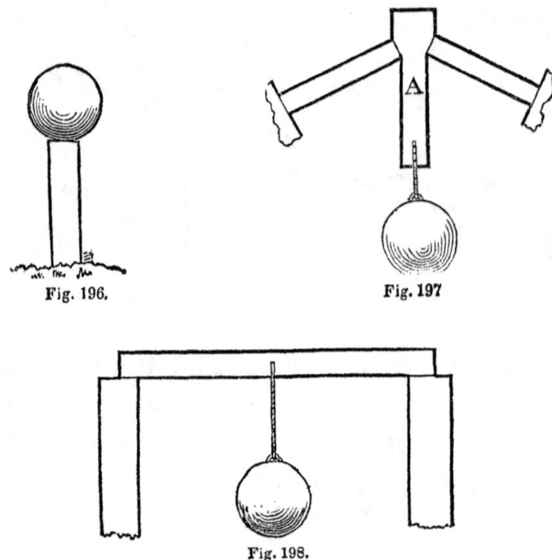

Fig. 196.

Fig. 197

Fig. 198.

The strength of a piece of timber, is to be considered in accordance with the direction in which the strain is applied upon it. When it is compressed in the direction of its length, as in *Fig.* 196, its strength is termed the *resistance to compression.* When the force tends to pull it asunder in the direction of its length, (*A*, *Fig.* 197,) it is termed the *resistance to tension.* And when strained by a force tending to break it crosswise, as at *Fig.* 198, its strength is called the *resistance to cross strains.*

261.—***Resistance to compression.*** When the height of a piece of timber exceeds about 10 times its diameter if round, or 10 times its thickness if rectangular, it will bend before crushing. The first of the following cases, therefore, refers to such posts as would be *crushed* if overloaded, and the other two to such as would *bend* before crushing. In estimating the strength of timber for this kind of resistance, it is provided in the following rules that the pressure be exactly in a line with the axis of the post.

Case 1.—To find the area of a post that will safely bear a given weight—when the height of the post is less than 10 times its least thickness. *Rule.*—Divide the given weight in pounds by 1000 for pine and 1400 for oak, and the quotient will be the least area of the post in inches. This rule requires that the area of the *abutting surface* be equal to the result: should there be, therefore, a tenon on the end of the post, this quotient will be too small. *Example.*—What should be the least area of a pine post that will safely sustain 48,000 pounds? 48,000, divided by 1000, gives 48—the required area in inches. Such a post may be 6×8 inches, and will bear to be of any length within 10 times 6 inches, its least thickness.

Case 2.—To find the area of a *rectangular* post that will safely bear a given weight—when its height is 10 times its least thickness or more. *Rule.*—Multiply the given weight or pressure in pounds by the square of the length in feet; and multiply this product by the decimal, ·0015, for oak, ·0021, for pitch pine and ·0016 for white pine; then divide this product by the breadth in inches, and the cube-root of the quotient will be the thickness in inches. *Example.*—What should be the thickness of a pine post, 8 feet high and 8 inches wide, in order to support a weight of 12 tons, or 26,880 pounds? The square of the length is 64 feet; this, multiplied by the weight in pounds, gives 1,730,320; this product, multiplied by the decimal, ·0016, gives 2768·512; and this again, divided by the breadth in inches, gives 346·064; by reference to the table of cube-roots in the appendix, the cube-root of this number will be found to be 7 inches large—which is the thickness required. The stiffest rectangular post is that in which the sides are as 10 to 6.

Case 3.—To find the area of a *round*, or *cylindrical*, post, that will safely bear a given weight—when its height is 10 times its least diameter or more. *Rule.*—Multiply the given weight or pressure in pounds by 1·7, and the product by ·0015 for oak, ·0021 for pitch pine and ·0016 for white pine; then multiply the square-root of this product by the height in feet, and the square-root of the last product will be the diameter required, in inches. *Example.*—What should be the diameter of a cylindrical oak post, 8 feet high, in order to support a weight of 12 tons, or 26,880 pounds? This weight in pounds, multiplied by 1·7, gives 45,696; and this, by ·0015, gives 68·544; the square-root of this product is (by the table in the appendix) 8·28, nearly—which, multiplied by 8, gives 66·24; the square-root of this number is 8·14, nearly; therefore, 8·14 inches is the diameter required.

Experiments have shown that the pressure should never be more than 1000 pounds per square inch on a joint in yellow pine —when the end of the grain of one piece is pressed against the side of the grain of the other.

262.—*Resistance to tension.* A bar of oak of an inch square, pulled in the direction of its length, has been torn asunder by a weight of - - - - 11,500 lbs.

Of white pine - - - 11,000

Of pitch pine - - - 10,000

Therefore, when the strain is applied in a line with the axis of the piece, the following rule must be observed.

To find the area of a piece of timber to resist a given strain in the direction of its length. *Rule.*—Divide the given weight to be sustained, by the weight that will tear asunder a bar an inch square of the same kind of wood, (as above,) and the product will be the area in inches of a piece that will just sustain the given weight; but the area should be at least 4 times this, to safely sustain a constant load of the given weight. *Example.*—What should be the area of a stick of pitch pine timber, which is required to sustain safely a constant load of 60,000 pounds? 60,000, divided by 10,000, (as above,) gives 6, and this, multiplied by 4, give 24 inches—the answer.

263.—*Resistance to cross strains.* To find the scantling of a piece of timber to sustain a given weight, when such piece is supported at the ends in a horizontal position.

Case 1.—When the breadth is given. *Rule.*—Multiply the square of the length in feet by the weight in pounds, and this product by the decimal, ·009, for oak, ·011 for white pine and ·016 for pitch pine; divide the product by the breadth in inches, and the cube-root of the quotient will be the depth required in inches. *Example.*—What should be the depth of a beam of white pine, having a bearing of 24 feet and a breadth of 6 inches, in order to support 900 pounds? The square of 24 is 576, and this, multiplied by 900, gives 518·400; and this again, by ·011, gives 5702·400; this, divided by 6, gives 950·400; the cube-root of which is 9·83 inches—the depth required.

Case 2.—When the depth is given. *Rule.*—Multiply the square of the length in feet by the weight in pounds, and multiply this product by the decimal, ·009, for oak, ·011 for white pine and ·016 for pitch pine; divide the last product by the cube of the depth in inches, and the quotient will be the breadth in inches required. *Example.*—What should be the breadth of a beam of oak, having a bearing of 16 feet and a depth of 12 inches, in order to support a weight of 4000 pounds? The square of 16 is 256, which, multiplied by 4000, gives 1,024,000; this, multiplied by ·009, gives 9216; and this again, divided by 1728, the cube of 12, gives 5⅓ inches—which is the breadth required.

Case 3.—When the breadth bears a certain proportion to the depth. When neither the breadth nor depth is given, it will be best to fix on some proportion which the breadth should have to the depth; for instance, suppose it be convenient to make the breadth to the depth as 0·6 is to 1, then the rule would become as follows: *Rule.*—Multiply the weight in pounds by the decimal, ·009, for oak, ·011 for white pine and ·016 for pitch pine; divide the product by 0·6, and extract the square-root; multiply this root by the length in feet, and extract the square-root a second time, which will be the depth in inches required. The breadth is equal to the depth multiplied by the decimal, 0·6. It is obvious that any other proportion of the breadth and depth may be obtained by merely changing the decimal, 0·6, in the rule. *Example.*—What should be the depth and breadth of a beam of pitch pine, having a proportion to one another as 0·6 to 1, and a bearing of 22 feet, in order to sustain a ton weight, or 2240 pounds? This, multiplied by ·016, gives 35·84, which, divided by 0·6, gives 59·73; the square-root of this is 7·7, which, multiplied by 22, the length, gives 169·4; the square-root of this is 13—which is the depth required. Then 13, multiplied by 0·6, gives 7·8 inches—the required breadth.

Case 4.—When the beam is inclined, as *A B*, *Fig.* 193. *Rule.*—Multiply together the weight in pounds, the length of the beam in feet, the horizontal distance, *A c*, between the supports, in feet, and the decimal, ·009, for oak, ·011 for white pine, and ·016 for pitch pine; divide this product by 0·6, and the fourth root of the quotient will give the depth in inches. The breadth is equal to the depth multiplied by the decimal, 0·6. *Example.*—What should be the size of an oak beam, the sides to bear a proportion to one another as 0·6 to 1, in order to support a ton weight or 2240 pounds, the beam being inclined so that, its length being 20 feet, its horizontal distance between the points of support will be 16 feet? 2240, multiplied by 20, gives 44,800, which, multiplied by 16, gives 716,800; and this again, by the decimal, ·009, gives 6451·2; this last, divided by 0·6, gives 10,752, the fourth root of which is 10·18, nearly; and this, multiplied by 0·6, gives 6·1; therefore, the size of the beam should be 10·18 inches by 6·1 inches.

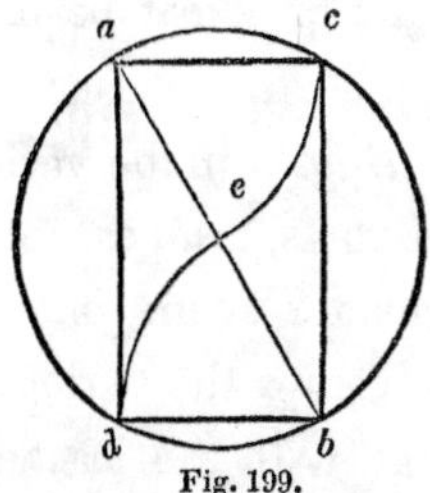

Fig. 199.

264.—*To ascertain the scantling of the stiffest beam that can be cut from a cylinder.* Let *d a c b*, (*Fig.* 199,) be the section, and *e* the centre, of a given cylinder. Draw the diameter, *a b*; upon *a* and *b*, with the radius of the section, describe the arcs, *d e* and *e c*; join *d* and *a*, *a* and *c*, *c* and *b*, and *b* and *d*; then the rectangle, *d a c b*, will be a section of the beam required.

265.—The greater the depth of a beam in proportion to the thickness, the greater the strength. But when the difference between the depth and the breadth is great, the beam must be stayed, (as at *Fig.* 202,) to prevent its falling over and breaking sideways. Their shrinking is another objection to deep beams; but where these evils can be remedied, the advantage of increasing the depth is considerable. The following rule is, *to find the strongest form for a beam out of a given quantity of timber. Rule.*—Multiply the length in feet by the decimal, 0·6, and divide the given area in inches by the product; and the square of the quotient will give the depth in inches. *Example.*—What is the strongest form for a beam whose given area of section is 48 inches, and length of bearing 20 feet? The length in feet, 20, multiplied by the decimal, 0·6, gives 12; the given area in inches, 48, divided by 12, gives a quotient of 4, the square of which is 16—this is the depth in inches; and the breadth must be 3 inches. A beam 16 inches by 3 would bear twice as much as a square beam of the same area of section; which shows how important it is to make beams deep and thin. In many old buildings, and even in new ones, in country places, the very reverse of this has been practised; the principal beams being oftener laid on the broad side than on the narrower one.

266.—*Systems of Framing.* In the various parts of framing known as floors, partitions, roofs, bridges, &c., each has a specific object; and, in all designs for such constructions, this object should be kept clearly in view; the various parts being so disposed as to serve the design with the least quantity of material. The simplest form is the best, not only because it is the most economical, but for many other reasons. The great number of joints, in a complex design, render the construction liable to derangement by multiplied compressions, shrinkage, and, in consequence, highly increased oblique strains; by which its stability and durability are greatly lessened.

FLOORS.

267.—Floors have been constructed in various ways, and are known as *single-joisted, double,* and *framed.* In a single-joisted floor, the timbers, or floor-joists, are disposed as is shown in *Fig.* 200. Where strength is the principal object, this manner of disposing the floor-joists is far preferable; as experiments have proved that, with the same quantity of material, single-joisted floors are much stronger than either double or framed floors. To obtain the greatest strength, the joists should be thin and deep.

268.—*To find the depth of a joist, the length of bearing and thickness being given, when the distance from centres is*

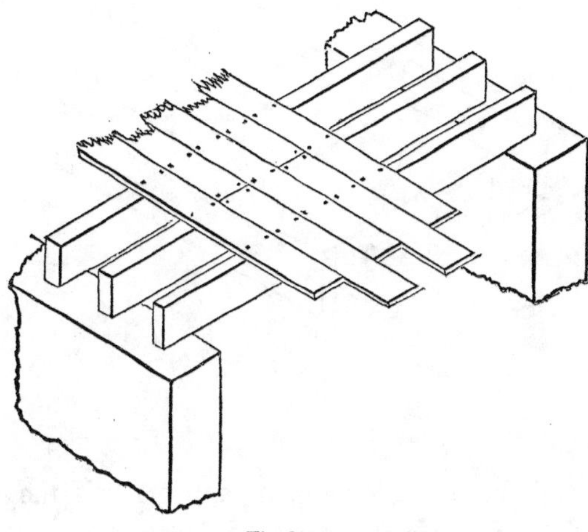

Fig. 200.

12 *inches.* *Rule.*—Divide the square of the length in feet, by the breadth in inches; and the cube-root of the quotient, multiplied by 2·2 for pine, or 2·3 for oak, will give the depth in inches. *Example.*—What should be the depth of floor-joists, having a bearing of 12 feet and a thickness of 3 inches, when said joists are of pine and placed 12 inches from centres? The square of 12 is 144, which, divided by 3, gives 48; the cube-root of this number is 3·63, which, multiplied by 2·2, gives 7·986 inches, the depth required; or 8 inches will be found near enough for practice.

269.—Where chimneys, flues, stairs, &c., occur to interrupt the bearing, the joists are framed into a piece, (*b*, *Fig.* 201,) called a *trimmer.* The beams, *a*, *a*, into which the trimmer is framed, are called *trimming-beams*, *trimming-joists*, or *carriage-beams.* They need to be stronger than the common joists, in proportion to the number of beams, *c*, *c*, which they support. The trimmers have to be made strong enough to support half the weight which the joists, *c*, *c*, support, (the wall, or another trimmer, at the other end supporting the other half,) and the *carriage-*

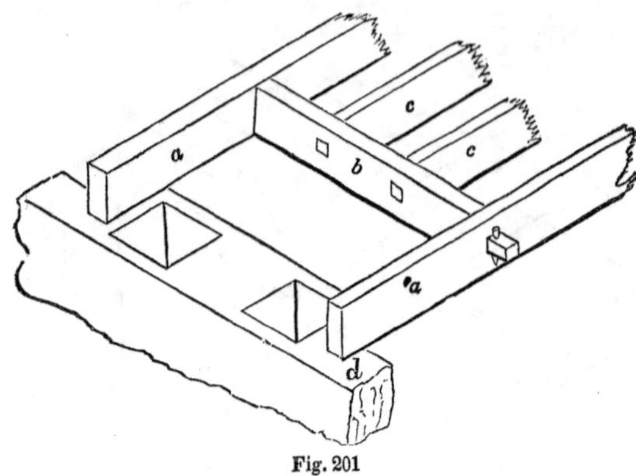

Fig. 201

beams must each be strong enough to support half the weight which the trimmer supports. In calculating for the dimensions of floor-timbers, regard must be had to the fact that the weight which they generally support—such as persons of 150 pounds moving over the floor—exerts a much greater influence than equal weights at rest. When the trimmer, *b*, is not more distant from the bearing, *d*, than is necessary for ordinary hearths, &c., it will be sufficient to add $\frac{1}{8}$ of an inch to the thickness of the carriage-beam for every joist, *c*, that is supported. Thus, if the thickness of *c* is 3 inches, and the number of joists supported be 6, add 6 eighths, or $\frac{3}{4}$ of an inch, making the carriage-beams $3\frac{3}{4}$ inches thick. It is generally the practice in dwellings to make the carriage-beam, in all situations, one inch thicker than the common joists. But it is well to have a rule for determining the size more accurately in extreme cases.

270.—When the bearing exceeds 8 feet, there should be *struts*, as *a* and *a*, (*Fig*. 202,) well nailed between the joists. These will prevent the turning or twisting of the floor-joists, and will greatly stiffen the floor. For, in the event of a heavy weight resting upon one of the joists, these struts will prevent that joist from settling below the others, to the injury of the plastering

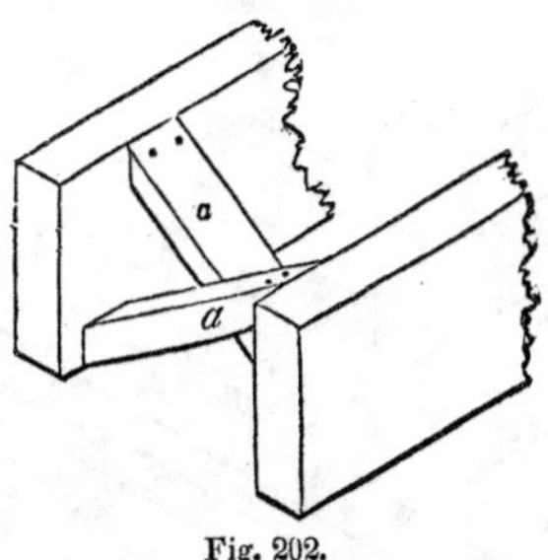

Fig. 202.

upon the underside. When the length of bearing is great, struts should be inserted at about every 4 feet.

271.—Single-joisted floors may be constructed for as great a length of bearing as timber of sufficient depth can be obtained; but, in such cases, where perfect ceilings are desirable, either double or framed floors are considered necessary. Yet the ceilings under a single-joisted floor may be rendered more durable by *cross-furring*, as it is termed—which consists of nailing a series of narrow strips of board on the under edge of the beams and at right angles to them. To these, instead of the beams, the laths are nailed. The strips should be not over 2 inches wide—enough to join the laths upon is all that is wanted in width—and not more than 12 inches apart. It is necessary that all furring for plastering be narrow, in order that the mortar may have a sufficient *clinch*.

When it is desirable to prevent the passage of sound, the openings between the beams, at about 3 inches from the upper edge, are closed by short pieces of boards, which rest on cleets nailed to the beam along its whole length. This forms a floor upon which mortar is laid to the depth of about 2 inches, leaving but about half an inch from its upper surface to the under side of the floor-plank.

272.—*Double floors.* A double floor consists, as at *Fig.* 203, of three tiers of joists or timbers; viz., *bridging-joists, a, a, binding-joists, b, b,* and *ceiling-joists, c, c.* The binding-joists

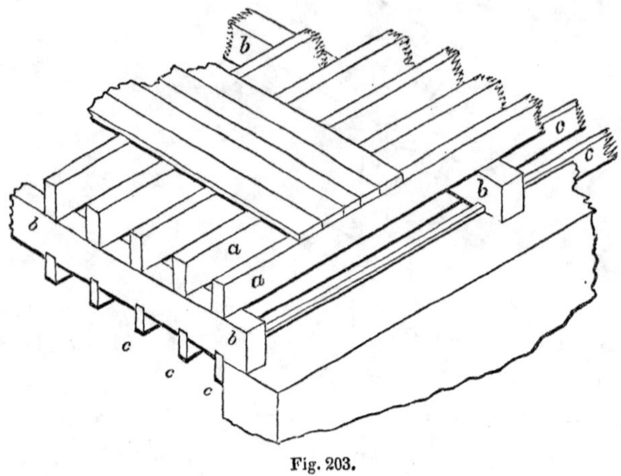

Fig. 203.

are the principal support, and of course reach from wall to wall. The bridging-joists, which support the floor-plank, are laid upon the binding-joists, to which they are nailed; sometimes they are notched into the binding-joists, but they are sufficiently firm when well nailed. The ceiling-joists are notched into the under side of the binders, and nailed; they are the support of the lath and plastering.

273.—Binders are laid 6 feet apart. At this distance the following rules will give the scantling.

Case 1.—To find the depth of a binding-joist, the length and breadth being given. *Rule.*—Divide the square of the length in feet, by the breadth in inches; and the cube-root of the quotient, multiplied by 3·42 for pine, or by 3·53 for oak, will give the depth in inches. *Example.*—What should be the depth of a binding-joist, having a length of 12 feet and a breadth of 6 inches, when the kind of timber is pine? The square of 12 is 144, which, divided by 6, gives 24; the cube-root of this is 2·88, which, multiplied by 3·42, gives 9·85, the depth in inches.

Case 2.—To find the breadth, when the depth and length are given. *Rule.*—Divide the square of the length in feet, by the cube of the depth in inches; and multiply the quotient by 40 for pine, or by 44 for oak, which will give the breadth in inches. *Example.*—What should be the breadth of a binding-joist, having a length of 12 feet and a depth of 10 inches, when the kind of wood is pine? The cube of 10 is 1000; the square of 12 is 144; this, divided by 1000, gives a quotient of ·144; and this quotient, multiplied by 40, gives 5·76, the breadth in inches.

274.—Bridging-joists are laid from 12 to 20 inches apart. The scantling may be found by the rule at *Art.* 268.

275.—Ceiling-joists are generally placed 12 inches apart from centres. They are arranged to suit the length of the lath; this being, in most cases, 4 feet long. What is said at *Art.* 271, in regard to the width of furring for plastering, will apply to the thickness of ceiling-joists.

To find the depth of a ceiling-joist, when the length of bearing and thickness are given. *Rule.*—Divide the length in feet by the cube-root of the breadth in inches; and multiply the quotient by 0·64 for pine, or by 0·67 for oak, which will give the depth in inches. *Example.*—What should be the depth of a ceiling-joist of pine, when the length of bearing is 6 feet and the thickness 2 inches? The length in feet, 6, divided by the cube-root of the breadth in inches, 1·26, gives a quotient of 4·76, which, being multiplied by the decimal, 0·64, gives 3 inches, the depth required.

When the thickness of a ceiling-joist is 2 inches, the depth in inches will be equal to half the length of bearing in feet. Thus, if the bearing is 6 feet, the depth will be 3 inches; bearing 8 feet, depth 4 inches, &c.

276.—*Framed floors.* When a good ceiling is required, and the distance of bearing is great, the binding-joists, instead of reaching from wall to wall, are framed into *girders.* These are heavy timbers, as *d*, (*Fig.* 204,) which reach from wall to wall, being the chief support of the floor. Such an arrangement is termed a *framed* floor. The binding, the bridging and the ceil

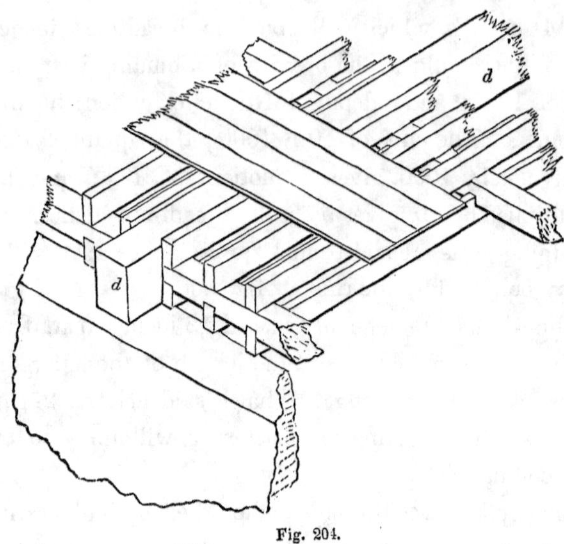

Fig. 204.

ing-joists in these, are the same as those in double floors just described. The distinctive feature of this kind of floor is the girder.

277.—Girders should be made as deep as the timber will allow: if their being increased in size should reduce the height of a story a few inches, it would be better than to have a house suffer from defective ceilings and insecure floors. In the following rules for the scantling of girders, they are supposed to be placed at 10 feet apart.

Case 1.—To find the depth, when the breadth of the girder and the length of bearing are given. *Rule.*—Divide the square of the length in feet, by the breadth in inches; and the cube-root of the quotient, multiplied by 4·2 for pine, or by 4·3 for oak, will give the depth required in inches. *Example.*—What should be the depth of a pine girder, having a length of 20 feet and a breadth of 13 inches? The square of 20 is 400, which, divided by 13, gives 30·77; the cube-root of this is 3·12, which, multiplied by 4·2, gives 13 inches, the depth required.

Case 2.—To find the breadth, when the length of bearing and depth are given. *Rule.*—Divide the square of the length in feet, by the cube of the depth in inches; and the quotient, multiplied by 74 for pine, or by 82 for oak, will give the breadth in inches. *Example.*—What should be the breadth of a pine girder, having a length of 18 feet and a depth of 14 inches? The square of the length in feet, 324, divided by the cube of the depth in inches, 2744, gives ·118; and this, multiplied by 74, gives 8·73 inches, the breadth required.

278.—When the breadth of a girder is more than about 12 inches, it is recommended to divide it by sawing from end to end, vertically through the middle, and then to bolt it together with the sawn sides outwards. This is not to strengthen the girder, as some have supposed, but to reduce the size of the timber, in order that it may dry sooner. The operation affords also an opportunity to examine the heart of the stick—a necessary precaution; as large trees are frequently in a state of decay at the heart, although outwardly they are seemingly sound. When the halves are bolted together, thin slips of wood should be inserted between them at the several points at which they are bolted, in order to leave sufficient space for the air to circulate between. This tends to prevent decay; which will be found first at such parts as are not exactly tight, nor yet far enough apart to permit the escape of moisture.

279.—When girders are required for a long bearing, it is usual to truss them; that is, to insert between the halves two pieces of oak which are inclined towards each other, and which meet at the centre of the length of the girder, like the rafters of a roof-truss, though nearly if not quite concealed within the girder. This, and many similar methods, though extensively practised, are generally worse than useless; since it has been ascertained that, in nearly all such cases, the operation has positively *weakened* the girder.

A girder may be strengthened by mechanical contrivance, when

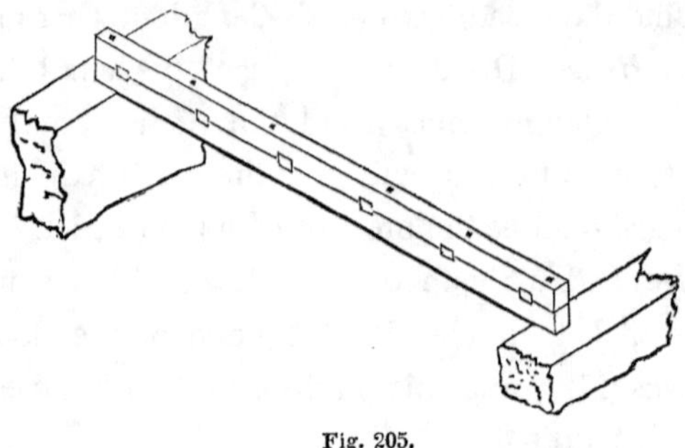

Fig. 205.

its depth is required to be greater than any one piece of timber will allow. *Fig.* 205 shows a very simple yet scientific method of doing this. The two pieces of which the girder is composed are bolted, or pinned, together, having keys inserted between to prevent the pieces from sliding. The keys should be of hard wood, well seasoned. The two pieces should be about equal in depth, in order that the joint between them may be in the neutral line. (See *Art.* 254.) The thickness of the keys should be about half their breadth, and the amount of their united thicknesses should be equal to a trifle over the depth and one-third of the depth of the girder. Instead of bolts or pins, iron hoops are sometimes used; and when they can be procured, they are far preferable. In this case, the girder is diminished at the ends, and the hoops driven from each end towards the middle.

280.—Beams may be spliced, if none of a sufficient length can be obtained, though not at or near the middle, if it can be avoided. (See *Art.* 259 and 332.) Girders should rest from 9 to 12 inches on the wall, and a space should be left for the air to circulate around the ends, that the dampness may evaporate. Floor-timbers are supported at their ends by walls of considerable height. They should not be permitted to rest upon intervening partitions, which are not likely to settle as much as the walls; otherwise the unequal settlements will derange the level of the floor. As all floors, however well-constructed, settle in some degree, it is advisable to frame the joists a little higher at the middle of the room than at its sides,—as also the ceiling-joists and cross-furring, when either are used. In single-joisted floors, for the same reason, the rounded edge of the stick, if it have one, should be placed uppermost.

If the floor-plank are laid down temporarily at first, and left to season a few months before they are finally driven together and secured, the joints will remain much closer. But if the edges of the plank are planed after the first laying, they will shrink again; as it is the nature of wood to shrink after *every* planing however dry it may have been before.

PARTITIONS.

281.—Too little attention has been given to the construction of this part of the frame-work of a house. The settling of floors and the cracking of ceilings and walls, which disfigure to so great an extent the apartments of even our most costly houses, may be attributed almost solely to this negligence. A square of partitioning weighs about half a ton, a greater weight, when added to its customary load, such as furniture, storage, &c., than any ordinary floor is calculated to sustain. Hence the timbers bend, the ceilings and cornices crack, and the whole interior part of the house settles; showing the necessity for providing adequate supports independent of the floor-timbers. A partition should, if practicable, be supported by the walls with which it is connected, in order, if the walls settle, that it may settle with them. This would prevent the separation of the plastering at the angles of rooms. For the same reason, a firm connection with the ceiling is an important object in the construction of a partition.

282.—The joists in a partition should be so placed as to discharge the weight upon the points of support. All oblique pieces in a partition, that tend not to this object, are much better omitted. *Fig.* 206 represents a partition having a door in the middle. Its

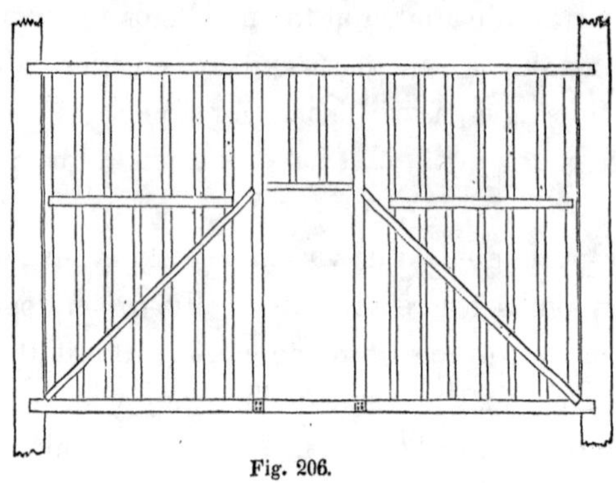

Fig. 206.

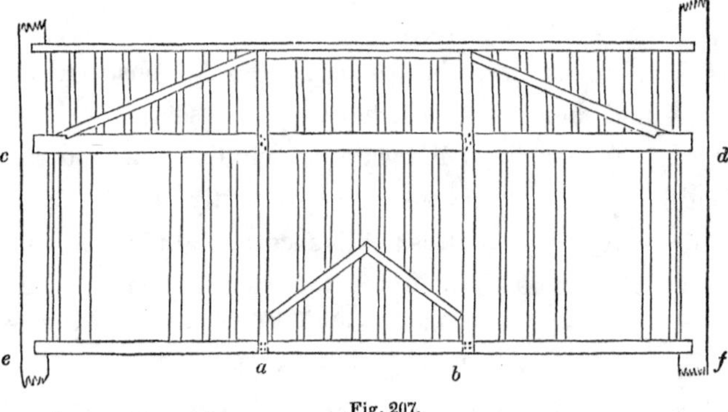

Fig. 207.

construction is simple but effective. *Fig.* 207 shows the manner of constructing a partition having doors near the ends. The truss is formed above the door-heads, and the lower parts are suspended from it. The posts, *a* and *b*, are halved, and nailed to the tie, *c d*, and the sill, *e f*. The braces in a trussed partition should be placed so as to form, as near as possible, an angle of 40 degrees with the horizon. In partitions that are intended to support only their own weight, the principal timbers may be 3×4 inches for a 20 feet span, 3½×5 for 30 feet, and 4×6 for 40. The thickness of the filling-in stuff may be regulated according to what is said at *Art.* 271, in regard to the width of furring for plastering. The filling-in pieces should be stiffened at about every three feet by short struts between.

All superfluous timber, besides being an unnecessary load upon the points of support, tends to injure the stability of the plastering; for, as the strength of the plastering depends, in a great measure, upon its clinch, formed by pressing the mortar through the space between the laths, the narrower the surface, therefore, upon which the laths are nailed, the less will be the quantity of plastering unclinched, and hence its greater security from fractures. For this reason, the principal timbers of the partition should have their edges reduced, by chamfering off the corners.

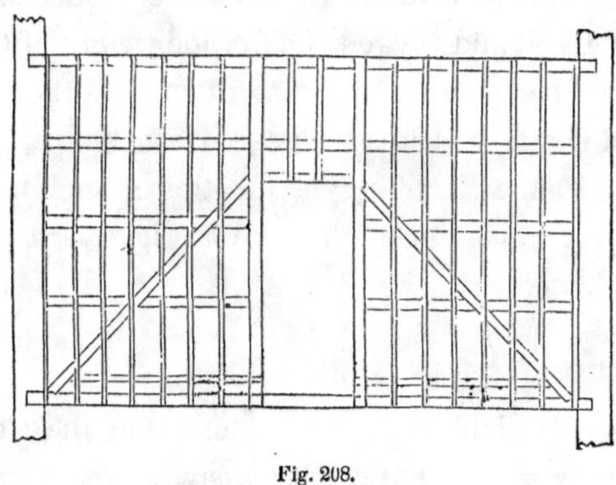

Fig. 208.

283.—When the principal timbers of a partition require to be large for the purpose of greater strength, it is a good plan to omit the upright filling-in pieces, and in their stead, to place a few horizontal pieces; in order, upon these and the principal timbers, to nail upright battens at the proper distances for lathing, as in *Fig.* 208. A partition thus constructed requires a little more space than others; but it has the advantage of insuring greater stability to the plastering, and also of preventing to a good degree the conversation of one room from being heard in the other. When a partition is required to support, in addition to its own weight, that of a floor or some other burden resting upon it, the dimensions of the timbers may be ascertained, by applying the principles which regulate the laws of pressure and those of the resistance of timber, as explained at the first part of this section. The following data, however, may assist in calculating the amount of pressure upon partitions:

284.—The weight of a square, (that is, a hundred square feet,) of partitioning may be estimated at from 1500 to 2000 lbs.; a square of single-joisted flooring, at from 1200 to 2000 lbs.; a square of framed flooring, at from 2700 to 4500 lbs.; and the weight of a square of *deafening*, (as described at the latter part of *Art.* 271,) at about 1500 lbs.

When a floor is supported at two opposite extremities, and by a partition introduced midway, one-half of the weight of the whole floor will then be supported by the partition. As the settling of partitions and floors, which is so disastrous to plastering, is frequently owing to the shrinking of the timber and to ill-made joints, it is very important that the timber be seasoned and the work well executed.

ROOFS.*

285.—In ancient buildings, the Norman and the Gothic, the walls and buttresses were erected so massive and firm, that it was customary to construct their roofs without a tie-beam; the walls being abundantly capable of resisting the lateral pressure exerted by the rafters. But in modern buildings, the walls are so slightly built as to be incapable of resisting scarcely any oblique pressure; and hence the necessity of constructing the roof so that all oblique and lateral strains may be removed; as, also, that instead of having a tendency to separate the walls, the roof may contribute to bind and steady them.

286.—In estimating the pressures upon any certain roof, for the purpose of ascertaining the proper sizes for the timbers, calculation must be made for the pressure exerted by the wind, and, if

* See also *Art.* 228.

in a cold climate, for the weight of snow, in addition to the weight of the materials of which the roof is composed. The force of wind may be calculated at 40 lbs. on a square foot. The weight of snow will be of course according to the depth it acquires. (See *weight of materials*, in Appendix.) In a severe climate, roofs ought to be constructed steeper than in a milder one; in order that the snow may have a tendency to slide off before it becomes of sufficient weight to endanger the safety of the roof. The inclination should be regulated in accordance with the qualities of the material with which the roof is to be covered. The following table may be useful in determining the inclination, and in estimating the weight of the various kinds of covering:

MATERIAL.	INCLINATION.	WEIGHT UPON A SQUARE FOOT.
Tin, - -	Rise 1 inch to a foot.	$\frac{5}{8}$ to $1\frac{1}{4}$ lbs.
Copper, - -	" 1 " "	1 to $1\frac{1}{2}$ "
Lead, - -	" 2 inches "	4 to 7 "
Zinc, - -	" 3 " "	$1\frac{1}{4}$ to 2 "
Short pine shingles,	" 5 " "	$1\frac{1}{2}$ to $2\frac{1}{2}$ "
Long cypress shingles,	" 6 " "	4 to 5 "
Slate, - -	" 6 " "	5 to 9 "

The weight of the covering, as above estimated, is that of the material only, added to the weight of whatever is used to fix it to the roof, such as nails, &c.; what the material is laid on, such as plank, boards or lath, is not included.

287.—*Fig.* 209 to 212 give a general idea of the usual manner of constructing trusses for roofs: *c*, (*Fig.* 209,) is a common

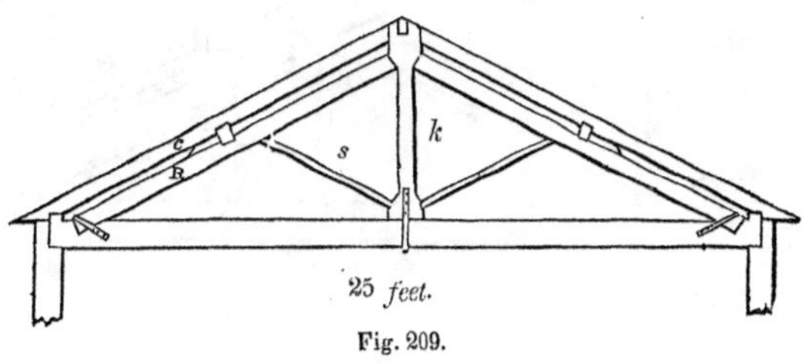

Fig. 209.

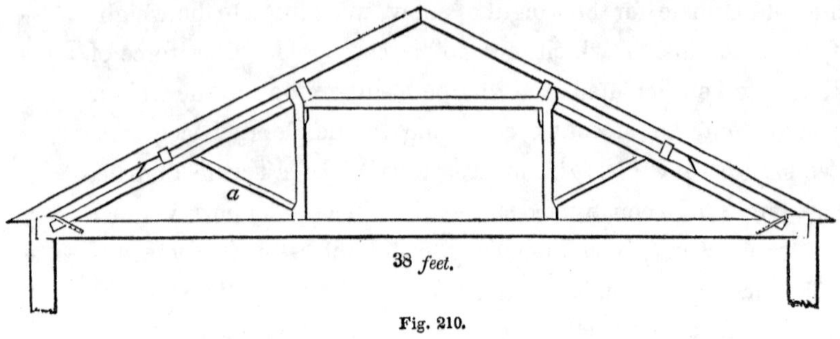

Fig. 210.

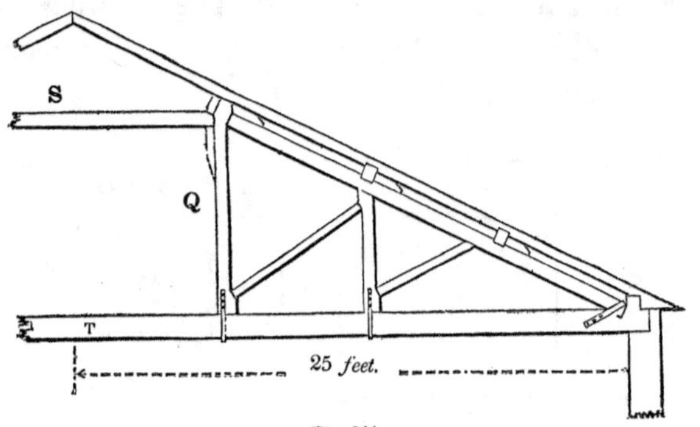

Fig. 211.

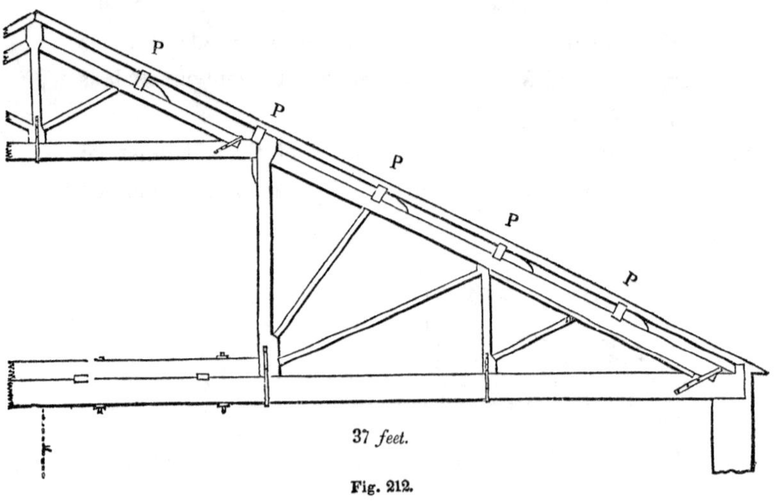

Fig. 212.

rafter; *R* is a principal rafter; *k* is a king-post; *s* is a strut; *S*, (*Fig*. 211,) is a straining-beam; *Q* is a queen-post; *T* is a tie-beam; and *P*, *P*, (*Fig*. 212,) are purlins. In constructing a roof of importance, the trusses should be placed not over 10 feet apart, the principal rafter supported by a strut at every purlin, the purlin *notched on* instead of being framed into the principal rafters, and the tie-beam supported at proper distances, according to the weight of the ceiling or whatever else it is required to support.

288.—The dimensions of the timbers may be found in accordance with the principles explained at the first part of this section; but for general purposes, the following rules, deduced from the experience of practical builders and from scientific principles, may be found useful: these rules give the dimensions of the piece at its smallest part.

289.—*To find the dimensions of a king-post.* *Rule.*—Multiply the length of the post in feet by the span in feet. Then multiply this product by the decimal, 0·12, for pine, or by 0·13 for oak, which will give the area of the king-post in inches; and divide this area by the breadth, and it will give the thickness; or by the thickness for the breadth. *Example.*—What should be the dimensions of a pine king-post, 8 feet long, for a roof having a span of 25 feet? 8 times 25 is 200; this, multiplied by the decimal, 0·12, gives 24 inches for the area; 4×6, therefore, would be a good size at the smallest part.

290.—*To find the dimensions of a queen-post.* *Rule.*—Multiply the length in feet, of the queen-post or suspending-piece, by that part of the length of the tie-beam it supports, also in feet. This product, multiplied by the decimal, 0·27, for pine, or by 0·32 for oak, will give the area of the post in inches; and dividing this area by the thickness will give the breadth. *Example.*—The queen-posts in *Fig*. 210 support each $\frac{1}{3}$ of the tie-beam, which is 12$\frac{2}{3}$ feet. To make them of pine, 6 feet long, what should be their dimensions? 12$\frac{2}{3}$, multiplied by 6, gives 76, which, multiplied by 0·27, gives 20·52; which indicates a size of about 4×5¼.

291.—*To find the dimensions of a tie-beam, that is required to support a ceiling only. Rule.*—Divide the length of the longest unsupported part by the cube-root of the breadth; and the quotient, multiplied by 1·47 for pine, or by 1·52 for oak, will give the depth in inches. *Example.*—The length of the longest unsupported part of the tie-beam in *Fig.* 210 is 12⅔ feet. What should be the depth of the tie-beam, the breadth being 6 inches, and the kind of wood, pine? The cube-root of 6 is 1·82, and 12⅔, divided by 1·82, gives a quotient of 6·956; this, multiplied by 1·47, gives 10·225. The size of the tie-beam, therefore, may be 6×10¼. When there are rooms in the roof, the dimensions for the tie-beam can be found by the rule for girders, (*Art.* 277.)

292.—*To find the dimensions of a principal rafter when there is a king-post in the middle. Rule.*—Multiply the square of the length of the rafter in feet, by the span in feet; and divide the product by the cube of the thickness in inches. For pine, multiply the quotient by ·096, which will give the depth in inches. *Example.*—What should be the depth of a rafter of pine, 22·36 feet long, and 6 inches thick, the roof having a span of 40 feet? The square of 22·36 is 500 nearly, this, multiplied by 40, gives 20000; and this, divided by 216, the cube of the thickness, gives 92·59; which, multiplied by ·096, equals 8·888. The size of the rafter should, therefore, be 6×8⅞.

293.—*To find the dimensions of a principal rafter when two queen-posts are used instead of a king-post. Rule.*—The same as the last, except that the decimal, 0·155, must be used instead of ·096. *Example.*—What should be the dimensions of a principal rafter, having a length of 14 feet, (as in *Fig.* 210,) and a thickness of 6 inches, when the span of the roof is 38 feet and the wood is pine? The square of 14 is 196, which, multiplied by 38, gives 7448; this, divided by 216, the cube of 6, gives

34·48, which, multiplied by 0·155, gives 5·34. The size of the rafter should, therefore, be $6 \times 5\frac{3}{8}$.

294.—*To find the dimensions of a straining-beam.* In order that this beam may be the strongest possible, its depth should be to its thickness as 10 is to 7. *Rule.*—Multiply the square-root of the span in feet, by the length of the straining-beam in feet, and extract the square-root of the product. Multiply this root by 0·9 for pine, which will give the depth in inches To find the thickness, multiply the depth by the decimal, 0·7. *Example.*—What should be the dimensions of a pine straining-beam, 12 feet long, for a span of 38 feet? The square-root of the span is 6·164, which, multiplied by 12, gives 73·968; the square-root of this is nearly 8·60, which, multiplied by 0·9, gives 7·74—the depth. This, multiplied by 0·7, gives 5·418—the thickness. Therefore, the beam should be $5\frac{3}{8} \times 7\frac{3}{4}$, or $5\frac{1}{4} \times 8$.

295.—*To find the dimensions of struts and braces. Rule.*—Multiply the square-root of the length supported in feet, by the length of the brace or strut in feet; and the square-root of the product, multiplied by 0·8 for pine, will give the depth in inches; and the depth, multiplied by the decimal, 0·6, will give the thickness in inches. *Example.*—In *Fig.* 210, the part supported by the brace or strut, *a*, is equal to half the length of the principal rafter, or 7 feet; and the length of the brace is 6 feet: what should be the size of a pine brace? The square-root of 7 is 2·65, which, multiplied by 6, gives 15·9; the square-root of this is 3·99, which, multiplied by 0·8, gives 3·192—the depth. This, multiplied by 0·6, gives 1·9152, the thickness. Therefore, the brace should be 2×3 inches.

It is customary to make the principal rafters, tie-beam, posts and braces, all of the same thickness, that the whole truss may be of the same thickness throughout.

296.—*To find the dimensions of purlins. Rule.*—Multiply the cube of the length of the purlin in feet, by the distance the purlins are apart in feet; and the fourth root of the product for pine will give the depth in inches; or multiply by 1·04 to obtain the depth for oak; and the depth, multiplied by the decimal, 0·6, will give the thickness. *Example.*—What should be the dimensions of pine purlins, 9 feet long and 6 feet apart? The cube of 9 is 729, which, multiplied by 6, gives 4374; the fourth root of this is 8·13—the required depth. This, multiplied by 0·6, gives 4·878—the thickness. A proper size for them would be about 5×8 inches. Purlins should be long enough to extend over two, three or more trusses.

297.—*To find the dimensions of common rafters.* The following rule is for slate roofs, having the rafters placed 12 inches apart. Shingle roofs may have rafters placed 2 feet apart. The dimensions of rafters for other kinds of covering may be found by reference to the table at *Art.* 286, and the laws of pressure at the first part of this section. *Rule.*—Divide the length of bearing in feet, by the cube-root of the breadth in inches; and the quotient, multiplied by 0·72 for pine, or 0·74 for oak, will give the depth in inches. *Example.*—What should be the depth of a pine rafter, 7 feet long and 2 inches thick? 7 feet, divided by 1·26, the cube-foot of 2, gives 5·55, which, multiplied by 0·72, gives nearly 4 inches—the depth required.

298.—If, instead of framing the principal rafters and straining-beam into the king and the queen posts, they be permitted to abut against each other, and the king and the queen posts be made in halves, notched on and bolted, or strapped to each other and to the tie-beam, much of the ill effects of shrinking in the heads of the king and the queen posts will be avoided. (See *Art.* 339 and 340.)

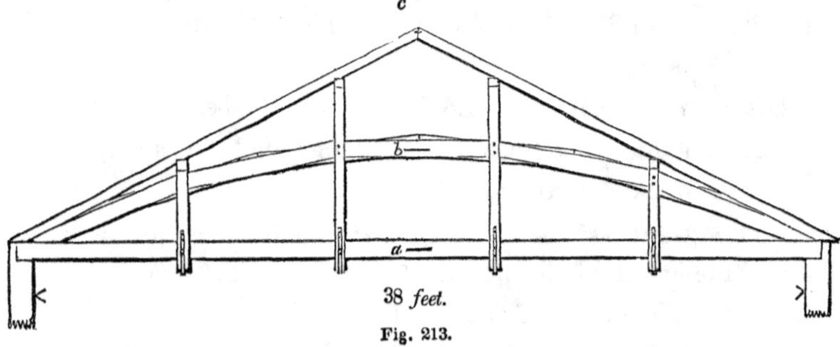

Fig. 213.

299.—*Fig.* 213 shows a method of constructing a truss having a *built-rib* in the place of principal rafters. The proper form for the curve is that of a parabola, (*Art.* 127.) This curve, when as flat as is described in the figure, approximates so near to that of the circle, that the latter may be used in its stead. The height, *a b*, is just half of *a c*, the curve to pass through the middle of the rib. The rib is composed of two series of abutting pieces, bolted together. These pieces should be as long as the dimensions of the timber will admit, in order that there may be but few joints. The suspending pieces are in halves, notched and bolted to the tie-beam and rib, and a purlin is framed upon the upper end of each. A truss of this construction needs, for ordinary roofs, no diagonal braces between the suspending pieces, but if extra strength is required the braces may be added. The best place for the suspending pieces is at the joints of the rib. A rib of this kind will be sufficiently strong, if the area of its section contain about one-fourth more timber, than is required for that of a straining-beam for a roof of the same size. The proportion of the depth to the thickness should be about as 10 is to 7.

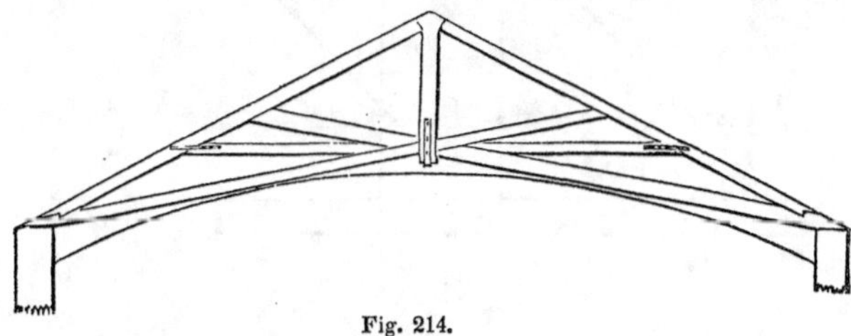

Fig. 214.

300.—Some writers have given designs for roofs similar to *Fig.* 214, having the tie-beam omitted for the accommodation of an arch in the ceiling. This and all similar designs are seriously objectionable, and should always be avoided; as the small height gained by the omission of the tie-beam can never compensate for the powerful lateral strains, which are exerted by the oblique position of the supports, tending to separate the walls. Where an arch is required in the ceiling, the best plan is to carry up the walls as high as the top of the arch. Then, by using a horizontal tie-beam, the oblique strains will be entirely removed. Many a public building in this place and vicinity, has been all but ruined by the settling of the roof, consequent upon a defective plan in the formation of the truss in this respect. It is very necessary, therefore, that the horizontal tie-beam be used, except where the walls are made so strong and firm by abutments, or other support, as to prevent a possibility of their separating.

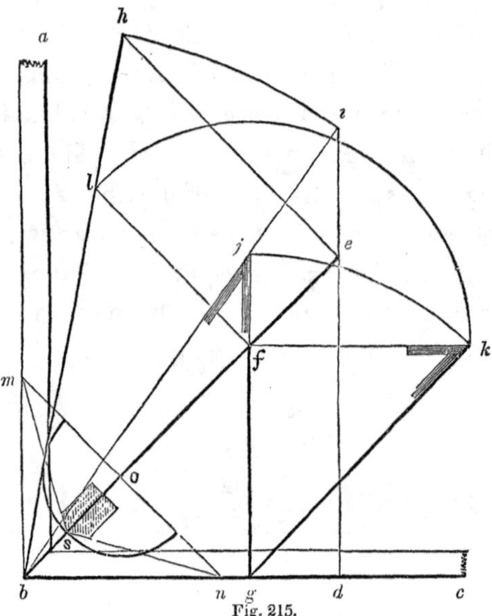

Fig. 215.

301.—*Fig.* 215 is a method of obtaining the proper lengths and bevils for rafters in a hip-roof, *a b* and *b c* are walls at the angle of the building; *b e* is the seat of the hip-rafter and *g f* of a jack or cripple rafter. Draw *e h*, at right angles to *b e*, and make it equal to the rise of the roof; join *b* and *h*, and *h b* will be the length of the hip-rafter. Through *e*, draw *d i*, at right angles to *b c*; upon *b*, with the radius, *b h*, describe the arc, *h i*, cutting *d i* in *i*; join *b* and *i*, and extend *g f* to meet *b i* in *j*; then *g j* will be the length of the jack-rafter. The length of each jack-rafter is found in the same manner—by extending its seat to cut the line, *b i*. From *f*, draw *f k*, at right angles to *f g*, also *f l*, at right angles to *b e*; make *f k* equal to *f l* by the arc, *l k*, or make *g k* equal to *g j* by the arc, *j k*; then the angle at *j* will be the *top-bevil* of the jack-rafters, and the one at *k* will be the *down-bevil*.*

302.—*To find the backing of the hip-rafter.* At any convenient place in *b e*, (*Fig*. 215,) as *o*, draw *m n*, at right angles to *b e*; from *o*, tangical to *b h*, describe a semi-circle, cutting *b e* in *s*; join *m* and *s* and *n* and *s*; then these lines will form at *s* the proper angle for beviling the top of the hip-rafter.

DOMES.†

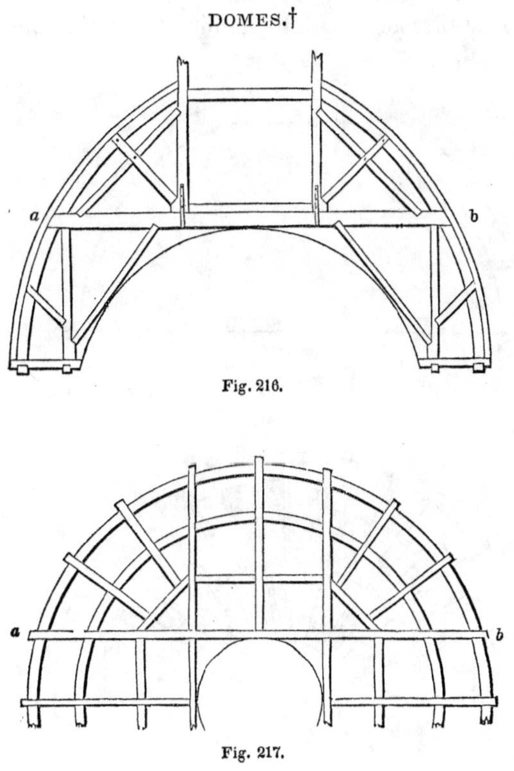

Fig. 216.

Fig. 217.

* The lengths and bevils of rafters for roof-*valleys* can also be found by the above process

† See also *Art.* 227

303.—The most usual form for domes is that of the sphere, the base being circular. When the interior dome does not rise too high, a horizontal tie may be thrown across, by which any degree of strength required may be obtained. *Fig.* 216 shows a section, and *Fig.* 217 the plan, of a dome of this kind, *a b* being the tie-beam in both. Two trusses of this kind, (*Fig.* 216,) parallel to each other, are to be placed one on each side of the opening in the top of the dome. Upon these the whole framework is to depend for support, and their strength must be calculated accordingly. (See the first part of this section, and *Art.* 286.) If the dome is large and of importance, two other trusses may be introduced at right angles to the foregoing, the tie-beams being preserved in one continuous length by framing them high enough to pass over the others.

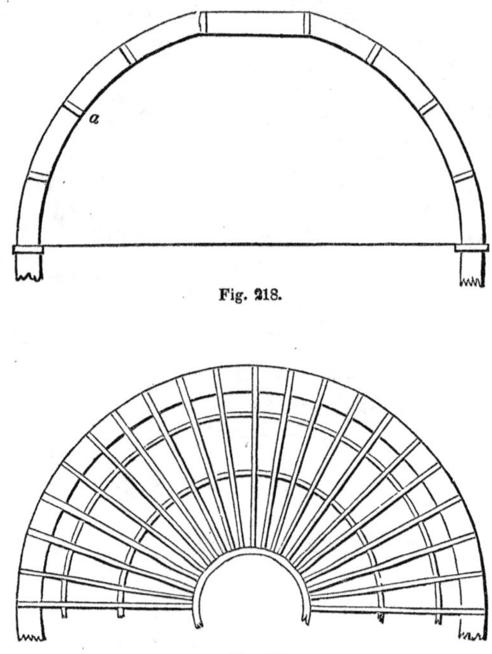

Fig. 218.

Fig. 219.

304.—When the interior dome rises too high to admit of a level tie-beam, the framing may be composed of a succession of ribs standing upon a continuous circular curb of timber, as seen at *Fig.* 218 and 219,—the latter being a plan and the former a section. This curb must be well secured, as it serves in the place of a tie-beam to resist the lateral thrust of the ribs. In small domes, these ribs may be easily cut from wide plank; but, where an extensive structure is required, they must be built in two thicknesses so as to *break joints*, in the same manner as is described for a roof at *Art.* 299. They should be placed at about two feet apart at the base, and strutted as at *a* in *Fig.* 218.

305.—The scantling of each thickness of the rib may be as follows:

For domes of	24	feet diameter,	1×8	inches.
" "	36	"	1½×10	"
" "	60	"	2×13	"
" "	90	"	2½×13	"
" "	108	"	3×13	"

306.—Although the outer and the inner surfaces of a dome may be finished to any curve that may be desired, yet the framing should be constructed of such a form, as to insure that the *curve of equilibrium* will pass through the middle of the depth of the framing. The nature of this curve is such that, if an arch or dome be constructed in accordance with it, no one part of the structure will be less capable than another of resisting the strains and pressures to which the whole fabric may be exposed. The curve of equilibrium for an arched vault or a roof, where the load is equally diffused over the whole surface, is that of a parabola, (*Art.* 127;) for a dome, having no *lantern*, tower or cupola above it, a *cubic parabola*, (*Fig.* 220;) and for one having a tower, &c., above it, a curve approaching that of an hyperbola must be adopted, as the greatest strength is required at its upper parts. If the curve of a dome be circular, (as in the vertical section, *Fig.* 218,) the pressure will have a tendency to burst the dome outwards at about one-third of its height. Therefore, when this form is used in the construction of an extensive dome, an iron band should be placed around the framework at that height; and whatever may be the form of the curve, a band or tie of some kind is necessary around or across the base.

If the framing be of a form less convex than the curve of equilibrium, the weight will have a tendency to crush the ribs inwards, but this pressure may be effectually overcome by strutting between the ribs; and hence it is important that the struts be so placed as to form continuous horizontal circles.

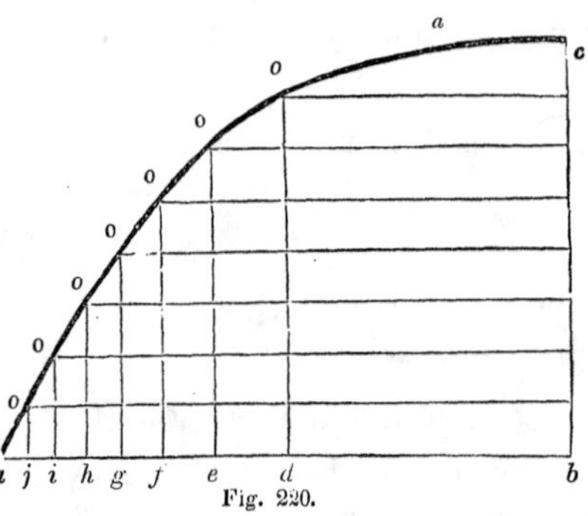

Fig. 220.

307.—*To describe a cubic parabola.* Let *a b*, (*Fig.* 220,) be the base and *b c* the height. Bisect *a b* at *d*, and divide *a d* into 100 equal parts; of these give *d e* 26, *e f* 18¼, *f g* 14½, *g h* 12¼, *h i* 10¾, *i j* 9½, and the balance, 8¾, to *j a;* divide *b c* into 8 equal parts, and, from the points of division, draw lines parallel to *a b*, to meet perpendiculars from the several points of division in *a b*, at the points, *o*, *o*, *o*, &c. Then a curve traced through these points will be the one required.

308.—Small domes to light stairways, &c., are frequently made elliptical in both plan and section; and as no two of the ribs in one quarter of the dome are alike in form, a method for obtaining the curves is necessary.

309.—*To find the curves for the ribs of an elliptical dome.* Let *a b c d*, (*Fig.* 221,) be the plan of a dome, and *e f* the seat

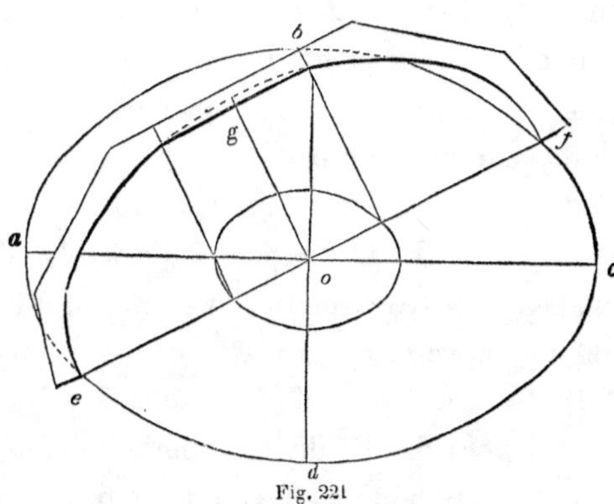

Fig. 221

of one of the ribs. Then take *e f* for the transverse *axis* and twice the rise, *o g*, of the dome for the conjugate, and describe, (according to *Art.* 115, 116, &c.,) the semi-ellipse, *e g f*, which will be the curve required for the rib, *e g f*. The other ribs are found in the same manner.

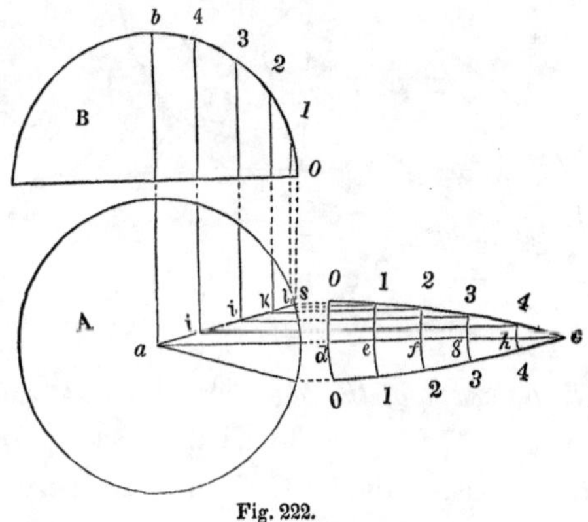

Fig. 222.

310.—*To find the shape of the covering for a spherical dome.* Let *A*, (*Fig.* 222,) be the plan and *B* the section of a given dome. From *a*, draw *a c*, at right angles to *a b*; find the stretch-out, (*Art.* 92,) of *o b*, and make *d c* equal to it; divide the arc, *o b*, and the line, *d c*, each into a like number of equal parts, as 5, (a large number will insure greater accuracy than a small one;) upon *c*, through the several points of division in *c d*, describe the arcs, *o d o*, 1 *e* 1, 2 *f* 2, &c.; make *d o* equal to half the width of one of the boards, and draw *o s*, parallel to *a c;* join *s* and *a*, and from the points of division in the arc, *o b*, drop perpendiculars, meeting *a s* in *i j k l;* from these points, draw *i* 4, *j* 3, &c., parallel to *a c;* make *d o*, *e* 1, &c., on the lower side of *a c*, equal to *d o*, *e* 1, &c., on the upper side; trace a curve through the points, *o*, 1, 2, 3, 4, *c*, on each side of *d c;* then *o c o* will be the proper shape for the board. By dividing the circumference of the base, *A*, into equal parts, and making the bottom, *o d o*, of the board of a size equal to one of those parts, every board may be made of the same size. In the same manner as the above, the shape of the covering for sections of another form may be found, such as an ogee, cove, &c.

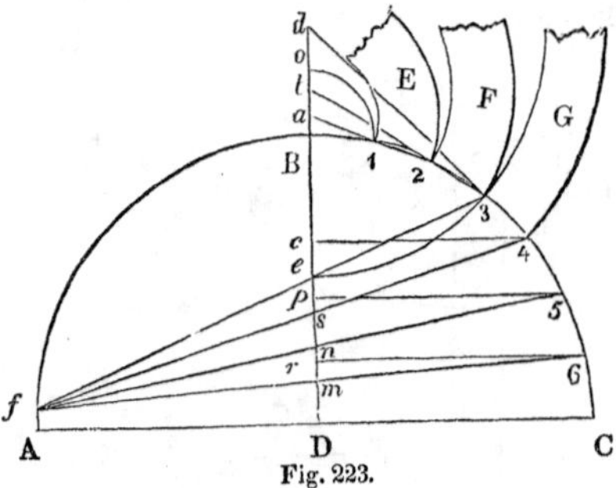

Fig. 223.

311.—*To find the curve of the boards when laid in horizontal courses.* Let *A B C*, (*Fig.* 223,) be the section of a given dome, and *D B* its axis. Divide *B C* into as many parts as there are to be courses of boards, in the points, 1, 2, 3, &c.; through 1 and 2, draw a line to meet the axis extended at *a;* then *a* will be the centre for describing the edges of the board, *E*. Through 3 and 2, draw 3 *b;* then *b* will be the centre for describing *F*. Through 4 and 3, draw 4 *d;* then *d* will be the centre for *G*. *B* is the centre for the arc, 1 *o*. If this method is taken to find the centres for the boards at the base of the dome, they would occur so distant as to make it impracticable : the following method is preferable for this purpose. *G* being the last board obtained by the above method, extend the curve of its inner edge until it meets the axis, *D B*, in *e ;* from 3, through *e*, draw 3 *f*, meeting the arc, *A B*, in *f ;* join *f* and 4, *f* and 5 and *f* and 6, cutting the axis, *D B*, in *s*, *n* and *m ;* from 4, 5 and 6, draw lines parallel to *A C* and cutting the axis in *c*, *p* and *r ;* make *c* 4, (*Fig.* 224,)

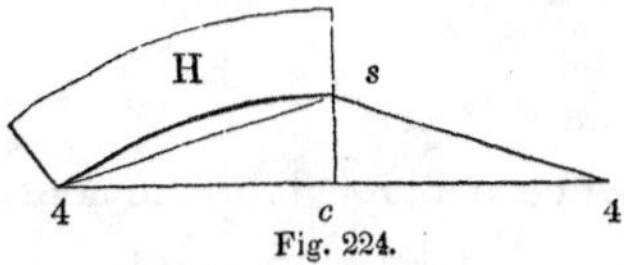

Fig. 224.

equal to *c* 4 in the previous figure, and *c s* equal to *c s* also in the previous figure; then describe the inner edge of the board, *H*, according to *Art.* 87 : the outer edge can be obtained by gauging from the inner edge. In like manner proceed to obtain the next board—taking *p* 5 for half the chord and *p n* for the height of the segment. Should the segment be too large to be described easily, reduce it by finding intermediate points in the curve, as at *Art.* 86.

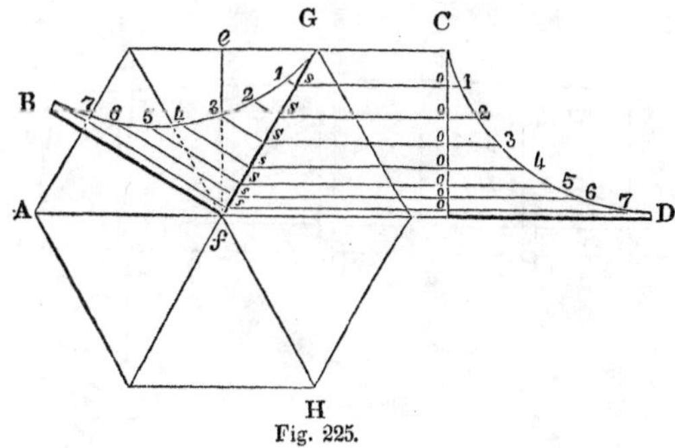

Fig. 225.

312.—*To find the shape of the angle-rib for a polygonal dome.* Let *A G H*, (*Fig.* 225,) be the plan of a given dome, and

C D a vertical section taken at the line, *e f*. From 1, 2, 3, &c., in the arc, *C D*, draw ordinates, parallel to *A D*, to meet *f G*; from the points of intersection on *f G*, draw ordinates at right-angles to *f G*; make *s* 1 equal to *o* 1, *s* 2 equal to *o* 2, &c.; then *G f B*, obtained in this way, will be the angle-rib required. The best position for the sheathing-boards for a dome of this kind is horizontal, but if they are required to be bent from the base to the vertex, their shape may be found in a similar manner to that shown at *Fig*. 222.

BRIDGES.

313.—Various plans have been adopted for the construction of bridges, of which perhaps the following are the most useful. *Fig*. 226 shows a method of constructing wooden bridges, where the banks of the river are high enough to permit the use of the tie-beam, *a b*. The upright pieces, *c d*, are notched and bolted on in pairs, for the support of the tie-beam. A bridge of this construction exerts no lateral pressure upon the abutments. This method may be employed even where the banks of the river are low, by letting the timbers for the roadway rest immediately upon the tie-beam. In this case, the framework above will serve the purpose of a railing.

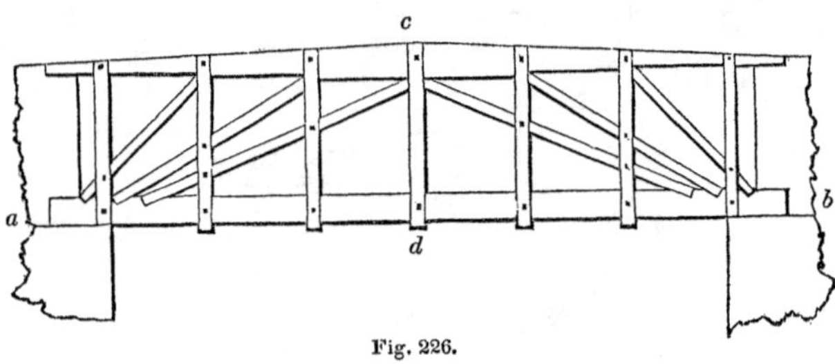

Fig. 226.

314.—*Fig*. 227 exhibits a wooden bridge without a tie-beam. Where staunch buttresses can be obtained, this method may be recommended; but if there is any doubt of their stability, it

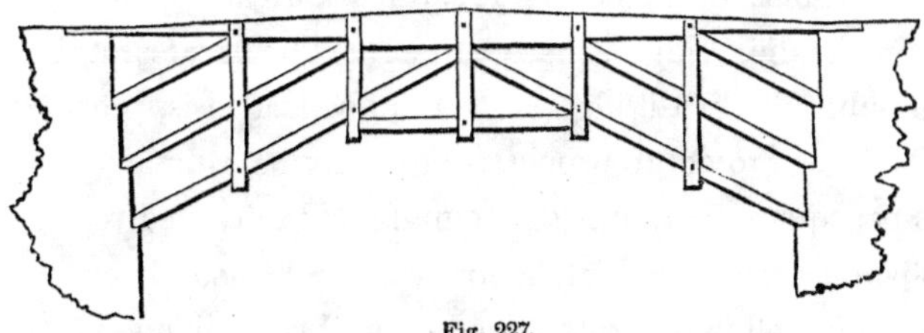

Fig. 227.

should not be attempted, as it is evident that such a system of framing is capable of a tremendous lateral thrust.

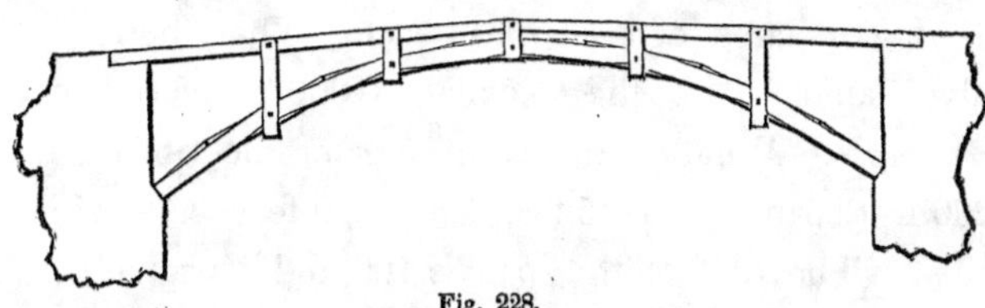

Fig. 228.

315.—*Fig.* 228 represents a wooden bridge in which a *built-rib*, (see *Art.* 299,) is introduced as a chief support. The curve of equilibrium will not differ much from that of a parabola: this, therefore, may be used—especially if the rib is made gradually a little stronger as it approaches the buttresses. As it is desirable that a bridge be kept low, the following table is given to show the least rise that may be given to the rib.

Span in feet.	Least rise in feet.	Span in feet.	Least rise in feet.	Span in feet.	Least rise in feet.
30	0·5	120	7	280	24
40	0·8	140	8	300	28
50	1·4	160	10	320	32
60	2	180	11	350	39
70	$2\frac{1}{2}$	200	12	380	47
80	3	220	14	400	53
90	4	240	17		
100	5	260	20		

The rise should never be made less than this, but in all cases greater if practicable; as a small rise requires a greater quantity of timber to make the bridge equally strong. The greatest uniform weight with which a bridge is likely to be loaded is, probably, that of a dense crowd of people. This may be estimated at 120 pounds per square foot, and the framing and gravelled roadway at 180 pounds more; which amounts to 300 pounds on a square foot. The following rule, based upon this estimate, may be useful in determining the area of the ribs. *Rule.*—Multiply the width of the bridge by the square of half the span, both in feet; and divide this product by the rise in feet, multiplied by the number of ribs; the quotient, multiplied by the decimal, 0·0011, will give the area of each rib in feet. When the roadway is only planked, use the decimal, 0·0007, instead of 0·0011. *Example.*—What should be the area of the ribs for a bridge of 200 feet span, to rise 15 feet, and be 30 feet wide, with 3 curved ribs? The half of the span is 100 and its square is 10,000; this, multiplied by 30, gives 300,000, and 15, multiplied by 3, gives 45; then 300,000, divided by 45, gives 6666⅔, which, multiplied by 0·0011, gives 7·333 feet, or 1056 inches for the area of each rib. Such a rib may be 24 inches thick by 44 inches deep, and composed of 6 pieces, 2 in width and 3 in depth.

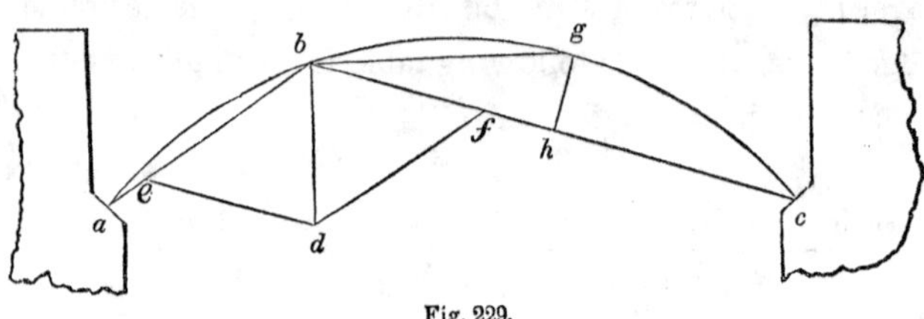

Fig. 229.

316.—The above rule gives the area of a rib, that would be requisite to support the greatest possible *uniform* load. But in large bridges, a *variable* load, such as a heavy wagon, is capable of exerting much greater strains; in such cases, therefore, the rib should be made larger. The greatest concentrated load a bridge will be likely to encounter, may be estimated at from about 20 to 50 thousand pounds, according to the size of the bridge. This is capable of exerting the greatest strain, when placed at about one-third of the span from one of the abutments, as at *b*, (*Fig.* 229.) The weakest point of the segment, *b g c*, is at *g*, the most distant point from the chord line. The pressure exerted at *b* by the above weight, may be considered to be in the direction of the chord lines, *b a* and *b c*; then, by constructing the parallelogram of forces, *e b f d*, according to *Art.* 248, *b f* will show the pressure in the direction, *b c*. Then the scantling for the rib may be found by the following rule.

Rule.—Multiply the pressure in pounds in the direction, *b c*, by the decimal, 0·0016, for white pine, 0·0021 for pitch pine, and 0·0015 for oak, and the product by the decimal representing the sine of the angle, *g b h*, to a radius of unity. Divide this product by the united breadth in inches of the several ribs, and the cube-root of the quotient, multiplied by the distance, *b c*, in feet, will give the depth of the rib. *Example.*—In a bridge of 200 feet span, 15 feet rise, having 3 ribs each 24 inches thick, or 72 inches whole thickness, the pressure in the direction, *b c*, is found to be 166,000 lbs., and the sine of the angle, *g b h*, is 0·1—what should be the depth of the rib for white pine? 166,000, multiplied by 0·0016, gives 265·6, which, multiplied by 0·1, gives 26·56; this, divided by 72, gives 0·3689. The cube-root of the last sum is 0·717 nearly, and the distance, *b c*, is 135 feet: then, 0·717, multiplied by 135, gives 96¾ inches, the depth required. By this, each rib will require to be 24×97 inches, in order to encounter without injury the greatest possible load.

317.—In constructing these ribs, if the span be not over 50 feet, each rib may be made in two or three thicknesses of timber, (three thicknesses is preferable,) of convenient lengths bolted together; but, in larger spans, where the rib will be such as to render it difficult to procure timber of sufficient breadth, they may be constructed by bending the pieces to the proper curve, and bolting them together. In this case, where timber of sufficient length to span the opening cannot be obtained, and scarfing is necessary, such joints must be made as will resist both tension and compression, (see *Fig.* 238.) To ascertain the greatest depth for the pieces which compose the rib, so that the process of bending may not injure their elasticity, multiply the radius of curvature in feet by the decimal, 0·05, and the product will be the depth in inches. *Example.*—Suppose the curve of the rib to be described with a radius of 100 feet, then what should be the depth? The radius in feet, 100, multiplied by 0·05, gives a product of 5 inches. White pine or oak timber, 5 inches thick, would freely bend to the above curve; and, if the required depth of such a rib be 20 inches, it would have to be composed of at least 4 pieces. Pitch pine is not quite so elastic as white pine or oak—its thickness may be found by using the decimal, 0·046, instead of 0·05.

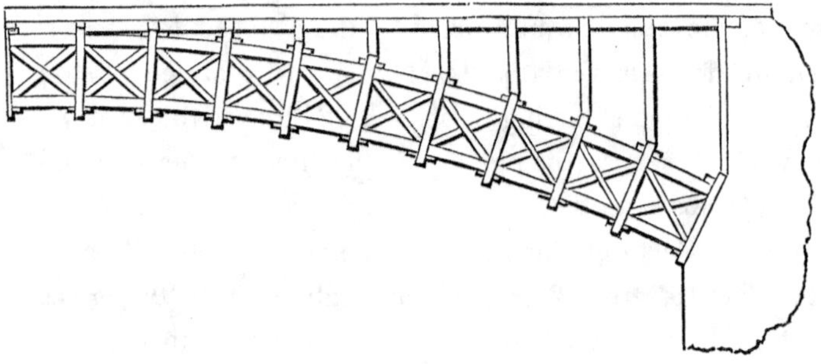

Fig. 230.

318.—When the span is over 250 feet, a *framed* rib, formed as in *Fig.* 230, would be preferable to the foregoing. Of this, the upper and the lower edges are formed as just described, by bending the timber to the proper curve. The pieces that tend to the centre of the curve, called *radials*, are notched and bolted on in pairs, and the cross-braces are halved together in the middle, and abut end to end between the radials. The distance between the ribs of a bridge should not exceed about 8 feet. The roadway should be supported by vertical standards bolted to the ribs at about every 10 to 15 feet. At the place where they rest on the ribs, a double, horizontal tie should be notched and bolted on the back of the ribs, and also another on the under side; and diagonal braces should be framed between the standards, over the space between the ribs, to prevent lateral motion. The timbers for the roadway may be as light as their situation will admit, as all useless timber is only an unnecessary load upon the arch.

319.—It is found that if a roadway be 18 feet wide, two carriages can pass one another without inconvenience. Its width, therefore, should be either 9, 18, 27 or 36 feet, according to the amount of travel. The width of the foot-path should be 2 feet for every person. When a stream of water has a rapid current, as few piers as practicable should be allowed to obstruct its course; otherwise the bridge will be liable to be swept away by freshets. When the span is not over 300 feet, and the banks of the river are of sufficient height to admit of it, only one arch should be employed. The rise of the arch is limited by the form of the roadway, and by the height of the banks of the river (See *Art.* 315.) The rise of the roadway should not exceed one in 24 feet, but, as the framing settles about one in 72, the roadway should be framed to rise one in 18, that it may be one in 24 after settling. The commencement of the arch at the abutments—the *spring*, as it is termed, should not be below high-water mark: and the bridge should be placed at right angles with the course of the current.

320.—The best material for the abutments and piers of a bridge, is stone; and, if possible, stone should be procured for the purpose. The following rule is to determine the extent of the abutments, they being rectangular, and built with stone weighing 120 lbs. to a cubic-foot. *Rule.*—Multiply the square of the height of the abutment by 160, and divide this product by the weight of a square foot of the arch, and by the rise of the arch; add unity to the quotient, and extract the square-root. Diminish the square-root by unity, and multiply the root, so diminished, by half the span of the arch, and by the weight of a square-foot of the arch. Divide the last product by 120 times the height of the abutment, and the quotient will be the thickness of the abutment. *Example.*—Let the height of the abutment from the base to the springing of the arch be 20 feet, half the span 100 feet, the weight of a square foot of the arch, including the greatest possible load upon it, 300 pounds, and the rise of the arch 18 feet—what should be its thickness? The square of the height of the abutment, 400, multiplied by 160, gives 64,000, and 300 by 18, gives 5400; 64,000, divided by 5400, gives a quotient of 11·852, one added to this makes 12·852, the square-root of which is 3·6; this, less one, is 2·6; this, multiplied by 100, gives 260, and this again by 300, gives 78,000; this, divided by 120 times the height of the abutment, 2400, gives 32 feet 6 inches, the thickness required.

The dimensions of a pier will be found by the same rule. For, although the thrust of an arch may be balanced by an adjoining arch, when the bridge is finished, and while it remains uninjured; yet, during the erection, and in the event of one arch being destroyed, the pier should be capable of sustaining the entire thrust of the other.

321.—Piers are sometimes constructed of timber, their principal strength depending on piles driven into the earth, but such piers should never be adopted where it is possible to avoid them; for, being alternately wet and dry, they decay much sooner than the upper parts of the bridge. Spruce and elm are considered good for piles. Where the height from the bottom of the river to the roadway is great, it is a good plan to cut them off at a little below low-water mark, cap them with a horizontal tie, and upon this erect the posts for the support of the roadway. This method cuts off the part that is continually wet from that which is only occasionally so, and thus affords an opportunity for replacing the upper part. The pieces which are immersed will last a great length of time, especially when of elm; for it is a well-established fact, that timber is less durable when subject to alternate dryness and moisture, than when it is either continually wet or continually dry. It has been ascertained that the piles under London bridge, after having been driven about 600 years, were not materially decayed. These piles are chiefly of elm, and vholly immersed.

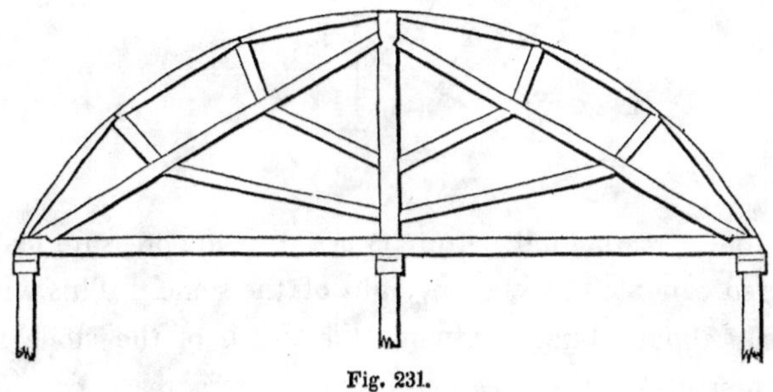

Fig. 231.

322.—*Centres for stone bridges.* *Fig.* 231 is a design for a centre for a stone bridge where intermediate supports, as piles driven into the bed of the river, are practicable. Its timbers are so distributed as to sustain the weight of the arch-stones as they are being laid, without destroying the original form of the centre; and also to prevent its destruction or settlement, should any of the piles be swept away. The most usual error in badly-constructed centres is, that the timbers are disposed so as to cause the framing to rise at the crown, during the laying of the arch-stones up the sides. To remedy this evil, some have loaded the crown with heavy stones; but a centre properly constructed will need no such precaution.

Experiments have shown that an arch-stone does not press upon the centring, until its bed is inclined to the horizon at an angle of from 30 to 45 degrees, according to the hardness of the stone, and whether it is laid in mortar or not. For general purposes, the point at which the pressure commences, may be considered to be at that joint which forms an angle of 32 degrees with the horizon. At this point, the pressure is inconsiderable, but gradually increases towards the crown. At an angle of 45 degrees, the pressure equals about one-quarter the weight of the stone; at 57 degrees, half the weight; and when a vertical line, as *a b*, (*Fig.* 232,) passing through the centre of gravity of

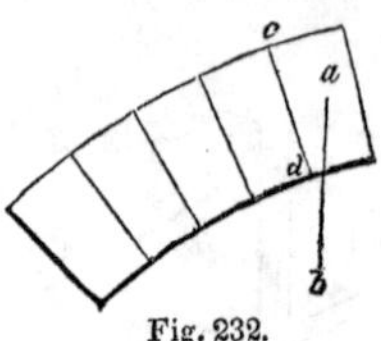

Fig. 232.

the arch-stone, does not fall within its bed, *c d*, the pressure may be considered equal to the whole weight of the stone. This will be the case at about 60 degrees, when the depth of the stone is double its breadth. The direction of these pressures is considered in a line with the radius of the curve. The weight upon a centre being known, the pressure may be estimated and the timber calculated accordingly. But it must be remembered that the whole weight is never placed upon the framing at once—as seems to have been the idea had in view by the designers of some centres. In building the arch, it should be commenced at each buttress at the same time, (as is generally the case,) and each side should progress equally towards the crown. In designing the framing, the effect produced by each successive layer of stone should be considered. The pressure of the stones upon one side should, by the arrangement of the struts, be counterpoised by that of the stones upon the other side.

323.—Over a river whose stream is rapid, or where it is necessary to preserve an uninterrupted passage for the purposes of navigation, the centre must be constructed without intermediate supports, and without a continued horizontal tie at the base; such a centre is shown at *Fig.* 233. In laying the stones from the base up to *a* and *c*, the pieces, *b d* and *b d*, act as ties to prevent any rising at *b*. After this, while the stones are being laid from *a* and from *c* to *b*, they act as struts: the piece, *f g*, is added for

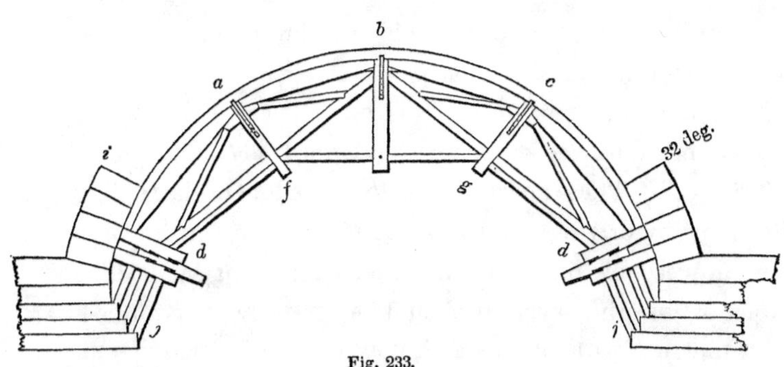

Fig. 233.

additional security. Upon this plan, with some variation to suit circumstances, centres may be constructed for any span usual in stone-bridge building.

324.—In bridge centres, the principal timbers should abut, and not be intercepted by a suspension or radial piece between. These should be in halves, notched on each side and bolted. The timbers should intersect as little as possible, for the more joints the greater is the settling; and halving them together is a bad practice, as it destroys nearly one-half the strength of the timber. Ties should be introduced across, especially where many timbers meet; and as the centre is to serve but a temporary purpose, the whole should be designed with a view to employ the timber afterwards for other uses. For this reason, all unnecessary cutting should be avoided.

325.—Centres should be sufficiently strong to preserve a staunch and steady form during the whole process of building; for any shaking or trembling will have a tendency to prevent the mortar or cement from *setting*. For this purpose, also, the centre should be lowered a trifle immediately after the key-stone is laid, in order that the stones may take their bearing before the mortar is set; otherwise the joints will open on the under side. The trusses, in centring, are placed at the distance of from 4 to 6 feet apart, according to their strength and the weight of the arch. Between every two trusses, diagonal braces should be introduced to prevent lateral motion.

326.—In order that the centre may be easily lowered, the frames, or trusses, should be placed upon wedge-formed sills; as is shown at *d*, (*Fig.* 233.) These are contrived so as to admit of the settling of the frame by driving the wedge, *d*, with a maul, or, in large centres, a piece of timber mounted as a battering-ram. The operation of lowering a centre should be very slowly performed, in order that the parts of the arch may take their bearing uniformly. The wedge pieces, instead of being placed parallel with the truss, are sometimes made sufficiently long and laid through the arch, in a direction at right angles to that shown at *Fig.* 233. This method obviates the necessity of stationing men beneath the arch during the process of lowering; and was originally adopted with success soon after the occurrence of an accident, in lowering a centre, by which nine men were killed.

327.—To give some idea of the manner of estimating the pressures, in order to select timber of the proper scantling, calculate the pressure of the arch-stones from *i* to *b*, (*Fig.* 233,) and suppose half this pressure concentrated at *a*, and acting in the direction, *a f*. Then, by reference to the laws of pressure and the resistance of timber at *Art.* 248, 260, &c., the scantlings of the several pieces composing the frame, *b d a*, may be computed. Again, calculate the pressure of that portion of the arch included between *a* and *c*, and consider half of it collected at *b*, and acting in a vertical direction; then the amount of pressure on the beams, *b d* and *b d*, may be found by reference to the first part of this section, as above. Add the pressure of that portion of the arch which is included between *i* and *b* to half the weight of the centre, and consider this amount concentrated at *d*, and acting in a vertical direction; then, by constructing the parallelogram of forces, the pressure upon *d j* may be ascertained.

328.—As a short rule for calculating the scantlings of the timbers, let every strut be sufficiently braced, so that it will yield to crushing before it will bend under the pressure—(*Art.* 261.) Then divide the pressure in pounds by 1000, and the quotient will be the area of the strut in inches. For example, let the pressure upon a strut, in the direction of its axis, be 60,000 lbs. This, divided by 1000, gives 60, the area of the strut in inches; the size of the strut, therefore, might be 6×10. This rule is based upon experiments by which it has been ascertained, that 1000 pounds is the greatest load that can be trusted upon a square inch of timber, without more indentation than would be compatible with the stability of the framing. The area ascertained by the rule, therefore, must have reference to the actual amount of surface upon which the load bears; and should the strut have a tenon on the end, the area of the shoulders, instead of a section of the whole piece, must be equal to the amount given by the rule.

329.—In the construction of arches, the *voussoirs*, or arch-stones, are so shaped that the joints between them are perpendicular to the curve of the arch, or to its tangent at the point at which the joint intersects the curve. In a circular arch, the joints tend toward the centre of the circle: in an elliptical arch, the joints may be found by the following process:

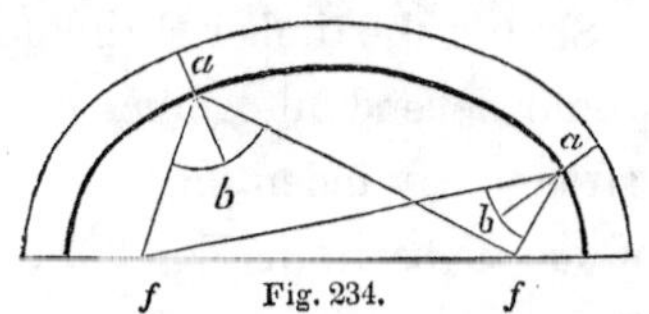

Fig. 234.

330.—*To find the direction of the joints for an elliptical arch.* A joint being wanted at *a*, (*Fig.* 234,) draw lines from that point to the foci, *f* and *f*; bisect the angle, *f a f*, with the line, *a b*; then *a b* will be the direction of the joint.

331.—*To find the direction of the joints for a parabolic arch.* A joint being wanted at *a*, (*Fig.* 235,) draw *a e*, at right angles to the axis, *e g*; make *c g* equal to *c e*, and join *a* and *g*; draw *a h*, at right angles to *a g*; then *a h* will be the direction of the joint

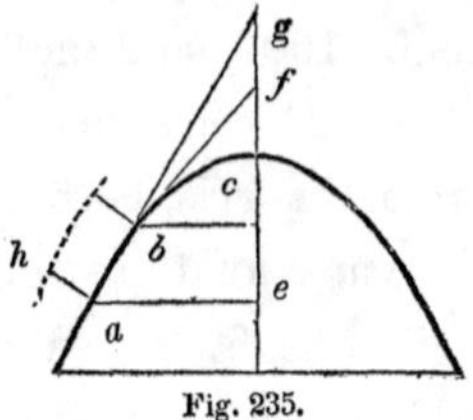

Fig. 235.

The direction of the joint from *b* is found in the same manner. The lines, *a g* and *b f*, are tangents to the curve at those points respectively; and any number of joints in the curve may be obtained, by first ascertaining the tangents, and then drawing lines at right angles to them.

JOINTS.

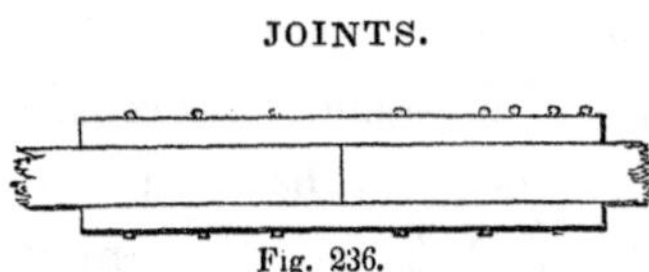
Fig. 236.

332.—*Fig.* 236 shows a simple and quite strong method of lengthening a tie-beam; but the strength consists wholly in the bolts, and in the friction of the parts produced by screwing the pieces firmly together. Should the timber shrink to even a small degree, the strength would depend altogether on the bolts. It would be made much stronger by indenting the pieces together; as at the upper edge of the tie-beam in *Fig.* 237; or by placing

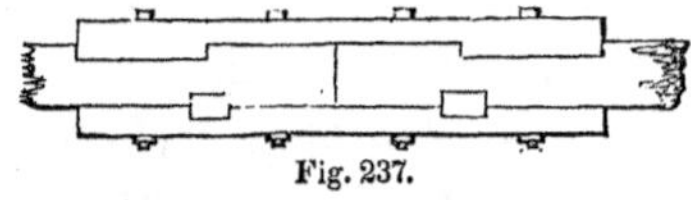
Fig. 237.

keys in the joints, as at the lower edge in the same figure. This process, however, weakens the beam in proportion to the depth of the indents.

333.—*Fig.* 238 shows a method of scarfing, or splicing, a tie-beam without bolts. The keys are to be of well-seasoned, hard

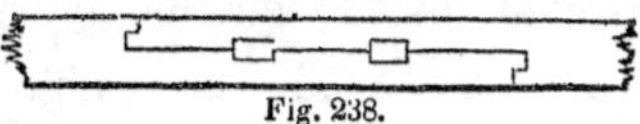
Fig. 238.

wood, and, if possible, very cross-grained. The addition of bolts would make this a very strong splice, or even white-oak pins would add materially to its strength.

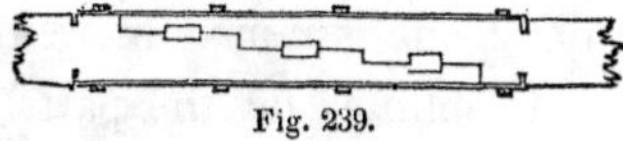
Fig. 239.

334.—*Fig.* 239 shows about as strong a splice, perhaps, as can well be made. It is to be recommended for its simplicity; as, on account of their being no oblique joints in it, it can be readily and accurately executed. A complicated joint is the worst that can be adopted; still, some have proposed joints that seem to have little else besides complication to recommend them.

335.—In proportioning the parts of these scarfs, the depths of all the indents taken together should be equal to one-third of the depth of the beam. In oak, ash or elm, the whole length of the scarf should be six times the depth, or thickness, of the beam, when there are no bolts; but, if bolts instead of indents are used, then three times the breadth; and, when both methods are combined, twice the depth of the beam. The length of the scarf in pine and similar soft woods, depending wholly on indents, should be about 12 times the thickness, or depth, of the beam; when depending wholly on bolts, 6 times the breadth; and, when both methods are combined, 4 times the depth.

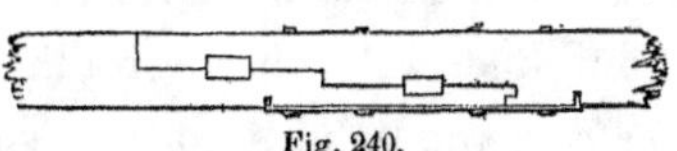
Fig. 240.

336.—Sometimes beams have to be pieced that are required to resist cross strains—such as a girder, or the tie-beam of a roof when supporting the ceiling. In such beams, the fibres of the wood in the upper part are compressed; and therefore a simple butt joint at that place, (as in *Fig*. 240,) is far preferable to any other. In such case, an oblique joint is the very worst. The under side of the beam being in a state of tension, it must be indented or bolted, or both; and an iron plate under the heads of the bolts, gives a great addition of strength.

Scarfing requires accuracy and care, as all the indents should bear equally; otherwise, one being strained more than another, there would be a tendency to splinter off the parts. Hence the simplest form that will attain the object, is by far the best. In all beams that are compressed endwise, abutting joints, formed at right angles to the direction of their length, are at once the simplest and the best. For a temporary purpose, *Fig*. 236 would do very well; it would be improved, however, by having a piece bolted on all four sides. *Fig*. 237, and indeed each of the others, since they have no oblique joints, would resist compression well.

337.—In framing one beam into another for bearing purposes, such as a floor-beam into a trimmer, the best place to make the mortice in the trimmer, is in the neutral line, (see *Art*. 254,) which is in the middle of its depth. Some have thought that, as the fibres of the upper edge are compressed, a mortice might be made there, and the tenon be driven in tight enough to make the parts as capable of resisting the compression, as they would be without it; and they have therefore concluded that plan to be the best. This could not be the case, even if the tenon would not shrink; for a joint between two pieces cannot possibly be made to resist compression, so well as a solid piece without joints. The proper place, therefore, for the mortice, is at the middle of the depth of the beam; but the best place for the tenon, in the floor-beam, is at its bottom edge. For the nearer this is placed to the upper edge, the greater is the liability for it to splinter off; if the joint is formed, therefore, as at *Fig*. 241, it will combine all the advantages that can be obtained. Double tenons are objectionable, because the piece framed into is needlessly weakened,

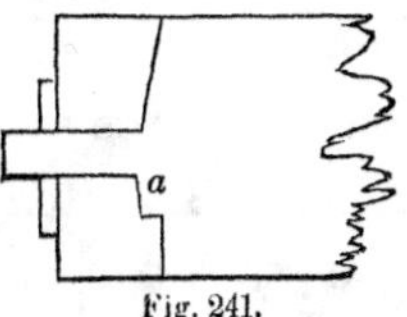

Fig. 241.

and the tenons are seldom so accurately made as to bear equally. For this reason, unless the tusk at *a* in the figure fits exactly, so as to bear equally with the tenon, it had better be omitted. And in sawing the shoulders, care should be taken not to saw into the tenon in the least, as it would wound the beam in the place least able to bear it.

338.—Thus it will be seen that framing weakens both pieces, more or less. It should, therefore, be avoided as much as possible; and where it is practicable one piece should rest *upon* the other, rather than be framed into it. This remark applies to the bridging-joists in a framed floor, to the purlins and jack-rafters of a roof, &c.

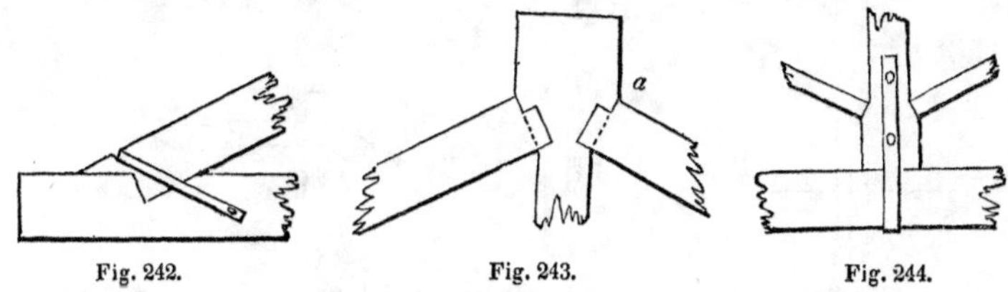

Fig. 242. Fig. 243. Fig. 244.

339.—In a framed truss for a roof, bridge, partition, &c., the joints should be so constructed as to direct the pressures through the axes of the several pieces, and also to avoid every tendency of the parts to slide. To attain this object, the abutting surface on the end of a strut should be at right angles to the direction of the pressure; as at the joint shown in *Fig*. 242 for the foot of a rafter, (see *Art*. 257,) in *Fig*. 243 for the head of a rafter, and in *Fig*. 244 for the foot of a strut or brace. The joint at *Fig*. 242 is not cut completely across the tie-beam, but a narrow lip is left standing in the middle, and a corresponding indent is made in the rafter, to prevent the parts from separating sideways. The abutting surface should be made as large as the attainment of other necessary objects will admit. The iron strap is added to prevent the rafter from sliding out, should the end of the tie-beam, by decay or otherwise, splinter off. In making the joint shown at *Fig*. 243, it should be left a little open at *a*, so as to bring the parts to a fair bearing at the settling of the truss, which must necessarily take place from the shrinking of the king-post and other parts. If the joint is made fair at first, when the truss settles it will cause it to open at the under side of the rafter, thus throwing the whole pressure upon the sharp edge at *a*. This will cause an indentation in the king-post, by which the truss will be made to settle further; and this pressure not being in the axis of the rafter, it will be greatly increased, thereby rendering the rafter liable to split and break.

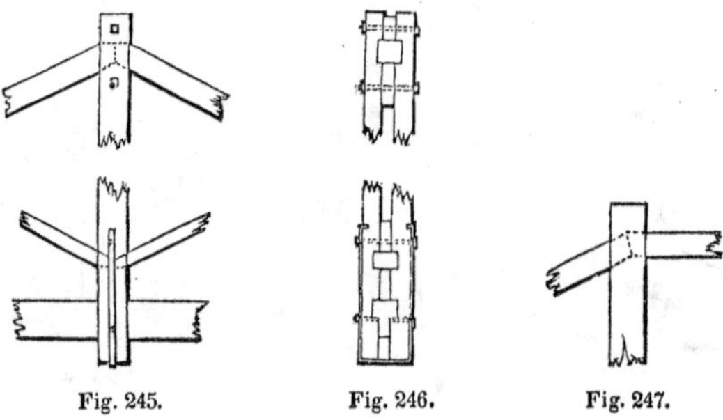

Fig. 245. Fig. 246. Fig. 247.

340.—If the rafters and struts were made to abut end to end, as in *Fig*. 245, 246 and 247, and the king or queen post notched on in halves and bolted, the ill effects of shrinking would be avoided. This method has been practised with success, in some of the most celebrated bridges and roofs in Europe; and, were its use adopted in this country, the unseemly sight of a *hogged* ridge would seldom be met with. A plate of cast iron between the abutting surfaces, will equalize the pressure.

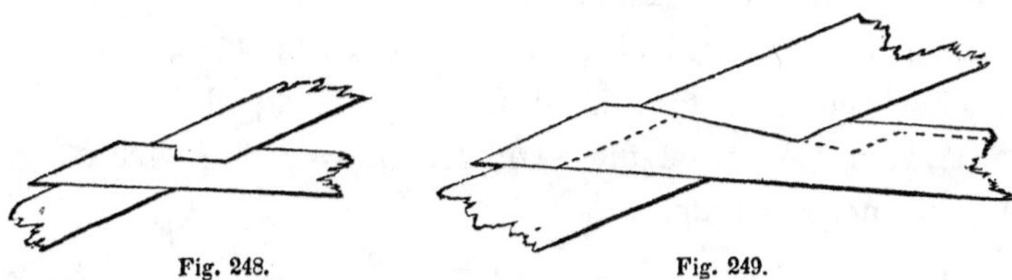

Fig. 248. Fig. 249.

341.—*Fig.* 248 is a proper joint for a collar-beam in a small roof: the principle shown here should characterize all tie-joints. The dovetail joint, although extensively practised in the above and similar cases, is the very worst that can be employed. The shrinking of the timber, if only to a small degree, permits the tie to withdraw—as is shown at *Fig.* 249. The dotted line shows the position of the tie after it has shrunk.

342.—Locust and white-oak pins are great additions to the strength of a joint. In many cases, they would supply the place of iron bolts; and, on account of their small cost, they should be used in preference wherever the strength of iron is not requisite. In small framing, good cut nails are of great service at the joints; but they should not be trusted to bear any considerable pressure, as they are apt to be brittle. Iron straps are seldom necessary, as all the joinings in carpentry may be made without them. They can be used to advantage, however, at the foot of suspending-pieces, and for the rafter at the end of the tie-beam. In roofs for ordinary purposes, the iron straps for suspending-pieces may be as follows: When the longest unsupported part of the tie-beam is

10 feet, the strap may be	1	inch wide by	$\frac{3}{16}$	thick.
15 " "	$1\frac{1}{2}$	"	$\frac{1}{4}$	"
20 " "	2	"	$\frac{1}{4}$	"

In fastening a strap, its hold on the suspending-piece will be much increased, by turning its ends into the wood. Iron straps should be protected from rust; for thin plates of iron decay very soon especially when exposed to dampness. For this purpose, as soon as the strap is made, let it be heated to about a blue heat, and, while it is hot, pour over its entire surface raw linseed oil, or rub it with beeswax. Either of these will give it a coating which dampness will not penetrate.

SECTION V.—DOORS, WINDOWS, &c.

DOORS.

343.—Among the several architectural arrangements of an edifice, the door is by no means the least in importance; and, if properly constructed, it is not only an article of use, but also of ornament, adding materially to the regularity and elegance of the apartments. The dimensions and style of finish of a door, should be in accordance with the size and style of the building, or the apartment for which it is designed. As regards the utility of doors, the principal door to a public building should be of sufficient width to admit of a free passage for a crowd of people; while that of a private apartment will be wide enough, if it permit one person to pass without being incommoded. Experience has determined that the least width allowable for this is 2 feet 8 inches; although doors leading to inferior and unimportant rooms may, if circumstances require it, be as narrow as 2 feet 6 inches; and doors for closets, where an entrance is seldom required, may be but 2 feet wide. The width of the principal door to a public building may be from 6 to 12 feet, according to the size of the building; and the width of doors for a dwelling may be from 2 feet 8 inches, to 3 feet 6 inches. If the importance of an apartment in a dwelling be such as to require a door of greater width than 3 feet 6 inches, the opening should be closed with two doors, or a door in two folds; generally, in such cases, where the opening is from 5 to 8 feet, folding or sliding doors are adopted. As to the height of a door, it should in no case be less than about 6 feet 3 inches; and generally not less than 6 feet 8 inches.

344.—The proportion between the width and height of single doors, for a dwelling, should be as 2 is to 5; and, for entrance-doors to public buildings, as 1 is to 2. If the width is given and the height required of a door for a dwelling, multiply the width by 5, and divide the product by 2; but, if the height is given and the width required, divide by 5, and multiply by 2. Where two or more doors of different widths show in the same room, it is well to proportion the dimensions of the more important by the above rule, and make the narrower doors of the same height as the wider ones; as all the doors in a suit of apartments, except the folding or sliding doors, have the best appearance when of one height. The proportions for folding or sliding doors should be such that the width may be equal to $\frac{4}{5}$ of the height; yet this rule needs some qualification: for, if the width of the opening be greater than one-half the width of the room, there will not be a sufficient space left for opening the doors; also, the height should be about one-tenth greater than that of the adjacent single doors.

345.—Where doors have but two panels in width, let the stiles and muntins be each $\frac{1}{7}$ of the width; or, whatever number of panels there may be, let the united widths of the stiles and the muntins, or the whole width of the solid, be equal to $\frac{3}{7}$ of the width of the door. Thus: in a door, 35 inches wide, containing two panels in width, the stiles should be 5 inches wide; and in a door, 3 feet 6 inches wide, the stiles should be 6 inches. If a door, 3 feet 6 inches wide, is to have 3 panels in width, the stiles and muntins should be each $4\frac{1}{2}$ inches wide, each panel being 8 inches. The bottom rail and the lock rail ought to be each equal in width to $\frac{1}{10}$ of the height of the door; and the top rail, and all others, of the same width as the stiles. The moulding on the panel should be equal in width to ¼ of the width of the stile.

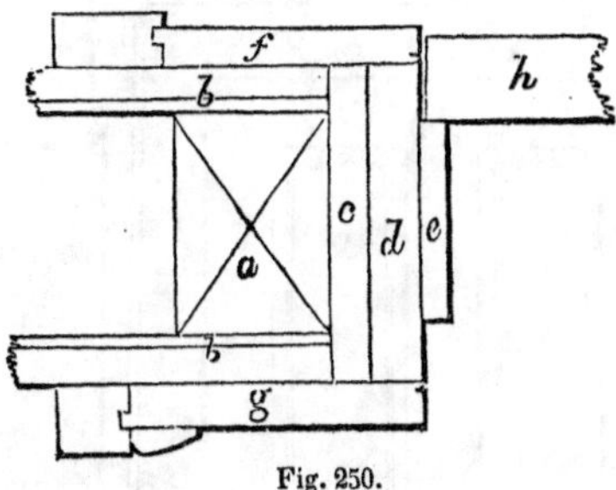

Fig. 250.

346.—*Fig*. 250 shows an approved method of trimming doors: *a* is the door stud; *b*, the lath and plaster; *c*, the *ground*; *d*, the jamb; *e*, the *stop*; *f* and *g*, architrave casings; and *h*, the door stile. It is customary in ordinary work to form the stop for the door by *rebating* the jamb. But, when the door is thick and heavy, a better plan is to nail on a piece as at *e* in the figure. This piece can be fitted to the door, and put on after the door is hung; so, should the door be a trifle *winding*, this will correct the evil, and the door be made to shut solid.

347.—*Fig*. 251 is an elevation of a door and trimmings suitable for the best rooms of a dwelling. (For trimmings generally, see Sect. III.) The number of panels into which a door should be divided, is adjusted at pleasure; yet the present style of finishing requires, that the number be as small as a proper regard for strength will admit. In some of our best dwellings, doors have been made having only two upright panels. A few years experience, however, has proved that the omission of the lock rail is at the expense of the strength and durability of the door; a four-panel door, therefore, is the best that can be made.

348.—The doors of a dwelling should all be hung so as to open into the principal rooms; and, in general, no door should be hung to open into the hall, or passage. As to the proper edge of the door on which to affix the hinges, no general rule can be assigned.

Fig. 251.

It may be observed, however, that a bed-room door should be hung so that, when half open, it will screen the bed; and a door leading from a hall, or passage, to a principal room, should screen the fire.

WINDOWS.

349.—A window should be of such dimensions, and in such a position, as to admit a sufficiency of light to that part of the apartment for which it is designed. No definite rule for the size can well be given, that will answer in all cases; yet, as an approximation, the following has been used for general purposes. Multiply together the length and the breadth in feet of the apartment to be lighted, and the product by the height in feet; then the square-root of this product will show the required number of square feet of glass.

350.—To ascertain the dimensions of window frames, add 4½ inches to the width of the glass for their width, and 6½ inches to the height of the glass for their height. These give the dimensions, in the clear, of ordinary frames for 12-light windows; the height being taken at the inside edge of the sill. In a brick wall, the width of the opening is 8 inches more than the width of the glass—4½ for the stiles of the sash, and 3½ for hanging stiles—and the height between the stone sill and lintel is about 10½ inches more than the height of the glass, it being varied according to the thickness of the sill of the frame.

351.—In hanging inside shutters to fold into *boxes*, it is necessary to have the box shutter about one inch wider than the flap, in order that the flap may not interfere when both are folded into the box. The usual margin shown between the face of the shutter when folded into the box and the quirk of the stop bead, or edge of the casing, is half an inch; and, in the usual method of letting the *whole* of the thickness of the butt hinge into the edge of the box shutter, it is necessary to make allowance for the *throw* of the hinge. This may, in general, be estimated at ¼ of an inch at each hinging; which being added to the margin, the entire width of the shutters will be 1½ inches more than the width of the frame in the clear. Then, to ascertain the width of the box shutter, add 1½ inches to the width of the frame in the clear, between the pulley stiles; divide this product by 4, and add half an inch to the quotient; and the last product will be the required width. For example, suppose the window to have 3 lights in width, 11 inches each. Then, 3 times 11 is 33, and 4½ added for the wood of the sash, gives 37½——37½ and 1½ is 39 and 39, divided by 4, gives $9\frac{3}{4}$; to which add half an inch, and the result will be $10\frac{1}{4}$ inches, the width required for the box shutter.

352.—In disposing and proportioning windows for the walls of a building, the rules of architectural taste require that they be of different heights in different stories, but of the same width. The windows of the upper stories should all range perpendicularly over those of the first, or principal, story; and they should be disposed so as to exhibit a balance of parts throughout the front of the building. To aid in this, it is always proper to place the front door in the middle of the front of the building; and, where the size of the house will admit of it, this plan should be adopted. (See the latter part of *Art.* 214.) The proportion that the height should bear to the width, may be, in accordance with general usage, as follows:

The height	of	basement windows,		$1\frac{1}{3}$	of the width.
"	"	principal-story	"	$2\frac{1}{8}$	"
"	"	second-story	"	$1\frac{7}{8}$	"
"	"	third-story	"	$1\frac{3}{4}$	"
"	"	fourth-story	"	$1\frac{1}{2}$	"
"	"	attic-story	"	the same as the width.	

But, in determining the height of the windows for the several stories, it is necessary to take into consideration the height of the story in which the window is to be placed. For, in addition to the height from the floor, which is generally required to be from 28 to 30 inches, room is wanted above the head of the window for the window-trimming and the cornice of the room, besides some respectable space which there ought to be between these.

353.—The present style of finish requires the heads of windows in general to be horizontal, or *square-headed;* yet, it is well to be possessed of information for trimming circular-headed windows, as repairs of these are occasionally needed. If the jambs of a door or window be placed at right angles to the face of the wall, the edges of the *soffit*, or surface of the head, would be straight, and its length be found by getting the stretch-out of the circle, (*Art.* 92;) but, when the jambs are placed obliquely to the face of the wall, occasioned by the demand for light in an oblique direction, the form of the soffit will be obtained as in the following article: and, when the face of the wall is circular, as in the succeeding one.

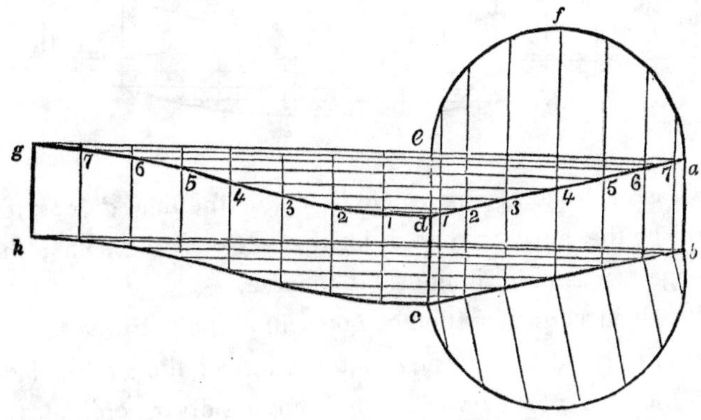

Fig. 252.

354.—*To find the form of the soffit for circular window-heads, when the light is received in an oblique direction.* Let *a b c d*, (*Fig.* 252,) be the ground-plan of a given window, and *e f a*, a vertical section taken at right angles to the face of the jambs. From *a*, through *e*, draw *a g*, at right angles to *a b*; obtain the stretch-out of *e f a*, and make *e g* equal to it; divide *e g* and *e f a*, each into a like number of equal parts, and drop perpendiculars from the points of division in each; from the points of intersection, 1, 2, 3, &c., in the line, *a d*, draw horizontal lines to meet corresponding perpendiculars from *e g*; then those points of intersection will give the curve line, *d g*, which will be the one required for the edge of the soffit. The other edge, *c h*, is found in the same manner.

355.—*To find the form of the soffit for circular window-heads, when the face of the wall is curved.* Let *a b c d*, (*Fig.* 253,) be the ground-plan of a given window, and *e f a*, a vertical section of the head taken at right angles to the face of the jambs.

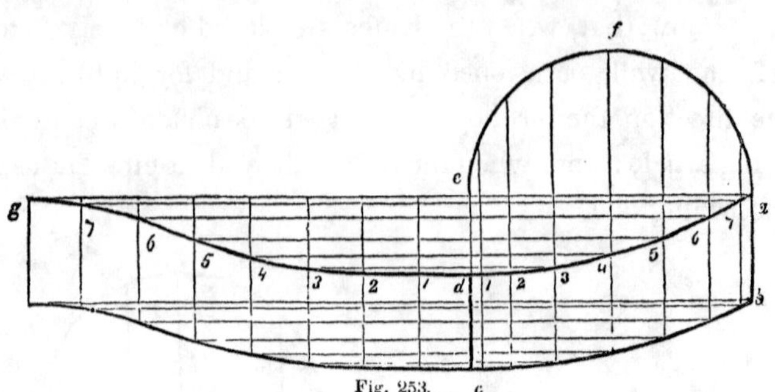

Fig. 253.

Proceed as in the foregoing article to obtain the line, *d g*; then that will be the curve required for the edge of the soffit; the other edge being found in the same manner.

If the given vertical section be taken in a line with the face of the wall, instead of at right angles to the face of the jambs, place it upon the line, *c b*, (*Fig.* 252;) and, having drawn ordinates at right angles to *c b*, transfer them to *e f a*; in this way, a section at right angles to the jambs can be obtained.

SECTION VI.—STAIRS.

356.—The **STAIRS** is that mechanical arrangement in a building by which access is obtained from one story to another. Their position, form and finish, when determined with discriminating taste, add greatly to the comfort and elegance of a structure. As regards their position, the first object should be to have them near the middle of the building, in order that an equally easy access may be obtained from all the rooms and passages. Next in importance is light; to obtain which they would seem to be best situated near an outer wall, in which windows might be constructed for the purpose; yet a sky-light, or opening in the roof, would not only provide light, and so secure a central position for the stairs, but may be made, also, to assist materially as an ornament to the building, and, what is of more importance, afford an opportunity for better ventilation.

357.—It would seem that the length of the raking side of the *pitch-board*, or the distance from the top of one riser to the top of the next, should be about the same in all cases; for, whether stairs be intended for large buildings or for small, for public or for private, the accommodation of men of the same stature is to be consulted in every instance. But it is evident that, with the same effort, a longer step can be taken on level than on rising ground;

and that, although the tread and rise cannot be proportioned merely in accordance with the style and importance of the building, yet this may be done according to the angle at which the flight rises. If it is required to ascend gradually and easy, the length from the top of one rise to that of another, or the hypothenuse of the pitch-board, may be long; but, if the flight is steep, the length must be shorter. Upon this data the following problem is constructed.

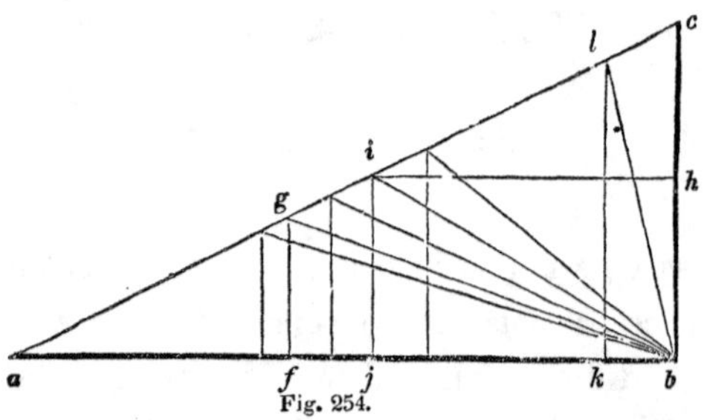

Fig. 254.

358.—*To proportion the rise and tread to one another.* Make the line, *a b*, (*Fig.* 254,) equal to 24 inches; from *b*, erect *b c*, at right angles to *a b*, and make *b c* equal to 12 inches; join *a* and *c*, and the triangle, *a b c*, will form a scale upon which to graduate the sides of the pitch-board. For example, suppose a very easy stairs is required, and the tread is fixed at 14 inches. Place it from *b* to *f*, and from *f*, draw *f g*, at right angles to *a b*; then the length of *f g* will be found to be 5 inches, which is a proper rise for 14 inches tread, and the angle, *f b g*, will show the degree of inclination at which the flight will ascend. But, in a majority of instances, the height of a story is fixed, while the length of tread, or the space that the stairs occupy on the lower floor, is optional. The height of a story being determined, the height of each rise will of course depend upon the number into which the whole height is divided; the angle of ascent being more easy if the number be great, than if it be smaller. By dividing the whole height of a story into a certain number of rises, suppose the length of each is found to be 6 inches. Place this length from *b* to *h*, and draw *h i*, parallel to *a b*; then *h i*, or *b j* will be the proper tread for that rise, and *j b i* will show the angle of ascent. On the other hand, if the angle of ascent be given, as *a b l*, (*b l* being 10½ inches, the proper *length of run* for a step-ladder,) drop the perpendicular, *l k*, from *l* to *k*; then *l k b* will be the proper proportion for the sides of a pitch-board for that *run*.

359.—The angle of ascent will vary according to circumstances. The following treads will determine about the right inclination for the different classes of buildings specified.

In public edifices,	tread about	14	inches.
In first-class dwellings	"	12½	"
In second-class "	"	11	"
In third-class " and cottages	"	9	"

Step-ladders to ascend to scuttles, &c., should have from 10 to 11 inches *run* on the rake of the string. (See notes at *Art.* 103.)

360.—The length of the steps is regulated according to the extent and importance of the building in which they are placed, varying from 3 to 12 feet, and sometimes longer. Where two persons are expected to pass each other conveniently, the shortest length that will admit of it is 3 feet; still, in crowded cities where land is so valuable, the space allowed for passages being very small, they are frequently executed at 2½ feet.

361.—*To find the dimensions of the pitch-board.* The first thing in commencing to build a stairs, is to make the *pitch*-board; this is done in the following manner. Obtain very accurately, in feet and inches, the perpendicular height of the story in which the stairs are to be placed. This must be taken from the top of the floor in the lower story to the top of the floor in the upper story. Then, to obtain the number of rises, the height in inches thus obtained must be divided by 5, 6, 7, 8, or 9, according to the quality and style of the building in which the stairs are to be built. For instance, suppose the building to be a first-class dwelling, and the height ascertained is 13 feet 4 inches, or 160 inches. The proper rise for a stairs in a house of this class is about 6 inches. Then, 160 divided by 6, gives 26⅔ inches. This being nearer 27 than 26, the number of risers, should be 27. Then divide the height, 160 inches, by 27, and the quotient will give the height of one rise. On performing this operation, the quotient will be found to be 5 inches, $\frac{7}{8}$ and $\frac{1}{16}$ of an inch.

Then, if the space for the extension of the stairs is not limited, the tread can be found as at *Art.* 358. But, if the contrary is the case, the whole distance given for the treads must be divided by the number of treads required. On account of the upper floor forming a step for the last riser, the number of treads is always one less than the number of risers. Having obtained this rise and tread, the pitch-board may be made in the following manner. Upon a piece of well-seasoned board about $\frac{5}{8}$ of an inch thick, having one edge jointed straight and square, lay the corner of a carpenters'-square, as shown at *Fig.* 255. Make ***a b***

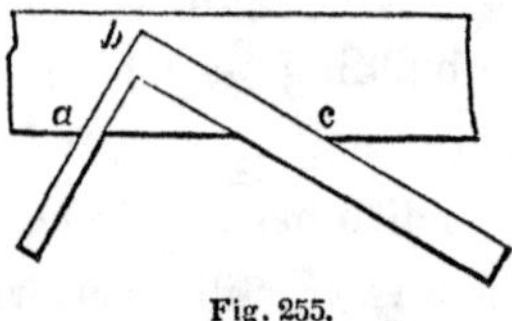

Fig. 255.

equal to the rise, and *b c* equal to the tread; mark along those edges with a knife, and cut it out by the marks, making the edges perfectly square. The grain of the wood must run in the direction indicated in the figure, because, if it shrinks a trifle, the rise and the tread will be equally affected by it. When a pitch-board is first made, the dimensions of the rise and tread should be preserved in figures, in order that, should the first shrink, a second could be made.

362.—*To lay out the string.* The space required for timber

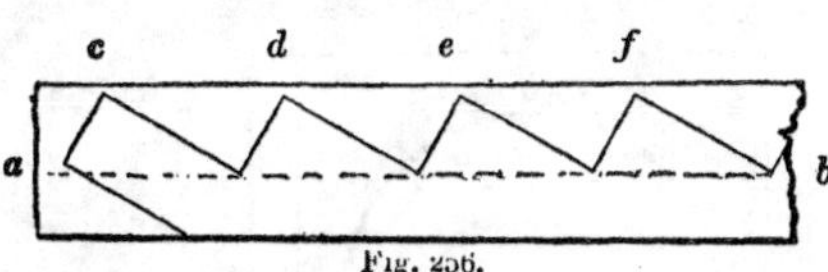

Fig. 256.

and plastering under the steps, is about 5 inches for ordinary stairs; set a gauge, therefore, at 5 inches, and run it on the lower edge of the plank, as *a b*, (*Fig.* 256.) Commencing at one end, lay the longest side of the pitch-board against the gauge-mark, *a b*, as at *c*, and draw by the edges the lines for the first rise and tread; then place it successively as at *d*, *e* and *f*, until the required number of risers shall be laid down.

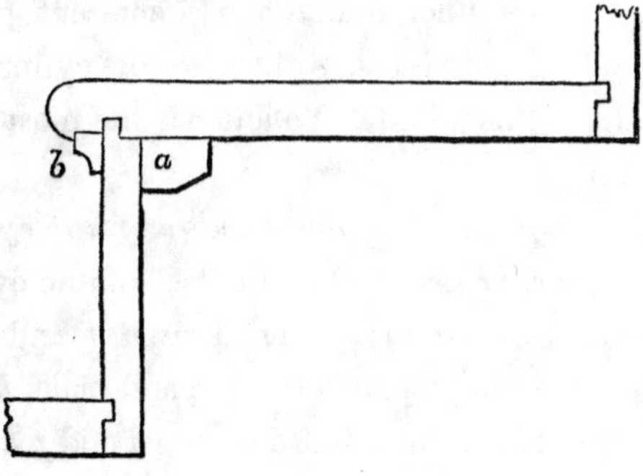

Fig. 257.

363.—*Fig.* 257 represents a section of a step and riser, joined after the most approved method. In this, *a* represents the end of a block about 2 inches long, two of which are glued in the corner in the length of the step. The cove at *b* is planed up square, glued in, and *stuck* after the glue is set.

PLATFORM STAIRS.

364.—A platform stairs ascends from one story to another in two or more flights, having platforms between for resting and to change their direction. This kind of stairs is the most easily constructed, and is therefore the most common. The cylin-

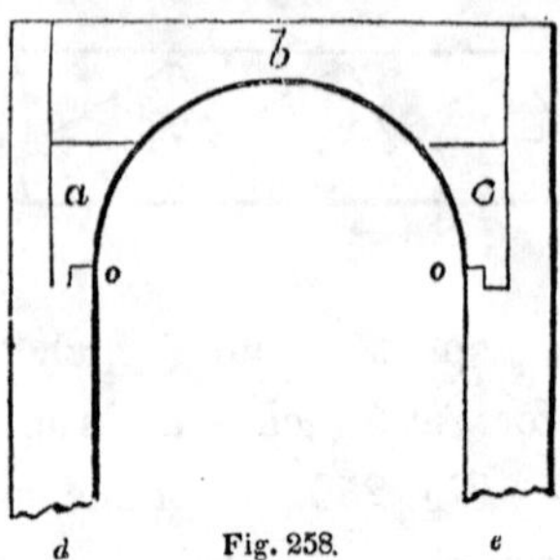

Fig. 258.

der is generally of small diameter, in most cases about 6 inches. It may be worked out of one solid piece, but a better way is to glue together three pieces, as in *Fig.* 258; in which the pieces, *a*, *b* and *c*, compose the cylinder, and *d* and *e* represent parts of the strings. The strings, after being glued to the cylinder, are secured with screws. The joining at *o* and *o* is the most proper for that kind of joint.

365.—*To obtain the form of the lower edge of the cylinder.* Find the stretch-out, *d e*, (*Fig.* 259,) of the face of the cylinder, *a b c*, according to *Art.* 92; from *d* and *e*, draw *d f* and *e g*, at right angles to *d e;* draw *h g*, parallel to *d e*, and make *h f* and *g i*, each equal to one rise; from *i* and *f*, draw *i j* and *f k*, parallel to *h g;* place the tread of the pitch-board at these last lines, and draw by the lower edge the lines, *k h* and *i l;* parallel to these, draw *m n* and *o p*, at the requisite distance for the dimensions of the string; from *s*, the centre of the plan, draw *s q*, parallel to *d f;* divide *h q* and *q g*, each into 2 equal parts, as at *v* and *w;* from *v* and *w*, draw *v n* and *w o*, parallel to *f d;* join *n* and *o*, cutting *q s* in *r;* then the angles, *u n r* and *r o t*, being eased off according to *Art.* 89, will give the proper curve for the bottom edge of the cylinder. A centre may be found upon which to describe these curves thus: from *u*, draw *u x*, at right angles to *m n;* from *r*, draw *r x*, at right angles to *n o;* then *x* will be the centre for the curve, *u r*. The centre for the curve, *r t*, is found in the same manner.

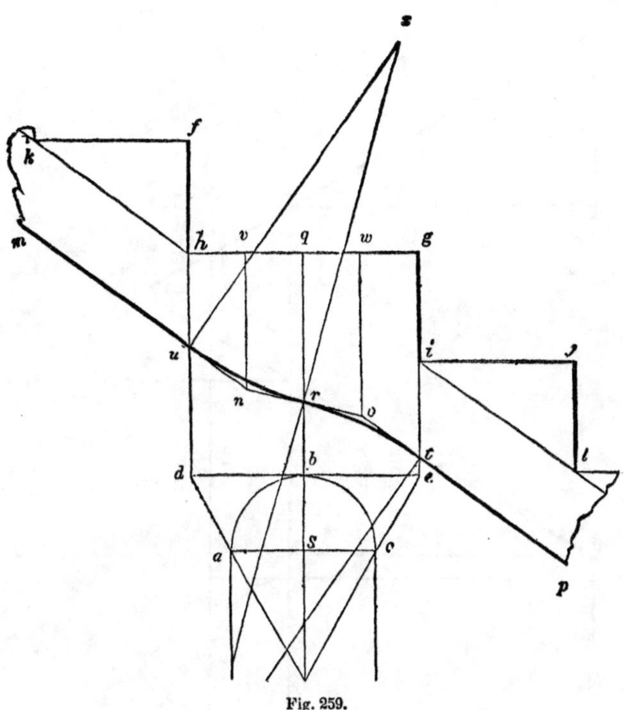

Fig. 259.

366.—*To find the position for the balusters.* Place the centre of the first baluster, (*b. Fig.* 260,) ½ its diameter from the face of the riser, *c d*, and ⅓ its diameter from the end of the step, *e d*; and place the centre of the other baluster, *a*, half the tread from the centre of the first. The centre of the rail must be placed over the centre of the balusters. Their usual length is 2 feet 5 inches, and 2 feet 9 inches, for the short and the long balusters respectively.

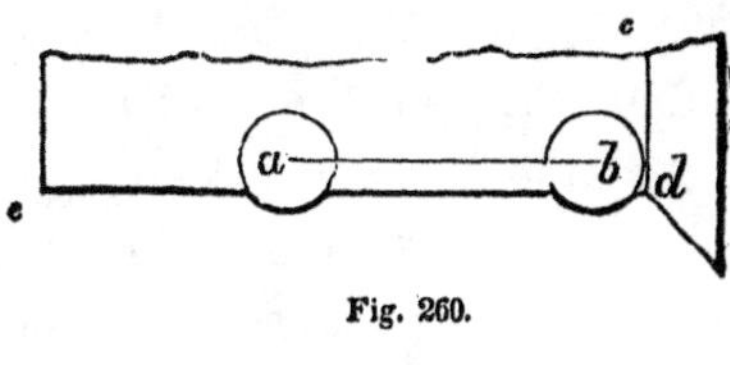

Fig. 260.

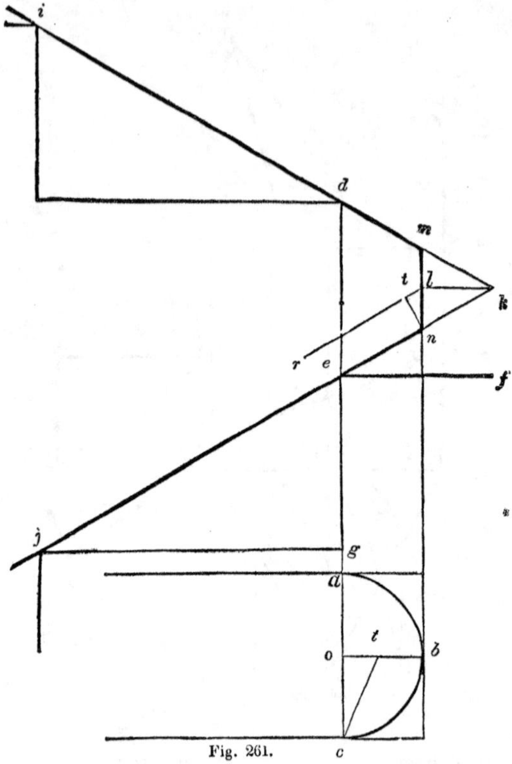

Fig. 261.

367.—*To find the face-mould for a round hand-rail to platform stairs.* CASE 1.—*When the cylinder is small.* In *Fig.* 261, *j* and *e* represent a vertical section of the last two steps of the first flight, and *d* and *i* the first two steps of the second flight, of a platform stairs, the line, *e f*, being the platform; and *a b c* is the plan of a line passing through the centre of the rail around the cylinder. Through *i* and *d*, draw *i k*, and through *j* and *e*, draw *j k*; from *k*, draw *k l*, parallel to *f e*; from *b*, draw *b m*, parallel to *g d*; from *l*, draw *l r*, parallel to *k j*; from *n*, draw *n t*, at right angles to *j k*; on the line, *o b*, make *o t* equal to *n t*; join *c* and *t*: on the line, *j c*, (*Fig.* 262,) make *e c* equal to *e n* at *Fig.* 261; from *c*, draw *c t*, at right angles to *j c*, and make *c t*

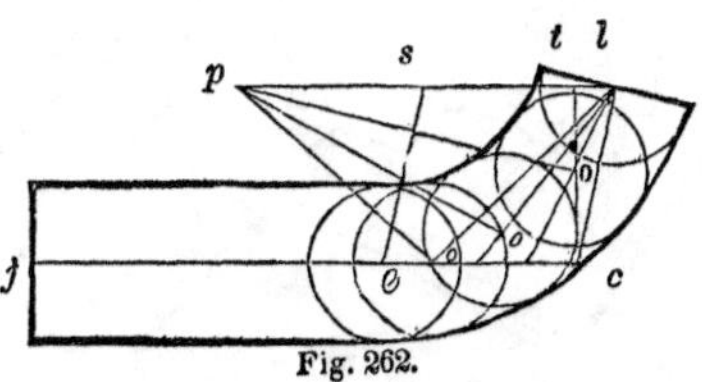

Fig. 262.

equal to *c t* at *Fig*. 261; through *t*, draw *p l*, parallel to *j c*, and make *t l* equal to *t l* at *Fig*. 261; join *l* and *c*, and complete the parallelogram, *e c l s;* find the points, *o*, *o*, *o*, according to *Art*. 118; upon *e*, *o*, *o*, *o*, and *l*, successively, with a radius equal to half the width of the rail, describe the circles shown in the figure; then a curve traced on both sides of these circles and just touching them, will give the proper form for the mould. The joint at *l* is drawn at right angles to *c l*.

368.—*Elucidation of the foregoing method.* This excellent plan for obtaining the face-moulds for the hand-rail of a platform stairs, has never before been published. It was communicated to me by an eminent stair-builder of this city: and having seen rails put up from it, I am enabled to give it my unqualified recommendation. In order to have it fully understood, I have introduced *Fig*. 263; in which the cylinder, for this purpose, is made rectangular instead of circular. The figure gives a perspective view of a part of the upper and of the lower flights, and a part of the platform about the cylinder. The heavy lines, *i m*, *m c* and *c j*, show the direction of the rail, and are supposed to pass through the centre of it. When the rake of the second flight is the same as that of the first, which is here and is generally the case, the face-mould for the lower twist will, when reversed, do for the upper flight: that part of the rail, therefore, which passes from *e* to *c* and from *c* to *l*, is all that will need explanation.

Suppose, then, that the parallelogram, *e a o c*, represent a plane lying perpendicularly over *e a b f*, being inclined in the direction, *e c*, and level in the direction, *c o*; suppose this plane, *e a o c*,

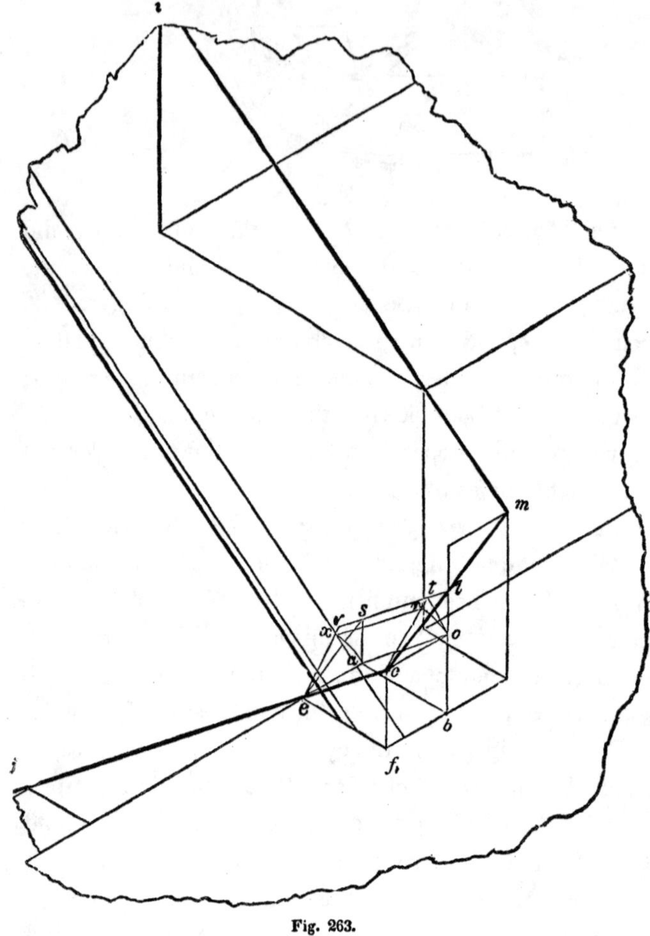

Fig. 263.

be revolved on *e c* as an axis, in the manner indicated by the arcs, *o n* and *a x*, until it coincides with the plane, *e r t c;* the line, *a o*, will then be represented by the line, *x n;* then add the parallelogram, *x r t n*, and the triangle, *c t l*, deducting the triangle, *e r s;* and the edges of the plane, *e s l c*, inclined in the direction, *e c*, and also in the direction, *c l*, will lie perpendicularly over the plane, *e a b f*. From this we gather that the line, *c o*, being at right angles to *e c*, must, in order to reach the point, *l*, be lengthened the distance, *n t*, and the right angle, *e c t*, be made obtuse by the addition to it of the angle, *t c l*. By reference to *Fig*. 261, it will be seen that this lengthening is performed by forming the right-angled triangle, *c o t*, corresponding to the triangle, *c o t*, in *Fig*. 263. The line, *c t*, is then transferred to *Fig*. 262, and placed at right angles to *e c;* this angle, *e c t*, being increased by adding the angle, *t c l*, corresponding to *t c l*, *Fig*. 263, the point, *l*, is reached, and the proper position and length of the lines, *e c* and *c l* obtained. To obtain the face-mould for a rail over a cylindrical well-hole, the same process is necessary to be followed until the the length and position of these lines are found; then, by forming the parallelogram, *e c l s*, and describing a quarter of an ellipse therein, the proper form will be given.

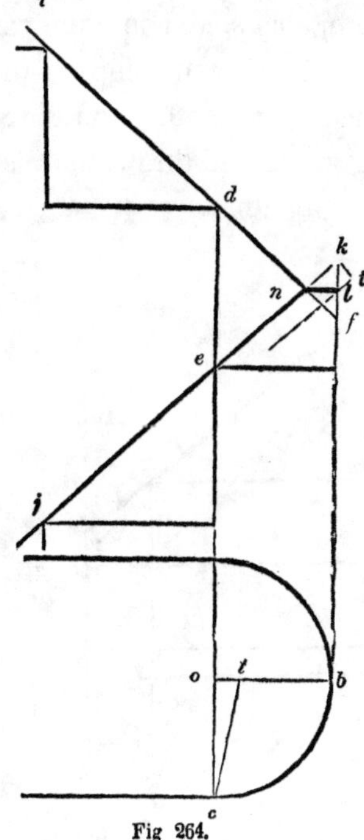

Fig 264.

369.—Case 2.— *When the cylinder is large.* *Fig*. 264 represents a plan and a vertical section of a line passing through the centre of the rail as before. From *b*, draw *b k*, parallel to *c d*; extend the lines, *i d* and *j e*, until they meet *k b* in *k* and *f*; from *n*, draw *n l*, parallel to *o b*; through *l*, draw *l t*, parallel to *j k*; from *k*, draw *k t*, at right angles to *j k*; on the line, *o b*, make *o t* equal to *k t*. Make *e c*, (*Fig.* 265.) equal to *e k* at *Fig.* 264; from *c*,

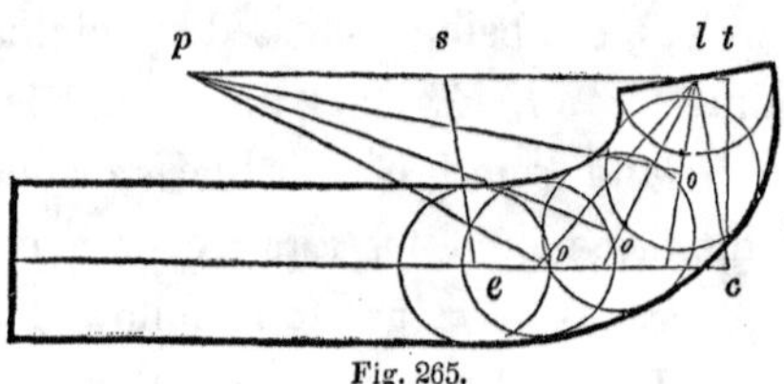

Fig. 265.

draw *c t*, at right angles to *e c*, and equal to *c t* at *Fig.* 264; from *t*, draw *t p*, parallel to *c e*, and make *t l* equal to *t l* at *Fig.* 264; complete the parallelogram, *e c l s*, and find the points, *o*, *o*, *o*, as before; then describe the circles and complete the mould as in *Fig.* 262. The difference between this and Case 1 is, that the line, *c t*, instead of being raised and thrown out, is lowered and drawn in. (See note at page 255.)

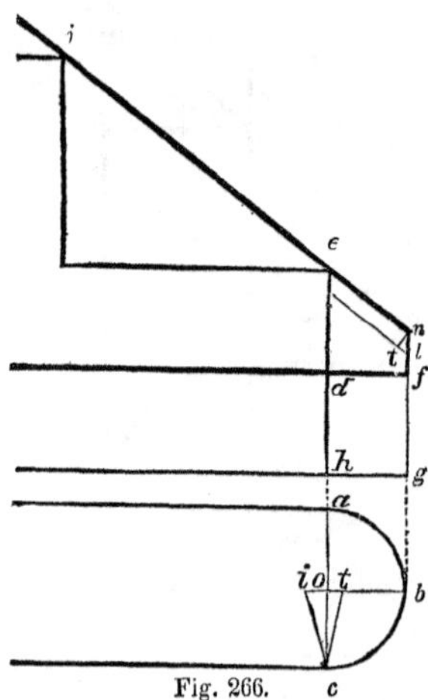

Fig. 266.

370.—Case 3.—*Where the rake meets the level.* In *Fig.*

266, *a b c* is the plan of a line passing through the centre of the rail around the cylinder as before, and *j* and *e* is a vertical section of two steps starting from the floor, *h g*. Bisect *e h* in *d*, and through *d*, draw *d f*, parallel to *h g;* bisect *f n* in *l*, and from *l*, draw *l t*, parallel to *n j;* from *n*, draw *n t*, at right angles to *j n;* on the line, *o b*, make *o t* equal to *n t*. Then, to obtain a mould for the twist going up the flight, proceed as at *Fig.* 262; making *e c* in that figure equal to *e n* in *Fig.* 266, and the other lines of a length and position such as is indicated by the letters of reference in each figure. To obtain the mould for the level rail, extend *b o*, (*Fig.* 266,) to *i;* make *o i* equal to *f l*, and join *i* and *c;* make *c i*, (*Fig.* 267,) equal to *c i* at *Fig.* 266; through *c*, draw *c d*, at

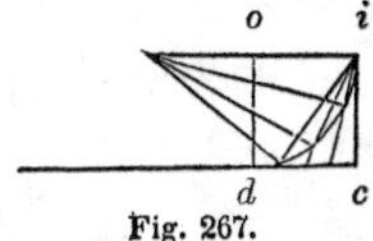

Fig. 267.

right angles to *c i;* make *d c* equal to *d f* at *Fig.* 266, and complete the parallelogram, *o d c i;* then proceed as in the previous cases to find the mould.

371.—All the moulds obtained by the preceding examples have been for round rails. For these, the mould may be applied to a plank of the same thickness as the rail is intended to be, and the plank sawed square through, the joints being cut square from the face of the plank. A twist thus cut and truly rounded will hang in a proper position over the plan, and present a perfect and graceful wreath.

372.—*To bore for the balusters of a round rail before rounding it.* Make the angle, *o c t*, (*Fig.* 268,) equal to the angle, *o c t*, at *Fig.* 261; upon *c*, describe a circle with a radius equal to half the thickness of the rail; draw the tangent, *b d*, parallel to *t c*, and complete the rectangle, *e b d f*, having sides tangical to the circle; from *c*, draw *c a*, at right angles to *o c;* then, *b d* being the bottom of the rail, set a gauge from *b* to *a*, and run it the whole length of the stuff; in boring, place the centre of the

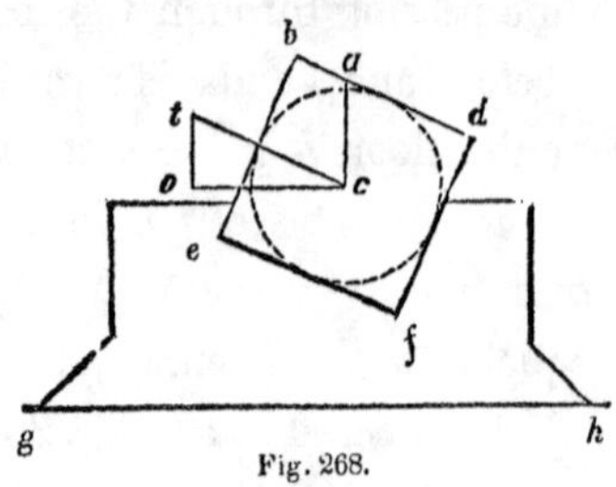

Fig. 268.

bit in the gauge-mark at *a*, and bore in the direction, *a c*. To do this easily, make *chucks* as represented in the figure, the bottom edge, *g h*, being parallel to *o c*, and having a place sawed out, as *e f*, to receive the rail. These being nailed to the bench, the rail will be held steadily in its proper place for boring vertically. The distance apart that the balusters require to be, on the under side of the rail, is one-half the length of the *rake-side* of the pitch-board.

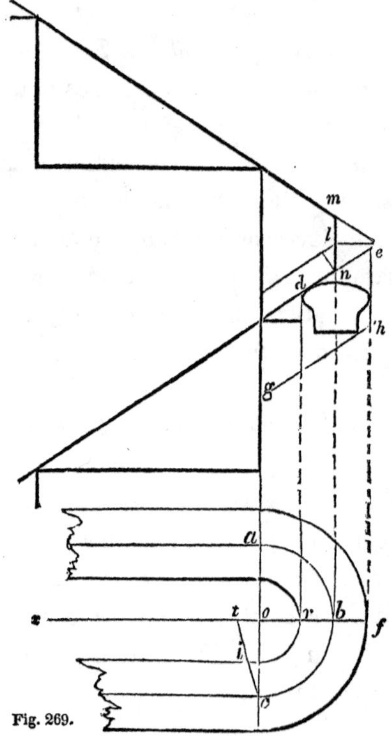

Fig. 269.

373.—*To obtain, by the foregoing principles, the face-mould for the twists of a moulded rail upon platform stairs.* In *Fig.* 269, *a b c* is the plan of a line passing through the centre of the rail around the cylinder as before, and the lines above it are a vertical section of steps, risers and platform, with the lines for the rail obtained as in *Fig.* 261. Set half the width of the rail from *b* to *f* and from *b* to *r*, and from *f* and *r*, draw *f e* and *r d*, parallel to *c a*. At *Fig.* 270, the centre lines of the

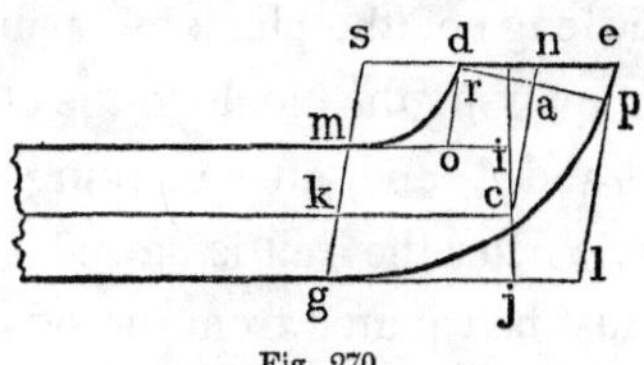

Fig. 270.

rail, *k c* and *c n*, are obtained as in the previous examples. Make *c i* and *c j*, each equal to *c i* at *Fig.* 269, and draw the lines, *i m* and *j g*, parallel to *c k*; make *n e* and *n d* equal to *n e* and *n d* at *Fig.* 269, and draw *d o* and *e l*, parallel to *n c*; also, through *k*, draw *s g*, parallel to *n c*; then, in the parallelograms, *m s d o* and *g s e l*, find the elliptic curves, *d m* and *e g*, according to *Art.* 118, and they will define the curves. The line, *d e*, being drawn through *n* parallel to *k c*, defines the joint, which is to be cut through the plank vertically. If the rail crosses the platform rather steep, a butt joint will be preferable, to obtain which see *Art.* 405.

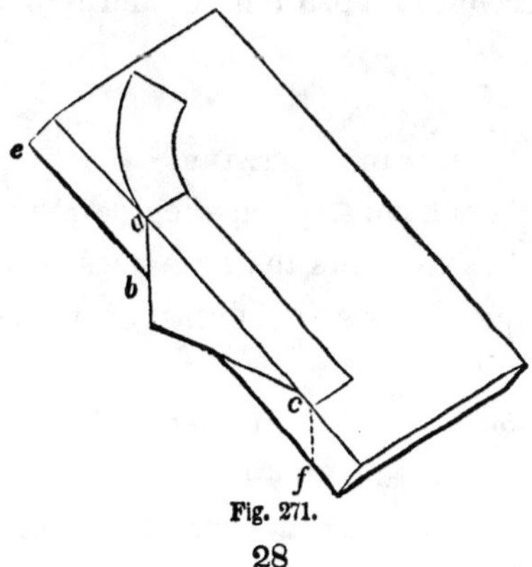

Fig. 271.

374.—*To apply the mould to the plank.* The mould obtained according to the last article must be applied to both sides of the plank, as shown at *Fig.* 271. Before applying the mould, the edge, *e f*, must be bevilled according to the angle, *c t x*, at *Fig.* 269; if the rail is to be canted *up*, the edge must be bevilled at an *obtuse* angle with the upper face; but if it is to be canted *down*, the angle that the edge makes with the upper face mnst be *acute.* From the spring of the curve, *a*, and the end, *c*, draw vertical lines across the edge of the plank by applying the pitch-board, *a b c;* then, in applying the mould to the other side, place the points, *a* and *c*, at *b* and *f;* and, after marking around it, saw the rail out vertically. After the rail is sawed out, the bottom and the top surfaces must be squared from the sides.

375.—*To ascertain the thickness of stuff required for the twists.* The thickness of stuff required for the twists of a round rail, as before observed, is the same as that for the straight; but for a moulded rail, the stuff for the twists must be thicker than that for the straight. In *Fig.* 269, draw a section of the rail between the lines, *d r* and *e f*, and as close to the line, *d e*, as possible; at the lower corner of the section, draw *g h*, parallel to *d e;* then the distance that these lines are apart, will be the thickness required for the twists of a moulded rail.

The foregoing method of finding moulds for rails is applicable to all stairs which have continued rails around cylinders, and are without winders.

WINDING STAIRS.

376.—Winding stairs have steps tapering narrower at one end than at the other. In some stairs, there are steps of parallel width incorporated with tapering steps; the former are then called *flyers* and the latter *winders.*

377.—*To describe a regular geometrical winding stairs.* In *Fig.* 272, *a b c d* represents the inner surface of the wall enclosing the space allotted to the stairs, *a e* the length of the steps, and *e f g h* the cylinder, or face of the front string. The line,

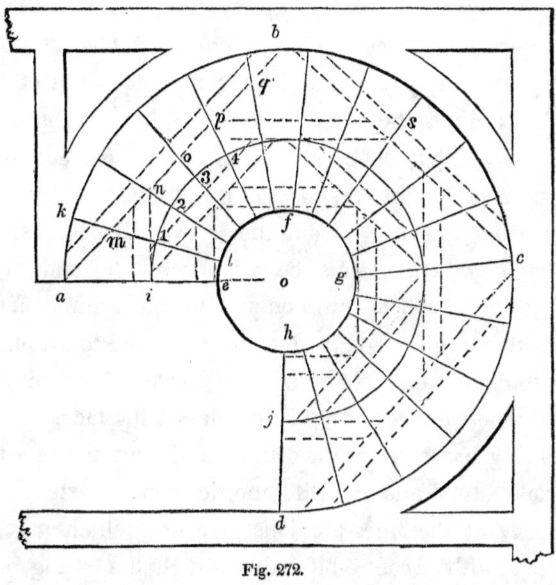

Fig. 272.

a e, is given as the face of the first riser, and the point, *j*, for the limit of the last. Make *e i* equal to 18 inches, and upon *o*, with *o i* for radius, describe the arc, *i j;* obtain the number of risers and of treads required to ascend to the floor at *j*, according to *Art.* 361, and divide the arc, *i j*, into the same number of equal parts as there are to be treads; through the points of division, 1, 2, 3, &c., and from the wall-string to the front-string, draw lines tending to the centre, *o;* then these lines will represent the face of each riser, and determine the form and width of the steps. Allow the necessary projection for the nosing beyond *a e*, which should be equal to the thickness of the step, and then *a e l k* will be the dimensions for each step. Make a pitch-board for the wall-string having *a k* for the tread, and the rise as previously ascertained; with this, lay out on a thicknessed plank the several risers and treads, as at *Fig.* 256, gauging from the upper edge of the string for the line at which to set the pitch-board.

Upon the back of the string, with a $1\frac{1}{4}$ inch dado plane, make a succession of grooves $1\frac{1}{4}$ inches apart, and parallel with the lines for the risers on the face. These grooves must be cut along the whole length of the plank, and deep enough to admit of the plank's bending around the curve, *a b c d*. Then construct a drum, or cylinder, of any common kind of stuff, and made to fit a curve having a radius the thickness of the string less than *o a*; upon this the string must be bent, and the grooves filled with strips of wood, called *keys*, which must be very nicely fitted and glued in. After it has dried, a board thin enough to bend around on the outside of the string, must be glued on from one end to the other, and nailed with clout nails. In doing this, be careful not to nail into any place where a riser or step is to enter on the face.

After the string has been on the drum a sufficient time for the glue to set, take it off, and cut the mortices for the steps and risers on the face at the lines previously made; which may be done by boring with a centre-bit half through the string, and nicely chiseling to the line. The drum need not be made so large as the whole space occupied by the stairs, but merely large enough to receive one piece of the wall-string at once—for it is evident that more than one will be required. The front string may be constructed in the same manner; taking *e l* instead of *a k* for the tread of the pitch-board, dadoing it with a smaller dado plane, and bending it on a drum of the proper size.

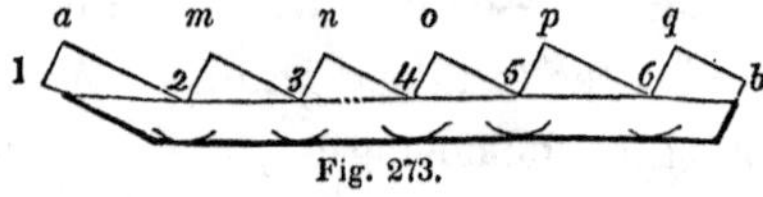

Fig. 273.

378.—*To find the shape and position of the timbers necessary to support a winding stairs.* The dotted lines in *Fig.* 272 show the proper position of the timbers as regards the plan: the shape of each is obtained as follows. In *Fig.* 273, the line, 1 *a*, is equal to a riser, less the thickness of the floor, and the lines, 2 *m*, 3 *n*, 4 *o*, 5 *p* and 6 *q*, are each equal to one riser. The line, *a* 2, is equal to *a m* in *Fig.* 272, the line, *m* 3 to *m n* in that figure, &c. In drawing this figure, commence at *a*, and make the lines, *a* 1 and *a* 2, of the length above specified, and draw them at right angles to each other; draw 2 *m*, at right angles to *a* 2, and *m* 3, at right angles to *m* 2, and make 2 *m* and *m* 3 of the lengths as above specified; and so proceed to the end. Then, through the points, 1, 2, 3, 4, 5 and 6, trace the line, 1 *b;* upon the points, 1, 2, 3, 4, &c., with the size of the timber for radius, describe arcs as shown in the figure, and by these the lower line may be traced parallel to the upper. This will give the proper shape for the timber, *a b*, in *Fig.* 272; and that of the others may be found in the same manner. In ordinary cases, the shape of one face of the timber will be sufficient, for a good workman can easily hew it to its proper level by that; but where great accuracy is desirable, a pattern for the other side may be found in the same manner as for the first.

379.—*To find the falling-mould for the rail of a winding stairs.* In *Fig.* 274, *a c b* represents the plan of a rail around half the cylinder, *A* the cap of the newel, and 1, 2, 3, &c., the face of the risers in the order they ascend. Find the stretch-out, *e f*, of *a c b*, according to *Art.* 92; from *o*, through the point of the mitre at the newel-cap, draw *o s;* obtain on the tangent, *e d*, the position of the points, *s* and h^2,* as at *t* and f^2; from *e t* f^2 and *f*, draw *e x*, *t u*, f^2 g^2 and *f h*, all at right angles to *e d;* make *e g* equal to one rise and f^2 g^2 equal to 12, as this line is drawn from the 12th riser; from *g*, through g^2, draw *g i;* make *g x* equal to about three-fourths of a rise, (the top of the newel, *x*, should be 3½ feet from the floor;) draw *x u*, at right angles to *e x*, and ease off the angle at *u;* at a distance equal to the thickness of

* In the above, the references, a^2, b^2, &c., are introduced for the first time. During the time taken to refer to the figure, the memory of the *form* of these may pass from the mind, while that of the *sound* alone remains; they may then be mistaken for *a* 2, *b* 2, &c. This can be avoided in reading by giving them a sound corresponding to their meaning, which is *second a second b*, &c. or *a second, b second.*

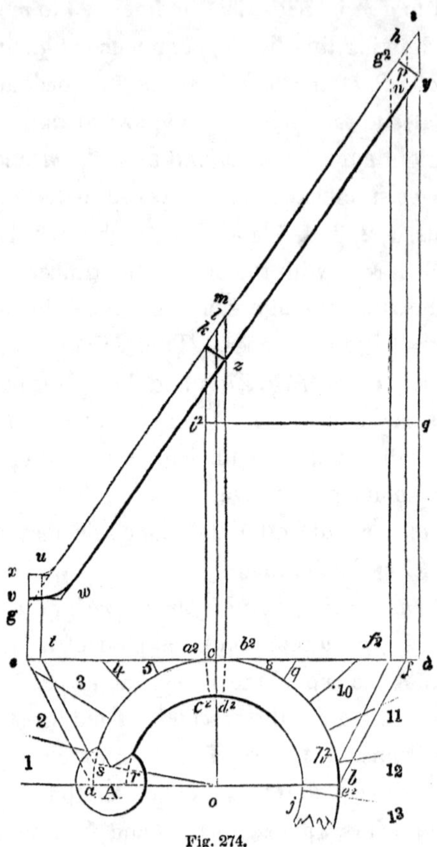

Fig. 274.

the rail, draw $v\ w\ y$, parallel to $x\ u\ i$; from the centre of the plan, o, draw $o\ l$, at right angles to $e\ d$; bisect $h\ n$ in p, and through p, at right angles to $g\ i$, draw a line for the joint; in the same manner, draw the joint at k; then $x\ y$ will be the falling-mould for that part of the rail which extends from s to b on the plan.

380.—*To find the face-mould for the rail of a winding-stairs.* From the extremities of the joints in the falling-mould, as k, z and y, (*Fig.* 274,) draw $k\ a^2$, $z\ b^2$ and $y\ d$, at right angles to $e\ d$; make $b\ e^2$ equal to $f\ d$. Then, to obtain the direction of the joint, $a^2\ c^2$, or $b^2\ d^2$, proceed as at *Fig.* 275, at which the parts are

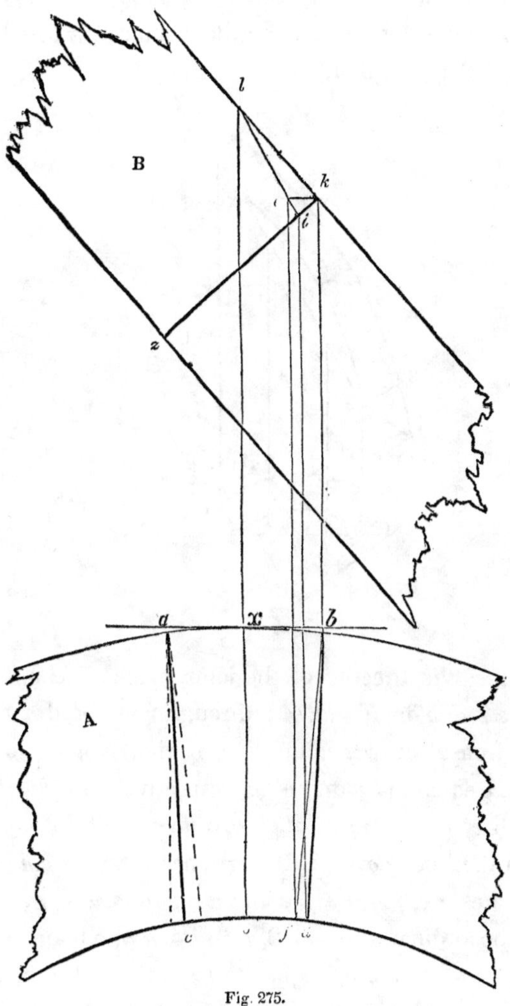

Fig. 275.

shown at half their full size. *A* is the plan of the rail, and *B* is the falling-mould ; in which *k z* is the direction of the butt-joint. From *k*, draw *k b*, parallel to *l o*, and *k e*, at right angles to *k b ;* from *b*, draw *b f*, tending to the centre of the plan, and from *f*, draw *f e*, parallel to *b k ;* from *l*, through *e*, draw *l i*, and from *i*, draw *i d*, parallel to *e f ;* join *d* and *b*, and *d b* will be the proper direction for the joint on the plan. The direction of the joint on the other side, *a c*, can be found by transferring the distances, *x b* and *o d*, to *x a* and *o c*. (See *Art.* 384.)

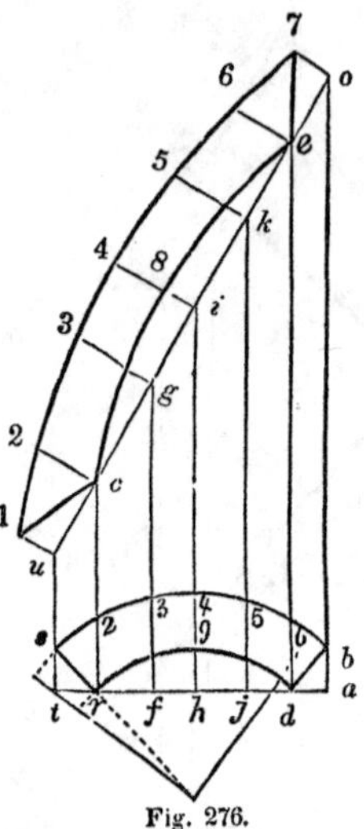

Fig. 276.

Having obtained the direction of the joint, make *s r d b*, (*Fig.* 276,) equal to *s r* d^2 b^2 in *Fig.* 274; through *r* and *d*, draw *t a*; through *s* and from *d*, draw *t u* and *d e*, at right angles to *t a*; make *t u* and *d e* equal to *t u* and b^2 *m*, respectively, in *Fig.* 274; from *u*, through *e*, draw *u o*; through *b*, from *r*, and from as many other points in the line, *t a*, as is thought necessary, as *f*, *h* and *j*, draw the ordinates, *r c*, *f g*, *h i*, *j k* and *a o*; from *u*, *c*, *g*, *i*, *k*, *e* and *o*, draw the ordinates, *u* 1, *c* 2, *g* 3, *i* 4, *k* 5, *e* 6 and *o* 7, at right angles to *u o*; make *u* 1 equal to *t s*, *c* 2 equal to *r* 2, *g* 3 equal to *f* 3, &c., and trace the curve, 1 7, through the points thus found; find the curve, *c e*, in the same manner, by transferring the distances between the line, *t a*, and the arc, *r d*; join 1 and *c*, also *e* and 7; then, 1 *c e* 7 will be the face-mould required for that part of the rail which is denoted by the letters, *s r* d^2 b^2, on the plan at *Fig.* 274.

To ascertain the mould for the next quarter, make *a c j e*, (*Fig.*

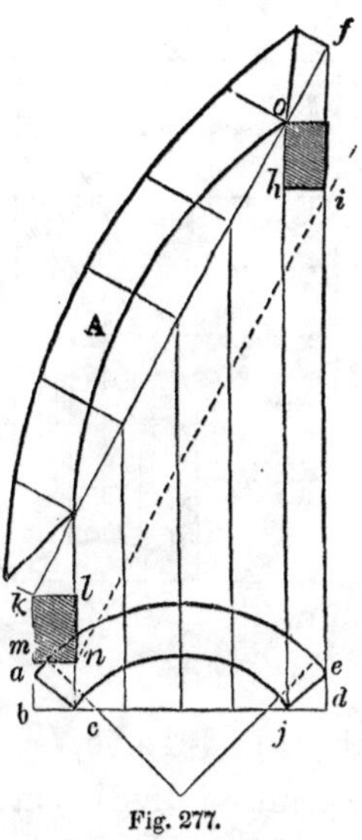

Fig. 277.

277,) equal to a^2 c^2 j e^2 at *Fig.* 274; at any convenient height on the line, *d i*, in that figure, draw q i^2, parallel to *e d;* through *c* and *j*, (*Fig.* 277,) draw *b d;* through *a*, and from *j*, draw *b k* and *j o*, at right angles to *b d;* make *b k* and *j o* equal to i^2 *k* and *q i*, respectively, in *Fig.* 274; from *k*, through *o*, draw *k f;* and proceed as in the last figure to obtain the face-mould, *A*.

381.—*To ascertain the requisite thickness of stuff.* CASE 1.—*When the falling-mould is straight.* Make *o h* and *k m*, (*Fig.* 277,) equal to *i y* at *Fig.* 274; draw *h i* and *m n*, parallel to *b d;* through the corner farthest from *k f*, as *n* or *i*, draw *n i*, parallel to *k f;* then the distance between *k f* and *n i* will give the thickness required.

382.—CASE 2.—*When the falling-mould is curved.* In *Fig.* 278, *s r d b* is equal to *s r* d^2 b^2 in *Fig.* 274. Make *a c* equal to the stretch-out of the arc, *s b*, according to *Art.* 92, and divide *a c* and *s b*, each into a like number of equal parts; from *a* and *c*, and from each point of division in the line, *a c*, draw *a k*, *e l*, &c., at right angles to *a c;* make *a k* equal to *t u* in *Fig.* 274, and *c j* equal to b^2 *m*

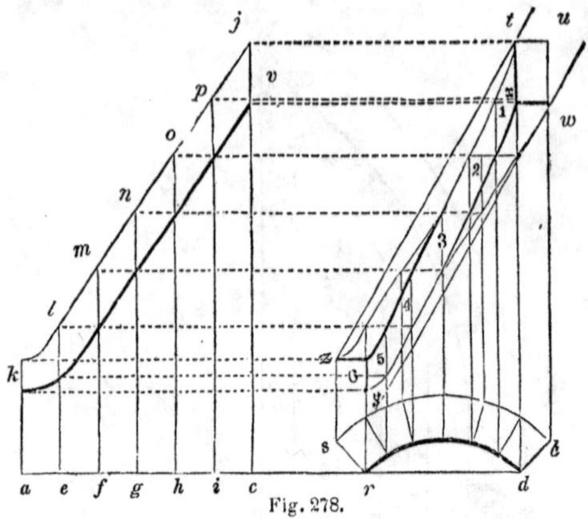

Fig. 278.

in that figure, and complete the falling-mould, *k j*, every way equal to *u m* in *Fig*. 274; from the points of division in the arc, *s b*, draw lines radiating towards the centre of the circle, dividing the arc, *r d*, in the same proportion as *s b* is divided; from *d* and *b*, draw *d t* and *b u*, at right angles to *a d*, and from *j* and *v*, draw *j u* and *v w*, at right angles to *j c*; then *x t u w* will be a vertical projection of the joint, *d b*. Supposing every radiating line across *s r d b*—corresponding to the vertical lines across *k j*—to represent a joint, find their vertical projection, as at 1, 2, 3, 4, 5 and 6; through the corners of those parallelograms, trace the curve lines shown in the figure; then 6 *u* will be a *helinet*, or vertical projection, of *s r d b*. To find the thickness of plank necessary to get out this part of the rail, draw the line, *z t*, touching the upper side of the helinet in two places: through the corner farthest projecting from that line, as *w*, draw *y w*, parallel to *z t;* then the distance between those lines will be the proper thickness of stuff for this part of the rail. The same process is necessary to find the thickness of stuff in all cases in which the falling-mould is in any way curved.

383.—*To apply the face-mould to the plank.* In *Fig*. 279, *A* represents the plank with its best side and edge in view, and *B* the same plank turned up so as to bring in view the other side

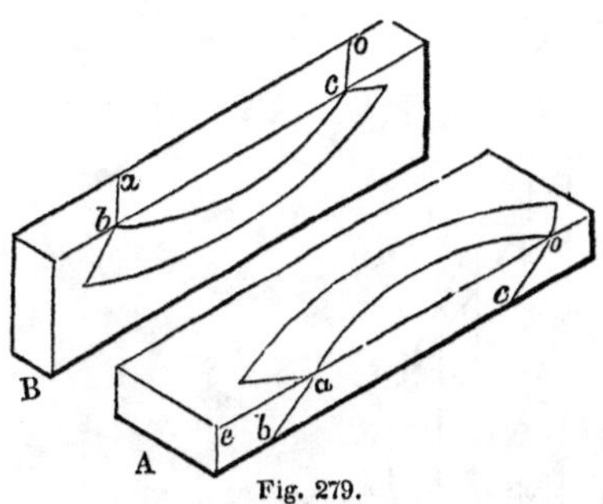

Fig. 279.

and the same edge, this being square from the face. Apply the tips of the mould at the edge of the plank, as at *a* and *o*, (*A*,) and mark out the shape of the twist; from *a* and *o*, draw the lines, *a b* and *o c*, across the edge of the plank, the angles, *e a b* and *e o c*, corresponding with *k f d* at *Fig.* 277; turning the plank up as at *B*, apply the tips of the mould at *b* and *c*, and mark it out as shown in the figure. In sawing out the twist, the saw must be be moved in the direction, *a b*; which direction will be perpendicular when the twist is held up in its proper position.

In sawing by the face-mould, the *sides* of the rail are obtained; the top and bottom, or the upper and the lower surfaces, are obtained by squaring from the sides, after having bent the falling-mould around the outer, or convex side, and marked by its edges. Marking across by the ends of the falling-mould will give the position of the butt-joint.

384.—*Elucidation of the process by which the direction of the butt-joint is obtained in Art.* 380. Mr. Nicholson, in his *Carpenter's Guide*, has given the joint a different direction to that here shown; he radiates it towards the centre of the cylinder. This is erroneous—as can be shown by the following operation:

In *Fig.* 280, *a r j i* is the plan of a part of the rail about the joint, *s u* is the stretch-out of *a i*, and *g p* is the helinet, or vertical projection of the plan, *a r j i*, obtained according to *Art.*

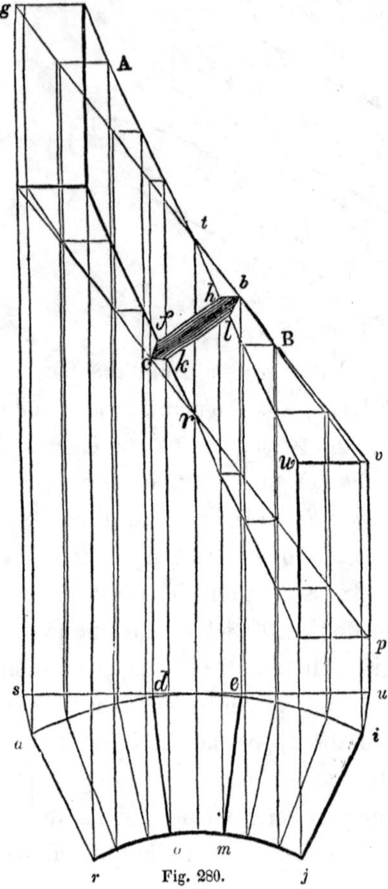

Fig. 280.

382. Bisect *r t*, part of an ordinate from the centre of the plan, and through the middle, draw *c b*, at right angles to *g v;* from *b* and *c*, draw *c d* and *b e*, at right angles to *s u;* from *d* and *e*, draw lines radiating towards the centre of the plan: then *d o* and *e m* will be the direction of the joint on the plan, according to Nicholson, and *c b* its direction on the falling-mould. It will be admitted that all the lines on the upper or the lower side of the rail which radiate towards the centre of the cylinder, as *d o*, *e m* or *i j*, are level; for instance, the level line, *w v*, on the top of the

rail in the helinet, is a true representation of the radiating line, *j i*, on the plan. The line, *b h*, therefore, on the top of the rail in the helinet, is a true representation of *e m* on the plan, and *k c* on the bottom of the rail truly represents *d o*. From *k*, draw *k l*, parallel to *c b*, and from *h*, draw *h f*, parallel to *b c*; join *l* and *b*, also *c* and *f*; then *c k l b* will be a true representation of the end of the lower piece, *B*, and *c f h b* of the end of the upper piece, *A*; and *f k* or *h l* will show how much the joint is open on the inner, or concave side of the rail.

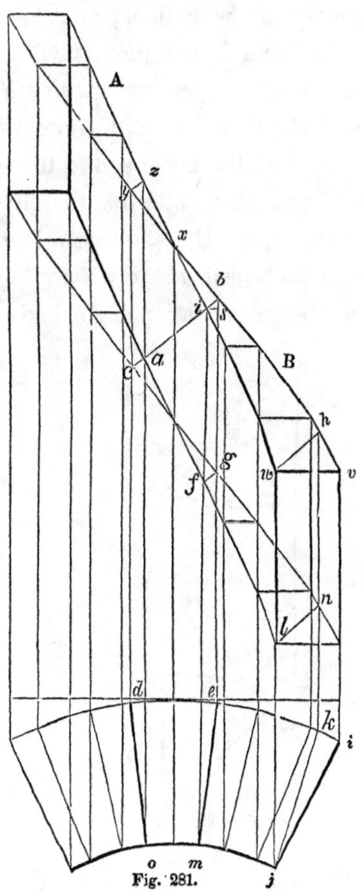

Fig. 281.

To show that the process followed in *Art.* 380 is correct, let *d o* and *e m*, (*Fig.* 281,) be the direction of the butt-joint found as at *Fig.* 275. Now, to project, on the top of the rail in the helinet, a line that does not radiate towards the centre of the cylinder, as *j k*, draw vertical lines from *j* and *k* to *w* and *h*, and join *w* and *h*; then it will be evident that *w h* is a true representation in the helinet of *j k* on the plan, it being in the same plane as *j k*, and also in the same winding surface as *w v*. The line, *l n*, also, is a true representation on the bottom of the helinet of the line, *j k*, in the plan. The line of the joint, *e m*, therefore, is projected in the same way and truly by *i b* on the top of the helinet; and the line, *d o*, by *c a* on the bottom. Join *a* and *i*, and then it will be seen that the lines, *c a*, *a i* and *i b*, exactly coincide with *c b*, the line of the joint on the convex side of the rail; thus proving the lower end of the upper piece, *A*, and the upper end of the lower piece, *B*, to be in one and the same plane, and that the direction of the joint on the plan is the true one. By reference to *Fig.* 275, it will be seen that the line, *l i*, corresponds to *x i* in *Fig.* 281; and that *e k* in that figure is a representation of *f b*, and *i k* of *d b*.

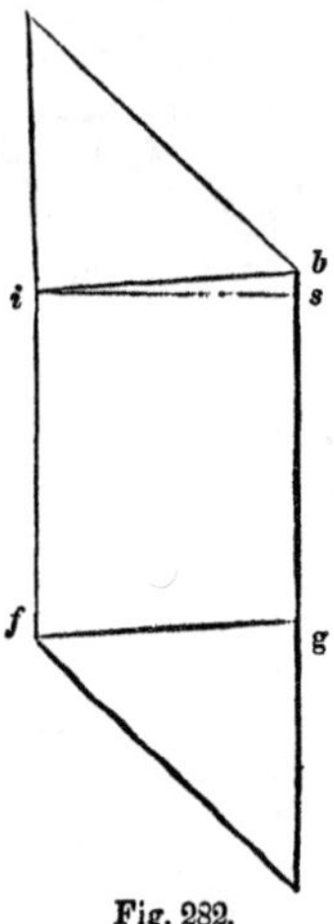

Fig. 282.

In getting out the twists, the joints, before the falling-mould is applied, are cut perpendicularly, the face-mould being long enough to include the overplus necessary for a butt-joint. The face-mould for *A*, therefore, would have to extend to the line, *i b;* and that for *B*, to the line, *y z*. Being sawed vertically at first, a section of the joint at the end of the face-mould for *A*, would be represented in the helinet by *b i f g*. To obtain the position of the line, *b i*, on the end of the twist, draw *i s*, (*Fig*. 282,) at right angles to *i f*, and make *i s* equal to *m e* at *Fig*. 281; through *s*, draw *s g*, parallel to *i f*, and make *s b* equal to *s b* at *Fig*. 281; join *b* and *i;* make *i f* equal to *i f* at *Fig*. 281, and from *f*, draw *f g*, parallel to *i b;* then *i b g f* will be a perpendicular section of the rail over the line, *e m*, on the plan at *Fig*. 281, corresponding to *i b g f* in the helinet at that figure; and when the rail is squared, the top, or back, must be trimmed off to the line, *i b*, and the bottom to the line, *f g*.

385.—*To grade the front string of a stairs, having winders in a quarter-circle at the top of the flight connected with flyers at the bottom.* In *Fig*. 283, *a b* represents the line of the facia along the floor of the upper story, *b e c* the face of the cylinder, and *c d* the face of the front string. Make *g b* equal to $\frac{1}{3}$ of the diameter of the baluster, and draw the centre-line of the rail, *f g*, *g h i* and *i j*, parallel to *a b*, *b e c* and *c d;* make *g k* and *g l* each equal to half the width of the rail, and through *k* and *l*, draw lines for the convex and the concave sides of the rail, parallel to the centre-line; tangical to the convex side of the rail, and parallel to *k m*, draw *n o;* obtain the stretch-out, *q r*, of the semi-circle, *k p m*, according to *Art*. 92; extend *a b* to *t*, and *k m* to *s;* make *c s* equal to the length of the steps, and *i u* equal to 18 inches, and describe the arcs, *s t* and *u* 6, parallel to *m p;* from *t*, draw *t w*, tending to the centre of the cylinder; from 6, and on the line, 6 *u x*, run off the regular tread, as at 5, 4, 3, 2, 1 and *v;* make *u x* equal to half the arc, *u* 6, and make the point of division nearest to *x*, as *v*, the limit of the parallel steps, or flyers; make *r o* equal to *m z;* from *o*, draw $o\ a^2$, at right angles to *n o*, and equal to one rise;

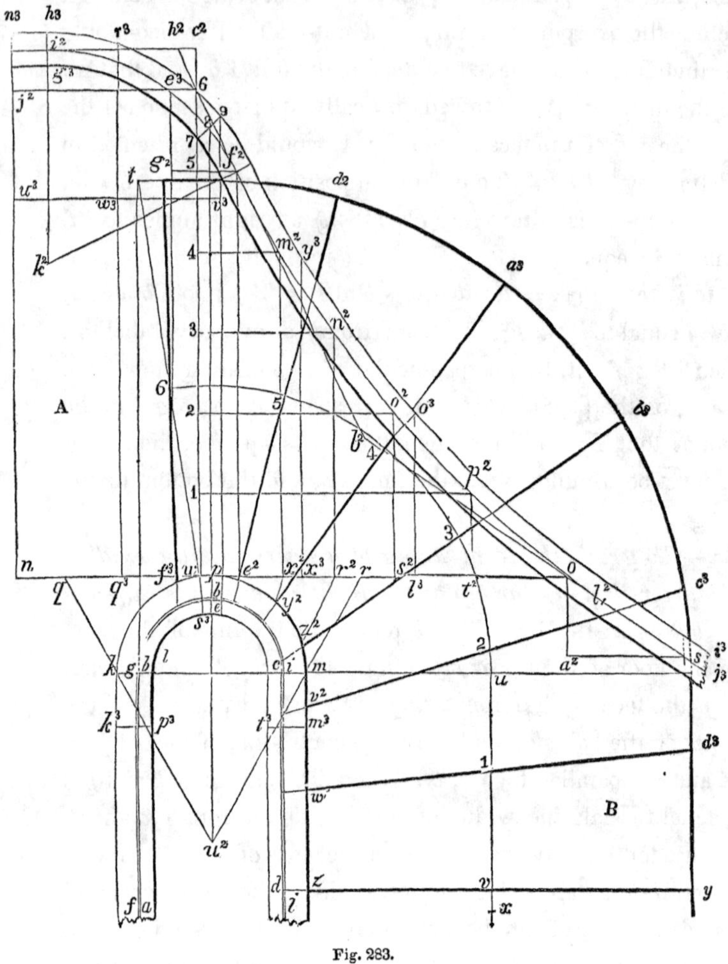

Fig. 283.

from a^2, draw $a^2\ s$, parallel to $n\ o$, and equal to one tread; from s, through o, draw $s\ b^2$.

Then from w, draw $w\ c^2$, at right angles to $n\ o$, and set up, on the line, $w\ c^2$, the same number of risers that the floor, A, is above the first winder, B, as at 1, 2, 3, 4, 5 and 6; through 5, (on the arc, 6 u,) draw $d^2\ e^2$, tending to the centre of the cylinder; from e^2, draw $e^2\ f^2$, at right angles to $n\ o$, and through 5, (on the line,

$w\ c^2$,) draw $g^2\ f^2$, parallel to $n\ o$; through 6, (on the line, $w\ c^2$,) and f^2, draw the line, $h^2\ b^2$; make 6 c^2 equal to half a rise, and from c^2 and 6, draw $c^2\ i^2$ and 6 j^2, parallel to $n\ o$; make $h^2\ i^2$ equal to $h^2\ f^2$; from i^2, draw $i^2\ k^2$, at right angles to $i^2\ h^2$, and from f^2, draw $f^2\ k^2$, at right angles to $f^2\ h^2$; upon k^2, with $k^2\ f^2$ for radius, describe the arc, $f^2\ i^2$; make $b^2\ l^2$ equal to $b^2\ f^2$, and ease off the angle at b^2 by the curve, $f^2\ l^2$. In the figure, the curve is described from a centre, but in a full-size plan, this would be impracticable; the best way to ease the angle, therefore, would be with a tanged-curve, according to *Art.* 89. Then from 1, 2, 3 and 4, (on the line, $w\ c^2$,) draw lines parallel to $n\ o$, meeting the curve in m^2, n^2, o^2 and p^2; from these points, draw lines at right angles to $n\ o$, and meeting it in x^2, r^2, s^2 and t^2; from x^2 and r^2, draw lines tending to u^2, and meeting the convex side of the rail in y^2 and z^2; make $m\ v^2$ equal to $r\ s^2$, and $m\ w^2$ equal to $r\ t^2$; from y^2, z^2, v^2, and w^2, through 4, 3, 2 and 1, draw lines meeting the line of the wall-string in a^3, b^3, c^3 and d^3; from e^3, where the centre-line of the rail crosses the line of the floor, draw $e^3\ f^3$, at right angles to $n\ o$, and from f^3, through 6, draw $f^3\ g^2$; then the heavy lines, $f^3\ g^2$, $e^2\ d^2$, $y^2\ a^3$, $z^2\ b^3$, $v^2\ c^3$, $w^2\ d^3$, and $z\ y$, will be the lines for the risers, which, being extended to the line of the front string, $b\ e\ c\ d$, will give the dimensions of the winders, and the grading of the front string, as was required.

386.—*To obtain the falling-mould for the twists of the last-mentioned stairs.* Make $i^2\ g^3$ and $i^2\ h^3$, (*Fig.* 283,) each equal to half the thickness of the rail; through h^3 and g^3, draw $h^3\ i^3$ and $g^3\ j^3$, parallel to $i^2\ s$; assuming $k\ k^3$ and $m\ m^3$ on the plan as the amount of straight to be got out with the twists, make $n\ q$ equal to $k\ k^3$, and $r\ l^3$ equal to $m\ m^3$; from n and l^3, draw lines at right angles to $n\ o$, meeting the top of the falling-mould in n^3 and o^3; from o^3, draw a line crossing the falling-mould at right angles to a chord of the curve, $f^2\ l^2$; through the centre of the cylinder, draw u^2 8, at right angles to $n\ o$; through 8, draw 7 9, tending to k^2; then n^3 7 will be the falling-mould for the upper twist, and 7 o^3 the falling-mould for the lower twist.

387.—*To obtain the face-moulds.* The moulds for the twists of this stairs may be obtained as at *Art.* 380; but, as the falling-mould in its course departs considerably from a straight line, it would, according to that method, require a very thick plank for the rail, and consequently cause a great waste of stuff. In order, therefore, to economize the material, the following method is to be preferred—in which it will be seen that the heights are taken in three places instead of two only, as is done in the previous method.

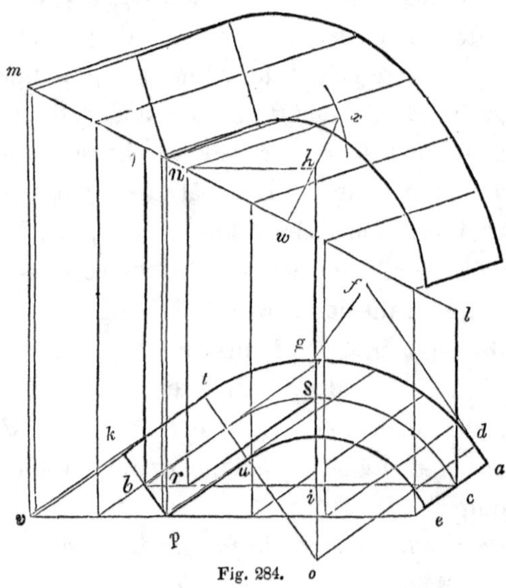

Fig. 284.

Case 1.—*When the middle height is above a line joining the other two.* Having found at *Fig.* 283 the direction of the joint, $w\ s^3$ and $p\ e$, according to *Art.* 380, make $k\ p\ e\ a$, (*Fig.* 284,) equal to $k^3\ p^3\ e\ p$ in *Fig.* 283; join b and c, and from o, draw $o\ h$, at right angles to $b\ c$; obtain the stretch-out of $d\ g$, as $d\ f$, and at *Fig.* 283, place it from the axis of the cylinder, p, to q^3; from q^3 in that figure, draw $q^3\ r^3$, at right angles to $n\ o$; also, at a convenient height on the line, $n\ n^3$, in that figure, and at right angles to that line, draw $u^3\ v^3$; from b and c, in *Fig.* 284, draw $b\ j$ and $c\ l$, at right angles to $b\ c$; make $b\ j$ equal to $u^3\ n^3$ in *Fig.* 283, $i\ h$ equal to $w^3\ r^3$ in that figure, and $c\ l$ equal to $v^3\ 9$; from l, through j, draw $l\ m$; from h, draw $h\ n$, parallel to $c\ b$; from n, draw $n\ r$, at right angles to $b\ c$, and join r and s; through the lowest corner of the plan, as p, draw $v\ e$, parallel to $b\ c$; from a, e, u, p, k, t, and from as many other points as is thought necessary, draw ordinates to the base-line, $v\ e$, parallel to $r\ s$; through h, draw $w\ x$, at right angles to $m\ l$; upon n, with $r\ s$ for radius, describe an intersecting arc at x, and join n and x; from the points at which the ordinates from the plan meet the base-line, $v\ e$, draw ordinates to meet the line, $m\ l$, at right angles to $v\ e$; and from the points of intersection on $m\ l$, draw corresponding ordinates, parallel to $n\ x$; make the ordinates which are parallel to $n\ x$ of a length corresponding to those which are parallel to $r\ s$, and through the points thus found, trace the face-mould as required.

CASE 2.—*When the middle height is below a line joining the other two.* The lower twist in *Fig.* 283 is of this nature. The face-mould for this is found at *Fig.* 285 in a manner similar to that at *Fig.* 284. The heights are all taken from the top of the falling-mould at *Fig.* 283; $b\ j$ being equal to w 6 in *Fig.* 283, $i\ h$ equal to $x^3\ y^3$ in that figure, and $c\ l$ to $l^3\ o^3$. Draw a line through j and l, and from h, draw $h\ n$, parallel to $b\ c$; from n, draw $n\ r$, at right angles to $b\ c$, and join r and s; then $r\ s$ will be the bevil for the lower ordinates. From h, draw $h\ x$, at right angles to $j\ l$; upon n, with $r\ s$ for radius, describe an intersecting arc at x, and join n and x; then $n\ x$ will be the bevil for the upper ordinates, upon which the face-mould is found as in Case 1.

388.—*Elucidation of the foregoing method.*—This method of finding the face-moulds for the handrailing of winding stairs, being founded on principles which govern cylindric sections, may be illustrated by the following figures. *Fig.* 286 and 287 represent solid blocks, or prisms, standing upright on a level base, $b\ d$; the upper surface, $j\ a$ forming oblique angles with the face, $b\ l$—

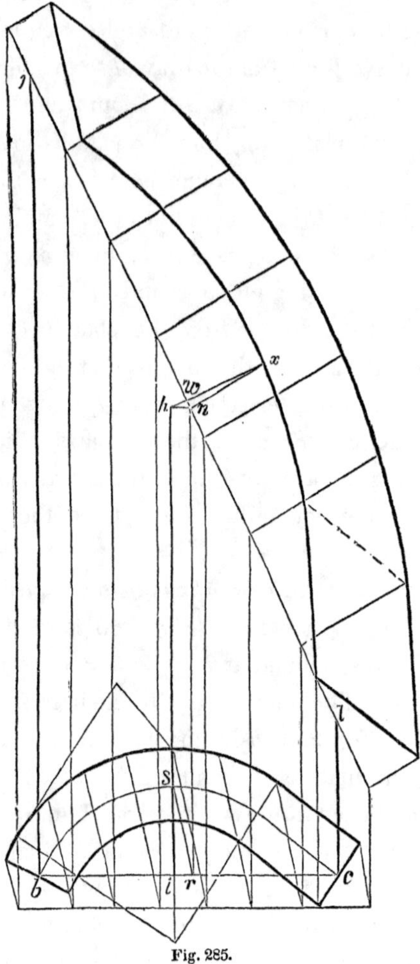

Fig. 285.

in *Fig.* 286 obtuse, and in *Fig.* 287 acute. Upon the base, describe the semi-circle, *b s c;* from the centre, *i*, draw *i s*, at right angles to *b c;* from *s*, draw *s x*, at right angles to *e d*, and from *i*, draw *i h*, at right angles to *b c;* make *i h* equal to *s x*, and join *h* and *x;* then, *h* and *x* being of the same height, the line, *h x*, joining them, is a level line. From *h*, draw *h n*, parallel to *b c*, and from *n*, draw *n r*, at right angles to *b c;* join *r* and *s*, also *n*

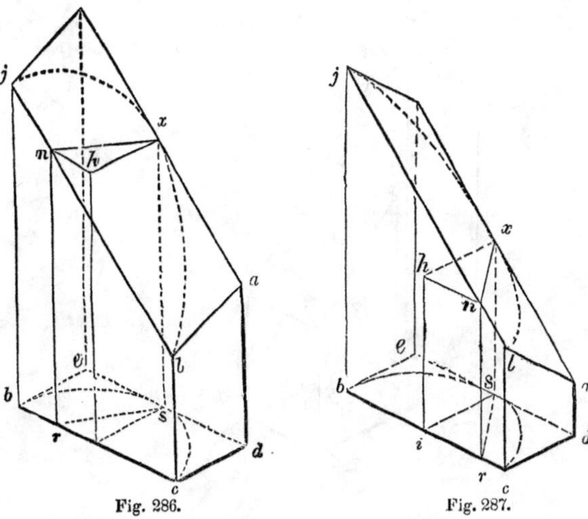

Fig. 286. Fig. 287.

and x; then, n and x being of the same height, $n\ x$ is a level line; and this line lying perpendicularly over $r\ s$, $n\ x$ and $r\ s$ must be of the same length. So, all lines on the top, drawn parallel to $n\ x$, and perpendicularly over corresponding lines drawn parallel to $r\ s$ on the base, must be equal to those lines on the base; and by drawing a number of these on the semi-circle at the base and others of the same length at the top, it is evident that a curve, $j\ x\ l$, may be traced through the ends of those on the top, which shall lie perpendicularly over the semi-circle at the base.

It is upon this principle that the process at *Fig.* 284 and 285 is founded. The plan of the rail at the bottom of those figures is supposed to lie perpendicularly under the face-mould at the top; and each ordinate at the top over a corresponding one at the base. The ordinates, $n\ x$ and $r\ s$, in those figures, correspond to $n\ x$ and $r\ s$ in *Fig.* 286 and 287.

In *Fig.* 288, the top, $e\ a$, forms a right angle with the face, $d\ c$; all that is necessary, therefore, in this figure, is to find a line corresponding to $h\ x$ in the last two figures, and that will lie level and in the upper surface; so that all ordinates at right angles to $d\ r$ on the base, will correspond to those that are at right angles

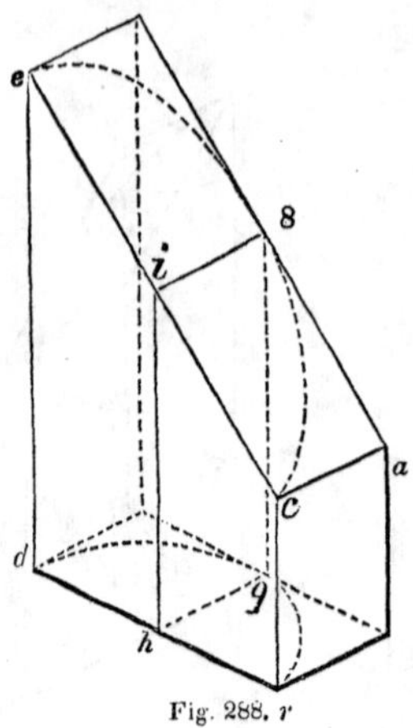

Fig. 288.

to *e c* on the top. This elucidates *Fig.* 276; at which the lines, *h* 9 and *i* 8, correspond to *h* 9 and *i* 8 in this figure.

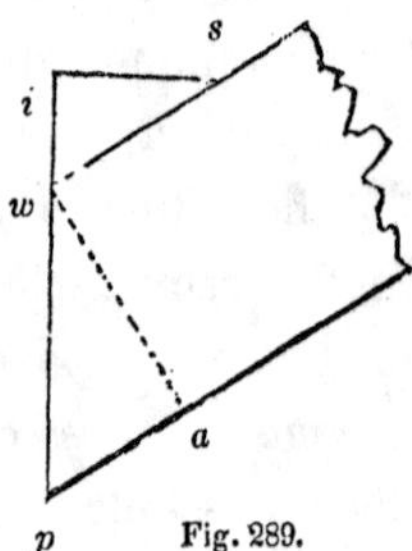

Fig. 289.

389.—*To find the bevil for the edge of the plank.* The plank, before the face-mould is applied, must be bevilled according to the angle which the top of the imaginary block, or prism, in the previous figures, makes with the face. This angle is determined in the following manner: draw *w i*, (*Fig.* 289,) at right angles to *i s*, and equal to *w h* at *Fig.* 284; make *i s* equal to *i s* in that figure, and join *w* and *s*; then *s w p* will be the bevil required in order to apply the face-mould at *Fig.* 284. In *Fig.* 285, the middle height being below the line joining the other two, the bevil is therefore acute. To determine this, draw *i s*, (*Fig.* 290,) at

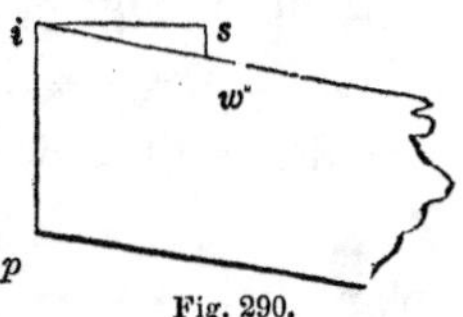

Fig. 290.

right angles to *i p*, and equal to *i s* in *Fig*. 285; make *s w* equal to *h w* in *Fig*. 285, and join *w* and *i*; then *w i p* will be the bevil required in order to apply the face-mould at *Fig*. 285. Although the falling-mould in these cases is curved, yet, as the plank is *sprung*, or bevilled on its edge, the thickness necessary to get out the twist may be ascertained according to *Art*. 381—taking the vertical distance across the falling-mould at the joints, and placing it down from the two outside heights in *Fig*. 284 or 285. After bevilling the plank, the moulds are applied as at *Art*. 383—applying the pitch-board on the bevilled instead of a square edge, and placing the tips of the mould so that they will bear the same relation to the edge of the plank, as they do to the line, *j l*, in *Fig*. 284 or 285.

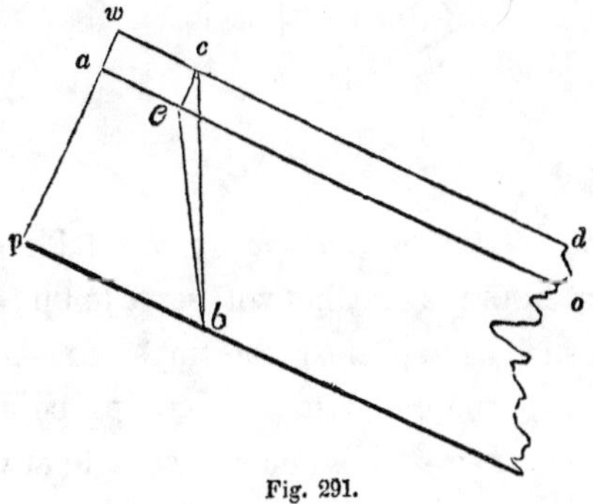

Fig. 291.

390.—*To apply the moulds without bevilling the plank.* Make *w p*, (*Fig*. 291,) equal to *w p* at *Fig*. 289, and the angle, *b c d*, equal to *b j l* in *Fig*. 284; make *p a* equal to the thickness of the plank, as *w a* in *Fig*. 289, and from *a* draw *a o*, parallel to *w d*; from *c*, draw *c e*, at right angles to *w d*, and join *e* and *b*; then the angle, *b e o*, on a square edge of the plank, having a line on the upper face at the distance, *p a*, in *Fig.* 289, at which to apply the tips of the mould—will answer the same purpose as bevilling the edge.

If the bevilled edge of the plank, which reaches from *p* to *w*, is supposed to be in the plane of the paper, and the point, *a*, to be above the plane of the paper as much as *a*, in *Fig.* 289, is distant from the line, *w p*; and the plank to be revolved on *p b* as an axis until the line, *p w*, falls below the plane of the paper, and the line, *p a*, arrives in it; then, it is evident that the point, *c*, will fall, in the line, *c e*, until it lies directly behind the point, *e*, and the line, *b c*, will lie directly behind *b e*.

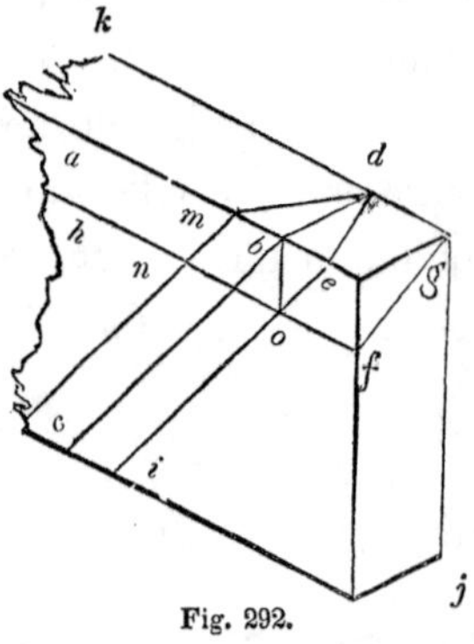

Fig. 292.

391.—*To find the bevils for splayed work.* The principle employed in the last figure is one that will serve to find the bevils for *splayed* work—such as hoppers, bread-trays, &c.—and a way of applying it to that purpose had better, perhaps, be introduced in this connection. In *Fig.* 292, *a b c* is the angle at which the work is splayed, and *b d*, on the upper edge of the board, is at right angles to *a b*; make the angle, *f g j*, equal to *a b c*, and from *f*, draw *f h*, parallel to *e a*; from *b*, draw *b o*, at right angles to *a b*; through *o*, draw *i e*, parallel to *c b*, and join *e* and *d*; then the angle, *a e d*, will be the proper bevil for the ends from the inside, or *k d e* from the outside. If a mitre-joint is required, set *f g*, the thickness of the stuff on the level, from *e* to *m*, and join *m* and *d*; then *k d m* will be the proper bevil for a mitre-joint.

If the upper edges of the splayed work is to be bevilled, so as to be horizontal when the work is placed in its proper position, *f g j*, being the same as *a b c*, will be the proper bevil for that purpose. Suppose, therefore, that a piece indicated by the lines, *k g*, *g f* and *f h*, were taken off; then a line drawn upon the bevilled surface from *d*, at right angles to *k d*, would show the true position of the joint, because it would be in the direction of the board for the other side; but a line so drawn would pass through the point, *o*,—thus proving the principle correct. So, if a line were drawn upon the bevilled surface from *d*, at an angle of 45 degrees to *k d*, it would pass through the point, *n*.

392.—*Another method for face-moulds.* It will be seen by reference to *Art.* 388, that the principal object had in view in the preparatory process of finding a face-mould, is to ascertain upon it the direction of a horizontal line. This can be found by a method different from any previously proposed; and as it requires fewer lines, and admits of less complication, it is probably to be preferred. It can be best introduced, perhaps, by the following explanation.

In *Fig.* 293, *j d* represents a prism standing upon a level base, *b d*, its upper surface forming an acute angle with the face, *b l*, as at *Fig.* 287. Extend the base line, *b c*, and the raking line, *j l*, to meet at *f*; also, extend *e d* and *g a*, to meet at *k*; from *f*, through *k*, draw *f m*. If we suppose the prism to stand upon a level floor, *o f m*, and the plane, *j g a l*, to be extended to meet that floor, then it will be obvious that the intersection between that plane and the plane of the floor would be in the line, *f k*; and the line, *f k*, being in the plane of the floor, and also in the inclined plane, *j g k f*, any line made in the plane, *j g k f*, parallel to *f k*, must be a level line. By finding the position of a perpendicular plane, at right angles to the raking plane, *j f k g*, we shall greatly shorten the process for obtaining ordinates.

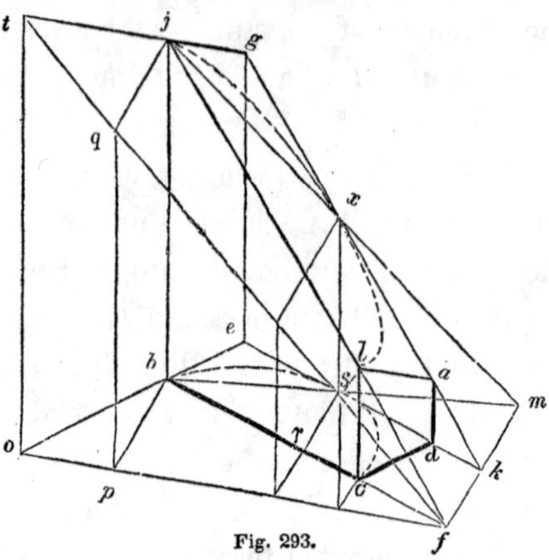

Fig. 293.

This may be done thus : from *f*, draw *f o*, at right angles to *f m ;* extend *e b* to *o*, and *g j*, to *t ;* from *o*, draw *o t*, at right angles to *o f*, and join *t* and *f ;* then *t o f* will be a perpendicular plane, at right angles to the inclined plane, *t g k f;* because the base of the former, *o f*, is at right angles to the base of the latter, *f k*, both these lines being in the same plane. From *b*, draw *b p*, at right angles to *o f*, or parallel to *f m ;* from *p*, draw *p q*, at right angles to *o f*, and from *q*, draw a line on the upper plane, parallel to *f m*, or at right angles to *t f ;* then this line will obviously be drawn to the point, *j*, and the line, *q j*, be equal to *p b*. Proceed, in the same way, from the points, *s* and *c*, to find *x* and *l*.

Now, to apply the principle here explained, let the curve, *b s c*, (*Fig.* 294,) be the base of a cylindric segment, and let it be required to find the shape of a section of this segment, cut by a plane passing through three given points in its curved surface: one perpendicularly over *b*, at the height, *b j ;* one perpendicularly over *s*, at the height, *s x ;* and the other over *c*, at the height, *c l*—these lines being drawn at right angles to the chord of the base, *b c*. From *j*, through *l*, draw a line to meet the chord line extended to *f ;* from *s*, draw *s k*, parallel to *b f*, and from *x*, draw *x k*, parallel to *j f ;* from *f*, through *k*, draw *f m ;* then *f m* will be the intersecting line of the plane of the section with the

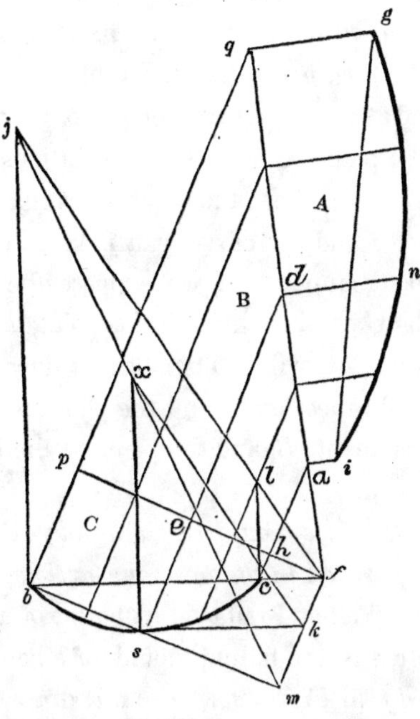

Fig. 294.

plane of the base. This line can be proved to be the intersection of these planes in another way; from *b*, through *s*, and from *j*, through *x*, draw lines meeting at *m;* then the point, *m*, will be in the intersecting line, as is shown in the figure, and also at *Fig*. 293.

From *f*, draw *f p*, at right angles to *f m;* from *b* and *c*, and from as many other points as is thought necessary, draw ordinates, parallel to *f m;* make *p q* equal to *b j*, and join *q* and *f;* from the points at which the ordinates meet the line, *q f*, draw others at right angles to *q f;* make each ordinate at *A* equal to its corresponding ordinate at *C*, and trace the curve, *g n i*, through the points thus found.

Now it may be observed that *A* is the plane of the section, *B* the plane of the segment, corresponding to the plane, *q p f*, of *Fig*. 293, and *C* is the plane of the base. To give these planes their proper position, let *A* be turned on *q f* as an axis until it stands perpendicularly over the line, *q f*, and at right angles to the plane, *B;* then, while *A* and *B* are fixed at right angles, let *B* be turned on the line, *p f*, as an axis until it stands perpendicularly over *p f*, and at right angles to the plane, *C;* then the plane, *A*, will lie over the plane, *C*, with the several lines on one corresponding to those on the other; the point, *i*, resting at *l*, the point, *n*, at *x*, and *g* at *j;* and the curve, *g n i*, lying perpendicularly over *b s c*—as was required. If we suppose the cylinder to be cut by a level plane passing through the point, *l*, (as is done in finding a face-mould,) it will be obvious that lines corresponding to *q f* and *p f* would meet in *l;* and the plane of the section, *A*, the plane of the segment, *B*, and the plane of the base, *C*, would all meet in that point.

393.—*To find the face-mould for a hand-rail according to the principles explained in the previous article.* In *Fig.* 295, *a e c f* is the plan of a hand-rail over a quarter of a cylinder; and in *Fig.* 296, *a b c d* is the falling-mould; *f e* being equal to the stretch-out of *a d f* in *Fig.* 295. From *c*, draw *c h*, parallel to *e f;* bisect *h c* in *i*, and find a point, as *b*, in the arc, *d f*, (*Fig.* 295,) corresponding to *i* in the line, *h c;* from *i*, (*Fig.* 296,) to the top of the falling-mould, draw *i j*, at right angles to *h c;* at *Fig.* 295, from *c*, through *b*, draw *c g*, and from *b* and *c*, draw *b j* and *c k*, at right angles to *g c;* make *c k* equal to *h g* at *Fig.* 296, and *b j* equal to *i j* at that figure; from *k*, through *j*, draw *k g*, and from *g*, through *a*, draw *g p;* then *g p* will be the intersecting line, corresponding to *f m* in *Fig.* 293 and 294; through *e*, draw *p* 6, at right angles to *g p*, and from *c*, draw *c q*, parallel to *g p;* make *r q* equal to *h g* at *Fig.* 296; join *p* and *q*, and proceed as in the previous examples to find the face-mould, *A*. The joint of the face-mould, *u v*, will be more accurately determined by finding the projection of the centre of the plan, *o*, as at *w;* joining *s* and *w*, and drawing *u v*, parallel to *s w*.

It may be noticed that *c k* and *b j* are not of a length corresponding to the above directions: they are but ⅓ the length given.

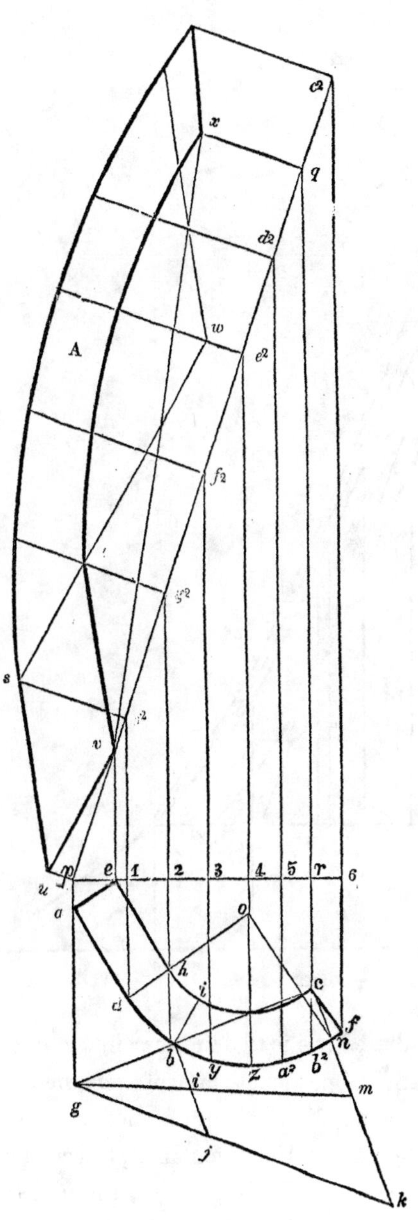

Fig. 295.

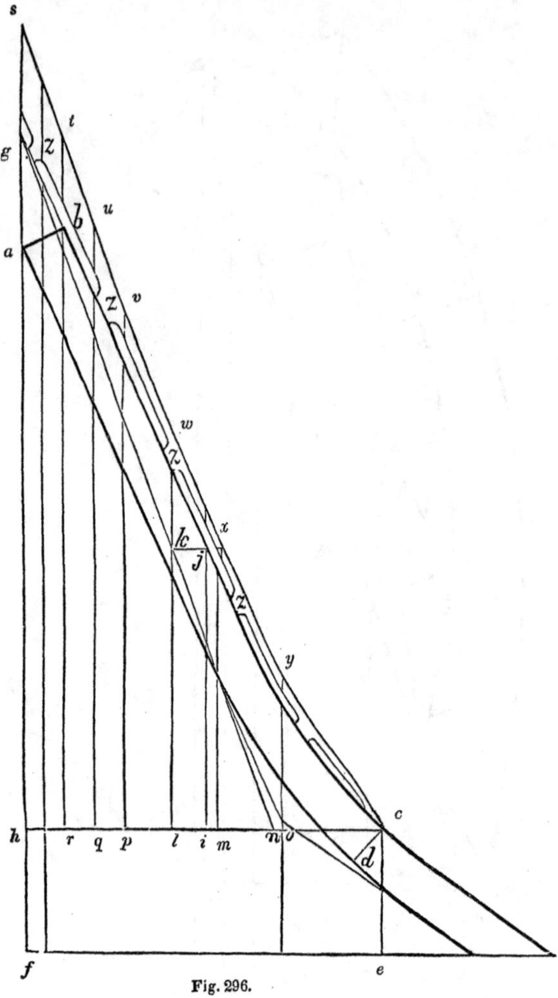

Fig. 296.

The object of drawing these lines is to find the point, *g*, and that can be done by taking any proportional parts of the lines given, as well as by taking the whole lines. For instance, supposing *c k* and *b j* to be the full length of the given lines, bisect one in *i* and the other in *m*; then a line drawn from *m*, through *i*, will give the point, *g*, as was required. The point, *g*, may also be obtained thus: at *Fig.* 296, make *h l* equal to *c b* in *Fig.* 295; from *l*, draw *l k*, at right angles to *h c;* from *j*, draw *j k*, parallel to *h c;* from *g*, through *k*, draw *g n;* at *Fig.* 295, make *b g* equal to *l n* in *Fig.* 296; then *g* will be the point required.

The reason why the points, *a*, *b* and *c*, in the plan of the rail at *Fig.* 295, are taken for resting points instead of *e*, *i* and *f*, is this: the top of the rail being level, it is evident that the points, *a* and *e*, in the section *a e*, are of the same height; also that the point, *i*, is of the same height as *b*, and *c* as *f*. Now, if *a* is taken for a point in the inclined plane rising from the line *g p*, *e* must be below that plane; if *b* is taken for a point in that plane, *i* must be below it; and if *c* is in the plane, *f* must be below it. The rule, then, for taking these points, is to take in each section the one that is nearest to the line, *g p*. Sometimes the line of intersection, *g p*, happens to come almost in the direction of the line, *e r:* in such case, after finding the line, see if the points from which the heights were taken agree with the above rule; if the heights were taken at the wrong points, take them according to the rule above, and then find the true line of intersection, which will not vary much from the one already found.

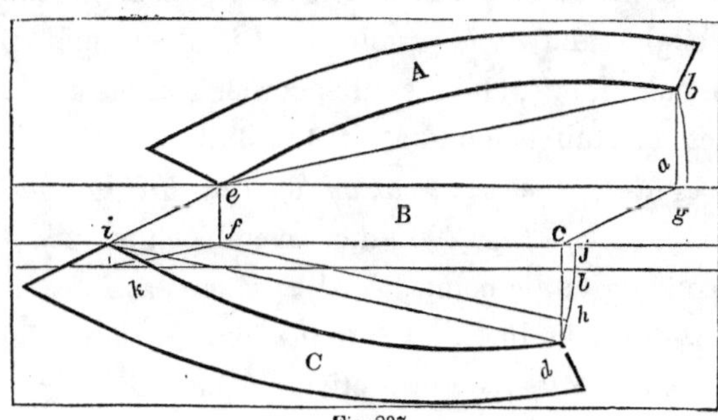

Fig. 297.

394.—*To apply the face-mould thus found to the plank.* The face-mould, when obtained by this method, is to be applied to a square-edged plank, as directed at *Art.* 383, with this difference: instead of applying both tips of the mould to the edge of the plank, one of them is to be set as far from the edge of the plank, as *x*, in *Fig.* 295, is from the chord of the section *p q*—as is shown at *Fig.* 297. *A*, in this figure, is the mould applied on the upper side of the plank, *B*, the edge of the plank, and *C*, the mould applied on the under side; *a b* and *c d* being made equal to *q x* in *Fig.* 295, and the angle, *e a c*, on the edge, equal to the angle, *p q r*, at *Fig.* 295. In order to avoid a waste of stuff, it would be advisable to apply the tips of the mould, *e* and *b*, immediately at the edge of the plank. To do this, suppose the moulds to be applied as shown in the figure; then let *A* be revolved upon *e* until the point, *b*, arrives at *g*, causing the line, *e b*, to coincide with *e g:* the mould upon the under side of the plank must now be revolved upon a point that is perpendicularly beneath *e*, as *f;* from *f*, draw *f h*, parallel to *i d*, and from *d*, draw *d h*, at right angles to *i d;* then revolve the mould, *C*, upon *f*, until the point, *h*, arrives at *j*, causing the line, *f h*, to coincide with *f j*, and the line, *i d*, to coincide with *k l;* then the tips of the mould will be at *k* and *l*.

The rule for doing this, then, will be as follows: make the angle, *i f k*, equal to the angle *q v x*, at *Fig.* 295; make *f k* equal to *f i*, and through *k*, draw *k l*, parallel to *i j;* then apply the corner of the mould, *i*, at *k*, and the other corner *d*, at the line, *k l*.

The thickness of stuff is found as at *Art.* 381.

395.—*To regulate the application of the falling-mould.* Obtain, on the line, *h c*, (*Fig.* 296,) the several points, *r*, *q*, *p*, *l* and *m*, corresponding to the points, b^2, a^2, *z*, *y*, &c., at *Fig.* 295; from *r q p*, &c., draw the lines, *r t*, *q u*, *p v*, &c., at right angles to *h c;* make *h s*, *r t*, *q u*, &c., respectively equal to 6 c^2, *r q*, 5 d^2, &c., at *Fig.* 295; through the points thus found, trace the curve, *s w c*. Then get out the piece, *g s c*, attached to the falling-mould at several places along its length, as at *z*, *z*, *z*, &c. In applying the falling-mould with this strip thus attached, the edge, *s w c*, will coincide with the upper surface of the rail piece before it is squared; and thus show the proper position of the falling-mould along its whole length. (See *Art.* 403.)

SCROLLS FOR HAND-RAILS.

396.—*General rule for finding the size and position of the regulating square.* The breadth which the scroll is to occupy, the number of its revolutions, and the relative size of the regulating square to the eye of the scroll, being given, multiply the number of revolutions by 4, and to the product add the number of times a side of the square is contained in the diameter of the eye, and the sum will be the number of equal parts into which the breadth is to be divided. Make a side of the regulating square equal to one of these parts. To the breadth of the scroll add one of the parts thus found, and half the sum will be the length of the longest ordinate.

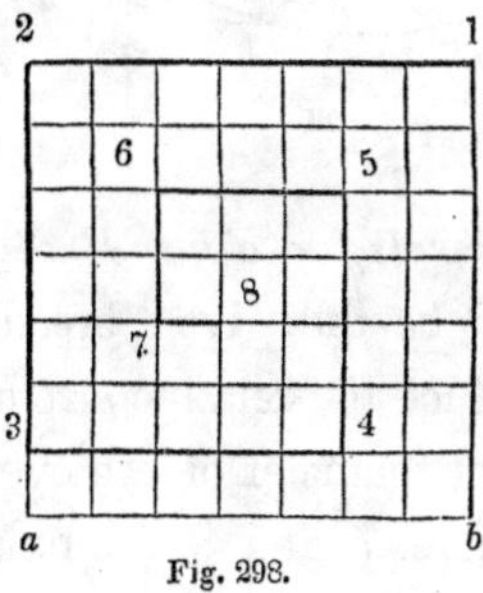

Fig. 298.

397.—*To find the proper centres in the regulating square.* Let *a* 2 1 *b*, (*Fig.* 298,) be the size of a regulating square, found according to the previous rule, the required number of revolutions being $1\frac{3}{4}$. Divide two adjacent sides, as *a* 2 and 2 1, into as many equal parts as there are quarters in the number of revolutions, as seven; from those points of division, draw lines across the square, at right angles to the lines divided; then, 1 being the first centre, 2, 3, 4, 5, 6 and 7, are the centres for the other quarters, and 8 is the centre for the eye; the heavy lines that deter-

32

mine these centres being each one part less in length than its preceding line.

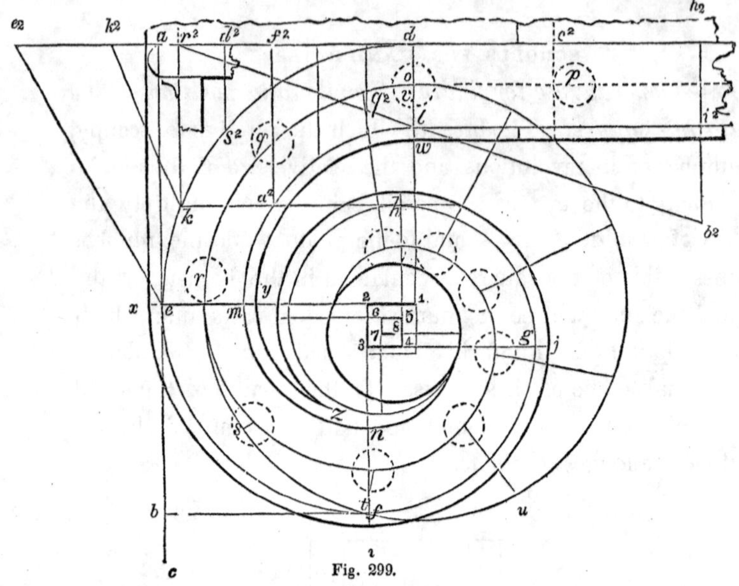

Fig. 299.

398.—*To describe the scroll for a hand-rail over a curtail step.* Let *a b*, (*Fig.* 299,) be the given breadth, $1\frac{3}{4}$ the given number of revolutions, and let the relative size of the regulating square to the eye be $\frac{1}{3}$ of the diameter of the eye. Then, by the rule, $1\frac{3}{4}$ multiplied by 4 gives 7, and 3, the number of times a side of the square is contained in the eye, being added, the sum is 10. Divide *a b*, therefore, into 10 equal parts, and set one from *b* to *c*; bisect *a c* in *e*; then *a e* will be the length of the longest ordinate, (1 *d* or 1 *e*.) From *a*, draw *a d*, from *e*, draw *e* 1, and from *b*, draw *b f*, all at right angles to *a b*; make *e* 1 equal to *e a*, and through 1, draw 1 *d*, parallel to *a b*; set *b c* from 1 to 2, and upon 1 2, complete the regulating square; divide this square as at *Fig.* 298; then describe the arcs that compose the scroll, as follows: upon 1, describe *d e*; upon 2, describe *e f*; upon 3, describe *f g*; upon 4, describe *g h*, &c.; make *d l* equal to the width of the rail, and upon 1, describe *l m*; upon 2, describe *m n*, &c.; describe the eye upon 8, and the scroll is completed.

399.—*To describe the scroll for a curtail step.* Bisect *d l*, (*Fig.* 299,) in *o*, and make *o v* equal to ⅓ of the diameter of a baluster; make *v w* equal to the projection of the nosing, and *e x* equal to *w l*; upon 1, describe *w y*, and upon 2, describe *y z*; also upon 2, describe *x i*; upon 3, describe *i j*, and so around to *z*; and the scroll for the step will be completed.

400.—*To determine the position of the balusters under the scroll.* Bisect *d l*, (*Fig.* 299,) in *o*, and upon 1, with 1 *o* for radius, describe the circle, *o r u*; set the baluster at *p* fair with the face of the second riser, c^2, and from *p*, with half the tread in the dividers, space off as at *o*, *q*, *r*, *s*, *t*, *u*, &c., as far as q^2; upon 2, 3, 4 and 5, describe the centre-line of the rail around to the eye of the scroll; from the points of division in the circle, *o r u*, draw lines to the centre-line of the rail, tending to the centre of the eye, 8; then, the intersection of these radiating lines with the centre-line of the rail, will determine the position of the balusters, as shown in the figure.

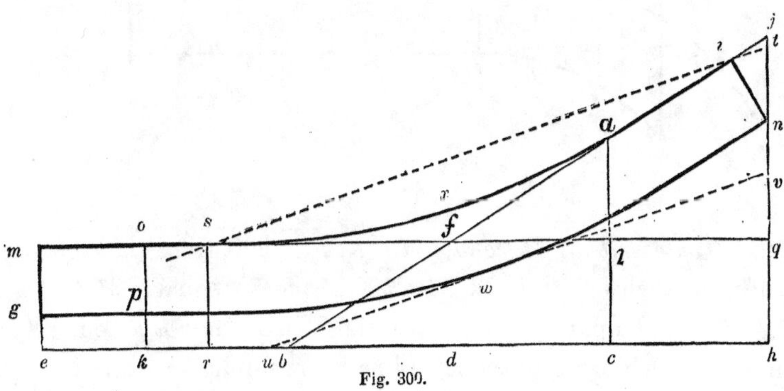

Fig. 300.

401.—*To obtain the falling-mould for the raking part of the scroll.* Tangical to the rail at *h*, (*Fig.* 299,) draw *h k*, parallel to *d a*; then *k* a^2 will be the joint between the twist and the other part of the scroll. Make *d* e^2 equal to the stretch-out of *d e*, and upon *d*

e^2, find the position of the point, k, as at k^2; at *Fig.* 300, make $e\,d$ equal to $e^2\,d$ in *Fig.* 299, and $d\ c$ equal to $d\ c^2$ in that figure; from c, draw $c\ a$, at right angles to $e\ c$, and equal to one rise; make $c\ b$ equal to one tread, and from b, through a, draw $b\ j$; bisect $a\ c$ in l, and through l, draw $m\ q$, parallel to $e\ h$; $m\ q$ is the height of the level part of a scroll, which should always be about 3½ feet from the floor; ease off the angle, $m\ f\ j$, according to *Art.* 89, and draw $g\ w\ n$, parallel to $m\ x\ j$, and at a distance equal to the thickness of the rail; at a convenient place for the joint, as i, draw $i\ n$, at right angles to $b\ j$; through n, draw $j\ h$, at right angles to $e\ h$; make $d\ k$ equal to $d\ k^2$ in *Fig.* 299, and from k, draw $k\ o$, at right angles to $e\ h$; at *Fig.* 299, make $d\ h^2$ equal to $d\ h$ in *Fig.* 300, and draw $h^2\ b^2$, at right angles to $d\ h^2$; then $k\ a^2$ and $h^2\ i^2$ will be the position of the joints on the plan, and at *Fig.* 300, $o\ p$ and $i\ n$, their position on the falling-mould; and $p\ o\ i\ n$, (*Fig.* 300,) will be the falling-mould required.

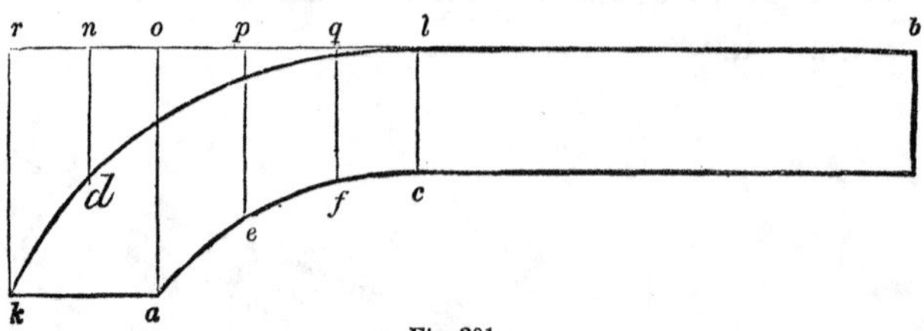

Fig. 301.

402.—*To describe the face-mould.* At *Fig.* 299, from k, draw $k\ r^2$, at right angles to $r^2\ d$; at *Fig.* 300, make $h\ r$ equal to $h^2\ r^2$ in *Fig.* 299, and from r, draw $r\ s$, at right angles to $r\ h$; from the intersection of $r\ s$ with the level line, $m\ q$, through i, draw $s\ t$; at *Fig.* 299, make $h^2\ b^2$ equal to $q\ t$ in *Fig.* 300, and join b^2 and r^2; from a^2, and from as many other points in the arcs, $a^2\ l$ and $k\ d$, as is thought necessary, draw ordinates to $r^2\ d$, at right angles to the latter; make $r\ b$, (*Fig.* 301,) equal in its length and in its divisions to the line, $r^2\ b^2$, in *Fig.* 299; from r, n, o, p, q

and *l*, draw the lines, *r k*, *n d*, *o a*, *p e*, *q f* and *l c*, at right angles to *r b*, and equal to $r^2\ k$, $d^2\ s^2$, $f^2\ a^2$, &c., in *Fig.* 299; through the points thus found, trace the curves, *k l* and *a c*, and complete the face-mould, as shown in the figure. This mould is to be applied to a square-edged plank, with the edge, *l b*, parallel to the edge of the plank. The rake lines upon the edge of the plank are to be made to correspond to the angle, *s t h*, in *Fig.* 300. The thickness of stuff required for this mould is shown at *Fig.* 300, between the lines *s t* and *u v*—*u v* being drawn parallel to *s t*.

403.—All the previous examples given for finding face-moulds over winders, are intended for *moulded* rails. For *round* rails, the same process is to be followed with this difference: instead of working from the sides of the rail, work from a centre-line. After finding the projection of that line upon the upper plane, describe circles upon it, as at *Fig.* 262, and trace the sides of the moulds by the points so found. The thickness of stuff for the twists of a round rail, is the same as for the straight; and the twists are to be sawed square through.

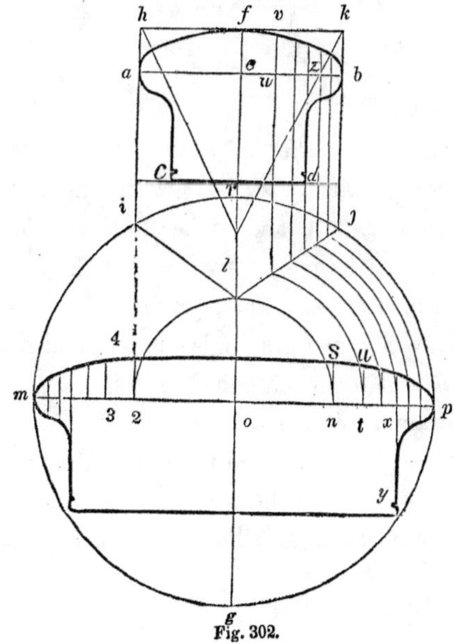

Fig. 302.

404.—*To ascertain the form of the newel-cap from a section of the rail.* Draw *a b*, (*Fig.* 302,) through the widest part of the given section, and parallel to *c d*; bisect *a b* in *e*, and through *a*, *e* and *b*, draw *h i*, *f g*, and *k j*, at right angles to *a b*; at a convenient place on the line, *f g*, as *o*, with a radius equal to half the width of the cap, describe the circle, *i j g*; make *r l* equal to *e b* or *e a*; join *l* and *j*, also *l* and *i*; from the curve, *f b*, to the line, *l j*, draw as many ordinates as is thought necessary, parallel to *f g*; from the points at which these ordinates meet the line, *l j*, and upon the centre, *o*, describe arcs in continuation to meet *o p*; from *n*, *t*, *x*, &c., draw *n s*, *t u*, &c., parallel to *f g*; make *n s*, *t u*, &c., equal to *e f*, *w v*, &c.; make *x y*, &c., equal to *z d*, &c.; make *o* 2, *o* 3, &c., equal to *o n*, *o t*, &c.; make 2 4 equal to *n s*, and in this way find the length of the lines crossing *o m*; through the points thus found, describe the section of the newel-cap, as shown in the figure.

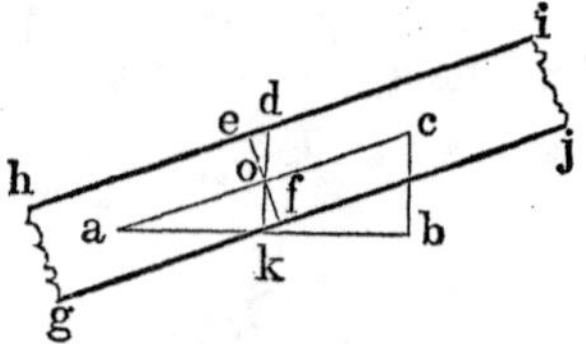

Fig. 303.

405.—*To find the true position of a butt joint for the twists of a moulded rail over platform stairs.* Obtain the shape of the mould according to *Art.* 373, and make the line *a b*, *Fig.* 303, equal to *a c*, *Fig.* 269; from *b*, draw *b c*, at right angles to *a b*, and equal in length to *n m*, *Fig.* 269; join *a* and *c*, and bisect *a c* in *o*; through *o* draw *e f*, at right angles to *a c*, and *d k*, parallel to *c b*; make *o d* and *o k* each equal to half *e h* at *Fig.* 269; through *e* and *f*, draw *h i* and *g j*, parallel to *a c*. At *Fig.* 270, make *n a* equal to *e d*, *Fig.* 303, and through *a*, draw *r p*, at right angles to *n c*; then *r p* will be the true position on the face-mould for a butt joint, as was required. The sides must be sawn vertically as described at *Art.* 374, but the joint is to be sawn square through the plank. The moulds obtained for round rails, (*Art.* 371,) give the line for the joint, when applied to either side of the plank; but here, for moulded rails, the line for the joint can be obtained from only one side. When the rail is canted up, the joint is taken from the mould laid on the upper side of the lower twist, and on the under side of the upper twist; but when it is canted down, a course just the reverse of this is to be pursued. When the rail is not canted, either up or down, the vertical joint, obtained as at *Art.* 373, will be a butt joint, and therefore, in such a case, the process described in this article will be unnecessary

---

NOTE TO ARTICLE 369.

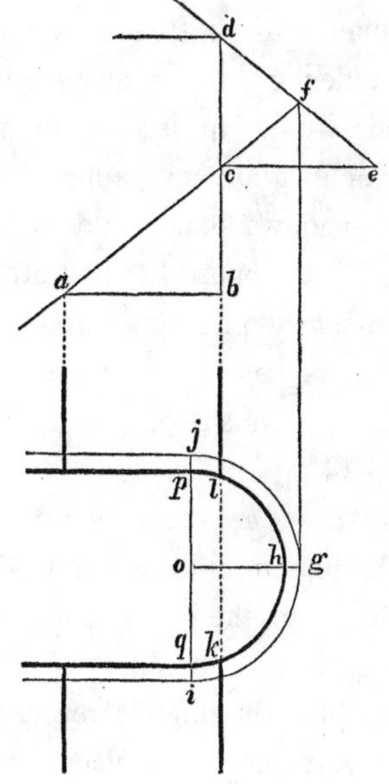

Platform stairs with a large cylinder. Instead of placing the platform-risers at the spring of the cylinder, a more easy and graceful appearance may be given to the rail, and the necessity of canting either of the twists entirely obviated, by fixing the place of the above risers at a certain distance within the cylinder, as shown in the annexed cut—the lines indicating the face of the risers cutting the cylinder at *k* and *l*, instead of at *p* and *q*, the spring of the cylinder. To ascertain the position of the risers, let *a b c* be the pitch-board of the lower flight, and *c d e* that of the upper flight, these being placed so that *b c* and *c d* shall form a right line. Extend *a c* to cut *d e* in *f*; draw *f g* parallel to *d b*, and of indefinite length: draw *g o* at right angles to *f g*, and equal in length to the radius of the circle formed by the centre of the rail in passing around the cylinder; on *o* as centre describe the semicircle *j g i;* make *o h* equal to the radius of the cylinder, and describe on *o* the face of the cylinder *p h q;* then extend *d b* across the cylinder, cutting it in *l* and *k*—giving the position of the face of the risers, as required. To find the face-mould for the twists is simple and obvious: it being merely a quarter of an ellipse, having *o j* for semi-minor axis, and the distance on the rake corresponding to *o g*, on the plan, for the semi-major axis, found thus,—extend *i j* to meet *a f*, then from this point of meeting to *f* is the semi-major axis.

SECTION VII.—SHADOWS.

406.—The art of drawing consists in representing solids upon a plane surface: so that a curious and nice adjustment of lines is made to present the same appearance to the eye, as does the human figure, a tree, or a house. It is by the effects of light, in its reflection, shade, and shadow, that the presence of an object is made known to us; so, upon paper, it is necessary, in order that the delineation may appear real, to represent fully all the shades and shadows that would be seen upon the object itself. In this section I propose to illustrate, by a few plain examples, the simple elementary principles upon which shading, in architectural subjects, is based. The necessary knowledge of drawing, preliminary to this subject, is treated of in the Introduction, from *Art.* 1 to 14.

407.—*The inclination of the line of shadow.* This is always, in architectural drawing, 45 degrees, both on the elevation and the plan; and the sun is supposed to be behind the spectator, and over his left shoulder. This can be illustrated by reference to *Fig.* 304, in which *A* represents a horizontal plane, and *B* and *C* two vertical planes placed at right angles to each other. *A* represents the plan, *C* the elevation, and *B* a vertical projection from the elevation. In finding the shadow of the plane, *B*, the

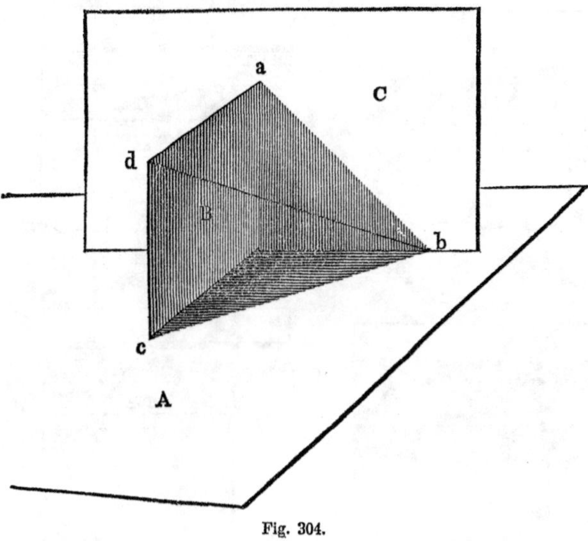

Fig. 304.

line, *a b*, is drawn at an angle of 45 degrees with the horizon, and the line, *c b*, at the same angle with the vertical plane, *B*. The plane, *B*, being a rectangle, this makes the true direction of the sun's rays to be in a course parallel to *d b;* which direction has been proved to be at an angle of 35 degrees and 16 minutes with the horizon. It is convenient, in shading, to have a set-square with the two sides that contain the right angle of equal length; this will make the two acute angles each 45 degrees; and will give the requisite bevil when worked upon the edge of the T-square. One reason why this angle is chosen in preference to another, is, that when shadows are properly made upon the drawing by it, the depth of every recess is more readily known, since the breadth of shadow and the depth of the recess will be equal.

To distinguish between the terms *shade* and *shadow*, it will be understood that all such parts of a body as are not exposed to the direct action of the sun's rays, are in *shade;* while those parts which are deprived of light by the interposition of other bodies, are in *shadow*.

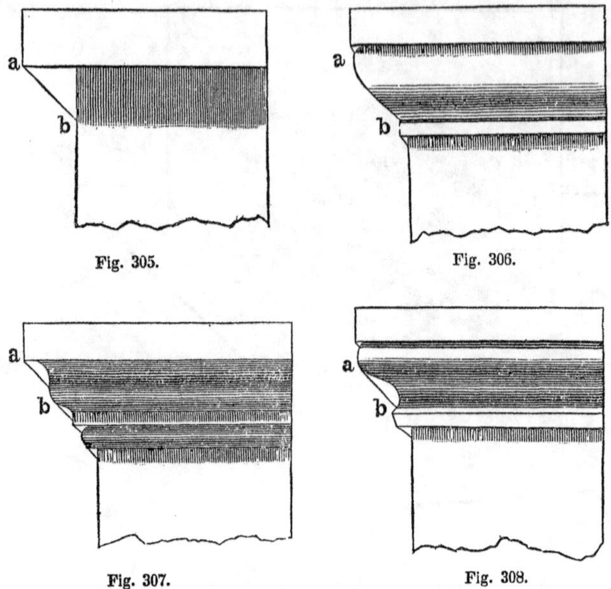

Fig. 305. Fig. 306.

Fig. 307. Fig. 308.

408.—*To find the line of shadow on mouldings and other horizontally straight projections.* *Fig.* 305, 306, 307 and 308, represent various mouldings in elevation, returned at the left, in the usual manner of mitreing around a projection. A mere inspection of the figures is sufficient to see how the line of shadow is obtained; bearing in mind that the ray, *a b*, is drawn from the projections at an angle of 45 degrees. Where there is no return at the end, it is necessary to draw a section, at any place in the length of the mouldings, and find the line of shadow from that.

409.—*To find the line of shadow cast by a shelf.* In *Fig.* 309, *A* is the plan, and *B* is the elevation of a shelf attached to a wall. From *a* and *c*, draw *a b* and *c d*, according to the angle previously directed; from *b*, erect a perpendicular intersecting *c d* at *d;* from *d*, draw *d e*, parallel to the shelf; then the lines, *c d* and *d e*, will define the shadow cast by the shelf. There is another method of finding the shadow, without the plan, *A*. Extend the lower line of the shelf to *f*, and make *c f* equal to the projection of the shelf

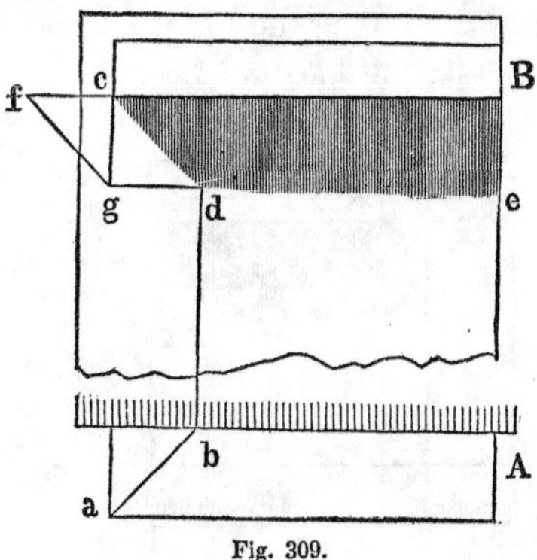

Fig. 309.

from the wall; from *f*, draw *f g*, at the customary angle, and from *c*, drop the vertical line, *c g*, intersecting *f g* at *g*; from *g*, draw *g e*, parallel to the shelf, and from *c*, draw *c d*, at the usual angle; then the lines, *c d* and *d e*, will determine the extent of the shadow as before.

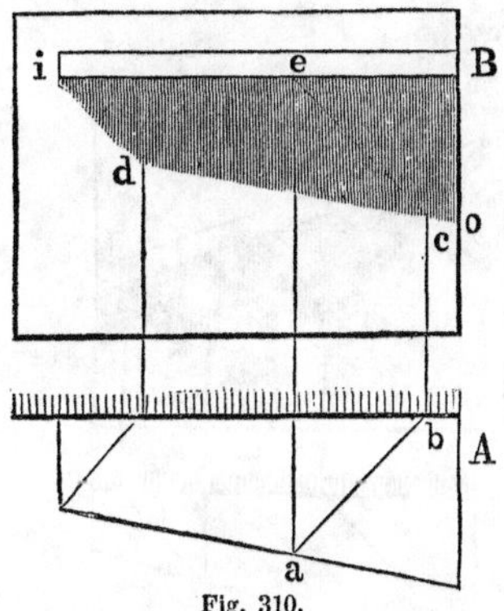

Fig. 310.

410.—*To find the shadow cast by a shelf, which is wider at one end than at the other.* In *Fig.* 310, *A* is the plan, and *B* the elevation. Find the point, *d*, as in the previous example, and from any other point in the front of the shelf, as *a*, erect the perpendicular, *a e*; from *a* and *e*, draw *a b* and *e c*, at the proper angle, and from *b*, erect the perpendicular, *b c*, intersecting *e c* in *c*;

from *d*, through *c*, draw *d o ;* then the lines, *i d* and *d o*, will give the limit of the shadow cast by the shelf.

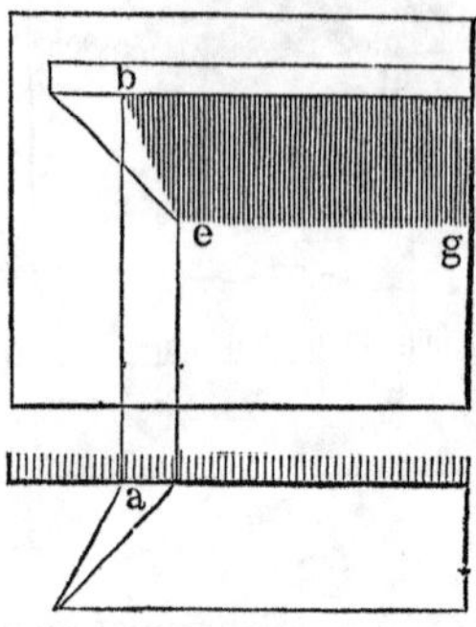

Fig. 311.

411.—*To find the shadow of a shelf having one end acute or obtuse angled. Fig.* 311 shows the plan and elevation of an acute-angled shelf. Find the line, *e g*, as before; from *a*, erect the perpendicular, *a b ;* join *b* and *e ;* then *b e* and *e g* will define the boundary of shadow.

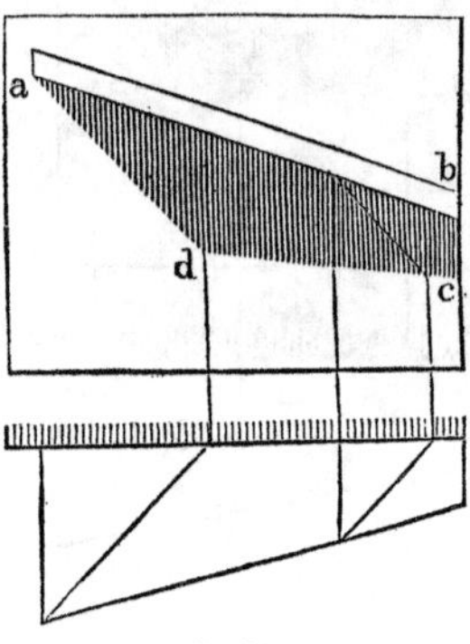

Fig. 312.

412.—*To find the shadow cast by an inclined shelf.* In *Fig.* 312, the plan and elevation of such a shelf is shown, having also one end wider than the other. Proceed as directed for finding the shadows of *Fig.* 310, and find the points, *d* and *c ;* then *a d* and *d c* will be the shadow required. If the shelf had been parallel in width on the plan, then the line, *d c*, would have been parallel with the shelf, *a b*.

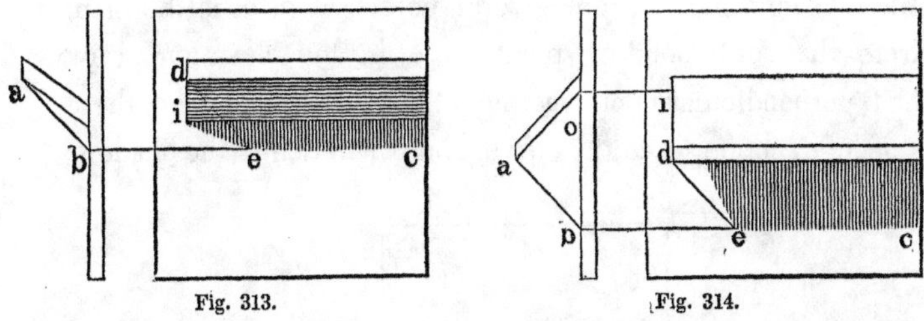

Fig. 313. Fig. 314.

413.—*To find the shadow cast by a shelf inclined in its vertical section either upward or downward.* From *a*, (*Fig.* 313 and 314,) draw *a b*, at the usual angle, and from *b*, draw *b c*, parallel with the shelf; obtain the point, *e*, by drawing a line from *d*, at the usual angle. In *Fig.* 313, join *e* and *i*; then *i e* and *e c* will define the shadow. In *Fig.* 314, from *o*, draw *o i*, parallel with the shelf; join *i* and *e*; then *i e* and *e c* will be the shadow required.

The projections in these several examples are bounded by straight lines; but the shadows of curved lines may be found in the same manner, by projecting shadows from several points in the curved line, and tracing the curve of shadow through these points. Thus—

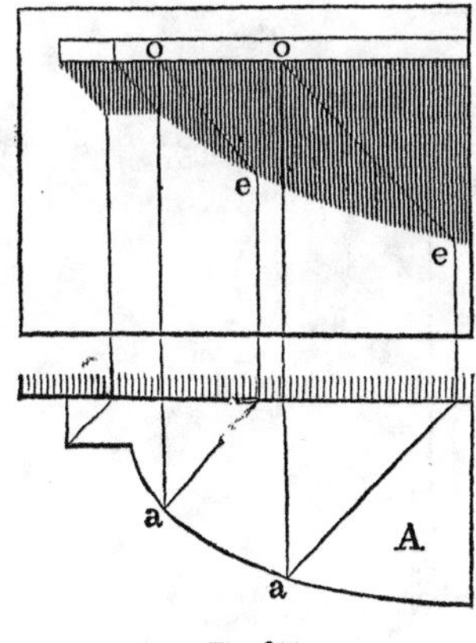

Fig. 315.

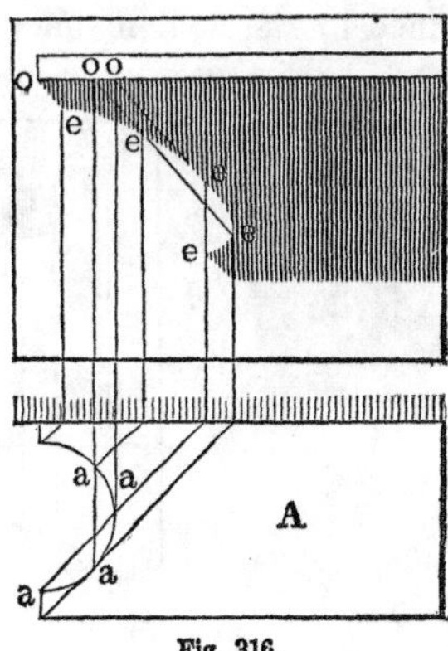

Fig. 316.

414.—*To find the shadow of a shelf having its front edge, or end, curved on the plan.* In *Fig.* 315 and 316, *A* and *A* show an example of each kind. From several points, as *a*, *a*, in the plan, and from the corresponding points, *o*, *o*, in the elevation, draw rays and perpendiculars intersecting at *e*, *e*, &c.; through these points of intersection trace the curve, and it will define the shadow.

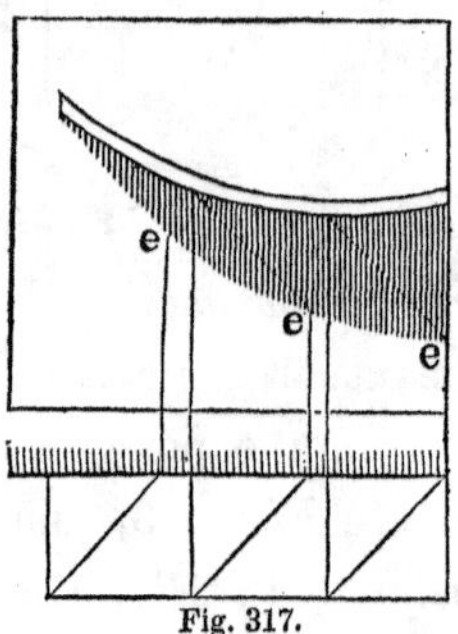

Fig. 317.

415.—*To find the shadow of a shelf curved in the elevation.* In *Fig.* 317, find the points of intersection, *e*, *e* and *e*, as in the last examples, and a curve traced through them will define the shadow.

The preceding examples show how to find shadows when cast upon a *vertical plane;* shadows thrown upon *curved surfaces* are ascertained in a similar manner. Thus—

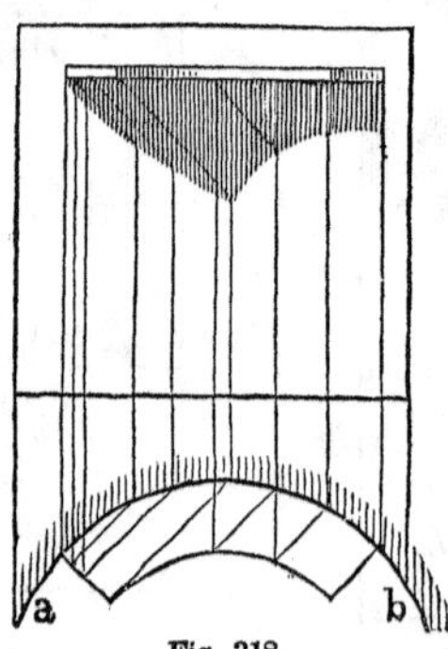

Fig. 318.

416.—*To find the shadow cast upon a cylindrical wall by a projection of any kind.* By an inspection of *Fig.* 318, it will be seen that the only difference between this and the last examples, is, that the rays in the plan die against the circle, *a b*, instead of a straight line.

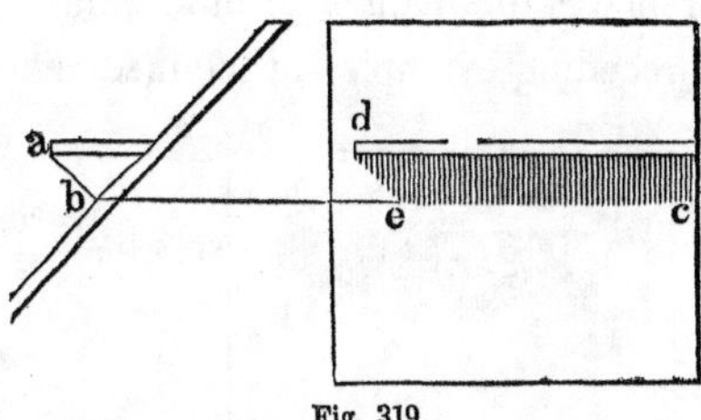

Fig. 319.

417.—*To find the shadow cast by a shelf upon an inclined wall.* Cast the ray, *a b*, (*Fig.* 319,) from the end of the shelf to the face of the wall, and from *b*, draw *b c*, parallel to the shelf; cast the ray, *d e*, from the end of the shelf; then the lines, *d e* and *e c*, will define the shadow.

These examples might be multiplied, but enough has been given to illustrate the general principle, by which shadows in all instances are found. Let us attend now to the application of this principle to such familiar objects as are likely to occur in practice.

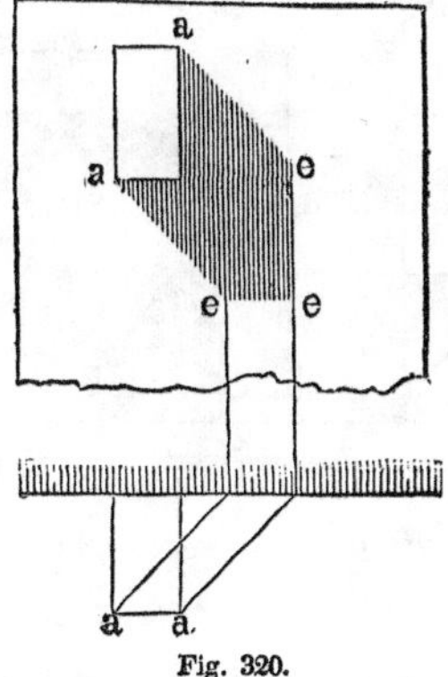

Fig. 320.

418.—*To find the shadow of a projecting horizontal beam.* From the points, *a, a,* &c., (*Fig.* 320,) cast rays upon the wall; the intersections, *e, e, e,* of those rays with the perpendiculars drawn from the plan, will define the shadow. If the beam be inclined, either on the plan or elevation, at any angle other than a right angle, the difference in the manner of proceeding can be seen by reference to the preceding examples of inclined shelves, &c.

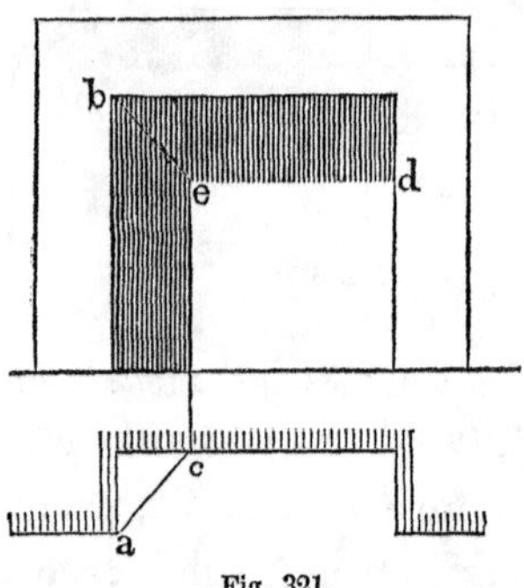

Fig. 321.

419.—*To find the shadow in a recess.* From the point, *a,* (*Fig.* 321,) in the plan, and *b* in the elevation, draw the rays, *a c* and *b e;* from *c,* erect the perpendicular, *c e,* and from *e,* draw the horizontal line, *e d;* then the lines, *c e* and *e d,* will show the extent of the shadow. This applies only where the back of the recess is parallel with the face of the wall.

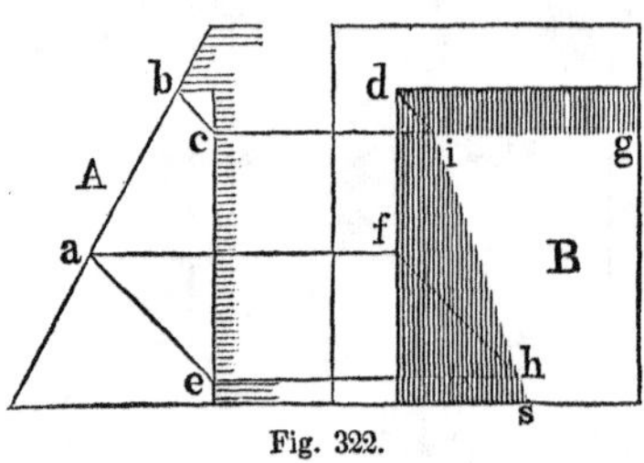

Fig. 322.

420.—*To find the shadow in a recess, when the face of the wall is inclined, and the back of the recess is vertical.* In *Fig.* 322, *A* shows the section and *B* the elevation of a recess of this kind. From *b*, and from any other point in the line, *b a*, as *a*, draw the rays, *b c* and *a e;* from *c*, *a*, and *e*, draw the horizontal lines, *c g*, *a f*, and *e h;* from *d* and *f*, cast the rays, *d i* and *f h;* from *i*, through *h*, draw *i s;* then *s i* and *i g* will define the shadow.

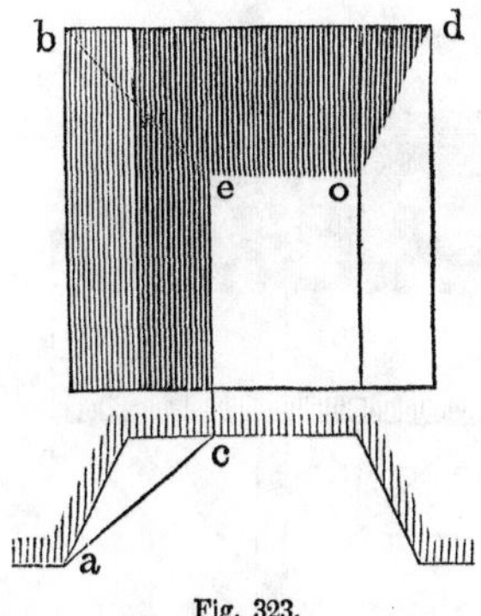

Fig. 323.

421.—*To find the shadow in a fireplace.* From *a* and *b*, (*Fig.* 323,) cast the rays, *a c* and *b e*, and from *c*, erect the perpendicular, *c e;* from *e*, draw the horizontal line, *e o*, and join *o* and *d;* then *c e*, *e o*, and *o d*, will give the extent of the shadow.

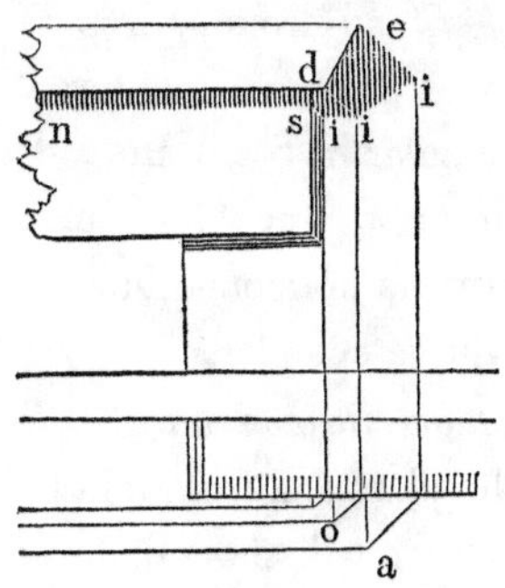

Fig. 324.

422.—*To find the shadow of a moulded window-lintel.* Cast rays from the projections, *a*, *o*, &c., in the plan, (*Fig.* 324,) and *d*, *e*, &c., in the elevation, and draw the usual perpendiculars intersecting the rays at *i*, *i*, and *i;* these intersections connected and horizontal lines drawn from them, will define the shadow. The shadow on the face of the lintel is found by casting a ray back from *i* to *s*, and drawing the horizontal line, *s n*.

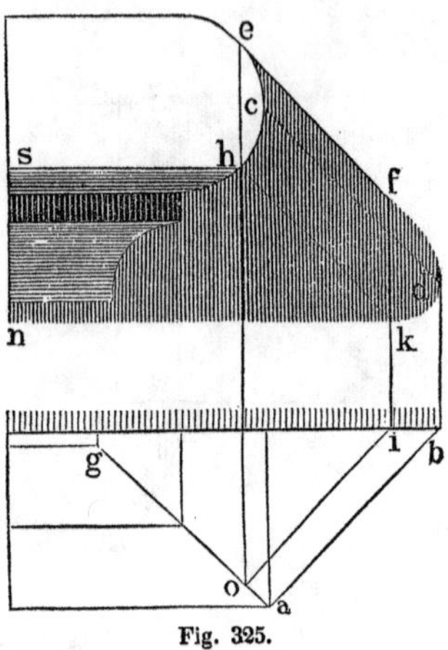

Fig. 325.

423.—*To find the shadow cast by the nosing of a step.* From *a*, (*Fig*. 325,) and its corresponding point, *c*, cast the rays, *a b* and *c d*, and from *b*, erect the perpendicular, *b d*; tangical to the curve at *e*, cast the ray, *e f*, and from *e*, drop the perpendicular, *e o*, meeting the mitre-line, *a g*, in *o*; cast a ray from *o* to *i*, and from *i*, erect the perpendicular, *i f*; from *h*, draw the ray, *h k*; from *f* to *d* and from *d* to *k*, trace the curve as shown in the figure; from *k* and *h*, draw the horizontal lines, *k n* and *h s*; then the limit of the shadow will be completed.

424.—*To find the shadow thrown by a pedestal upon steps.* From *a*, (*Fig*. 326,) in the plan, and from *c* in the elevation, draw the rays, *a b* and *c e*; then *a o* will show the extent of the shadow on the first riser, as at *A*; *f g* will determine the shadow on the second riser, as at *B*; *c d* gives the amount of shadow on the first tread, as at *C*, and *h i* that on the second tread, as at *D*; which completes the shadow of the left-hand pedestal, both on the plan and elevation. A mere inspection of the figure will be suf-

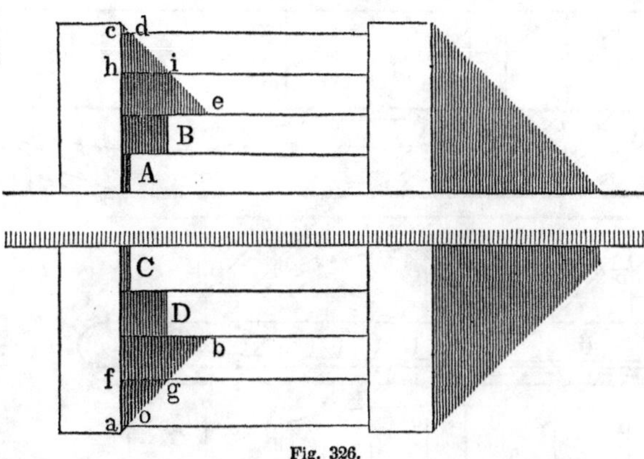

Fig. 326.

ficient to show how the shadow of the right-hand pedestal is obtained.

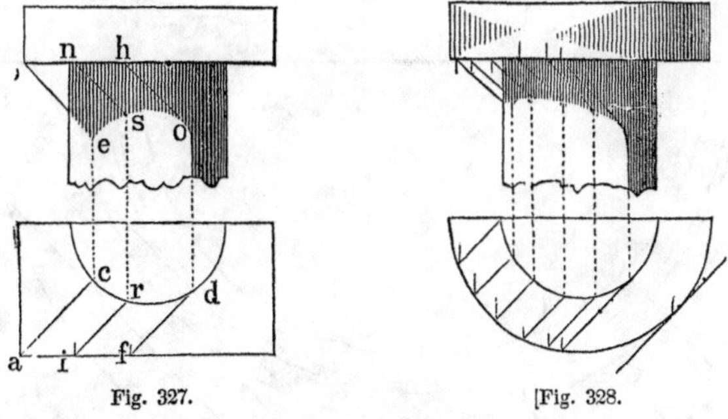

Fig. 327. Fig. 328.

425.—*To find the shadow thrown on a column by a square abacus.* From *a* and *b*, (*Fig.* 327,) draw the rays, *a c* and *b e*, and from *c*, erect the perpendicular, *c e*; tangical to the curve at *d*, draw the ray, *d f*, and from *h*, corresponding to *f* in the plan, draw the ray, *h o*; take any point between *a* and *f*, as *i*, and from this, as also from a corresponding point, *n*, draw the rays, *i r* and *n s*; from *r*, and from *d*, erect the perpendiculars, *r s* and *d o*; through the points, *e*, *s*, and *o*, trace the curve as shown in the figure; then the extent of the shadow will be defined.

426.—*To find the shadow thrown on a column by a circular abacus.* This is so near like the last example, that no explanation will be necessary farther than a reference to the preceding article.

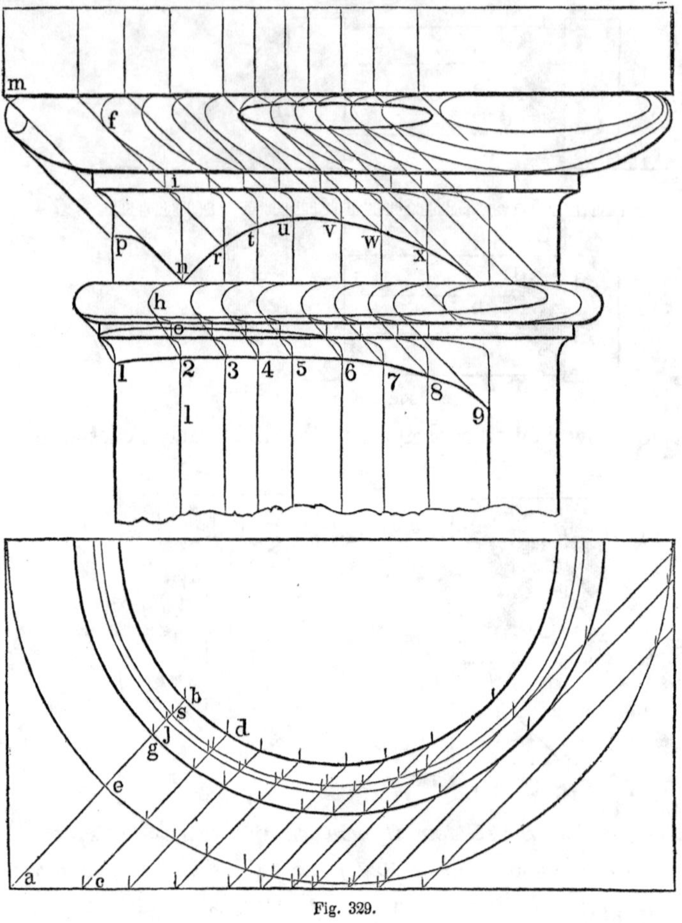

Fig. 329.

427.—*To find the shadows on the capital of a column.* This may be done according to the principles explained in the examples already given; a quicker way of doing it, however, is as follows. If we take into consideration one ray of light in connection with all those perpendicularly under and over it, it is evident that these several rays would form a vertical plane, standing at an angle of 45 degrees with the face of the elevation. Now, we may suppose the column to be *sliced*, so to speak, with planes of this

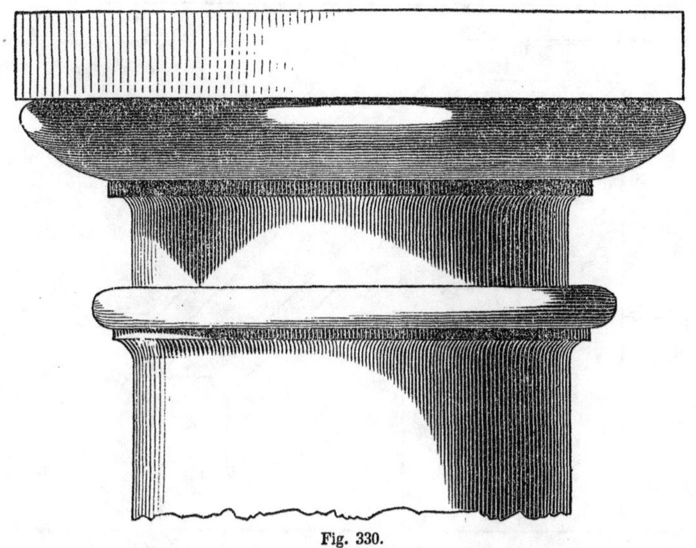

Fig. 330.

nature—cutting it in the lines, *a b*, *c d*, &c., (*Fig.* 329,) and, in the elevation, find, by squaring up from the plan, the *lines of section* which these planes would make thereupon. For instance: in finding upon the elevation the line of section, *a b*, the plane cuts the ovolo at *e*, and therefore *f* will be the corresponding point upon the elevation; *h* corresponds with *g*, *i* with *j*, *o* with *s*, and *l* with *b*. Now, to find the shadows upon this line of section, cast from *m*, the ray, *m n*, from *h*, the ray, *h o*, &c.; then that part of the section indicated by the letters, *m f i n*, and that part also between *h* and *o*, will be under shadow. By an inspection of the figure, it will be seen that the same process is applied to each line of section, and in that way the points, *p*, *r*, *t*, *u*, *v*, *w*, *x*, as also 1, 2, 3, &c., are successively found, and the lines of shadow traced through them.

Fig. 330 is an example of the same capital with all the shadows finished in accordance with the lines obtained on *Fig.* 329.

428.—*To find the shadow thrown on a vertical wall by a column and entablature standing in advance of said wall.* Cast

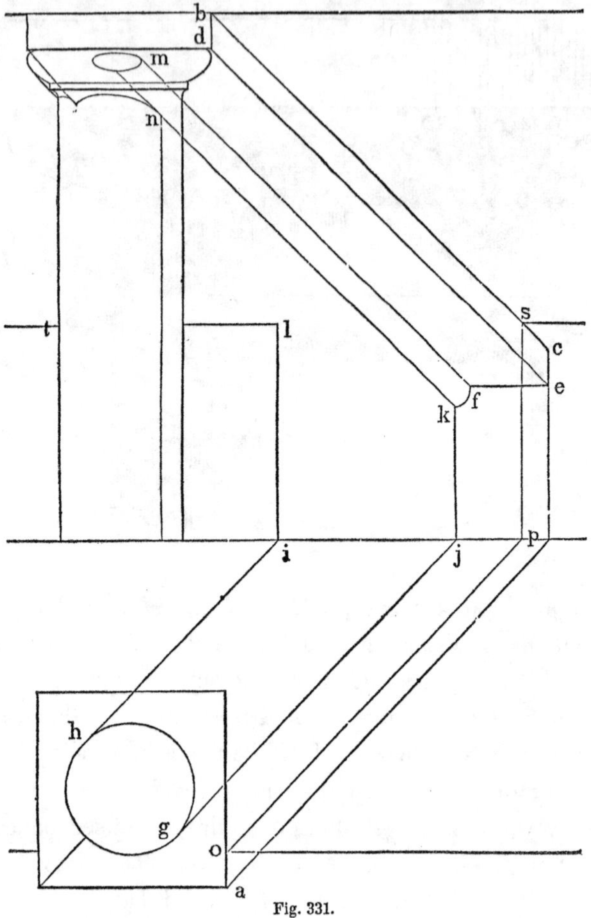

Fig. 331.

rays from *a* and *b*, (*Fig.* 331,) and find the point, *c*, as in the previous examples; from *d*, draw the ray, *d e*, and from *e*, the horizontal line, *e f;* tangical to the curve at *g* and *h*, draw the rays, *g j* and *h i*, and from *i* and *j*, erect the perpendiculars, *i l* and *j k;* from *m* and *n*, draw the rays, *m f* and *n k*, and trace the curve between *k* and *f;* cast a ray from *o* to *p*, a vertical line from *p* to *s*, and through *s*, draw the horizontal line, ***s t;*** **the** shadow as required will then be completed.

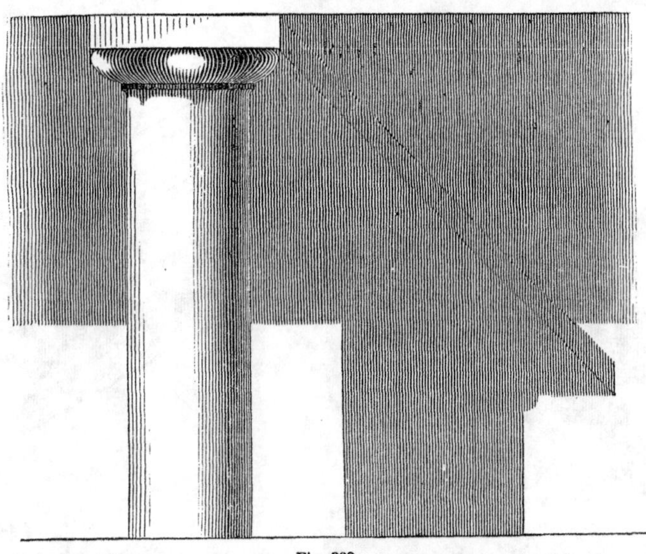

Fig. 332.

Fig. 332 is an example of the same kind as the last, with all the shadows filled in, according to the lines obtained in the preceding figure.

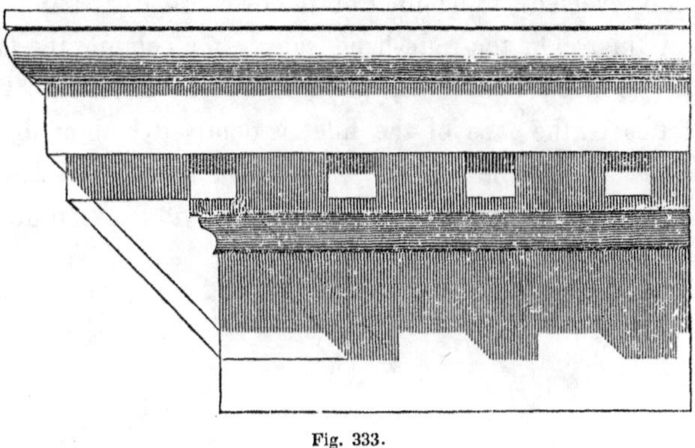

Fig. 333.

429.—*Fig.* 333 and 334 are examples of the Tuscan cornice. The manner of obtaining the shadows is evident.

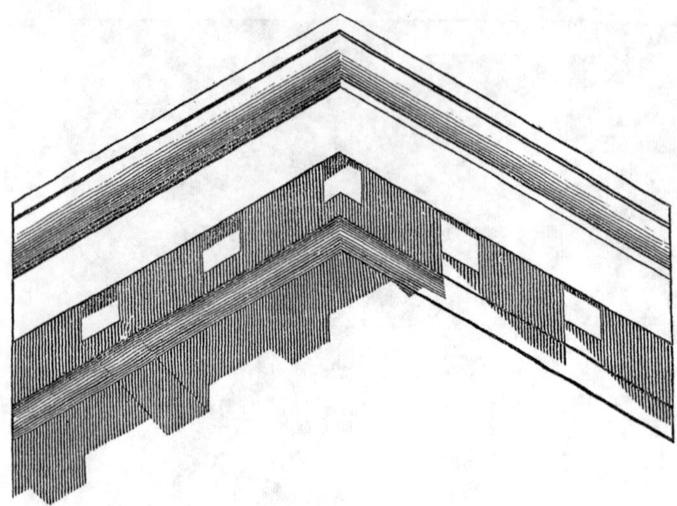

Fig. 334.

430.—*Reflected light.* In shading, the finish and life of an object depend much on reflected light This is seen to advantage in *Fig.* 330 and on the column in *Fig.* 332. Reflected rays are thrown in a direction exactly the reverse of direct rays; therefore, on that part of an object which is subject to reflected light, the shadows are reversed. The fillet of the ovolo in *Fig.* 330 is an example of this. On the right-hand side of the column, the face of the fillet is much darker than the cove directly under it. The reason of this is, the face of the fillet is deprived both of direct and reflected light, whereas the cove is subject to the latter. Other instances of the effect of reflected light will be seen in the other examples.

APPENDIX.

GLOSSARY.

Terms not found here can be found in the lists of definitions in other parts of this book, or in common dictionaries.

Abacus.—The uppermost member of a capital.

Abbatoir.—A slaughter-house.

Abbey.—The residence of an abbot or abbess.

Abutment.—That part of a pier from which the arch springs.

Acanthus.—A plant called in English, *bear's-breech.* Its leaves are employed for decorating the Corinthian and the Composite capitals.

Acropolis.—The highest part of a city; generally the citadel.

Acroteria.—The small pedestals placed on the extremities and apex of a pediment, originally intended as a base for sculpture.

Aisle.—Passage to and from the pews of a church. In Gothic architecture, the lean-to wings on the sides of the *nave.*

Alcove.—Part of a chamber separated by an *estrade,* or partition of columns. Recess with seats, &c., in gardens.

Altar.—A pedestal whereon sacrifice was offered. In modern churches, the area within the railing in front of the pulpit.

Alto-relievo.—High relief; sculpture projecting from a surface so as to appear nearly isolated.

Amphitheatre.—A double theatre, employed by the ancients for the exhibition of gladiatorial fights and other shows.

Ancones.—Trusses employed as an apparent support to a cornice upon the flanks of the architrave.

Annulet.—A small square moulding used to separate others; the fillets in the Doric capital under the ovolo, and those which separate the flutings of columns, are known by this term.

Antæ.—A pilaster attached to a wall.

Apiary.—A place for keeping beehives.

Arabesque.—A building after the Arabian style.

Areostyle.—An intercolumniation of from four to five diameters.

Arcade—A series of arches.

Arch.—An arrangement of stones or other material in a curvilinear form, so as to perform the office of a lintel and carry superincumbent weights.

Architrave.—That part of the entablature which rests upon the capital of a column, and is beneath the frieze. The casing and mouldings about a door or window.

Archivolt.—The ceiling of a vault: the under surface of an arch.

Area.—Superficial measurement. An open space, below the level of the ground, in front of basement windows.

Arsenal.—A public establishment for the deposition of arms and warlike stores.

Astragal.—A small moulding consisting of a half-round with a fillet on each side.

Attic.—A low story erected over an order of architecture. A low additional story immediately under the roof of a building.

Aviary.—A place for keeping and breeding birds.

Balcony.—An open gallery projecting from the front of a building.

Baluster.—A small pillar or pilaster supporting a rail.

Balustrade.—A series of balusters connected by a rail.

Barge-course.—That part of the covering which projects over the gable of a building.

Base.—The lowest part of a wall, column, &c.

Basement-story.—That which is immediately under the principal story, and included within the foundation of the building.

Basso-relievo.—Low relief; sculptured figures projecting from a surface one-half their thickness or less. See *Alto-relievo.*

Battering.—See *Talus.*

Battlement.—Indentations on the top of a wall or parapet.

Bay-window.—A window projecting in two or more planes, and not forming the segment of a circle.

Bazaar.—A species of mart or exchange for the sale of various articles of merchandise.

Bead.—A circular moulding.

Bed-mouldings.—Those mouldings which are between the corona and the frieze.

Belfry.—That part of a steeple in which the bells are hung: anciently called *campanile.*

Belvedere.—An ornamental turret or observatory commanding a pleasant prospect.

Bow-window.—A window projecting in curved lines.

Bressummer.—Abeam or iron tie supporting a wall over a gateway or other opening.

Brick-nogging.—The brickwork between studs of partitions.

Buttress.—A projection from a wall to give additional strength.

Cable.—A cylindrical moulding placed in flutes at the lower part of the column.

Camber.—To give a convexity to the upper surface of a beam.

Campanile.—A tower for the reception of bells, usually, in Italy, separated from the church.

Canopy.—An ornamental covering over a seat of state.

Cantalivers.—The ends of rafters under a projecting roof. Pieces of wood or stone supporting the eaves.

Capital.—The uppermost part of a column included between the shaft and the architrave.

Caravansera.—In the East, a large public building for the reception of travellers by caravans in the desert.

Carpentry.—(From the Latin, *carpentum,* carved wood.) That department of science and art which treats of the disposition, the construction and the relative strength of timber. The first is called descriptive, the second constructive, and the last mechanical carpentry.

Caryatides.—Figures of women used instead of columns to support an entablature.

Casino.—A small country-house.

Castellated.—Built with battlements and turrets in imitation of ancient castles.

Castle.—A building fortified for military defence. A house with towers, usually encompassed with walls and moats, and having a donjon, or keep, in the centre.

Catacombs.—Subterraneous places for burying the dead.

Cathedral.—The principal church of a province or diocese, wherein the throne of the archbishop or bishop is placed.

Cavetto.—A concave moulding comprising the quadrant of a circle.

Cemetery.—An edifice or area where the dead are interred.

Cenotaph.—A monument erected to the memory of a person buried in another place.

Centring.—The temporary woodwork, or framing, whereon any vaulted work is constructed.

Cesspool.—A well under a drain or pavement to receive the waste-water and sediment.

Chamfer.—The bevilled edge of any thing originally right-angled.

Chancel.—That part of a Gothic church in which the altar is placed.

Chantry.—A little chapel in ancient churches, with an endowment for one or more priests to say mass for the relief of souls out of purgatory.

Chapel.—A building for religious worship, erected separately from a church, and served by a chaplain.

Chaplet.—A moulding carved into beads, olives, &c.

Cincture.—The ring, listel, or fillet, at the top and bottom of a column, which divides the shaft of the column from its capital and base.

Circus.—A straight, long, narrow building used by the Romans for the exhibition of public spectacles and chariot races. At the present day, a building enclosing an arena for the exhibition of feats of horsemanship.

Clere-story.—The upper part of the nave of a church above the roofs of the aisles.

Cloister.—The square space attached to a regular monastery or large church, having a peristyle or ambulatory around it, covered with a range of buildings.

Coffer-dam.—A case of piling, water-tight, fixed in the bed of a river, for the purpose of excluding the water while any work, such as a wharf, wall, or the pier of a bridge, is carried up.

Collar-beam.—A horizontal beam framed between two principal rafters above the tie-beam.

Collonade.—A range of columns.

Columbarium.—A pigeon-house.

Column.—A vertical, cylindrical support under the entablature of an order.

Common-rafters.—The same as *jack-rafters*, which see

Conduit.—A long, narrow, walled passage underground, for secret communication between different apartments. A canal or pipe for the conveyance of water.

Conservatory.—A building for preserving curious and rare exotic plants.

Consoles.—The same as *ancones*, which see.

Contour.—The external lines which bound and terminate a figure.

Convent.—A building for the reception of a society of religious persons.

Coping.—Stones laid on the top of a wall to defend it from the weather.

Corbels.—Stones or timbers fixed in a wall to sustain the timbers of a floor or roof.

Cornice.—Any moulded projection which crowns or finishes the part to which it is affixed.

Corona.—That part of a cornice which is between the crown-moulding and the bed-mouldings.

Cornucopia.—The horn of plenty.

Corridor.—An open gallery or communication to the different apartments of a house.

Cove.—A concave moulding.

Cripple-rafters.—The short rafters which are spiked to the hip-rafter of a roof.

Crockets.—In Gothic architecture, the ornaments placed along the angles of pediments, pinnacles, &c.

Crosettes.—The same as *ancones*, which see.

Crypt.—The under or hidden part of a building.

Culvert.—An arched channel of masonry or brickwork, built beneath the bed of a canal for the purpose of conducting water under it. Any arched channel for water underground.

Cupola.—A small building on the top of a dome.

Curtail-step.—A step with a spiral end, usually the first of the flight.

Cusps.—The pendents of a pointed arch.

Cyma.—An ogee. There are two kinds; the *cyma-recta*, having the upper part concave and the lower convex, and the *cyma-reversa*, with the upper part convex and the lower concave.

Dado.—The die, or part between the base and cornice of a pedestal.

Dairy.—An apartment or building for the preservation of milk, and the manufacture of it into butter, cheese, &c.

Dead-shoar.—A piece of timber or stone stood vertically in brick-work, to support a superincumbent weight until the brickwork which is to carry it has set or become hard.

Decastyle.—A building having ten columns in front.

Dentils.—(From the Latin, *dentes*, teeth.) Small rectangular blocks used in the bed-mouldings of some of the orders.

Diastyle.—An intercolumniation of three, or, as some say, four diameters.

Die.—That part of a pedestal included between the base and the cornice; it is also called a *dado*.

Dodecastyle.—A building having twelve columns in front.

Donjon.—A massive tower within ancient castles to which the garrison might retreat in case of necessity.

Dooks.—A Scotch term given to wooden bricks.

Dormer.—A window placed on the roof of a house, the frame being placed vertically on the rafters.

Dormitory.—A sleeping-room.

Dovecote.—A building for keeping tame pigeons. A columbarium.

Echinus.—The Grecian ovolo.

Elevation.—A geometrical projection drawn on a plane at right angles to the horizon.

Entablature.—That part of an order which is supported by the columns; consisting of the architrave, frieze, and cornice.

Eustyle.—An intercolumniation of two and a quarter diameters.

Exchange.—A building in which merchants and brokers meet to transact business.

Extrados.—The exterior curve of an arch.

Façade.—The principal front of any building.

Face-mould—The pattern for marking the plank, out of which hand-railing is to be cut for stairs, &c.

Facia, or *Fascia.*—A flat member like a band or broad fillet.

Falling-mould.—The mould applied to the convex, vertical surface of the rail-piece, in order to form the back and under surface of the rail, and finish the squaring.

Festoon.—An ornament representing a wreath of flowers and leaves.

Fillet.—A narrow flat band, listel, or annulet, used for the separation of one moulding from another, and to give breadth and firmness to the edges of mouldings.

Flutes.—Upright channels on the shafts of columns.

Flyers.—Steps in a flight of stairs that are parallel to each other.

Forum.—In ancient architecture, a public market; also, a place where the common courts were held, and law pleadings carried on.

Foundry.—A building in which various metals are cast into moulds or shapes.

Frieze.—That part of an entablature included between the architrave and the cornice.

Gable.—The vertical, triangular piece of wall at the end of a roof, from the level of the eaves to the summit.

Gain.—A recess made to receive a tenon or tusk.

Gallery.—A common passage to several rooms in an upper story. A long room for the reception of pictures. A platform raised on columns, pilasters, or piers.

Girder.—The principal beam in a floor for supporting the binding and other joists, whereby the bearing or length is lessened.

Glyph.—A vertical, sunken channel. From their number, those in the Doric order are called *triglyphs*.

Granary.—A building for storing grain, especially that intended to be kept for a considerable time.

Groin.—The line formed by the intersection of two arches, which cross each other at any angle.

Guttæ.—The small cylindrical pendent ornaments, otherwise called *drops*, used in the Doric order under the triglyphs, and also pendent from the mutuli of the cornice.

Gymnasium.—Originally, a space measured out and covered with sand for the exercise of athletic games; afterwards, spacious buildings devoted to the mental as well as corporeal instruction of youth.

Hall.—The first large apartment on entering a house. The public room of a corporate body. A manor-house.

Ham.—A house or dwelling-place. A street or village: hence Notting*ham*, Bucking*ham*, &c. *Hamlet*, the diminutive of *ham*, is a small street or village.

Helix.—The small volute, or twist, under the abacus in the Corinthian capital.

Hem.—The projecting spiral fillet of the Ionic capital.

Hexastyle.—A building having six columns in front.

Hip-rafter.—A piece of timber placed at the angle made by two adjacent inclined roofs.

Homestall.—A mansion-house, or seat in the country.

Hotel, or *Hostel.*—A large inn or place of public entertainment. A large house or palace.

Hot-house.—A glass building used in gardening.

Hovel.—An open shed.

Hut.—A small cottage or hovel generally constructed of earthy materials, as strong loamy clay, &c.

Impost.—The capital of a pier or pilaster which supports an arch.

Intaglio.—Sculpture in which the subject is hollowed out, so that the impression from it presents the appearance of a bas-relief.

Intercolumniation.—The distance between two columns.

Intrados.—The interior and lower curve of an arch.

Jack-rafters.—Rafters that fill in between the principal rafters of a roof; called also *common-rafters.*

Jail.—A place of legal confinement.

Jambs.—The vertical sides of an aperture.

Joggle-piece.—A post to receive struts.

Joists.—The timbers to which the boards of a floor or the laths of a ceiling are nailed.

Keep.—The same as *donjon*, which see.

Key-stone.—The highest central stone of an arch.

Kiln.—A building for the accumulation and retention of heat, in order to dry or burn certain materials deposited within it.

King-post.—The centre-post in a trussed roof.

Knee.—A convex bend in the back of a hand-rail. See *Ramp.*

Lactarium.—The same as *dairy,* which see.

Lantern.—A cupola having windows in the sides for lighting an apartment beneath.

Larmier.—The same as *corona,* which see.

Lattice.—A reticulated window for the admission of air, rather than light, as in dairies and cellars.

Lever-boards.—Blind-slats: a set of boards so fastened that they may be turned at any angle to admit more or less light, or to lap upon each other so as to exclude all air or light through apertures.

Lintel.—A piece of timber or stone placed horizontally over a door, window, or other opening.

Listel.—The same as *fillet,* which see.

Lobby.—An enclosed space, or passage, communicating with the principal room or rooms of a house.

Lodge.—A small house near and subordinate to the mansion. A cottage placed at the gate of the road leading to a mansion.

Loop.—A small narrow window. *Loophole* is a term applied to the vertical series of doors in a warehouse, through which goods are delivered by means of a crane.

Luffer-boarding.—The same as *lever-boards,* which see.

Luthern.—The same as *dormer,* which see.

Mausoleum.—A sepulchral building—so called from a very celebrated one erected to the memory of Mausolus, king of Caria, by his wife Artemisia.

Metopa.—The square space in the frieze between the triglyphs of the Doric order.

Mezzanine.—A story of small height introduced between two of greater height.

Minaret.—A slender, lofty turret having projecting balconies, common in Mohammedan countries.

Minster.—A church to which an ecclesiastical fraternity has been or is attached.

Moat.—An excavated reservoir of water, surrounding a house, castle or town.

Modillion.—A projection under the corona of the richer orders, resembling a bracket.

Module.—The semi-diameter of a column, used by the architect as a measure by which to proportion the parts of an order.

Monastery.—A building or buildings appropriated to the reception of monks.

Monopteron.—A circular collonade supporting a dome without an enclosing wall.

Mosaic.—A mode of representing objects by the inlaying of small cubes of glass, stone, marble, shells, &c.

Mosque.—A Mohammedan temple, or place of worship.

Mullions.—The upright posts or bars, which divide the lights in a Gothic window.

Muniment-house.—A strong, fire-proof apartment for the keeping and preservation of evidences, charters, seals, &c., called muniments.

Museum.—A repository of natural, scientific and literary, curiosities, or of works of art.

Mutule.—A projecting ornament of the Doric cornice supposed to represent the ends of rafters.

Nave.—The main body of a Gothic church.

Newel.—A post at the starting or landing of a flight of stairs.

Niche.—A cavity or hollow place in a wall for the reception of a statue, vase, &c.

Nogs.—Wooden bricks.

Nosing.—The rounded and projecting edge of a step in stairs.

Nunnery.—A building or buildings appropriated for the reception of nuns.

Obelisk.—A lofty pillar of a rectangular form.

Octastyle.—A building with eight columns in front.

Odeum.—Among the Greeks, a species of theatre wherein the poets and musicians rehearsed their compositions previous to the public production of them.

Ogee.—See *Cyma.*

Orangery.—A gallery or building in a garden or parterre fronting the south.

Oriel-window.—A large bay or recessed window in a hall, chapel, or other apartment.

Ovolo.—A convex projecting moulding whose profile is the quadrant of a circle.

Pagoda.—A temple or place of worship in India.

Palisade.—A fence of pales or stakes driven into the ground.

Parapet.—A small wall of any material for protection on the sides of bridges, quays, or high buildings.

Pavilion.—A turret or small building generally insulated and comprised under a single roof.

Pedestal.—A square foundation used to elevate and sustain a column, statue, &c.

Pediment.—The triangular crowning part of a portico or aperture which terminates vertically the sloping parts of the roof: this, in Gothic architecture, is called a *gable.*

Penitentiary.—A prison for the confinement of criminals whose crimes are not of a very heinous nature.

Piazza.—A square, open space surrounded by buildings. This term is often improperly used to denote a *portico.*

Pier.—A rectangular pillar without any regular base or capital. The upright, narrow portions of walls between doors and windows are known by this term.

Pilaster.—A square pillar, sometimes insulated, but more commonly engaged in a wall, and projecting only a part of its thickness.

Piles.—Large timbers driven into the ground to make a secure foundation in marshy places, or in the bed of a river.

Pillar.—A column of irregular form, always disengaged, and always deviating from the proportions of the orders; whence the distinction between a pillar and a column.

Pinnacle.—A small spire used to ornament Gothic buildings.

Planceer.—The same as *soffit*, which see.

Plinth.—The lower square member of the base of a column, pedestal, or wall.

Porch.—An exterior appendage to a building, forming a covered approach to one of its principal doorways.

Portal.—The arch over a door or gate; the framework of the gate; the lesser gate, when there are two of different dimensions at one entrance.

Portcullis.—A strong timber gate to old castles, made to slide up and down vertically.

Portico.—A colonnade supporting a shelter over a walk, or ambulatory.

Priory.—A building similar in its constitution to a monastery or abbey, the head whereof was called a prior or prioress.

Prism.—A solid bounded on the sides by parallelograms, and on the ends by polygonal figures in parallel planes.

Prostyle.—A building with columns in front only.

Purlines.—Those pieces of timber which lie under and at right angles to the rafters to prevent them from sinking.

Pycnostyle.—An intercolumniation of one and a half diameters.

Pyramid.—A solid body standing on a square, triangular or polygonal basis, and terminating in a point at the top.

Quarry.—A place whence stones and slates are procured.

Quay.—(Pronounced, *key.*) A bank formed towards the sea or on the side of a river for free passage, or for the purpose of unloading merchandise.

Quoin.—An external angle. See *Rustic quoins.*

Rabbet, or *Rebate.*—A groove or channel in the edge of a board.

Ramp.—A concave bend in the back of a hand-rail.

Rampant arch.—One having abutments of different heights.

Regula.—The band below the tænia in the Doric order.

Riser.—In stairs, the vertical board forming the front of a step.

Rostrum.—An elevated platform from which a speaker addresses an audience.

Rotunda.—A circular building.

Rubble-wall.—A wall built of unhewn stone.

Rudenture.—The same as *cable*, which see.

Rustic quoins.—The stones placed on the external angle of a building, projecting beyond the face of the wall, and having their edges bevilled.

Rustic-work.—A mode of building masonry wherein the faces of the stones are left rough, the sides only being wrought smooth where the union of the stones takes place.

Salon, or *Saloon*.—A lofty and spacious apartment comprehending the height of two stories with two tiers of windows.

Sarcophagus.—A tomb or coffin made of one stone.

Scantling.—The measure to which a piece of timber is to be or has been cut.

Scarfing.—The joining of two pieces of timber by bolting or nailing transversely together, so that the two appear but one.

Scotia.—The hollow moulding in the base of a column, between the fillets of the tori.

Scroll.—A carved curvilinear ornament, somewhat resembling in profile the turnings of a ram's horn.

Sepulchre.—A grave, tomb, or place of interment.

Sewer.—A drain or conduit for carrying off soil or water from any place.

Shaft.—The cylindrical part between the base and the capital of a column.

Shoar.—A piece of timber placed in an oblique direction to support a building or wall.

Sill.—The horizontal piece of timber at the bottom of framing; the timber or stone at the bottom of doors and windows.

Soffit—The underside of an architrave, corona, &c. The underside of the heads of doors, windows, &c.

Summer.—The lintel of a door or window; a beam tenoned into a girder to support the ends of joists on both sides of it.

Systyle.—An intercolumniation of two diameters.

Tænia.—The fillet which separates the Doric frieze from the architrave.

Talus.—The slope or inclination of a wall, among workmen called *battering*.

Terrace.—An area raised before a building, above the level of the ground, to serve as a walk.

Tesselated pavement.—A curious pavement of Mosaic work, composed of small square stones.

Tetrastyle.—A building having four columns in front.

Thatch.—A covering of straw or reeds used on the roofs of cottages, barns, &c.

Theatre.—A building appropriated to the representation of dramatic spectacles.

Tile.—A thin piece or plate of baked clay or other material used for the external covering of a roof.

Tomb.—A grave, or place for the interment of a human body, including also any commemorative monument raised over such a place.

Torus.—A moulding of semi-circular profile used in the bases of columns.

Tower.—A lofty building of several stories, round or polygonal.

Transept.—The transverse portion of a cruciform church.

Transom.—The beam across a double-lighted window; if the window have no transom, it is called a *clere-story* window.

Tread.—That part of a step which is included between the face of its riser and that of the riser above.

Trellis.—A reticulated framing made of thin bars of wood for screens, windows, &c.

Triglyph.—The vertical tablets in the Doric frieze, chamfered on the two vertical edges, and having two channels in the middle.

Tripod.—A table or seat with three legs.

Trochilus.—The same as *scotia*, which see.

Truss.—An arrangement of timbers for increasing the resistance to cross-strains, consisting of a tie, two struts and a suspending-piece.

Turret.—A small tower, often crowning the angle of a wall, &c.

Tusk—A short projection under a tenon to increase its strength.

Tympanum.—The naked face of a pediment, included between the level and the raking mouldings.

Underpinning.—The wall under the ground-sills of a building.

University.—An assemblage of colleges under the supervision of a senate, &c.

Vault.—A concave arched ceiling resting upon two opposite parallel walls.

Venetian-door.—A door having side-lights.

Venetian-window.—A window having three separate apertures.

Veranda.—An awning. An open portico under the extended roof of a building.

Vestibule.—An apartment which serves as the medium of communication to another room or series of rooms.

Vestry.—An apartment in a church, or attached to it, for the preservation of the sacred vestments and utensils.

Villa.—A country-house for the residence of an opulent person.

Vinery.—A house for the cultivation of vines.

Volute.—A spiral scroll, which forms the principal feature of the Ionic and the Composite capitals.

Voussoirs.—Arch-stones

Wainscoting.—Wooden lining of walls, generally in panels.

Water-table.—The stone covering to the projecting foundation or other walls of a building.

Well.—The space occupied by a flight of stairs. The space left beyond the ends of the steps is called the *well-hole.*

Wicket.—A small door made in a gate.

Winders.—In stairs, steps not parallel to each other.

Zophorus.—The same as *frieze*, which see.

Zystos.—Among the ancients, a portico of unusual length, commonly appropriated to gymnastic exercises.

TABLE OF SQUARES, CUBES, AND ROOTS.

(From Hutton's Mathematics.)

No.	Square.	Cube.	Sq. Root.	CubeRoot.	No.	Square.	Cube.	Sq. Root.	CubeRoot.
1	1	1	1·0000000	1·000000	68	4624	314432	8·2462113	4·081655
2	4	8	1·4142136	1·259921	69	4761	328509	8·3066239	4·101566
3	9	27	1·7320508	1·442250	70	4900	343000	8·3666003	4·121285
4	16	64	2·0000000	1·587401	71	5041	357911	8·4261498	4·140818
5	25	125	2·2360680	1·709976	72	5184	373248	8·4852814	4·160168
6	36	216	2·4494897	1·817121	73	5329	389017	8·5440037	4·179339
7	49	343	2·6457513	1·912931	74	5476	405224	8·6023253	4·198336
8	64	512	2·8284271	2·000000	75	5625	421875	8·6602540	4·217163
9	81	729	3·0000000	2·080084	76	5776	438976	8·7177979	4·235824
10	100	1000	3·1622777	2·154435	77	5929	456533	8·7749644	4·254321
11	121	1331	3·3166248	2·223980	78	6084	474552	8·8317609	4·272659
12	144	1728	3·4641016	2·289429	79	6241	493039	8·8881944	4·290840
13	169	2197	3·6055513	2·351335	80	6400	512000	8·9442719	4·308869
14	196	2744	3·7416574	2·410142	81	6561	531441	9·0000000	4·326749
15	225	3375	3·8729833	2·466212	82	6724	551368	9·0553851	4·344481
16	256	4096	4·0000000	2·519842	83	6889	571787	9·1104336	4·362071
17	289	4913	4·1231056	2·571282	84	7056	592704	9·1651514	4·379519
18	324	5832	4·2426407	2·620741	85	7225	614125	9·2195445	4·396830
19	361	6859	4·3588989	2·668402	86	7396	636056	9·2736185	4·414005
20	400	8000	4·4721360	2·714418	87	7569	658503	9·3273791	4·431048
21	441	9261	4·5825757	2·758924	88	7744	681472	9·3808315	4·447960
22	484	10648	4·6904158	2·802039	89	7921	704969	9·4339811	4·464745
23	529	12167	4·7958315	2·843867	90	8100	729000	9·4868330	4·481405
24	576	13824	4·8989795	2·884499	91	8281	753571	9·5393920	4·497941
25	625	15625	5·0000000	2·924018	92	8464	778688	9·5916630	4·514357
26	676	17576	5·0990195	2·962496	93	8649	804357	9·6436508	4·530655
27	729	19683	5·1961524	3·000000	94	8836	830584	9·6953597	4·546836
28	784	21952	5·2915026	3·036589	95	9025	857375	9·7467943	4·562903
29	841	24389	5·3851648	3·072317	96	9216	884736	9·7979590	4·578857
30	900	27000	5·4772256	3·107232	97	9409	912673	9·8488578	4·594701
31	961	29791	5·5677644	3·141381	98	9604	941192	9·8994949	4·610436
32	1024	32768	5·6568542	3·174802	99	9801	970299	9·9498744	4·626065
33	1089	35937	5·7445626	3·207534	100	10000	1000000	10·0000000	4·641589
34	1156	39304	5·8309519	3·239612	101	10201	1030301	10·0498756	4·657009
35	1225	42875	5·9160798	3·271066	102	10404	1061208	10·0995049	4·672329
36	1296	46656	6·0000000	3·301927	103	10609	1092727	10·1488916	4·687548
37	1369	50653	6·0827625	3·332222	104	10816	1124864	10·1980390	4·702669
38	1444	54872	6·1644140	3·361975	105	11025	1157625	10·2469508	4·717694
39	1521	59319	6·2449980	3·391211	106	11236	1191016	10·2956301	4·732623
40	1600	64000	6·3245553	3·419952	107	11449	1225043	10·3440804	4·747459
41	1681	68921	6·4031242	3·448217	108	11664	1259712	10·3923048	4·762203
42	1764	74088	6·4807407	3·476027	109	11881	1295029	10·4403065	4·776856
43	1849	79507	6·5574385	3·503398	110	12100	1331000	10·4880885	4·791420
44	1936	85184	6·6332496	3·530348	111	12321	1367631	10·5356538	4·805895
45	2025	91125	6·7082039	3·556893	112	12544	1404928	10·5830052	4·820284
46	2116	97336	6·7823300	3·583048	113	12769	1442897	10·6301458	4·834588
47	2209	103823	6·8556546	3·608826	114	12996	1481544	10·6770783	4·848808
48	2304	110592	6·9282032	3·634241	115	13225	1520875	10·7238053	4·862944
49	2401	117649	7·0000000	3·659306	116	13456	1560896	10·7703296	4·876999
50	2500	125000	7·0710678	3·684031	117	13689	1601613	10·8166538	4·890973
51	2601	132651	7·1414284	3·708430	118	13924	1643032	10·8627805	4·904868
52	2704	140608	7·2111026	3·732511	119	14161	1685159	10·9087121	4·918685
53	2809	148877	7·2801099	3·756286	120	14400	1728000	10·9544512	4·932424
54	2916	157464	7·3484692	3·779763	121	14641	1771561	11·0000000	4·946087
55	3025	166375	7·4161985	3·802952	122	14884	1815848	11·0453610	4·959676
56	3136	175616	7·4833148	3·825862	123	15129	1860867	11·0905365	4·973190
57	3249	185193	7·5498344	3·848501	124	15376	1906624	11·1355287	4·986631
58	3364	195112	7·6157731	3·870877	125	15625	1953125	11·1803399	5·000000
59	3481	205379	7·6811457	3·892996	126	15876	2000376	11·2249722	5·013298
60	3600	216000	7·7459667	3·914868	127	16129	2048383	11·2694277	5·026526
61	3721	226981	7·8102497	3·936497	128	16384	2097152	11·3137085	5·039684
62	3844	238328	7·8740079	3·957891	129	16641	2146689	11·3578167	5·052774
63	3969	250047	7·9372539	3·979057	130	16900	2197000	11·4017543	5·065797
64	4096	262144	8·0000000	4·000000	131	17161	2248091	11·4455231	5·078753
65	4225	274625	8·0622577	4·020726	132	17424	2299968	11·4891253	5·091643
66	4356	287496	8·1240384	4·041240	133	17689	2352637	11·5325626	5·104469
67	4489	300763	8·1853528	4·061548	134	17956	2406104	11·5758369	5·117230

No.	Square.	Cube.	Sq. Root.	CubeRoot.	No.	Square.	Cube.	Sq. Root.	CubeRoot.
135	18225	2460375	11·6189500	5·129928	202	40804	8242408	14·2126704	5·867464
136	18496	2515456	11·6619038	5·142563	203	41209	8365427	14·2478068	5·877131
137	18769	2571353	11·7046999	5·155137	204	41616	8489664	14·2828569	5·886765
138	19044	2628072	11·7473401	5·167649	205	42025	8615125	14·3178211	5·896368
139	19321	2685619	11·7898261	5·180101	206	42436	8741816	14·3527001	5·905941
140	19600	2744000	11·8321596	5·192494	207	42849	8869743	14·3874946	5·915482
141	19881	2803221	11·8743422	5·204828	208	43264	8998912	14·4222051	5·924992
142	20164	2863288	11·9163753	5·217103	209	43681	9129329	14·4568323	5·934473
143	20449	2924207	11·9582607	5·229321	210	44100	9261000	14·4913767	5·943922
144	20736	2985984	12·0000000	5·241483	211	44521	9393931	14·5258390	5·953342
145	21025	3048625	12·0415946	5·253588	212	44944	9528128	14·5602198	5·962732
146	21316	3112136	12·0830460	5·265637	213	45369	9663597	14·5945195	5·972093
147	21609	3176523	12·1243557	5·277632	214	45796	9800344	14·6287388	5·981424
148	21904	3241792	12·1655251	5·289572	215	46225	9938375	14·6628783	5·990726
149	22201	3307949	12·2065556	5·301459	216	46656	10077696	14·6969385	6·000000
150	22500	3375000	12·2474487	5·313293	217	47089	10218313	14·7309199	6·009245
151	22801	3442951	12·2882057	5·325074	218	47524	10360232	14·7648231	6·018462
152	23104	3511808	12·3288280	5·336803	219	47961	10503459	14·7986486	6·027650
153	23409	3581577	12·3693169	5·348481	220	48400	10648000	14·8323970	6·036811
154	23716	3652264	12·4096736	5·360108	221	48841	10793861	14·8660687	6·045943
155	24025	3723875	12·4498996	5·371685	222	49284	10941048	14·8996644	6·055049
156	24336	3796416	12·4899960	5·383213	223	49729	11089567	14·9331845	6·064127
157	24649	3869893	12·5299641	5·394691	224	50176	11239424	14·9666295	6·073178
158	24964	3944312	12·5698051	5·406120	225	50625	11390625	15·0000000	6·082202
159	25281	4019679	12·6095202	5·417501	226	51076	11543176	15·0332964	6·091199
160	25600	4096000	12·6491106	5·428835	227	51529	11697083	15·0665192	6·100170
161	25921	4173281	12·6885775	5·440122	228	51984	11852352	15·0996689	6·109115
162	26244	4251528	12·7279221	5·451362	229	52441	12008989	15·1327460	6·118033
163	26569	4330747	12·7671453	5·462556	230	52900	12167000	15·1657509	6·126926
164	26896	4410944	12·8062485	5·473704	231	53361	12326391	15·1986842	6·135792
165	27225	4492125	12·8452326	5·484807	232	53824	12487168	15·2315462	6·144634
166	27556	4574296	12·8840987	5·495865	233	54289	12649337	15·2643375	6·153449
167	27889	4657463	12·9228480	5·506878	234	54756	12812904	15·2970585	6·162240
168	28224	4741632	12·9614814	5·517848	235	55225	12977875	15·3297097	6·171006
169	28561	4826809	13·0000000	5·528775	236	55696	13144256	15·3622915	6·179747
170	28900	4913000	13·0384048	5·539658	237	56169	13312053	15·3948043	6·188463
171	29241	5000211	13·0766968	5·550499	238	56644	13481272	15·4272486	6·197154
172	29584	5088448	13·1148770	5·561298	239	57121	13651919	15·4596248	6·205822
173	29929	5177717	13·1529464	5·572055	240	57600	13824000	15·4919334	6·214465
174	30276	5268024	13·1909060	5·582770	241	58081	13997521	15·5241747	6·223084
175	30625	5359375	13·2287566	5·593445	242	58564	14172488	15·5563492	6·231680
176	30976	5451776	13·2664992	5·604079	243	59049	14348907	15·5884573	6·240251
177	31329	5545233	13·3041347	5·614672	244	59536	14526784	15·6204994	6·248800
178	31684	5639752	13·3416641	5·625226	245	60025	14706125	15·6524758	6·257325
179	32041	5735339	13·3790882	5·635741	246	60516	14886936	15·6843871	6·265827
180	32400	5832000	13·4164079	5·646216	247	61009	15069223	15·7162336	6·274305
181	32761	5929741	13·4536240	5·656653	248	61504	15252992	15·7480157	6·282761
182	33124	6028568	13·4907376	5·667051	249	62001	15438249	15·7797338	6·291195
183	33489	6128487	13·5277493	5·677411	250	62500	15625000	15·8113883	6·299605
184	33856	6229504	13·5646600	5·687734	251	63001	15813251	15·8429795	6·307994
185	34225	6331625	13·6014705	5·698019	252	63504	16003008	15·8745079	6·316360
186	34596	6434856	13·6381817	5·708267	253	64009	16194277	15·9059737	6·324704
187	34969	6539203	13·6747943	5·718479	254	64516	16387064	15·9373775	6·333026
188	35344	6644672	13·7113092	5·728654	255	65025	16581375	15·9687194	6·341326
189	35721	6751269	13·7477271	5·738794	256	65536	16777216	16·0000000	6·349604
190	36100	6859000	13·7840488	5·748897	257	66049	16974593	16·0312195	6·357861
191	36481	6967871	13·8202750	5·758965	258	66564	17173512	16·0623784	6·366097
192	36864	7077888	13·8564065	5·768998	259	67081	17373979	16·0934769	6·374311
193	37249	7189057	13·8924440	5·778996	260	67600	17576000	16·1245155	6·382504
194	37636	7301384	13·9283883	5·788960	261	68121	17779581	16·1554944	6·390676
195	38025	7414875	13·9642400	5·798890	262	68644	17984728	16·1864141	6·398828
196	38416	7529536	14·0000000	5·808786	263	69169	18191447	16·2172747	6·406958
197	38809	7645373	14·0356688	5·818648	264	69696	18399744	16·2480768	6·415069
198	39204	7762392	14·0712473	5·828477	265	70225	18609625	16·2788206	6·423158
199	39601	7880599	14·1067360	5·838272	266	70756	18821096	16·3095064	6·431228
200	40000	8000000	14·1421356	5·848035	267	71289	19034163	16·3401346	6·439277
201	40401	8120601	14·1774469	5·857766	268	71824	19248832	16·3707055	6·447306

No.	Square.	Cube.	Sq. Root.	CubeRoot.	No.	Square.	Cube.	Sq Root.	CubeRoot.
269	72361	19465109	16·4012195	6·455315	336	112896	37933056	18·3303028	6·952053
270	72900	19683000	16·4316767	6·463304	337	113569	38272753	18 3575598	6·958943
271	73441	19902511	16·4620776	6·471274	338	114244	38614472	18·3847763	6·965820
272	73984	20123648	16·4924225	6·479224	339	114921	38958219	18·4119526	6·972683
273	74529	20346417	16·5227116	6·487154	340	115600	39304000	18·4390889	6·979532
274	75076	20570824	16·5529454	6·495065	341	116281	39651821	18·4661853	6·986368
275	75625	20796875	16·5831240	6·502957	342	116964	40001688	18·4932420	6·993191
276	76176	21024576	16·6132477	6·510830	343	117649	40353607	18·5202592	7·000000
277	76729	21253933	16·6433170	6·518684	344	118336	40707584	18·5472370	7·006796
278	77284	21484952	16·6733320	6·526519	345	119025	41063625	18·5741756	7·013579
279	77841	21717639	16·7032931	6·534335	346	119716	41421736	18·6010752	7·020349
280	78400	21952000	16·7332005	6·542133	347	120409	41781923	18·6279360	7·027106
281	78961	22188041	16·7630546	6·549912	348	121104	42144192	18·6547581	7·033850
282	79524	22425768	16·7928556	6·557672	349	121801	42508549	18·6815417	7·040581
283	80089	22665187	16·8226038	6·565414	350	122500	42875000	18·7082869	7·047299
284	80656	22906304	16·8522995	6·573139	351	123201	43243551	18·7349940	7·054004
285	81225	23149125	16·8819430	6·580844	352	123904	43614208	18·7616630	7·060697
286	81796	23393656	16 9115345	6·588532	353	124609	43986977	18·7882942	7·067377
287	82369	23639903	16·9410743	6·596202	354	125316	44361864	18·8148877	7·074044
288	82944	23887872	16·9705627	6·603854	355	126025	44738875	18·8414437	7·080699
289	83521	24137569	17·0000000	6·611489	356	126736	45118016	18·8679623	7·087341
290	84100	24389000	17·0293864	6·619106	357	127449	45499293	18·8944436	7·093971
291	84681	24642171	17·0587221	6·626705	358	128164	45882712	18·9208879	7·100588
292	85264	24897088	17·0880075	6·634287	359	128881	46268279	18·9472953	7·107194
293	85849	25153757	17·1172428	6·641852	360	129600	46656000	18·9736660	7·113787
294	86436	25412184	17·1464282	6·649400	361	130321	47045881	19·0000000	7·120367
295	87025	25672375	17·1755640	6·656930	362	131044	47437928	19·0262976	7·126936
296	87616	25934336	17·2046505	6·664444	363	131769	47832147	19·0525589	7·133492
297	88209	26198073	17·2336879	6·671940	364	132496	48228544	19·0787840	7·140037
298	88804	26463592	17·2626765	6·679420	365	133225	48627125	19·1049732	7·146569
299	89401	26730899	17·2916165	6·686883	366	133956	49027896	19·1311265	7 153090
300	90000	27000000	17·3205081	6·694329	367	134689	49430863	19·1572441	7·159599
301	90601	27270901	17·3493516	6·701759	368	135424	49836032	19·1833261	7·166096
302	91204	27543608	17·3781472	6·709173	369	136161	50243409	19·2093727	7·172581
303	91809	27818127	17·4068952	6·716570	370	136900	50653000	19·2353841	7·179054
304	92416	28094464	17·4355958	6·723951	371	137641	51064811	19·2613603	7·185516
305	93025	28372625	17·4642492	6·731316	372	138384	51478848	19·2873015	7·191966
306	93636	28652616	17·4928557	6·738664	373	139129	51895117	19·3132079	7·198405
307	94249	28934443	17·5214155	6·745997	374	139876	52313624	19·3390796	7·204832
308	94864	29218112	17·5499288	6·753313	375	140625	52734375	19·3649167	7·211248
309	95481	29503629	17 5783958	6·760614	376	141376	53157376	19·3907194	7·217652
310	96100	29791000	17·6068169	6·767899	377	142129	53582633	19·4164878	7·224045
311	96721	30080231	17·6351921	6·775169	378	142884	54010152	19·4422221	7·230427
312	97344	30371328	17·6635217	6·782423	379	143641	54439939	19·4679223	7·236797
313	97969	30664297	17·6918060	6·789661	380	144400	54872000	19·4935887	7·243156
314	98596	30959144	17·7200451	6·796884	381	145161	55306341	19·5192213	7·249504
315	99225	31255875	17·7482393	6·804092	382	145924	55742968	19·5448203	7·255841
316	99856	31554496	17·7763888	6·811285	383	146689	56181887	19·5703858	7·262167
317	100489	31855013	17·8044938	6·818462	384	147456	56623104	19·5959179	7·268482
318	101124	32157432	17·8325545	6·825624	385	148225	57066625	19·6214169	7·274786
319	101761	32461759	17·8605711	6·832771	386	148996	57512456	19·6468827	7·281079
320	102400	32768000	17·8885438	6·839904	387	149769	57960603	19·6723156	7·287362
321	103041	33076161	17·9164729	6·847021	388	150544	58411072	19·6977156	7·293633
322	103684	33386248	17·9443584	6·854124	389	151321	58863869	19·7230829	7·299894
323	104329	33698267	17·9722008	6·861212	390	152100	59319000	19·7484177	7·306144
324	104976	34012224	18·0000000	6·868285	391	152881	59776471	19·7737199	7·312383
325	105625	34328125	18·0277564	6·875344	392	153664	60236288	19·7989899	7·318611
326	106276	34645976	18·0554701	6·882389	393	154449	60698457	19·8242276	7·324829
327	106929	34965783	18·0831413	6·889419	394	155236	61162984	19·8494332	7·331037
328	107584	35287552	18·1107703	6·896435	395	156025	61629875	19·8746069	7·337234
329	108241	35611289	18·1383571	6·903436	396	156816	62099136	19·8997487	7·343420
330	108900	35937000	18·1659021	6·910423	397	157609	62570773	19·9248588	7·349597
331	109561	36264691	18·1934054	6·917396	398	158404	63044792	19·9499373	7·355762
332	110224	36594368	18·2208672	6·924356	399	159201	63521199	19·9749844	7·361918
333	110889	36926037	18·2482876	6·931301	400	160000	64000000	20·0000000	7·368063
334	111556	37259704	18·2756669	6·938232	401	160801	64481201	20·0249844	7·374198
335	112225	37595375	18·3030052	6·945150	402	161604	64964808	20·0499377	7·380323

No.	Square.	Cube.	Sq. Root.	CubeRoot.	No.	Square.	Cube.	Sq. Root.	CubeRoot.
403	162409	65450827	20·0748599	7·386437	470	220900	103823000	21·6794834	7·774980
404	163216	65939264	20·0997512	7·392542	471	221841	104487111	21·7025344	7·780490
405	164025	66430125	20·1246118	7·398636	472	222784	105154048	21·7255610	7·785993
406	164836	66923416	20·1494417	7·404721	473	223729	105823817	21·7485632	7·791487
407	165649	67419143	20·1742410	7·410795	474	224676	106496424	21·7715411	7·796974
408	166464	67917312	20·1990099	7·416859	475	225625	107171875	21·7944947	7·802454
409	167281	68417929	20·2237484	7·422914	476	226576	107850176	21·8174242	7·807925
410	168100	68921000	20·2484567	7·428959	477	227529	108531333	21·8403297	7·813389
411	168921	69426531	20·2731349	7·434994	478	228484	109215352	21·8632111	7·818846
412	169744	69934528	20·2977831	7·441019	479	229441	109902239	21·8860686	7·824294
413	170569	70444997	20·3224014	7·447034	480	230400	110592000	21·9089023	7·829735
414	171396	70957944	20·3469899	7·453040	481	231361	111284641	21·9317122	7·835169
415	172225	71473375	20·3715488	7·459036	482	232324	111980168	21·9544984	7·840595
416	173056	71991296	20·3960781	7·465022	483	233289	112678587	21·9772610	7·846013
417	173889	72511713	20·4205779	7·470999	484	234256	113379904	22·0000000	7·851424
418	174724	73034632	20·4450483	7·476966	485	235225	114084125	22·0227155	7·856828
419	175561	73560059	20·4694895	7·482924	486	236196	114791256	22·0454077	7·862224
420	176400	74088000	20·4939015	7·488872	487	237169	115501303	22·0680765	7·867613
421	177241	74618461	20·5182845	7·494811	488	238144	116214272	22·0907220	7·872994
422	178084	75151448	20·5426386	7·500741	489	239121	116930169	22·1133444	7·878368
423	178929	75686967	20·5669638	7·506661	490	240100	117649000	22·1359436	7·883735
424	179776	76225024	20·5912603	7·512571	491	241081	118370771	22·1585198	7·889095
425	180625	76765625	20·6155281	7·518473	492	242064	119095488	22·1810730	7·894447
426	181476	77308776	20·6397674	7·524365	493	243049	119823157	22·2036033	7·899792
427	182329	77854483	20·6639783	7·530248	494	244036	120553784	22·2261108	7·905129
428	183184	78402752	20·6881609	7·536122	495	245025	121287375	22·2485955	7·910460
429	184041	78953589	20·7123152	7·541987	496	246016	122023936	22·2710575	7·915783
430	184900	79507000	20·7364414	7·547842	497	247009	122763473	22·2934968	7·921099
431	185761	80062991	20·7605395	7·553689	498	248004	123505992	22·3159136	7·926408
432	186624	80621568	20·7846097	7·559526	499	249001	124251499	22·3383079	7·931710
433	187489	81182737	20·8086520	7·565355	500	250000	125000000	22·3606798	7·937005
434	188356	81746504	20·8326667	7·571174	501	251001	125751501	22·3830293	7·942293
435	189225	82312875	20·8566536	7·576985	502	252004	126506008	22·4053565	7·947574
436	190096	82881856	20·8806130	7·582786	503	253009	127263527	22·4276615	7·952848
437	190969	83453453	20·9045450	7·588579	504	254016	128024064	22·4499443	7·958114
438	191844	84027672	20·9284495	7·594363	505	255025	128787625	22·4722051	7·963374
439	192721	84604519	20·9523268	7·600138	506	256036	129554216	22·4944438	7·968627
440	193600	85184000	20·9761770	7·605905	507	257049	130323843	22·5166605	7·973873
441	194481	85766121	21·0000000	7·611663	508	258064	131096512	22·5388553	7·979112
442	195364	86350888	21·0237960	7·617412	509	259081	131872229	22·5610283	7·984344
443	196249	86938307	21·0475652	7·623152	510	260100	132651000	22·5831796	7·989570
444	197136	87528384	21·0713075	7·628881	511	261121	133432831	22·6053091	7·994788
445	198025	88121125	21·0950231	7·634607	512	262144	134217728	22·6274170	8·000000
446	198916	88716536	21·1187121	7·640321	513	263169	135005697	22·6495033	8·005205
447	199809	89314623	21·1423745	7·646027	514	264196	135796744	22·6715681	8·010403
448	200704	89915392	21·1660105	7·651725	515	265225	136590875	22·6936114	8·015595
449	201601	90518849	21·1896201	7·657414	516	266256	137388096	22·7156334	8·020779
450	202500	91125000	21·2132034	7·663094	517	267289	138188413	22·7376340	8·025957
451	203401	91733851	21·2367606	7·668766	518	268324	138991832	22·7596134	8·031129
452	204304	92345408	21·2602916	7·674430	519	269361	139798359	22·7815715	8·036293
453	205209	92959677	21·2837967	7·680086	520	270400	140608000	22·8035085	8·041451
454	206116	93576664	21·3072758	7·685733	521	271441	141420761	22·8254244	8·046603
455	207025	94196375	21·3307290	7·691372	522	272484	142236648	22·8473193	8·051748
456	207936	94818816	21·3541565	7·697002	523	273529	143055667	22·8691933	8·056886
457	208849	95443993	21·3775583	7·702625	524	274576	143877824	22·8910463	8·062018
458	209764	96071912	21·4009346	7·708239	525	275625	144703125	22·9128785	8·067143
459	210681	96702579	21·4242853	7·713845	526	276676	145531576	22·9346899	8·072262
460	211600	97336000	21·4476106	7·719443	527	277729	146363183	22·9564806	8·077374
461	212521	97972181	21·4709106	7·725032	528	278784	147197952	22·9782506	8·082480
462	213444	98611128	21·4941853	7·730614	529	279841	148035889	23·0000000	8·087579
463	214369	99252847	21·5174348	7·736188	530	280900	148877000	23·0217289	8·092672
464	215296	99897344	21·5406592	7·741753	531	281961	149721291	23·0434372	8·097759
465	216225	100544625	21·5638587	7·747311	532	283024	150568768	23·0651252	8·102839
466	217156	101194696	21·5870331	7·752861	533	284089	151419437	23·0867928	8·107913
467	218089	101847563	21·6101828	7·758402	534	285156	152273304	23·1084400	8·112980
468	219024	102503232	21·6333077	7·763936	535	286225	153130375	23·1300670	8·118041
469	219961	103161709	21·6564078	7·769462	536	287296	153990656	23·1516738	8·123093

No.	Square.	Cube.	Sq. Root.	CubeRoot.	No.	Square.	Cube.	Sq. Root.	CubeRoot.
537	288369	154854153	23·1732605	8·128145	604	364816	220348864	24·5764115	8·453028
538	289444	155720872	23·1948270	8·133187	605	366025	221445125	24·5967478	8·457691
539	290521	156590819	23·2163735	8·138223	606	367236	222545016	24·6170673	8·462348
540	291600	157464000	23·2379001	8·143253	607	368449	223648543	24·6373700	8·467000
541	292681	158340421	23·2594067	8·148276	608	369664	224755712	24·6576560	8·471647
542	293764	159220088	23·2808935	8·153294	609	370881	225866529	24·6779254	8·476289
543	294849	160103007	23·3023604	8·158305	610	372100	226981000	24·6981781	8·480926
544	295936	160989184	23·3238076	8·163310	611	373321	228099131	24·7184142	8·485558
545	297025	161878625	23·3452351	8·168309	612	374554	229220928	24·7386338	8·490185
546	298116	162771336	23·3666429	8·173302	613	375769	230346397	24·7588368	8·494806
547	299209	163667323	23·3880311	8·178289	614	376996	231475544	24·7790234	8·499423
548	300304	164566592	23·4093998	8·183269	615	378225	232608375	24·7991935	8·504035
549	301401	165469149	23·4307490	8·188244	616	379456	233744896	24·8193473	8·508642
550	302500	166375000	23·4520788	8·193213	617	380689	234885113	24·8394847	8·513243
551	303601	167284151	23·4733392	8·198175	618	381924	236029032	24·8596058	8·517840
552	304704	168196608	23·4946802	8·203132	619	383161	237176659	24·8797106	8·522432
553	305809	169112377	23·5159520	8·208082	620	384400	238328000	24·8997992	8·527019
554	306916	170031464	23·5372046	8·213027	621	385641	239483061	24·9198716	8·531601
555	308025	170953875	23·5584380	8·217966	622	386884	240641848	24·9399278	8·536178
556	309136	171879616	23·5796522	8·222898	623	388129	241804367	24·9599679	8·540750
557	310249	172808693	23·6008474	8·227825	624	389376	242970624	24·9799920	8·545317
558	311364	173741112	23·6220236	8·232746	625	390625	244140625	25·0000000	8·549880
559	312481	174676879	23·6431808	8·237661	626	391876	245314376	25·0199920	8·554437
560	313600	175616000	23·6643191	8·242571	627	393129	246491883	25·0399681	8·558990
561	314721	176558481	23·6854386	8·247474	628	394384	247673152	25·0599282	8·563538
562	315844	177504328	23·7065392	8·252371	629	395641	248858189	25·0798724	8·568081
563	316969	178453547	23·7276210	8·257263	630	396900	250047000	25·0998008	8·572619
564	318096	179406144	23·7486842	8·262149	631	398161	251239591	25·1197134	8·577152
565	319225	180362125	23·7697286	8·267029	632	399424	252435968	25·1396102	8·581681
566	320356	181321496	23·7907545	8·271904	633	400689	253636137	25·1594913	8·586205
567	321489	182284263	23·8117618	8·276773	634	401956	254840104	25·1793566	8·590724
568	322624	183250432	23·8327506	8·281635	635	403225	256047875	25·1992063	8·595238
569	323761	184220009	23·8537209	8·286493	636	404496	257259456	25·2190404	8·599748
570	324900	185193000	23·8746728	8·291344	637	405769	258474853	25·2388589	8·604252
571	326041	186169411	23·8956063	8·296190	638	407044	259694072	25·2586619	8·608753
572	327184	187149248	23·9165215	8·301030	639	408321	260917119	25·2784493	8·613248
573	328329	188132517	23·9374184	8·305865	640	409600	262144000	25.2982213	8·617739
574	329476	189119224	23·9582971	8·310694	641	410881	263374721	25·3179778	8·622225
575	330625	190109375	23·9791576	8·315517	642	412164	264609288	25·3377189	8·626706
576	331776	191102976	24·0000000	8·320335	643	413449	265847707	25·3574447	8·631183
577	332929	192100033	24·0208243	8·325147	644	414736	267089984	25·3771551	8·635655
578	334084	193100552	24·0416306	8·329951	645	416025	268336125	25·3968502	8.640123
579	335241	194104539	24·0624188	8·334755	646	417316	269586136	25·4165301	8·644585
580	336400	195112000	24·0831891	8·339551	647	418609	270840023	25·4361947	8·649044
581	337561	196122941	24·1039416	8·344341	648	419904	272097792	25·4558441	8·653497
582	338724	197137368	24·1246762	8·349126	649	421201	273359449	25·4754784	8·657946
583	339889	198155287	24·1453929	8·353905	650	422500	274625000	25·4950976	8·662391
584	341056	199176704	24·1660919	8·358678	651	423801	275894451	25·5147016	8·666831
585	342225	200201625	24·1867732	8·353447	652	425104	277167808	25·5342907	8·671266
586	343396	201230056	24·2074369	8·368209	653	426409	278445077	25·5538647	8·675697
587	344569	202262003	24·2280829	8·372967	654	427716	279726264	25·5734237	8·680124
588	345744	203297472	24·2487113	8·377719	655	429025	281011375	25·5929678	8·684546
589	346921	204336469	24·2693222	8·382465	656	430336	282300416	25·6124969	8·688963
590	348100	205379000	24·2899156	8·387206	657	431649	283593393	25·6320112	8·693376
591	349281	206425071	24·3104916	8·391942	658	432964	284890312	25·6515107	8·697784
592	350464	207474688	24·3310501	8·396673	659	434281	286191179	25·6709953	8·702188
593	351649	208527857	24·3515913	8·401398	660	435600	287496000	25·6904652	8·706588
594	352836	209584584	24·3721152	8·406118	661	436921	288804781	25·7099203	8·710983
595	354025	210644875	24·3926218	8·410833	662	438244	290117528	25·7293607	8·715373
596	355216	211708736	24·4131112	8·415542	663	439569	291434247	25·7487864	8·719760
597	356409	212776173	24·4335834	8·420246	664	440896	292754944	25·7681975	8·724141
598	357604	213847192	24·4540385	8·424945	665	442225	294079625	25·7875939	8·728518
599	358801	214921799	24.4744765	8·429638	666	443556	295408296	25·8069758	8·732892
600	360000	216000000	24·4948974	8·434327	667	444889	296740963	25·8263431	8·737260
601	361201	217081801	24·5153013	8·439010	668	446224	298077632	25·8456960	8·741625
602	362404	218167208	24·5356883	8·443688	669	447561	299418309	25·8650343	8·745985
603	363609	219256227	24·5560583	8·448360	670	448900	300763000	25·8843582	8·750340

No.	Square.	Cube.	Sq. Root.	CubeRoot.	No.	Square.	Cube.	Sq. Root.	CubeRoot.
671	450241	302111711	25·9036677	8·754691	738	544644	401947272	27·1661554	9·036886
672	451584	303464448	25·9229628	8·759033	739	546121	403583419	27·1845544	9·040965
673	452929	304821217	25·9422435	8·763331	740	547600	405224000	27·2029410	9·045042
674	454276	306182024	25·9615100	8·767719	741	549081	406869021	27·2213152	9·049114
675	455625	307546875	25·9807621	8·772053	742	550564	408518488	27·2396769	9·053183
676	456976	308915776	26·0000000	8·776383	743	552049	410172407	27·2580263	9·057248
677	458329	310288733	26·0192237	8·780708	744	553536	411830784	27·2763634	9·061310
678	459684	311665752	26·0384331	8·785030	745	555025	413493625	27·2946881	9·065368
679	461041	313046839	26.0576284	8·789347	746	556516	415160936	27·3130006	9·069422
680	462400	314432000	26·0768096	8·793659	747	558009	416832723	27·3313007	9·073473
681	463761	315821241	26·0959767	8·797968	748	559504	418508992	27·3495887	9·077520
682	465124	317214568	26·1151297	8·802272	749	561001	420189749	27·3678644	9·081563
683	466489	318611987	26·1342687	8·806572	750	562500	421875000	27·3861279	9·085603
684	467856	320013504	26·1533937	8·810868	751	564001	423564751	27·4043792	9·089639
685	469225	321419125	26·1725047	8·815160	752	565504	425259008	27·4226184	9·093672
686	470596	322828856	26·1916017	8·819447	753	567009	426957777	27·4408455	9·097701
687	471969	324242703	26·2106848	8·823731	754	568516	428661064	27·4590604	9·101726
688	473344	325660672	26·2297541	8·828010	755	570025	430368875	27·4772633	9·105748
689	474721	327082769	26·2488095	8·832285	756	571536	432081216	27·4954542	9·109767
690	476100	328509000	26·2678511	8·836556	757	573049	433798093	27·5136330	9·113782
691	477481	329939371	26·2868789	8·840823	758	574564	435519512	27·5317998	9·117793
692	478864	331373888	26·3058929	8·845085	759	576081	437245479	27·5499546	9·121801
693	480249	332812557	26·3248932	8·849344	760	577600	438976000	27·5680975	9·125805
694	481636	334255384	26·3438797	8·853598	761	579121	440711081	27·5862284	9·129806
695	483025	335702375	26·3628527	8·857849	762	580644	442450728	27·6043475	9·133803
696	484416	337153536	26·3818119	8·862095	763	582169	444194947	27·6224546	9·137797
697	485809	338608873	26·4007576	8.866337	764	583696	445943744	27·6405499	9·141787
698	487204	340068392	26·4196896	8·870576	765	585225	447697125	27·6586334	9·145774
699	488601	341532099	26·4386081	8·874810	766	586756	449455096	27·6767050	9·149758
700	490000	343000000	26·4575131	8·879040	767	588289	451217663	27·6947648	9·153737
701	491401	344472101	26·4764046	8·883266	768	589824	452984832	27·7128129	9·157714
702	492804	345948408	26·4952826	8·887488	769	591361	454756609	27·7308492	9·161687
703	494209	347428927	26·5141472	8·891706	770	592900	456533000	27·7488739	9·165656
704	495616	348913664	26·5329983	8·895920	771	594141	458314011	27·7668868	9·169623
705	497025	350402625	26·5518361	8·900130	772	595984	460099648	27·7848880	9·173585
706	498436	351895816	26·5706605	8·904337	773	597529	461889917	27·8028775	9·177544
707	499849	353393243	26·5894716	8·908539	774	599076	463684824	27·8208555	9·181500
708	501264	354894912	26·6082694	8·912737	775	600625	465484375	27·8388218	9·185453
709	502681	356400829	26·6270539	8·916931	776	602176	467288576	27·8567766	9·189402
710	504100	357911000	26·6458252	8·921121	777	603729	469097433	27·8747197	9·193347
711	505521	359425431	26·6645833	8·925308	778	605284	470910952	27·8926514	9·197290
712	506944	360944128	26·6833281	8·929490	779	606841	472729139	27·9105715	9·201229
713	508369	362467097	26·7020598	8·933669	780	608400	474552000	27·9284801	9·205164
714	509796	363994344	26·7207784	8·937843	781	609961	476379541	27·9463772	9·209096
715	511225	365525875	26·7394839	8·942014	782	611524	478211768	27·9642629	9·213025
716	512656	367061696	26·7581763	8·946181	783	613089	480048687	27·9821372	9·216950
717	514089	368601813	26·7768557	8·950344	784	614656	481890304	28·0000000	9·220873
718	515524	370146232	26·7955220	8·954503	785	616225	483736625	28·0178515	9·224791
719	516961	371694959	26·8141754	8·958658	786	617796	485587656	28·0356915	9·228707
720	518400	373248000	26·8328157	8·962809	787	619369	487443403	28·0535203	9·232619
721	519841	374805361	26·8514432	8·966957	788	620944	489303872	28·0713377	9·236528
722	521284	376367048	26·8700577	8·971101	789	622521	491169069	28·0891438	9·240435
723	522729	377933067	26·8886593	8·975241	790	624100	493039000	28·1069386	9·244335
724	524176	379503424	26·9072481	8·979377	791	625681	494913671	28·1247222	9·248234
725	525625	381078125	26·9258240	8·983509	792	627264	496793088	28·1424946	9·252130
726	527076	382657176	26·9443872	8·987637	793	628849	498677257	28·1602557	9·256022
727	528529	384240583	26·9629375	8·991762	794	630436	500566184	28·1780056	9·259911
728	529984	385828352	26·9814751	8·995883	795	632025	502459875	28·1957444	9·263797
729	531441	387420489	27·0000000	9·000000	796	633616	504358336	28·2134720	9·267680
730	532900	389017000	27·0185122	9·004113	797	635209	506261573	28·2311884	9·271559
731	534361	390617891	27·0370117	9·008223	798	636804	508169592	28·2488938	9·275435
732	535824	392223168	27·0554985	9·012329	799	638401	510082399	28·2665881	9·279308
733	527289	393832837	27·0739727	9·016431	800	640000	512000000	28·2842712	9·283178
734	538756	395446904	27·0924344	9·020529	801	641601	513922401	28·3019434	9·287044
735	540225	397065375	27.1108834	9·024624	802	643204	515849608	28·3196045	9·290907
736	541696	398688256	27·1293199	9·028715	803	644809	517781627	28·3372546	9·294767
737	543169	400315553	27·1477439	9·032802	804	646416	519718464	28·3548938	9·298624

No.	Square.	Cube.	Sq. Root.	CubeRoot.	No.	Square.	Cube.	Sq. Root.	CubeRoot.
805	648025	521660125	28·3725219	9·302477	872	760384	663054848	29·5296461	9·553712
806	649636	523606616	28·3901391	9·306328	873	762129	665338617	29·5465734	9·557363
807	651249	525557943	28·4077454	9·310175	874	763876	667627624	29·5634910	9·561011
808	652864	527514112	28·4253408	9·314019	875	765625	669921875	29·5803989	9·564656
809	654481	529475129	28·4429253	9·317860	876	767376	672221376	29·5972972	9·568298
810	656100	531441000	28·4604989	9·321697	877	769129	674526133	29·6141858	9·571938
811	657721	533411731	28·4780617	9·325532	878	770884	676836152	29·6310648	9·575574
812	659344	535387328	28·4956137	9·329363	879	772641	679151439	29·6479342	9·579208
813	660969	537367797	28·5131549	9·333192	880	774400	681472000	29·6647939	9·582840
814	662596	539353144	28·5306852	9·337017	881	776161	683797841	29·6816442	9·586468
815	664225	541343375	28·5482048	9·340839	882	777924	686128968	29·6984848	9·590094
816	665856	543338496	28·5657137	9·344657	883	779689	688465387	29·7153159	9·593717
817	667489	545338513	28·5832119	9·348473	884	781456	690807104	29·7321375	9·597337
818	669124	547343432	28·6006993	9·352286	885	783225	693154125	29·7489496	9·600955
819	670761	549353259	28·6181760	9·356095	886	784996	695506456	29·7657521	9·604570
820	672400	551368000	28·6356421	9·359902	887	786769	697864103	29·7825452	9·608182
821	674041	553387661	28·6530976	9·363705	888	788544	700227072	29·7993289	9·611791
822	675684	555412248	28·6705424	9·367505	889	790321	702595369	29·8161030	9·615398
823	677329	557441767	28·6879766	9·371302	890	792100	704969000	29·8328678	9·619002
824	678976	559476224	28·7054002	9·375096	891	793881	707347971	29·8496231	9·622603
825	680625	561515625	28·7228132	9·378887	892	795664	709732288	29·8663690	9·626202
826	682276	563559976	28·7402157	9·382675	893	797449	712121957	29·8831056	9·629797
827	683929	565609283	28·7576077	9·386460	894	799236	714516984	29·8998328	9·633391
828	685584	567663552	28·7749891	9·390242	895	801025	716917375	29·9165506	9·636981
829	687241	569722789	28·7923601	9·394021	896	802816	719323136	29·9332591	9·640569
830	688900	571787000	28·8097206	9·397796	897	804609	721734273	29·9499583	9·644154
831	690561	573856191	28·8270706	9·401569	898	806404	724150792	29·9666481	9·647737
832	692224	575930368	28·8444102	9·405339	899	808201	726572699	29·9833287	9·651317
833	693889	578009537	28·8617394	9·409105	900	810000	729000000	30·0000000	9·654894
834	695556	580093704	28·8790582	9·412869	901	811801	731432701	30·0166620	9·658468
835	697225	582182875	28·8963666	9·416630	902	813604	733870808	30·0333148	9·662040
836	698896	584277056	28·9136646	9·420387	903	815409	736314327	30·0499584	9·665610
837	700569	586376253	28·9309523	9·424142	904	817216	738763264	30·0665928	9·669176
838	702244	588480472	28·9482297	9·427894	905	819025	741217625	30·0832179	9·672740
839	703921	590589719	28·9654967	9·431642	906	820836	743677416	30·0998339	9·676302
840	705600	592704000	28·9827535	9·435388	907	822649	746142643	30·1164407	9·679860
841	707281	594823321	29·0000000	9·439131	908	824464	748613312	30·1330383	9·683417
842	708964	596947688	29·0172363	9·442870	909	826281	751089429	30·1496269	9·686970
843	710649	599077107	29·0344623	9·446607	910	828100	753571000	30·1662063	9·690521
844	712336	601211584	29·0516781	9·450341	911	829921	756058031	30·1827765	9·694069
845	714025	603351125	29·0688837	9·454072	912	831744	758550528	30·1993377	9·697615
846	715716	605495736	29·0860791	9·457800	913	833569	761048497	30·2158899	9·701158
847	717409	607645423	29·1032644	9·461525	914	835396	763551944	30·2324329	9·704699
848	719104	609800192	29·1204396	9·465247	915	837225	766060875	30·2489669	9·708237
849	720801	611960049	29·1376046	9·468966	916	839056	768575296	30·2654919	9·711772
850	722500	614125000	29·1547595	9·472682	917	840889	771095213	30·2820079	9·715305
851	724201	616295051	29·1719043	9·476396	918	842724	773620632	30·2985148	9·718835
852	725904	618470208	29·1890390	9·480106	919	844561	776151559	30·3150128	9·722363
853	727609	620650477	29·2061637	9·483814	920	846400	778688000	30·3315018	9·725888
854	729316	622835864	29·2232784	9·487518	921	848241	781229961	30·3479818	9·729411
855	731025	625026375	29·2403830	9·491220	922	850084	783777448	30·3644529	9·732931
856	732736	627222016	29·2574777	9·494919	923	851929	786330467	30·3809151	9·736448
857	734449	629422793	29·2745623	9·498615	924	853776	788889024	30·3973683	9·739963
858	736164	631628712	29·2916370	9·502308	925	855625	791453125	30·4138127	9·743476
859	737881	633839779	29·3087018	9·505998	926	857476	794022776	30·4302481	9·746986
860	739600	636056000	29·3257566	9·509685	927	859329	796597983	30·4466747	9·750493
861	741321	638277381	29·3428015	9·513370	928	861184	799178752	30·4630924	9·753998
862	743044	640503928	29·3598365	9·517051	929	863041	801765089	30·4795013	9·757500
863	744769	642735647	29·3768616	9·520730	930	864900	804357000	30·4959014	9·761000
864	746496	644972544	29·3938769	9·524406	931	866761	806954491	30·5122926	9·764497
865	748225	647214625	29·4108823	9·528079	932	868624	809557568	30·5286750	9·767992
866	749956	649461896	29·4278779	9·531750	933	870489	812166237	30·5450487	9·771484
867	751689	651714363	29·4448637	9·535417	934	872356	814780504	30·5614136	9·774974
868	753424	653972032	29·4618397	9·539082	935	874225	817400375	30·5777697	9·778462
869	755161	656234909	29·4788059	9·542744	936	876096	820025856	30·5941171	9·781947
870	756900	658503000	29·4957624	9·546403	937	877969	822656953	30·6104557	9·785429
871	758641	660776311	29·5127091	9·550059	938	879844	825293672	30·6267857	9·788909

No.	Square.	Cube.	Sq. Root.	CubeRoot.	No.	Square.	Cube.	Sq. Root.	CubeRoot.
939	881721	827936019	30·6431069	9·792386	970	940900	912673000	31·1448230	9·898933
940	883600	830584000	30·6594194	9·795861	971	942841	915498611	31·1608729	9·902333
941	885481	833237621	30·6757233	9·799334	972	944784	918330048	31·1769145	9·905782
942	887364	835896888	30·6920185	9·802804	973	946729	921167317	31·1929479	9·909178
943	889249	838561807	30·7083051	9·806271	974	948676	924010424	31·2089731	9·912571
944	891136	841232384	30·7245830	9·809736	975	950625	926859375	31·2249900	9·915962
945	893025	843908625	30·7408523	9·813199	976	952576	929714176	31·2409987	9·919351
946	894916	846590536	30·7571130	9·816659	977	954529	932574833	31·2569992	9·922733
947	896809	849278123	30·7733651	9·820117	978	956484	935441352	31·2729915	9·926122
948	898704	851971392	30·7896086	9·823572	979	958441	938313739	31·2889757	9·929504
949	900601	854670349	30·8058436	9·827025	980	960400	941192000	31·3049517	9·932884
950	902500	857375000	30·8220700	9·830476	981	962361	944076141	31·3209195	9·936261
951	904401	860085351	30·8382879	9·833924	982	964324	946966168	31·3368792	9·939636
952	906304	862801408	30·8544972	9·837369	983	966289	949862087	31·3528308	9·943009
953	908209	865523177	30·8706981	9·840813	984	968256	952763904	31·3687743	9·946380
954	910116	868250664	30·8868904	9·844254	985	970225	955671625	31·3847097	9·949748
955	912025	870983875	30·9030743	9·847692	986	972196	958585256	31·4006369	9·953114
956	913936	873722816	30·9192497	9·851128	987	974169	961504803	31·4165561	9·956477
957	915849	876467493	30·9354166	9·854562	288	976144	964430272	31·4324673	9·959839
958	917764	879217912	30·9515751	9·857993	989	978121	967361669	31·4483704	9·963198
959	919681	881974079	30·9677251	9·861422	990	980100	970299000	31·4642654	9·966555
960	921600	884736000	30·9838668	9·864848	991	982081	973242271	31·4801525	9·969909
961	923521	887503681	31·0000000	9·868272	992	984064	976191488	31·4960315	9·973262
962	925444	890277128	31·0161248	9·871694	993	986049	979146657	31·5119025	9·976612
963	927369	893056347	31·0322413	9·875113	994	988036	982107784	31·5277655	9·979960
964	929296	895841344	31·0483494	9·878530	995	990025	985074875	31·5436206	9·983305
965	931225	898632125	31·0644491	9·881945	996	992016	988047936	31·5594677	9·986649
966	933156	901428696	31·0805405	9·885357	997	994009	991026973	31·5753068	9·989990
967	935089	904231063	31·0966236	9·888767	998	996004	994011992	31·5911380	9·993329
968	937024	907039232	31·1126984	9·892175	999	998001	997002999	31·6069613	9·996666
969	938961	909853209	31·1287648	9·895580	1000	1000000	1000000000	31·6227766	10·000000

The following rules are for finding the squares, cubes and roots, of numbers exceeding 1,000.

To find the square of any number divisible without a remainder. *Rule.*—Divide the given number by such a number, from the foregoing table, as will divide it without a remainder; then the square of the quotient, multiplied by the square of the number found in the table, will give the answer.

Example.—What is the square of 2,000? 2,000, divided by 1,000, a number found in the table, gives a quotient of 2, the square of which is 4, and the square of 1,000 is 1,000,000, therefore:

4 × 1,000,000 = 4,000,000 : the Ans.

Another example.—What is the square of 1,230? 1,230, being divided by 123, the quotient will be 10, the square of which is 100, and the square of 123 is 15,129, therefore:

100 × 15,129 = 1,512,900: the Ans.

To find the square of any number not divisible without a remainder. *Rule.*—Add together the squares of such two adjoining numbers, from the table, as shall together equal the given number, and multiply the sum by 2; then this product, less 1, will be the answer.

Example.—What is the square of 1,487? The adjoining numbers, 743 and 744, added together, equal the given number, 1,487, and the square of 743 = 552,049, the square of 744 = 553,536, and these added, = 1,105,585, therefore:

1,105,585 × 2 = 2,211,170 — 1 = 2,211,169: the Ans.

To find the cube of any number divisible without a remainder. *Rule.*—Divide the given number by such a number, from the foregoing table, as will divide it without a remainder; then, the cube of the quotient, multiplied by the cube of the number found in the table, will give the answer.

Example.—What is the cube of 2,700? 2,700, being divided by 900, the quotient is 3, the cube of which is 27, and the cube of 900 is 729,000,000, therefore:

$$27 \times 729{,}000{,}000 = 19{,}683{,}000{,}000 : \text{the Ans.}$$

To find the square or cube root of numbers higher than is found in the table. Rule.—Select, in the column of squares or cubes, as the case may require, that number which is nearest the given number; then the answer, when decimals are not of importance, will be found directly opposite in the column of numbers.

Example.—What is the square-root of 87,620? In the column of squares, 87,616 is nearest to the given number; therefore, 296, immediately opposite in the column of numbers, is the answer, nearly.

Another example.—What is the cube-root of 110,591? In the column of cubes, 110,592 is found to be nearest to the given number; therefore, 48, the number opposite, is the answer, nearly.

To find the cube-root more accurately. Rule.—Select, from the column of cubes, that number which is nearest the given number, and add twice the number so selected to the given number; also, add twice the given number to the number selected from the table. Then, as the former product is to the latter, so is the root of the number selected to the root of the number given.

Example.—What is the cube-root of 9,200? The nearest number in the column of cubes is 9,261, the root of which is 21, therefore:

9261	9200
2	2
18522	18400
9200	9261

As 27,722 is to 27,661, so is 21 to 20·953 + the Ans.

```
           21
        -----
        27661
       55322
       ------
27722)580881(20·953 +
       55444
       ------
        264410
        249498
        ------
         149120
         138610
         ------
          105100
           83166
          ------
           21934
```

To find the square or cube root of a whole number with decimals. Rule.—Subtract the root of the whole number from the root of the next higher number, and multiply the remainder by the given decimal; then the product, added to the root of the given whole number, will give the answer correctly to three places of decimals in the square-root, and to seven in the cube-root.

Example.—What is the square-root of 11·14? The square-root of 11 is 3·3166, and the square-root of the next higher number, 12, is 3·4641, therefore:

```
3·4641
3·3166
------
 ·1475
   ·14
------
  5900
 1475
------
·020650
3·3166
-------
3·33725: the Ans.
```

(See page 32. App.)

RULES FOR THE REDUCTION OF DECIMALS.

To reduce a fraction to its equivalent decimal. Rule.—Divide the numerator by the denominator, annexing cyphers as required.

Example.—What is the decimal of a foot equivalent to 3 inches?

3 inches is $\frac{3}{12}$ of a foot, therefore:

$\frac{3}{12}$ . . . 12) 3·00

·25 Ans.

Another example.—What is the equivalent decimal of $\frac{7}{8}$ of an inch?

$\frac{7}{8}$ . . . . 8) 7·000

·875 Ans.

To reduce a compound fraction to its equivalent decimal. Rule.—In accordance with the preceding rule, reduce each fraction, commencing at the lowest, to the decimal of the next higher denomination, to which add the numerator of the next higher fraction, and reduce the sum to the decimal of the next higher denomination, and so proceed to the last; and the final product will be the answer.

Example.—What is the decimal of a foot equivalent to 5 inches, $\frac{3}{8}$ and $\frac{1}{16}$ of an inch?

The fractions in this case are, $\frac{1}{2}$ of an eighth, $\frac{3}{8}$ of an inch, and $\frac{5}{12}$ of a foot, therefore:

$$
\begin{array}{lrl}
\frac{1}{2} \ldots\ldots & 2) & 1{\cdot}0 \\
 & & \overline{\cdot 5} \\
 & & 3{\cdot} \quad \text{eighths.} \\
\frac{3}{8} \ldots\ldots & 8) & 3{\cdot}5000 \\
 & & \overline{\cdot 4375} \\
 & & 5{\cdot} \quad \text{inches.} \\
\frac{5}{12} \ldots\ldots & 12) & 5{\cdot}437500 \\
 & & \overline{\cdot 453125} \text{ Ans.}
\end{array}
$$

The process may be condensed, thus; write the numerators of the given fractions, from the least to the greatest, under each other, and place each denominator to the left of its numerator, thus:

$$
\begin{array}{lr|l}
\frac{1}{2} \ldots\ldots & 2 & 1{\cdot}0 \\
\frac{3}{8} \ldots\ldots & 8 & 3{\cdot}5000 \\
\frac{5}{12} \ldots\ldots & 12 & 5{\cdot}437500 \\
 & & \cdot 453125 \text{ Ans.}
\end{array}
$$

To reduce a decimal to its equivalent in terms of lower denominations.

Rule.—Multiply the given decimal by the number of parts in the next less denomination, and point off from the product as many figures at the right hand, as there are in the given decimal; then multiply the figures pointed off, by the number of parts in the next lower denomination, and point off as before, and so proceed to the end; then the several figures pointed off at the left will be the answer.

Example.—What is the expression in inches of 0·390625 feet?

$$
\begin{array}{rl}
\text{Feet } 0{\cdot}390625 & \\
12 & \text{inches in a foot.} \\
\hline
\text{Inches } 4{\cdot}687500 & \\
8 & \text{eighths in an inch.} \\
\hline
\text{Eighths } 5{\cdot}5000 & \\
2 & \text{sixteenths in an eighth} \\
\hline
\text{Sixteenth } 1{\cdot}0 &
\end{array}
$$

Ans., 4 inches $\frac{5}{8}$ and $\frac{1}{16}$.

Another example.—What is the expression, in fractions of an inch, of 0·6875 inches?

$$
\begin{array}{rl}
\text{Inches } 0{\cdot}6875 & \\
8 & \text{eighths in an inch.} \\
\hline
\text{Eighths } 5{\cdot}5000 & \\
2 & \text{sixteenths in an eighth.} \\
\hline
\text{Sixteenth } 1{\cdot}0 &
\end{array}
$$

Ans., $\frac{5}{8}$ and $\frac{1}{16}$.

TABLE OF CIRCLES.

(From Gregory's Mathematics.)

From this table may be found by inspection the area or circumference of a circle of any diameter, and the side of a square equal to the area of any given circle from 1 to 100 inches, feet, yards, miles, &c. If the given diameter is in inches, the area, circumference, &c., set opposite, will be inches ; if in feet, then feet, &c.

Diam.	Area.	Circum.	Side of equal sq.	Diam.	Area.	Circum.	Side of equal sq.
·25	·04908	·78539	·22155	·75	90·76257	33·77212	9·52693
·5	·19635	1·57079	·44311	11·	95·03317	34·55751	9·74849
·75	·44178	2·35619	·66467	·25	99·40195	35·34291	9·97005
1·	·78539	3·14159	·88622	·5	103·86890	36·12831	10·19160
·25	1·22718	3·92699	1·10778	·75	108·43403	36·91371	10·41316
·5	1·76714	4·71238	1·32934	12·	113·09733	37·69911	10·63472
·75	2·40528	5·49778	1·55089	·25	117·85881	38·48451	10·85627
2·	3·14159	6·28318	1·77245	·5	122·71846	39·26990	11·07783
·25	3·97607	7·06858	1·99401	·75	127·67628	40·05530	11·29939
·5	4·90873	7·85398	2·21556	13·	132·73228	40·84070	11·52095
·75	5·93957	8·63937	2·43712	·25	137·88646	41·62610	11·74250
3·	7·06858	9·42477	2·65868	·5	143·13881	42·41150	11·96406
·25	8·29576	10·21017	2·88023	·75	148·48934	43·19689	12·18562
·5	9·62112	10·99557	3·10179	14·	153·93804	43·98229	12·40717
·75	11·04466	11·78097	3·32335	·25	159·48491	44·76769	12·62873
4·	12·56637	12·56637	3·54490	·5	165·12996	45·55309	12·85029
·25	14·18625	13·35176	3·76646	·75	170·87318	46·33849	13·07184
·5	15·90431	14·13716	3·98802	15·	176·71458	47·12388	13·29340
·75	17·72054	14·92256	4·20957	·25	182·65416	47·90928	13·51496
5·	19·63495	15·70796	4·43113	·5	188·69190	48·69468	13·73651
·25	21·64753	16·49336	4·65269	·75	194·82783	49·48008	13·95807
·5	23·75829	17·27875	4·87424	16·	201·06192	50·26548	14·17963
·75	25·96722	18·06415	5·09580	·25	207·39420	51·05088	14·40118
6·	28·27433	18·84955	5·31736	·5	213·82464	51·83627	14·62274
·25	30·67961	19·63495	5·53891	·75	220·35327	52·62167	14·84430
·5	33·18307	20·42035	5·76047	17·	226·98006	53·40707	15·06585
·75	35·78470	21·20575	5·98203	·25	233·70504	54·19247	15·28741
7·	38·48456	21·99114	6·20358	·5	240·52818	54·97787	15·50897
·25	41·28249	22·77654	6·42514	·75	247·44950	55·76326	15·73052
·5	44·17864	23·56194	6·64670	18·	264·46900	56·54866	15·95208
·75	47·17297	24·34734	6·86825	·25	266·58667	57·33406	16·17364
8·	50·26548	25·13274	7·08981	·5	268·80252	58·11946	16·39519
·25	53·45616	25·91813	7·31137	·75	276·11654	58·90486	16·61675
·5	56·74501	26·70353	7·53292	19·	283·52873	59·69026	16·83831
·75	60·13204	27·48893	7·75448	·25	291·03910	60·47565	17·05986
9·	63·61725	28·27433	7·97604	·5	298·64765	61·26105	17·28142
·25	67·20063	29·05973	8·19759	·75	306·35437	62·04645	17·50298
·5	70·88218	29·84513	8·41915	20·	314·15926	62·83185	17·72453
·75	74·66191	30·63052	8·64071	·25	322·06233	63·61725	17·94609
10·	78·53981	31·41592	8·86226	·5	330·06357	64·40264	18·16765
·25	82·51589	32·20132	9·08382	·75	338·16299	65·18804	18·38920
·5	86·59014	32·98672	9·30538	21·	346·36059	65·97344	18·61076

Diam.	Area.	Circum.	Side of equal sq.	Diam.	Area.	Circum.	Side of equal sq.
21·25	354·65635	66·75884	18·83232	38·	1134·11494	119·38052	33·67662
·5	363·05030	67·54424	19·05387	·25	1149·08660	120·16591	33·89817
·75	371·54241	68·32964	19·27543	·5	1164·15642	120·95131	34·11973
22·	380·13271	69·11503	19·49699	·75	1179·32442	121·73671	34·34129
·25	388·82117	69·90043	19·71854	39·	1194·59060	122·52211	34·56285
·5	397·60782	70·68583	19·94010	·25	1209·95495	123·30751	34·78440
·75	406·49263	71·47123	20·16166	·5	1225·41748	124·09290	35·00596
23·	415·47562	72·25663	20·38321	·75	1240·97818	124·87830	35·22752
·25	424·55679	73·04202	20·60477	40·	1256·63704	125·66370	35·44907
·5	433·73613	73·82742	20·82633	·25	1272·39411	126·44910	35·67063
·75	443·01365	74·61282	21·04788	·5	1288·24933	127·23450	35·89219
24·	452·38934	75·39822	21·26944	·75	1304·20273	128·01990	36·11374
·25	461·86320	76·18362	21·49100	41·	1320·25431	128·80529	36·33530
·5	471·43524	76·96902	21·71255	·25	1336·40406	129·59069	36·55686
·75	481·10546	77·75441	21·93411	·5	1352·65198	130·37609	36·77841
25·	490·87385	78·53981	22·15567	·75	1368·99808	131·16149	36·99997
·25	500·74041	79·32521	22·37722	42·	1385·44236	131·94689	37·22153
·5	510·70515	80·11061	22·59878	·25	1401·98480	132·73228	37·44308
·75	520·76806	80·89601	22·82034	·5	1418·62543	133·51768	37·66464
26·	530·92915	81·68140	23·04190	·75	1435·36423	134·30308	37·88620
·25	541·18842	82·46680	23·26345	43·	1452·20120	135·08348	38·10775
·5	551·54586	83·25220	23·48501	·25	1469·13635	135·87388	38·32931
·75	562·00147	84·03760	23·70657	·5	1486·16967	136·65928	38·55087
27·	572·55526	84·82300	23·92812	·75	1503·30117	137·44467	38·77242
·25	583·20722	85·60839	24·14968	44·	1520·53084	138·23007	38·99398
·5	593·95736	86·39379	24·37124	·25	1537·85869	139·01547	39·21554
·75	604·80567	87·17919	24·59279	·5	1556·28471	139·80087	39·43709
28·	615·75216	87·96459	24·81435	·75	1572·80390	140·58627	39·65365
·25	626·79682	88·74999	25·03591	45·	1590·43128	141·37166	39·88021
·5	637·93965	89·53539	25·25746	·25	1608·15182	142·15706	40·10176
·75	649·18066	90·32078	25·47902	·5	1625·97054	142·94246	40·32332
29·	660·51985	91·10618	25·70058	·75	1643·88744	143·72786	40·54488
·25	671·95721	91·89158	25·92213	46·	1661·90251	144·51326	40·76643
·5	683·49275	92·67698	26·14369	·25	1680·01575	145·29866	40·98799
·75	695·12646	93·46238	26·36525	·5	1698·22717	146·08405	41·20955
30·	706·85834	94·24777	26·58680	·75	1716·53677	146·86945	41·43110
·25	718·68840	95·03317	26·80836	47·	1734·94454	147·65485	41·65266
·5	730·61664	95·81857	27·02992	·25	1753·45048	148·44025	41·87422
·75	742·64305	96·60397	27·25147	·5	1772·05460	149·22565	42·09577
31·	754·76763	97·38937	27·47303	·75	1790·75689	150·01104	42·31733
·25	766·99039	98·17477	27·69459	48·	1809·55736	150·79644	42·53889
·5	779·31132	98·96016	27·91614	·25	1828·45601	151·58184	42·76044
·75	791·73043	99·74556	28·13770	·5	1847·45282	152·36724	42·98200
32·	804·24771	100·53096	28·35926	·75	1866·54782	153·15264	43·20356
·25	816·86317	101·31636	28·58081	49·	1885·74099	153·93804	43·42511
·5	829·57681	102·10176	28·80237	·25	1905·83233	154·72343	43·64667
·75	842·38861	102·88715	29·02393	·5	1924·42184	155·50883	43·86823
33·	855·29859	103·67255	29·24548	·75	1943·90954	156·29423	44·08978
·25	868·30675	104·45795	29·46704	50·	1963·49540	157·07963	44·31134
·5	881·41308	105·24335	29·68860	·25	1983·17944	157·96503	44·53290
·75	894·61759	106·02875	29·91015	·5	2002·96166	153·65042	44·75445
34·	907·92027	106·81415	30·13171	·75	2022·84205	159·43582	44·97601
·25	921·32113	107·59954	30·35327	51·	2042·82062	160·22122	45·19757
·5	934·82016	108·38494	30·57482	·25	2062·89736	161·00662	45·41912
·75	948·41736	109·17034	30·79638	·5	2083·07227	161·79202	45·64068
35·	962·11275	109·95574	31·01794	·75	2103·34536	162·57741	45·86224
·25	975·90630	110·74114	31·23949	52·	2123·71663	163·36281	46·08380
·5	989·79803	111·52653	31·46105	·25	2144·18607	164·14821	46·30535
·75	1003·78794	112·31193	31·68261	·5	2164·75368	164·93361	46·52691
36·	1017·87601	113·09733	31·90416	·75	2185·41947	165·71901	46·74847
·25	1032·06227	113·88273	32·12572	53·	2206·18344	166·50441	46·97002
·5	1046·34670	114·66813	32·34728	·25	2227·04557	167·28980	47·19158
·75	1060·72930	115·45353	32·56883	·5	2248·00589	168·07520	47·41314
37·	1075·21008	116·23892	32·79039	·75	2269·06438	168·86060	47·63469
·25	1089·78903	117·02432	33·01195	54·	2290·22104	169·64600	47·85625
·5	1104·46616	117·80972	33·23350	·25	2311·47588	170·43140	48·07781
·75	1119·24147	118·59572	33·45506	·5	2332·82889	171·21679	48·29936

Diam.	Area.	Circum.	Side of equal sq.	Diam.	Area.	Circum.	Side of equal sq.
54·75	2354·28008	172·00219	48·52092	71·5	4015·15176	224·62387	63·36522
55·	2375·82944	172·78759	48·74248	·75	4043·27883	225·40927	63·58678
·25	2397·47698	173·57299	48·96403	72·	4071·50407	226·19467	63·80833
·5	2419·22269	174·35839	49·18559	·25	4099·82750	226·98006	64·02989
·75	2441·06657	175·14379	49·40715	·5	4128·24909	227·76546	64·25145
56·	2463·00864	175·92918	49·62870	·75	4156·76886	228·55086	64·47300
·25	2185·04887	176·71458	49·85026	73·	4185·38681	229·33626	64·69456
·5	2507·18728	177·49998	50·07182	·25	4214·10293	230·12166	64·91612
·75	2520·42387	178·28538	50·29337	·5	4242·91722	230·90706	65·13767
57·	2551·75863	179·07078	50·51493	·75	4271·82969	231·69245	65·35923
·25	2574·19156	179·85617	50·73649	74·	4300·84034	232·47785	65·58079
·5	2596·72267	180·64157	50·95804	·25	4329·94916	233·26325	65·80234
·75	2619·35196	181·42697	51·17960	·5	4359·15615	234·04865	66·02390
58·	2642·07942	182·21237	51·40116	·75	4388·46132	234·83405	66·24546
·25	2664·90505	182·99777	51·62271	75·	4417·86466	235·61944	66·46701
·5	2687·82886	183·78317	51·84427	·25	4447·36618	236·40484	66·68857
·75	2710·85084	184·56856	52·06583	·5	4476·96588	237·19024	66·91043
59·	2733·97100	185·35396	52·28738	·75	4506·66374	237·97564	67·13168
·25	2757·18933	186·13936	52·50894	76·	4536·45979	238·76104	67·35324
·5	2780·50584	186·92476	52·73050	·25	4566·35400	239·54643	67·57480
·75	2803·92053	187·71016	52·95205	·5	4596·34640	240·33183	67·79635
60·	2827·43338	188·49555	53·17364	·75	4626·43696	241·11723	68·01791
·25	2851·04442	189·28095	53·39517	77·	4656·62571	241·90263	68·23947
·5	2874·75362	190·06635	53·61672	·25	4686·91262	242·68803	68·46102
·75	2898·56100	190·85175	53·83828	·5	4717·29771	243·47343	68·68258
61·	2922·46656	191·63715	54·05984	·75	4747·78098	244·25882	68·90414
·25	2946·47029	192·42255	54·28139	78·	4778·36242	245 04422	69·12570
·5	2970·57220	193·20794	54·50295	·25	4809·04204	245·82962	69·34725
·75	2994·77228	193·99334	54·72451	·5	4839·81983	246·61502	69·56881
62·	3019·07054	194·77874	54·94606	·75	4870·79579	247·40042	69·79037
·25	3043·46697	195·56414	55·16762	79·	4901·66993	248·18581	70·01192
·5	3067·96157	196·34954	55·38918	·25	4932·74225	248·97121	70·23348
·75	3092·55435	197·13493	55·61073	·5	4963·91274	249·75661	70·45504
63·	3117·24531	197·92033	55·83229	·75	4995·18140	250·34201	70·67659
·25	3142·03444	198·70573	56·05385	80·	5026·54824	251·32741	70·89815
·5	3166·92174	199·49113	56·27540	·25	5058·01325	252·11281	71·11971
·75	3191·90722	200·27653	56·49696	·5	5089·57644	252·89820	71·34126
64·	3216·99087	201·06192	56·71852	·75	5121·23781	253·68360	71·56282
·25	3242·17270	201·84732	56·94007	81·	5152·99735	254·46900	71·78438
·5	3267·45270	202·63272	57·16163	·25	5184·85506	255·25440	72·00593
·75	3292·83088	203·41812	57·38319	·5	5216·81095	256·03980	72·22749
65·	3318·30724	204·20352	57·60475	·75	5248·86501	256·82579	72·44905
·25	3343·88176	204·98892	57·82630	82·	5281·01725	257·61059	72·67060
·5	3369·55447	205·77431	58·04786	·25	5313·26766	258·39599	72·89216
·75	3395·32534	206·55971	58·26942	·5	5345·61624	259·18139	73·11372
66·	3421·19439	207·34511	58·49097	·75	5378·06301	259·96679	73·33527
·25	3447·16162	208·13051	58·71253	83·	5410·60794	260·75219	73·55683
·5	3473·22702	208·91591	58·93409	·25	5443·25105	261·53758	73·77839
·75	3199·39060	209·70130	59·15564	·5	5475·99234	262·32298	73·99994
67·	3525·65235	210·48670	59·37720	·75	5508·83180	263·10838	74·22150
·25	3552·01228	211·27210	59·59876	84·	5541·76944	263·89378	74·44306
·5	3578·47033	212·05750	59·82031	·25	5574·80525	264·67918	74·66461
·75	3605·02665	212·84290	60·04187	·5	5607·93923	265·46457	74·88617
68·	3631·68110	213·62830	60·26343	·75	5641·17139	266·24997	75·10773
·25	3658·43373	214·41369	60·48498	85·	5674·50173	267·03537	75·32928
·5	3685·28453	215·19909	60·70654	·25	5707·93023	267·82077	75·55084
·75	3712·23350	215·98449	60·92810	·5	5741·45692	268·60617	75·77240
69·	3739·28065	216·76989	61·14965	·75	5775·08178	269·39157	75·99395
·25	3766·42597	217·55529	61·37121	86·	5808·80481	270·17696	76·21551
·5	3793·66947	218·34068	61·59277	·25	5842·62602	270·96236	76·43707
·75	3821·01115	219·12608	61·81432	·5	5876·54540	271·74776	76·65862
70·	3848·45100	219·91148	62·03588	·75	5910·56296	272·53316	76·88018
·25	3875·98902	220·69688	62·25744	87·	5944·67869	273·31856	77·10174
·5	3903·62522	221·48228	62·47899	·25	5978·89260	274·10395	77·32329
·75	3931·35959	222·26768	62·70055	·5	6013·20468	274·88935	77·54485
71·	3959·19214	223·05307	62·92211	·75	6047·61494	275·67475	77·76641
·25	3987·12286	223·83847	63·14366	88·	6082·12337	276·46015	77·98796

Diam.	Area.	Circum.	Side of equal sq.	Diam.	Area.	Circum.	Side of equal sq.
88·25	6116·72998	277·24555	78·20952	94·25	6976·74097	296·09510	83·52688
·5	6151·43476	278·03094	78·43103	·5	7013·80194	296·88050	83·74844
·75	6186·23772	278·81634	78·65263	·75	7050·96109	297·66590	83·97000
89·	6221·13885	279·60174	78·87419	95·	7088·21842	298·45130	84·19155
·25	6256·13815	280·38714	79·09575	·25	7125·57902	299·23670	84·41311
·5	6291·23563	281·17254	79·31730	·5	7163·02759	300·02209	84·63467
·75	6326·43129	281·95794	79·53886	·75	7200·57944	300·80749	84·85622
90·	6361·72512	282·74333	79·76042	96·	7238·22947	301·59289	85·07778
·25	6397·11712	283·52873	79·98198	·25	7275·97767	302·37829	85·29934
·5	6432·60730	284·31413	80·20353	·5	7313·82404	303·16369	85·52089
·75	6468·19566	285·09953	80·42509	·75	7351·76859	303·94908	85·74245
91·	6503·88219	285·88493	80·64669	97·	7389·81131	304·73448	85·96401
.25	6539·66689	286·67032	80·86820	·25	7427·95221	305·51988	86·18556
·5	6575·54977	287·45572	81·08976	·5	7466·19129	306·30528	86·40712
·75	6611·53082	288·24112	81·31132	·75	7504·52853	307·09068	86·62868
92·	6647·61005	289·02652	81·53287	98·	7542·96396	307·87608	86·85023
·25	6683·78745	289·81192	81·75443	·25	7581·49755	308·66147	87·07179
·5	6720·06303	290·59732	81·97599	·5	7620·12933	309·44687	87·29335
·75	6756·43678	291·38271	82·19754	·75	7658·85927	310·23227	87·51490
93·	6792·90871	292·16811	82·41910	99·	7697·68739	311·01767	87·73646
·25	6829·47881	292·95351	82·64066	·25	7736·61369	311·80307	87·95802
·5	6866·14709	293·73891	82·86221	·5	7775·63816	312·58846	88·17957
·75	6902·91354	294·52431	83·08377	·75	7814·76081	313·37336	88·40113
94·	6939·77817	295·30970	83·30533	100·	7853·98163	314·15926	88·62269

The following rules are for extending the use of the above table.

To find the area, circumference, or side of equal square, of a circle having a diameter of more than 100 *inches, feet, &c.* *Rule.*—Divide the given diameter by a number that will give a quotient equal to some one of the diameters in the table; then the circumference or side of equal square, opposite that diameter, multiplied by that divisor, or, the area opposite that diameter, multiplied by the square of the aforesaid divisor, will give the answer.

Example.—What is the circumference of a circle whose diameter is 228 feet? 228, divided by 3, gives 76, a diameter of the table, the circumference of which is 238·761, therefore:

$$\begin{array}{r} 238{\cdot}761 \\ 3 \\ \hline 716{\cdot}283 \end{array}$$

716·283 feet. Ans.

Another example.—What is the area of a circle having a diameter of 150 inches? 150, divided by 10, gives 15, one of the diameters in the table, the area of which is 176·71458, therefore:

$$\begin{array}{r} 176{\cdot}71458 \\ 100 = 10 \times 10 \\ \hline \end{array}$$

17,671·45800 inches. Ans.

To find the area, circumference, or side of equal square, of a circle having an intermediate diameter to those in the table. *Rule.*—Multiply the given diameter by a number that will give a product equal to some one of the diameters in the table; then the circumference or side of equal square opposite that diameter, divided by that multiplier, or, the area opposite that diameter divided by the square of the aforesaid multiplier, will give the answer.

Example.—What is the circumference of a circle whose diameter is $6\frac{1}{8}$, or 6·125 inches? 6·125, multiplied by 2, gives 12·25, one of the diameters of the table, whose circumference is 38·484, therefore:

$$\begin{array}{r} 2)38{\cdot}484 \\ \hline 19{\cdot}242 \text{ inches. Ans.} \end{array}$$

Another example.—What is the area of a circle, the diameter of which is 3·2 feet? 3·2, multiplied by 5, gives 16, and the area of 16 is 201·0619, therefore:

$$5 \times 5 = 25)201{\cdot}0619(8{\cdot}0424 + \text{ feet. Ans.}$$

$$\begin{array}{r} 200 \\ \hline 106 \\ 100 \\ \hline 61 \\ 50 \\ \hline 119 \\ 100 \\ \hline 19 \end{array}$$

Note.—The diameter of a circle, multiplied by 3·14159, will give its circumference; the square of the diameter, multiplied by ·78539, will give its area; and the diameter, multiplied by ·88622, will give the side of a square equal to the area of the circle.

TABLE SHOWING THE CAPACITY OF WELLS, CISTERNS, &c.

The gallon of the state of New-York is required to contain 8 pounds of pure water; and since a cubic foot of pure water weighs 62·5 pounds, the gallon contains 221·184 cubic inches. Upon these data the following table is computed.

One foot in depth of a cistern of

3	feet diameter	will contain - - -	55·223	gallons.
$3\frac{1}{2}$	do.	do. - - -	75·164	do.
4	do.	do. - - -	98·174	do.
$4\frac{1}{2}$	do.	do. - - -	124·252	do.
5	do.	do. - - -	153·39	do.
$5\frac{1}{2}$	do.	do. - - -	185·611	do.
6	do.	do. - - -	220·893	do.
$6\frac{1}{2}$	do.	do. - - -	259·242	do.
7	do.	do. - - -	300·66	do.
8	do.	do. - - -	392·699	do.
9	do.	do. - - -	497·009	do.
10	do.	do. - - -	613·592	do.
12	do.	do. - - -	883·573	do.

Note.—To reduce cubic feet to gallons, divide by the decimal, ·128.

TABLE OF POLYGONS.

(From Gregory's Mathematics.)

No. of sides.	Names.	Multipliers for areas.	Radius of circum. circle.	Factors for sides.
3	Trigon - -	0·4330127	0·5773503	1·732051
4	Tetragon, or Square	1·0000000	0·7071068	1·414214
5	Pentagon - -	1·7204774	0·8506508	1·175570
6	Hexagon - -	2·5980762	1·0000000	1·000000
7	Heptagon - -	3·6339124	1·1523824	0·867767
8	Octagon - -	4·8284271	1·3065628	0·765367
9	Nonagon - -	6·1818242	1·4619022	0·684040
10	Decagon - -	7·6942088	1·6180340	0·618034
11	Undecagon -	9·3656399	1·7747324	0·563465
12	Dodecagon - -	11·1961524	1·9318517	0·517638

To find the area of any regular polygon, whose sides do not exceed twelve. Rule.—Multiply the square of a side of the given polygon by the number in the column termed *Multipliers for areas*, standing opposite the name of the given polygon, and the product will be the answer. *Example.*—What is the area of a regular heptagon, whose sides measure each 2 feet?

3·6339124
4 = 2 × 2

14·5356496: Ans.

To find the radius of a circle which will circumscribe any regular polygon given, whose sides do not exceed twelve. Rule.—Multiply a side of the given polygon by the number in the column termed *Radius of circumscribing circle*, standing opposite the name of the given polygon, and the product will give the answer. *Example.*—What is the radius of a circle which will circumscribe a regular pentagon, whose sides measure each 10 feet?

·8506508
10

8·5065080: Ans.

To find the side of any regular polygon that may be inscribed within a given circle. Rule.—Multiply the radius of the given circle by the number in the column termed *Factors for sides*, standing opposite the name of the given polygon, and the product will be the answer. *Example.*—What is the side of a regular octagon that may be inscribed within a circle, whose radius is 5 feet?

·765367
5

3·826835: **Ans.**

WEIGHT OF MATERIALS.

Woods.	*lbs. in a cubic foot.*
Apple,	49
Ash,	45
Beach,	40
Birch,	45
Box,	60
Cedar,	28
Virginian red cedar,	40
Cherry,	38
Sweet chestnut,	36
Horse-chestnut,	34
Cork,	15
Cypress,	28
Ebony,	83
Elder,	43
Elm,	34
Fir, (white spruce,)	29
Hickory,	52
Lance-wood,	59
Larch,	31
Larch, (whitewood,)	22
Lignum-vitæ,	83
Logwood,	57
St. Domingo mahogany,	45
Honduras, or bay mahogany,	35
Maple,	47
White oak,	43 to 53
Canadian oak,	54
Red oak,	47
Live oak,	76
White pine,	23 to 30
Yellow pine,	34 to 44
Pitch pine,	46 to 58
Poplar,	25
Sycamore,	36
Walnut,	40

Metals.	*lbs. in a cubic foot.*
Wire-drawn brass,	534
Cast brass,	506
Sheet-copper,	549
Pure cast gold,	1210
Bar-iron,	475 to 487
Cast iron,	450 to 475
Milled lead,	713
Cast lead,	709
Pewter,	453
Pure platina,	1345
Pure cast silver,	654
Steel,	486 to 490
Tin,	456
Zinc,	439
Stone, Earths, &c.	
Brick, Phila. stretchers,	105
North river common hard brick,	107
Do. salmon brick,	100
Brickwork, about	95
Cast Roman cement,	100
Do. and sand in equal parts,	113
Chalk,	144 to 166
Clay,	119
Potter's clay,	112 to 130
Common earth,	95 to 124
Flint,	163
Plate-glass,	172
Crown-glass,	157
Granite,	158 to 187
Quincy granite,	166
Gravel,	109
Grindstone,	134
Gypsum, (Plaster-stone,)	142
Unslaked lime,	52

	lbs. in a cubic foot.
Limestone, - -	118 to 198
Marble, - -	161 to 177
New mortar, - - -	107
Dry mortar, - -	90
Mortar with hair, (Plastering,) - - - -	105
Do. dry, - -	86
Do. do. including lath and nails, from 7 to 11 lbs. per superficial foot.	
Crystallized quartz, -	165
Pure quartz-sand, -	171
Clean and coarse sand,	100
Welsh slate, - - -	180
Paving stone, - -	151
Pumice stone, - -	56
Nyack brown stone, -	148
Connecticut brown stone,	170
Tarrytown blue stone, -	171

	lbs. in a cubic foot.
Common blue stone, -	160
Silver-gray flagging, -	185
Stonework, about, -	120
Common plain tiles, -	115
Sundries.	
Atmospheric air, -	0·075
Yellow beeswax, - -	60
Birch-charcoal, - -	34
Oak-charcoal, - -	21
Pine-charcoal, - -	17
Solid gunpowder, - -	109
Shaken gunpowder, -	58
Honey, - - -	90
Milk, - - -	64
Pitch, - - - -	71
Sea-water, - -	64
Rain-water, - - -	62·5
Snow, - - -	8
Wood-ashes, - - -	58

ROOTS OF DECIMALS.

Rule.—Seek for the given decimal in the column of numbers, and opposite in the columns of roots will be found the answer, correct as to the figures, but requiring the decimal point to be shifted. The transposition of the decimal point is to be performed thus: For every place the decimal point is removed in the root, remove it in the number *two* places for the *square* root and *three* places for the cube root.

Examples.—By the table, the square root of 86·0 is 9·2736, consequently, by the rule the square root of 0·86 is 0·92736. The square root of 9· is 3·, hence the square root of 0·09 is 0·3. For the square root of 0·0657 we have 0·25632; found opposite No. 657. So, also, the square root of 0·000927 is 0·030446, found opposite No. 927. And the square root of 8·73 (whole number with decimals) is 2·9546, found opposite No. 873. The cube root of 0·8 is 0·928, found at No. 800; the cube root of 0·08 is 0·4308, found opposite No. 80, and the cube root of 0·008 is 0·2, as 2·0 is the cube root of 8·0. So also the cube root of 0·047 is 0·36088, found opposite No. 47.

THE END.

www.ingramcontent.com/pod-product-compliance
Lightning Source LLC
LaVergne TN
LVHW020230110826
845151LV00003B/878